PRINCES, PEASANTS, AND OTHER
POLISH SELVES

PRINCES, PEASANTS, AND OTHER POLISH SELVES

ETHNICITY IN AMERICAN LITERATURE

Thomas S. Gladsky

THE UNIVERSITY OF MASSACHUSETTS PRESS

AMHERST

Copyright © 1992 by The University of Massachusetts Press
All rights reserved
Printed in the United States of America
LC 91–42671
ISBN 0–87023–775–6
Designed by Susan Bishop
Set in Linotron Sabon by Keystone Typesetting, Inc.
Printed and bound by Thomson-Shore, Inc.

Library of Congress Cataloging-in-Publication Data
Gladsky, Thomas S., 1939–
　　Princes, peasants, and other Polish selves : ethnicity in American
literature / Thomas S. Gladsky.
　　　　p.　cm.
　　Includes bibliographical references and index.
　　ISBN 0–87023–775–6 (alk. paper)
　　　　1. American literature—Polish influences.　2. National
characteristics, Polish, in literature.　3. American literature—
Polish American authors—History and criticism.　4. Polish
Americans—Intellectual life.　5. Polish Americans in literature.
6. Ethnicity in literature.　7. Poland in literature.　8. Poles in
literature.　I. Title.
　　PS159.P7G53　1992
　　810.9′352039185—dc20　　91-42671

British Library Cataloguing in Publication data are available.

Parts of this manuscript have previously appeared in *Critique* 29
(Winter 1988); *The Future of American Modernism: Ethnic Writing
between the Wars*, ed. William Boelhower (1990); *The New England
Quarterly* 61 (1988); *Polish-Anglo Saxon Studies* 3–4 (1992);
The Polish Review 36 (1991); and *Studies in American Jewish
Literature* 5 (1986).

To Rita, who read and listened and shared

CONTENTS

ACKNOWLEDGMENTS

I wish to thank Donald Darnell for his guidance over the years in this and in all matters and Jay Martin, who in the early stages of this study pointed me in the right direction as he has always done. To Louis Budd who read and encouraged and to Jerry White, Mark Johnson, and Larry Olpin, who offered manuscript advice and a sympathetic ear, I am indebted. The staff of Ward Edwards Library kindly secured materials and provided a nest; and the College of Arts and Sciences granted time to write. Cate Nesler and Janet Cozza helped prepare the manuscript, and my daughter, Kristen Gladsky, typed the index. I am grateful also to the Council for the International Exchange of Scholars for Fulbright Awards to Poland and to the editors and reviewers of learned journals whose acceptance of my research motivated me. I acknowledge, finally, the efforts of scholars, such as Thomas Napierkowski, who first probed this topic, and descent writers who in words and in deeds helped me to understand "Polish selves."

PRINCES, PEASANTS, AND OTHER
POLISH SELVES

INTRODUCTION

*Can American literature help define the meaning
of ethnicity?* —WERNER SOLLORS

The ambiguity of the term "ethnic literature" is apparent in the definitions offered by contributors to one of the standard works on ethnic literary history, *Ethnic Perspectives in American Literature* (1983): Edward Ifkovic insists that ethnic literature must convey universal human concerns; Rose Basil Green argues that it must project continuing values unique to the group; Iniko Molnar Basa, speaking about Hungarian American literature, believes that it must be written by a member of the group; and Richard Tuerk states that Jewish American literature need not deal with the ethnic dimension at all as long as it is consciously concerned with the author's Jewishness. Others continue the debate largely on the grounds of inclusivity versus exclusivity. Objecting to ethnic exclusivity and biological insiderism, Werner Sollors has campaigned for a broader definition. In *Beyond Ethnicity,* he defines ethnic literature as works "written by, about, or for persons who perceived themselves, or were perceived by others, as members of ethnic groups" (7), to which he later adds, "including those nationally and internationally popular writings by 'major' authors and formally intricate and modernist texts" (243). However, Sollors's definition, which I have basically embraced in this study of Polish literary selves, is not without problems. According to him, the children's stories of Maia Wojciechowska and the poetry of Czeslaw Milosz, even though they do not speak directly to the notion of ethnicity, are ethnic literature while two texts about the ethnic self—William Styron's *Sophie's Choice* and Tennessee Williams's *A Streetcar Named Desire*—are not. I recognize the danger of disclaiming Milosz, the voice of a transplanted Pole, but Milosz's poetry and his public comments stake no claim to the ethnic Polish self.

The question that occupies me is not so much what is ethnic literature and who is the ethnic writer but rather what and where is literary ethnicity. That is to say, I differentiate between "ethnic literature" and "literary ethnicity," in that the latter term helps to avoid the pitfalls inherent in the definitions offered in *Ethnic Perspectives* and other works. Literary ethnicity provides us with an approach to texts not necessarily written "by, about, and for" but which—consciously and unconsciously, directly and in passing—may be read as contributing to the literary creation of ethnic selves and American ethnicity. With this in mind, I have not discussed emigré writers such as W. S. Kuniczak, who writes novels about Polish history; or Charles Bukoski, despite his descent; or Jewish American writers with roots in Poland who do not write about Polishness (defined for purposes of coherence—not necessarily of conviction—as Slavic, Christian, Polish-speaking). Yet I have discussed works and writers—Emma Southworth, Rupert Hughes, William Carlos Williams, James Michener—not likely to be regarded as ethnic by anyone. By approaching texts in terms of literary ethnicity, scholars, I believe, might venture into areas that not even Sollors's liberal model permits—although his concept of descent and consent must be the starting point for all discussions of literary ethnicity.

At the outset, Sollors contends that the conflict between descent, our position as "heirs, our hereditary qualities, liabilities, and entitlements," and consent, our position as "mature free agents and architects of our fate," is "at the root of the ambiguity surrounding the very terminology of American ethnic interaction" (5–6). His paradigm signals his uneasiness with conventional approaches to ethnicity and his belief that descent and consent are central to the way "ethnicity is symbolized in America" (4). Sollors's thesis aptly fits the struggle over Polish literary selves (as, I suspect, it does the study of any particular ethnic group) and the ways those selves have been invented by writers and perceived by scholars. In a 1985 address to the Polish American Historical Association, Stanislaus Blejwas stated that "remarkable as it may seem, there does not exist a Polish American literature, that is, a literature penned by Polish immigrants and Polish ethnics about their experiences in America" ("Voiceless" 5). Clearly, Blejwas sees ethnicity only in terms of descent filtered through American experience. This struggle for turf (descent and consent) permeates scholarship about the Polish literary selves so much so that some have tried to discover a tradition in unlikely places. Jerzy Maciuszko, for example, moves not only beyond consent and descent but beyond time and place in his essay, "Polish-American Literature." He includes Wawrzyniec Goslicki's *De Optimo Senatore* (1568), "not without its influence on the American Declaration of Independence" (163); Witold Gombrowicz, who—writing in Polish—lived most of his adult life in Argentina; Adam Mickiewicz; Nelson Algren; and others with a more genuine claim to Polish Americanness. Both Maciuszko's and Blejwas's essays exemplify the ambivalence and contention that raise the eyebrows of those, like Sollors, eager to break down self-imposed boundaries but careful to establish a coherent framework.

In part the ambiguity and indeterminacy of literary Polishness derives from history: from the many invasions, partitions, occupations, and border shifts that have changed, sometimes overnight, the national identity of large numbers of Poles; from the pluralistic nature of historical Poland (Jews, Ruthenians, Silesians, Highlanders, and so on); and from the ebb and flow of millions of Poles to the globe's far reaches where they have assumed bi-national, multicultural, ethnic, and other altered states. And in part the problem derives from the inability of scholars to reconstruct the literary tradition of Poles in America, including those who, by consent rather than descent, have written about Poles.

Studies of immigrant fiction such as those of David M. Fine and Elwood Lawrence generally disregard the Poles. Except for Joseph Zurawski's valuable but intuitive 1975 publication, no legitimate bibliography exists and precious little criticism is available. A. L. Waldo has written on Polish American theater, but his descriptive essay concentrates only on Polish language theater. Caroline Golab writes perceptively about the image of Slavs in Hollywood films, and Stanislaus Blejwas documents the New England literary image. "The Pattern of Polish-American Literary Relations," a 1976 seminal essay by Polish academic Franciszek Lyra, is especially important in establishing colonial America's awareness of Polish authors. Lyra has also written about the Polish connections of Louisa May Alcott and William James. Perhaps the most active scholar is Thomas Napierkowski who, in addition to surveying the image of Polish Americans, has championed the ethnic voices of Anne Pellowski and Anthony Bukoski, although Napierkowski at times indulges in heavy measures of ethos. In addition to these studies, a stray article here and there calls attention to Ruth Tabrah's *Pulaski Place,* Flannery O'Connor's "Displaced Person," or Nelson Algren's fiction. Styron's *Sophie's Choice* provoked a heated discussion and a number of essays in *Polish American Studies.* More recently conferences held at the University of Silesia (1989) and at Central Missouri State University (1991) have produced thoughtful papers on Silas Steele's *The Yankee in Poland,* Karl Harriman's *The Homebuilders,* Anne Pellowski's Latsch Valley tetralogy, and on Jerome Rothenberg, Anthony Bukoski, James Michener, Isaac Singer, Czeslaw Milosz, Henryk Sienkiewicz in Poland and America, and American Exceptionalism.

Needless to say, this study is indebted to all these efforts, although I have resisted encouraging the exclusivity suggested by some. *Princes and Peasants* is rather about consent and descent—the dialogue between majority *and* minority cultures, *and* the internal dialogue of descent writers working out their own literary images while reflecting upon their ethnic heritage. These debates characterize over 150 years of literary history. Beginning in the late eighteenth century—although one could start with John Smith's allusion to Polish craftsmen in his *History of Virginia*—host-culture writers have produced a surprising number of plays, poems, novels, and stories about Poles (the people of Poland *and* their American descendants). At times, Polishness is as oblique as Emerson's one-line reference to Poland's "stolen fruit" in "Ode Inscribed to W. H. Channing." On other occasions, host-culture writers have stepped forward as spokespersons for Poland. Dartmouth graduate Eric Kelly, assigned to Poland in 1918 with the American Relief Agency, had a lifelong association that included study at Jagiellonian University in Krakow and years of teaching Slavic studies at Dartmouth. More to the point, Kelly published a half dozen young readers' novels on Polish historical legends and myths, one of which, *The Trumpeter of Krakow,* won the prestigious Newberry Medal in 1929. The success of Kelly's books owes much to nineteenth-century America's view of Poland as a beau ideal among nations. In poems, stories, novels, and prose pieces, writers portrayed the Polish self as a mirror to our own national character, drawing comparisons between two Christian, democratic, freedom-loving, enlightened, and providentially guided countries. The tendency to view Poland romantically, as Poland viewed itself, continues into the present as attested to by James Michener's *Poland* and the adulation and support accorded to Lech Walesa and Solidarity.

In the twentieth century other Polish selves appear alongside the beau ideal: anarchists, peasant farmers, proletariat, war refugees, Jew-haters, and "others." While these labels are by nature reductive, they serve to show America's tendency to strip ethnicity to the bone and to interpret the Polish self to suit the historical temper, national preoccupations, literary movements, and changing attitudes toward minorities. Like Huck Finn, the Pole in host-culture literature is always someone but rarely himself; unlike Huck, he is not a three-dimensional self with the ability to tell his own story.

Nonetheless, Polish literary selves have their own journey, an episodic and quixotic one to be sure. Within given time periods and across genres, these selves tend to be very similar from work to work. And except for changes in costume (e.g., anarchist, farmer, worker, refugee), the portrayal of ethnicity remains fairly constant. In other words, Polishness is confined largely within what Frederik Barth calls "the ethnic boundary" (9), and it is presented in ways that support Sollors's claim that "the cultural content of ethnicity [the stuff that Barth's boundaries enclose] is largely interchangeable and rarely historically authenticated" (28). Host-culture writers have seemed determined to

4

show that—to paraphrase a popular song from *Cabaret*—if you could see her through my eyes, she wouldn't look Polish at all.

Inside the mask of social identity, Poles are remarkably uniform in character and cultural markings—not, I suspect, because of the failure of art but rather because of the felt recognition that ethnicity, as Herbert Gans points out, is largely a matter of symbols (193). To this end, host-culture writers have relied on cultural icons and symbols to distinguish ethnics from each other as well as from the majority and to present demystified and deculturized ethnics, compatible with the expectations of the reading audience. In the first third of the twentieth century, writers did this through what Sollors calls the "strategy of inversion": they portrayed Poles as a people with the capacity to become better Americans than most native-born citizens, and then fused this strategy to the American literary odyssey—journeys without and within—and to the pastoral vision described by Ralph Ellison as the "Aren't-Negroes-Wonderful? School" (*Shadow and Act* 87). This is especially true in fiction about war refugees and peasant farmers. In these works ethnicity is presented largely through typology, folk symbols, and sympathetic kinship: Poles are patriots and martyrs, redemptive agents and Old World Puritans. Polishness is the ubiquitous peasant wedding, foods, a sprinkling of myths, proverbs and Polish language phrases, and occasional references to history and geography. Writers emphasize folk culture, character, and such qualities as the work ethic, endurance, humility, morality, parsimony, and loyalty to family and nation.

In effect, writers constructed what William Boelhower calls a "cultural map of exegete" (109). They worked, moreover, to construct community-building images, always with an eye toward melting-pot assimilation rather than pluralism. The Poles in these works instinctively recognize the superiority of American culture. Their desire to retain their own culture, always a factor, gives way ultimately to their impulse (actually the author's) to contribute to a new national family often free of Polish distinctions. The symbolic marriages that so often occur in these texts drive this point home. Consent in the form of Anglo-Saxon "willingness" dominates descent. The difference between "them" and "us," these translators of ethnicity suggest, is not so much a question of character but rather the eccentricities of a folk culture easily transcended by the second generation.

While descent literature bears fundamental similarities to host-culture models—suggesting, at least in the Polish case, that the fabric of ethnicity differs only slightly between the two—literature by "Poles" does not fit so neatly into mainstream ethnic literary history. Polish immigrants, for example, did not publish (in English) the standard "autobiography" or the traditional journey/cultural collision novel in the style of Mary Antin's *From Plotzk to Boston* and O. E. Rolvaag's *Giants in the Earth,* nor did they record—like Anzia Yezierska, Abraham Cahan, and Pietro di Donato—the formative years or the crisis of individual transformation. Collectively, descent literature pales in comparison, qualitatively and quantitatively, to African and Jewish American literatures. And, even to this date, no Yezierskas, Kingstons, Angelous, or Morrisons have emerged to capture the unique story of the Slavic woman. In addition, descent literature is primarily a postwar development, more specially a product of the last quarter century.

The absence of immigrant literature together with the recent emergence of descent literature causes some problems in regard to outlines developed by such scholars as Daniel Aaron, whose three-stage paradigm dominates our view of hyphenated literary history. For Aaron, the hyphenated writer is at first a kind of local colorist who exploits the uniqueness of his material to win sympathy and to dissipate prejudice. In the second stage, writers lash out at restrictions and risk "double criticism" from the majority culture and from the group that wants a spokesperson but does not want attention called to itself. Aaron describes the third stage as a movement from the periphery to the center: the transcendence of "mere parochial allegiance," the acquisition of "double vision," and the transformation of ethnic concerns into those of the human condition and the human predicament (213 ff).

I review Aaron's model at length because of its widespread influence (Sollors discusses it in some detail in his essay, "Literature and Ethnicity" in the *Harvard Encyclopedia of American Ethnic Groups* 647–65), and because it illustrates that, in the absence of a literary tradition, Polish descent writers have had to perform on all three stages *simultaneously.* A casual survey of two recent anthologies, *Blood of Their Blood* and *Concert at Chopin's House,* reveals descent writers exploiting the uniqueness of their heritage, railing against discrimination and indifference, and yet criticizing ethnic parochialism—sometimes all in one breath. Others perfectly reflect Aaron's description of third-stage writers. Anne Pellowski transforms ethnicity into global cultures. Richard Bankowsky offers ethnicity as a metaphor for humankind. For Darryl Poniscan, the ethnic hero is a symbol of American discontent and disconnection. Actually, the phenomenon of "double consciousness," first noted by W.E.B. DuBois as the "sense of always looking at one's self through the eyes of others" (qtd. in Chametzky 4), characterizes the work of virtually all descent writers. From Monica Krawczyk's stories of the 1930s to Gary Gildner's "state of ethnicity" poems appearing in current magazines, descent literature is marked with a sense of otherness, an awareness that more than one audience is out there, that Poles remain on the edge of the mainstream, and that the writers themselves are sensitive to their own doubleness. The reflecting devices (ponds, mirrors, window panes, water) in Anthony Bukoski's fiction corroborate this double-triple vision, just as his rush to define and redefine old and new ethnic selves serves to illustrate the feeling of urgency on the part of descent writers who, as Mark Pawlak phrases it, believe that "it's 3 o'clock in our experience" (qtd. in Contoski 83).

Descent literature concentrates on intercultural differences, the passing of the immigrant generation, and the loss of a culture never fully realized nor quite grasped by its successors. Thus, "strangeness" turns both ways: as object and subject, as a culture dimly perceived and as a point of view still in the making. This, rather than the deliberate attempt to create a literature to be read differently by insiders and outsiders, is what particularizes the double-consciousness of descent literature about Poles. Along these lines, the tension between ancestry and diversity discussed by Sollors in *Beyond Ethnicity* takes on a somewhat different form. To a great degree, host-culture authors acted as surrogate stage-one and stage-two writers, offering examples of the bifurcated self torn between two traditions. For Stuart Dybek, Anthony Bukoski, Gary Gildner and others, however, the issue is not either/or but a question of enlarging the ethnic self beyond descent while still retaining a sense of ethnicity. In other words the idea of the divided self as the pivotal point in ethnic literature (Sollors) becomes for many descent writers an opportunity to reinvent the ethnic self to represent the human condition. Nowhere is this more evident than in Richard Bankowsky's Rose tetralogy.

"Invention," currently the buzz word for students of ethnicity (see *The Invention of Ethnicity* 1989), is thus a helpful and accurate way to look at the emergence of Polish selves in turn-of-the-century literature—when writers created a multiplicity of selves—and to see how descent writers later appropriated these selves in order to rewrite their own literary history. In the process, folk culture, functioning as an organizing agent for host-culture writers, loses its vitality and preciousness as descent authors move toward transethnicity—an approach that, Sollors reminds us, paradoxically denies and renews ethnicity. Moreover, the continual appearance of Polishness as a class marker, resisted but acknowledged, supports Sollors's assertion that ethnicity might be "inter-American," a demonstration of how we are "separated from each other by the same culture" (*Beyond* 36), especially the culture of class.

With few exceptions, the newly invented Polish self is separated from Old World culture and tradition but, nonetheless, is doggedly homeward bound. For some, that self is frozen in time, in images of a dying, static culture. Others mourn for the loss of cultural identity and the isolated self, cut off from the past and, by descent, from the present. Poniscan's and Bukoski's portrayal of the ethnic as cultural exile integrates ethnicity and modernism and illustrates how descent writers have at the same time reworked *The Catcher in the Rye* into an "ethnically Polish" story. Consequently, "lostness" for Bukoski and Dybek, as for Jerzy Kosinski, himself a bridge between host-culture and descent writers, becomes an opportunity to find ethnicity. Whether it is in Bukoski's decision to join his local Kosciuszko lodge or in Gildner's newly found fascination with the American in Poland, writers insist that the Polish self is alive and well somewhere, even if it no longer dwells in the old neighborhoods. "New material does exist for us," Bukoski writes, "intercultural, interracial, neopolitical" (TLS November 4, 1989). For Dybek it is place; for Pellowski, continuity; for Bankowsky, time; for Poniscan, region; for Gildner, Poland; and for Bukoski himself, spirituality.

In effect, descent writers have decided that ethnics are indeed the bearers of something, which—ironically but not surprisingly—is America as it might be. If Sollors is correct in claiming that ethnic study involves learning how America is achieved (*Beyond* 36), this study of Polish selves shows us that ethnicity is, as Jules Chametzky says, "a sacred space" (11) and that the other is us. The argument of descent writers that Polishness is, at one and the same time, ethnic, American, and universal perhaps flies in the face of insular notions of ethnicity. It also demonstrates that in American literary history, the Polish self has come full circle from the 1830s image as a kindred but separate spirit, to the late twentieth-century view that ethnicity is the heart of Americanness.

PART

I

★

POLISH SELVES—AMERICAN PERSPECTIVES

1

PRINCES AND PATRIOTS

Nineteenth-Century Writers and the
Polish Beau Ideal

Even the word Poland is touching. —ST. BEUVE

*Who would seek freedom must leave his country
and risk his life for her.* —MICKIEWICZ

I. A MIRROR TO THE NATION

In March 1831, a young West Point cadet, recently resigned, wrote to the superintendent about his future: "Having no longer any ties which can bind me to my native country—no prospects—nor any friends—I intend by the first opportunity to proceed to Paris with the view of obtaining thru' the interest of the Marquis de Lafayette an appointment (if possible) in the Polish Army. In the event of the interference of France in behalf of Poland this may easily be effected" (*Letters* 1:44). Edgar Allan Poe's plan was apparently not a very serious one. He did not journey to Paris, meet with Lafayette, or join the Polish army. That he would consider such a venture, says more, perhaps, about the times and the country's attitude toward Poland than it does about the youthful idealist and soon to be famous author.

In 1830, Poland—for the second time since the partition of the country by Russia, Austria, and Prussia—rose in revolt, and the United States responded, energetically and emotionally as Poe's letter makes plain. This response was, in part, a historical reflex extending back to the American Revolution when Poland had sent two of its most illustrious sons to help in the struggle for independence. The distinguished efforts of Thaddeus Kosciuszko and Casimir Pulaski, who gave his life in the cause of the Revolution, created an indelible impression in the mind of the nation. To America, Poland's rush to the call symbolized the recognition and approval of the Old World, especially as it came from one of Europe's most distinguished and democratic countries. America was honored, impressed, and indebted—a debt acknowledged in part by the many places scattered across the United States bearing the names of Kosciuszko and Pulaski. As a major participant, moreover, in both the Polish and American struggles for independence, Kosciuszko was a link between the destinies of the two nations and an expression of their kindred spirits. His triumphant return to the United States in 1797 and his stay in Philadelphia where "the famous in all fields . . . came to pay their respects" (Budka 36) testify to his reputation and esteem.

The memory and reputation of Kosciuszko served as a bridge between the Revolutionary years and the 1830s, when American-Polish relations took on a second breath of energy. In that intervening period, Americans such as Oliver Cromwell (pseud.) kept the Polish flame lit through literary works that sought to romanticize the Poles and to rekindle cultural connections. In *Kosciuszko, or The Fall of Warsaw* (1826), Cromwell features an aristocratic cast with Kosciuszko as the central figure. Set in Warsaw during the 1793 uprising, the verse play presents a melancholy Kosciuszko, resigned to Poland's dissolution despite its courageous stand for independence. Cromwell has little to say about Poles, Poland, or history for that matter. His version of history is barely recognizable at times. Rather his intention is to present a few, poignant images to his readers: Poland, a Christian nation, is a martyr to oppression; Poles are brave, patriotic, genteel, high-minded—characteristics that would find their way into literary portrayals of Polishness in the 1830s. As an afterthought, Cromwell links Poland and America as Kosciuszko decides to flee to the United States "where men are free" (72), thus providing a suggestion of cultural ties, which later writers would develop at some length.

As one of the earliest literary works about Poles, Cromwell's play says less about Poles than about the era of good feeling that resulted from Polish participation in the American Revolution. Polish and American travelers visited each other's country with happy results: John Paul Jones was delighted with the "greatest hospitality and politeness" of his host in Poland; Poles such as Thomas Wengierski wrote glowingly of their American experiences; and Julian Niemcewicz's *Under Their Vine and Fig Tree* remains a classic account of observations on America. The budding love affair of Pole and American found expression in other ways as well. Thomas Jefferson and others officially condemned the partition of Poland. Jefferson was himself elected to membership in the Royal Society of the Friends of Sciences in Warsaw. And when Washington died, the Polish legion in Italy draped their banners with shrouds (Wytrwal 95).

When the Poles rebelled against the tsar in 1830, America had the opportunity to reciprocate to an "old friend" and the response, as Jerzy Lerski has shown in *A Polish Chapter in Jacksonian America*, was vociferous and generous. Some, such as Poe, volunteered to join the

Polish forces; others marshalled support through proclamations, meetings, and fund raisings. Resolutions of support were drawn up by New York City's Council of Aldermen and the Boston Youth Association. Toasts to the Poles were drunk in New York City, Buffalo, Richmond, Lexington (Kentucky), and Columbia (South Carolina). A Committee of Help to Poland was organized in Boston where on September 12, 1831, an elaborate ceremony was held in Faneuil Hall. An impressively decorated set of flags, picturing Washington, Lafayette, and Kosciuszko surrounded by the colors of their respective countries was unveiled and then sent to Poland.

Perhaps the most significant expression of sympathy occurred not in the states but in Paris, where James Fenimore Cooper helped organize an American-Polish Committee. Cooper, through his friend Adam Mickiewicz with whom he had toured Rome, was already favorably disposed to the Polish situation. With the help of Marquis de Lafayette he brought together approximately "a hundred prominent Americans residing in Paris . . . some of the most illustrious American names of the day" (Lerski 35). Together they drew up resolutions to raise money, supplies, and public support. In addition, Cooper published his lengthy "An Appeal to the American People" in the *New York American,* focusing on Polish national qualities and a historical struggle that mirrored America's own. He referred to Poland as a republic, the fifth power of Christendom, and praised the Poles as gallant, freedom-loving people whose only crime was "too much liberty." While Cooper did not ingraciously remind Americans of their debt to Poland, he did draw an analogy between Poland and America as underdogs, reviled by many, envied by all. Cooper's appeal bore immediate results, including a subscription from Poe's classmates at West Point (Beard 2:124–29).

After the Polish defeat, America's offer of safe haven precipitated the first substantial immigration of Poles to the New World. The *Buffalo Journal,* under a heading "Blood of Poland," welcomed the "most abused and generous race" to resettle in America, and within months two ships carrying former officers (mostly aristocrats) caused a stir of excitement and curiosity when they docked in New York harbor. Albert Gallatin, former treasury secretary under Jefferson and Madison and one of the then most prominent statesmen, headed the welcome and relief delegation. Dinners, fund raisers, and public ceremonies took place in New York, Philadelphia, Boston, and Albany. William B. Sprague reminded his Albany congregation: "Let it be remembered that they are not vulgar and uneducated men, who were born to the prospect of a life of penury: on the contrary, they are men of considerable intellectual culture, of high and honorable feelings" (qtd. in Lerski 115). Americans signed petitions to Congress requesting a grant of land which could serve as a collective homeland for the exiles, and in June 1834, Congress passed a Donation Bill setting aside a tract in Illinois. Although the land was never settled by Poles, the people of Illinois enthusiastically welcomed their prospective neighbors.

America's response was literary as well as political. The many poems, prologues, portraits, fictions, and historical pieces published in the ensuing decade mark the 1830s as the seminal period in the history of the Pole in American literature: James Fletcher produced two works: a short *History of Poland* and *The Polish Revolution of 1830–1831;* Harro Harring wrote *Poland under the Dominion of Russia;* Charles V. Kraitser issued *The Poles in the United States of America.* Two exiles published memoirs: Joseph Hordynski's *History of the Late Polish Revolution and the Events of the Campaign* and August Jakubowski's *The Remembrances of a Polish Exile;* and another, J. K. Salomonski, translated Jozef Straszewicz's *The Life of the Countess Emily Plater.* In addition, Robin Carver produced an illustrated book of short stories for children; S. L. Knapp submitted a two-volume novel, *The Polish Chiefs* as well as *Tales of the Garden of Kosciuszko;* and Susan R. Morgan wrote two novels which drew upon the situation in Poland. Silas Steele brought the Pole to the American stage in *The Brazen Drum; or the Yankee in Poland,* and numerous writers penned poems. At a flag dedication in Faneuil Hall, two odes to Poland were read by Benjamin Thatcher and a writer known only as Miss Leslie. Other poems celebrating Poland's cause appeared in *The Philadelphia Journal, The Lady's Amaranth, Boston Sentinel, New Haven Herald, Buffalo Courier, Baltimore Gazette, Albany Argus,* and other newspapers and periodicals. Over a half dozen poems were published in New Haven newspapers alone, as Arthur Coleman points out in *A New England City and the November Uprising.*

In the poems we can see the roots of mutual admiration, the first signs of literary ethnicity (of Polishness), and the concerns that would occupy American writers throughout the nineteenth century and, to a lesser degree, the twentieth. The poems are one of a kind; that is, their singular aim is to praise Poland and vilify its oppressors. The Polish cause is described only in broad, general strokes and Polish character is imperfectly sketched. Even so, the Pole emerges as noble in spirit, tireless in his quest for freedom, possessed of a heart of steel, dedicated to homeland—warrior, patriot, martyr, symbol. Similarly, the Polish cause is rendered through high-sounding platitudes. We read about "tyrant's shackles," "ages of glory," "Poland's sun," "freedom's temple," "glorious liberty," "righteous cause," a spirit that "walks abroad," and a host of phrases reminiscent of the rhetoric of the poetry of the Revolution written by Trumbull, Barlow, Freneau, Hopkinson, and their colleagues. Clearly what American poets saw in the 1830s was a correspondence between Poland's struggle and America's earlier one. Florizel, the author of "Roll on, Roll on," links the two events inextricably. To identify Poland for his readers, he calls it "Pulaski's and Kosciuszko's land" and develops the Polish American analogy at length:

> Fondly do we remember yet
>> The days when fate seemed brooding o'er
> Our happy soil; when darkly met
>> For death on our devoted shore
>> Freedom's best friends—her sternest foes.
> When legions hovered round the spot
>> Where hung upon the thread of fate
>> The hopes of millions and the great,
> The good of distant lands, were not
>> Forgetful of our wrongs, they rose,
> They freely bared the arm of might;
> They poured their blood in freedom's fight—
>> And deeply we remember still
>> That heaven lent aid and ever will.
>> (Qtd. in Coleman 51)

In their proclamation to the members of the American Polish Committee, the citizens of Vandalia, Illinois, offered yet another example of this viewpoint. They explained that America's debt to Poland was still fresh in the minds of "a few gray-haired patriots who have united their exertions and mingled their blood with patriots of other countries in the achievements of American liberty" (qtd. in Lerski 181). The declaration called upon all to remember and honor Pulaski, Kosciuszko, Lafayette, and DeKalb and closed by pointing out the shared destiny of Poland and America. The Poles may even "engraft the indomitable spirit of Polish liberty on our American stock" (183) were they to emigrate, a note sounded later in twentieth-century fiction dealing with Polish farmers in New England and with World War II refugees. Cooper himself emphasized the universality of the Polish struggle and the bond between Pole and American in "An Appeal to the American People," when he told his readers "not a freeman falls, in the most remote quarter of the world, that you do not lose one who is enlisted in your own noble enterprise" (*Letters* 2:127). The Polish struggle was regarded by Americans as a symbolic one. The will to resist oppression represented the spirit of all nations during the Revolutionary age and stood as an object lesson to America—and a warning too. "Poles! Bid every heart awake / Bid every soul fresh courage take," the author of "To Poland" exclaimed in the *Albany Argus*. And H.U.C. in "Poland" tied together the fate of the two nations when he reminded his readers:

The star of glory has not set; its beams
Have reached the western world, and freedom's sons
In proud America shall hail its light.

(Qtd. in Coleman 54)

In letters and poems, resolutions and proclamations, the message was simple and consistent: Poland and America shared a destiny as democratic beacons in the Old and New Worlds; and Poland, of the highest intellectual, cultural, and moral fiber, was a model to imitate.

2. THE POLISH CONNECTION AND THE QUEST FOR A NATIONAL LITERATURE

Fiction writers, novelists, and playwrights were also swept up in the wave of enthusiasm about Poland, and works inspired by the events of 1830–31 soon appeared. Samuel Lorenzo Knapp published a lengthy two-volume novel, *The Polish Chiefs*, in 1832, and a year later Robin Carver's illustrated *Stories of Poland* appeared. Susan Rigby Morgan wrote two novels: *Swiss Heiress* (1836) and *Polish Orphan* (1838). And at least five plays with Polish themes were produced on American stages in New York, Boston, Philadelphia, and Baltimore: Jonas Phillips's *The Polish Wife* (1831), J. H. Payne's *Christine of Poland* (1837), *A Graceful Polander* (1843, author unknown), Silas Steele's *The Brazen Drum; or the Yankee in Poland* (1841), and *Emil Plater* (1845). Of these, only *The Brazen Drum* survives. These writers, naturally enough, took up the notions and attitudes introduced briefly and vaguely in poems and proclamations, but in so doing extended and developed an emerging perspective of Poland in the American cultural imagination. The leisure of fiction and the immediacy of theater allowed them to present a richer picture of Polish history, culture, and character; to introduce the Polish aristocrat into historical romance and frontier drama in ways understandable to Americans; and to implant romance and myth firmly into history. More importantly, they fused Polish and American history in ways that not only portrayed Poland as a mirror to the nation but also implied that ethnicity and Americanness were compatible.

Without exception, Poles are presented in positive, almost glowing terms. Aristocrats and political exiles—cultivated, pure in heart, noble in intention—they are superb representatives of pre-Napoleonic Europe. Courageous, compassionate, patriotic, self-sacrificing, educated, cultured, adventurous, high-minded—they represent the beau ideal of Western man. In part, this conception owes much to the conventional portraits of upper-class figures in English and American fiction of the period. As Norman Davies reminds us, for Americans, especially

16

the liberal democrats of the time, the Polish nobleman seemed to be a reflection of themselves. In addition, others saw a connection between the spirit of the Polish republic and primitive frontier anarchism (Davies 1:370–71). To still others, Poland's aristocratic landowners bore some resemblance to America's genteel southerners—a similarity which may have stirred Cooper's Polish sympathies, especially since he often fashioned his protagonists as southern gentry.

American writers saw the Polish connection as an integral chapter of America's history and incorporated the subject into the quest for a national literature, especially in their attempts to root fiction in history. For example, Robin Carver tells us that his stories owe much to Major Hordynski's *History,* the first work published in English by a Polish exile to America, although Carver proudly adds, "I have been to Poland" (2). To his novel, Samuel Knapp appends various historical documents including approximately twenty-five pages of biographical information on the first group of Polish officers to emigrate to the United States. (The sketches had earlier appeared in Thomas Campbell's new periodical, *The Metropolitan.*) And by using Kosciuszko's commentary on a "ruined Poland," Mrs. Morgan leaves no doubt that her novels were motivated by history itself. What these writers were after was nothing less than a version of history that would present a symbolic Poland whose fate was inextricably linked to America's.

Like the poets whose inspired verse described the Polish-American connection in historical and mythical terms, these writers further magnified Poland's largely symbolic role in the American Revolution. S. L. Knapp, for example, devotes virtually the entire first volume of his novel to Pulaski in the American Revolution, emphasizing Pulaski's selfless behavior in the pursuit of liberty. He explains that General Warren wrote to Count Pulaski seeking his expertise and aid, and that Pulaski sorrowfully but dutifully left the "misery and desolation" of conquered Poland to take up arms against America's enemies. As he would later with Kosciuszko, Knapp treats Pulaski as a savior and eventual martyr to the American cause. He has Pulaski say, "I have no ambition, sir, but to be useful, no hopes of glory, but to shed my blood in your cause" (32). Recording every detail of Pulaski's campaigns, Knapp ends volume one with a ten-page elegy to Pulaski, who fell at the battle of Charleston in 1779. Kosciuszko's role and America's implicit debt to Poland occupy Knapp in volume two.

Knapp's scheme in *The Polish Chiefs* is subtle and intricate. For one thing, he presents the novel as if it were narrative history; for another, he links Polish and American fortunes so as to forge an indissoluble bond between the present and the past. America and Poland are one, Knapp seems to say, as he fashions the past to create a future. In his dedication he invokes the Washington-Lafayette-Kosciuszko trinity and reminds us of those who earlier "breasted the wave of oppression for the rights of man" (iii). Next he notes America's long association with Poland and explains that "we felt strongly for the Poles in 1794, and we feel strongly for them now" (vi). As he had done with Pulaski, Knapp records Kosciuszko's achievements in Poland and America, viewing the two struggles as essentially one event occurring on both sides of the Atlantic. Like others of the period, Knapp believed that America had passed on the mantle of freedom to countries such as Poland, which in turn were now responsible for protecting and nurturing democracy. Knapp incorporates this notion into a conversation between Casimir Pulaski, the count's son, and Joel Barlow. Barlow reminds Pulaski that if Poland is to be "a great and happy people," she must free the peasants, educate the people, and conquer her prejudices. In short, she must follow America's democratic lead. Knapp demonstrates America's power of moral persuasion when Kosciuszko, wounded and captured by Russians, is treated honorably only after his captors recognize the sword given to him by the American Congress. When Knapp describes Kosciuszko's death in 1817, it is again with an eye toward developing Polish and American connections. Kosciuszko, we learn, treasures above all else the order of the Cincinnatus and dies with a blessing for young America on his lips. Knapp eventually works the plot toward the events of 1831, stressing the interconnected paths of the two nations through such incidents as the election of Pulaski's grandson as commander of the Polish forces in 1831.

Whereas Knapp's novel concentrates on the Revolution in America, Robin Carver's *Stories of Poland,* published the following year in 1833, is basically a primer on Poland. Amply illustrated, it includes chapters entitled, "Exercises and Amusements," "Cracow," "About the Salt Mines," and "A Splendid Entertainment." In the second half, however, Carver's aim is similar to Knapp's. He too recalls America's unpaid debt to Poland when he writes about Pulaski's service and sacrifice and when he briefly but tellingly traces Kosciuszko's activities. Carver describes Kosciuszko as a "friend of liberty," a man whom "Washington loved dearly," and a great patriot who rushed "to assist our fathers in the Revolutionary War" (86). By directing his appeal to America's children, Carver extends America's good will, debt of gratitude, and sense of responsibility into the next generation. He reminds his young readers that their Polish counterparts do not enjoy freedom, peace, and happiness of mind and cautions them to remember as adults that "other distant nations have claims upon your warmest sympathy" (142).

In *Swiss Heiress* and its sequel, *Polish Orphans,* Susan Rigby Morgan is somewhat less concerned with but no less insistent on the virtues of the historical alliance between Poland and America. One of her main characters, the Swiss Polish Captain Montargis, dies in combat at the battle of Yorktown. His death is justified by his belief that "she will, she must be free" (209). Morgan also employs the iconic Kosciuszko who, melancholy with grief over his distressed country, reminds Morgan's partly Polish heroine to "remember your native blood" (86), which neither she nor Morgan seems able to do. Interested primarily in manners and courtship, and not in politics, Morgan seizes upon the Pole as a representative European aristocrat who embodies the behavior, traditions, and breeding that America had come to associate with the beau ideal. By making her characters Polish, when virtually any European nationality would do, Morgan takes advantage of the spirit of the times and seizes upon a recognizable and appealing "ethnic" type.

The good will expressed in these works was reciprocal; Poland and America comprised an exclusive mutual admiration society. Everything about Poland bespoke splendor, chivalry, historical nobility; everything about America, to Polish eyes, was worthy of transplanting to central Europe. This is evident in the account of Polish travelers to America. Thomas Cajetan Wengierski, touring the United States in 1783, praised America's leaders, cities, customs, and family life. He was especially attracted to the American farmer whom he described in terms similar to Crevecoeur's. "There is," he wrote, "no man less dependent in the world than the farmer in this land; removed from his neighbors, he reigns over his family, does not pay any taxes and has no obligations; he feels that he is equal to anybody in the world and does not even hear of government officials" (qtd. in Haiman 140). In 1805 another celebrated Polish traveler, Julian Ursyn Niemcewicz, praised the United States in *Under Their Vine and Fig Tree*: "Everybody who wants to work has here an assured income in quantity sufficient to live on it and, to save something besides. . . . The equality provided by law exists to the greatest extent possible . . . in daily life all are on equal footing" (9–10). Although Joseph Hordynski was not a traveler like his countrymen Wengierski and Niemcewicz, he prefaces his *History of the Late Polish Revolution* with equally flattering comments "to the great and free nation." Hordynski cites "these happy shores," "fair country," "hearty benevolence," and "the asylum of the persecuted" in his opening remarks. What is more, he notes that every Pole looks toward America "with love and esteem" (v).

Knapp, Carver, and Morgan place similar remarks in the mouths of their fictional Poles, who comment often on the rising glory of America, its people, institutions, and natural blessings. Their high praise serves further to ingratiate them, and by extension all Poles, with the American reading public. How can anyone, these writers seem to ask, not look kindly on those who are so sensitive to America's greatness? That Morgan has her Polish and American characters move back and forth from Europe to America, enjoying Vermont as much as Warsaw, endorses the kindred nature of the cultures. Knapp, however, goes on at some length documenting Polish enthusiasm for America. He devotes almost 100 pages to the journal of Petros Polandski, warrior, scholar, poet, and classmate of Kosciuszko. Knapp supplies an endless number of anecdotes to illustrate Polandski's admiration of the regularity, economy, industry, and determination of the American people. Polandski concludes that, in effect, "this is the best germ of a great nation that ever sprung up since time began" (1:169). Knapp also quotes liberally from Julian Niemcewicz's book. Impressed with America's sublimity and grandeur, Knapp's Niemcewicz limits himself primarily to praise of the political system and natural resources. But he also has kind words for an emerging literary culture headed by Washington Irving. Like Polandski, Niemcewicz finds a country where all is well, one whose "fountains were pure" (2:76).

Similarly, in American eyes, the complexities of Polish history, politics, and culture were reduced to a simple, understandable, romantic image: the Poles were longstanding champions of freedom, defenders of Christianity, and martyrs to oppression. Their history was a mirror to the Old World just as America's was the destiny of the New. For Samuel Knapp, Polish history records the conflict between the standard-bearers of truth and enlightenment, the Poles, and the barbaric dark forces, the Russians. He cites the Constitution of 1791 as a model of liberal thought and a forerunner of democracies to come. For Robin Carver, Polish history is an unbroken line of heroic gestures against tyranny. Early in his book, he promises "to tell you all about the country and the people who live in it" (2); but after a few comments on manners and traditions, he presents a romanticized version of Polish politics from the mid-seventeenth century to 1831—200 years of heroic struggle against the Eastern threats (Turkey and Russia). Beginning with Sobieski's oft-cited defense of Vienna, Carver works his way through the various partitions and insurrections without ever departing from his view of Poland as a divine union of God and people in league against darkness. His stories of schoolboys flogged for writing "the third of May forever" on their benches and of sixteen-year-old Antoinette Tomaszewska, who joins the army to defend her nation, best represent his intentions.

In works like these, American writers created a country akin to theirs without necessarily understanding either the people or the culture. Susan Morgan's knowledge of Poland is limited at best. As for Knapp and Carter, their impressions appear to have evolved from an acquaintance with a few Polish emigrés and their works and from the highly stylized, emotional reports of the American press written, in turn, by those whose only contact with Poles and Poland was second hand. By and large, the real Poland remained unknown to Americans and unrepresented in American letters. Peasants, Jews, and the other ethnic and minority groups that made up the majority of the Polish population did not exist for Knapp or Morgan. Carver at one point pauses to say, "I must tell you a word or two about the Jews" (21), and he is faithful to his word. In a short, unflattering paragraph, he tries to introduce ten percent of Poland's population. And in a few hundred words, he surveys the peasant, the heart and soul of the country, without any apparent enthusiasm or insight. The allegiance of certain Polish leaders to foreign monarchs, the petty squabbling of the gentry, the failure to accommodate itself to the age of exploration, science, and industry, the day-to-day life of the people—all are ignored by American writers. Catholicism, synonymous with the Polish nation, is rarely mentioned. Carver's avoidance of the subject in his introduction to the land of the Poles seems almost deliberate. For Susan Morgan, Catholicism is perhaps the one national characteristic that tarnishes Poland. *Swiss Heiress* deals in part with Protestant-Catholic animosity, as Morgan's heroine resists the courtship of a Polish count precisely because he is Catholic. Nonetheless, the religious question, becoming increasingly important to nativist groups at mid-century, is resolved rather easily in the novel.

3. THE BEAU IDEAL

For the most part, Poles in nineteenth-century American literature are "just like us." Even better, to a democratic audience still enamored of European titles, they are an idealized us, a blend of democrat and aristocrat whose character and breeding resemble the portrait of the American gentleman described by Cooper in *The American Democrat*. Rather than pointing out cultural differences, which might have repelled American readers, writers stressed only similarities between Poles and Americans. The Poles we meet in Morgan's novels would be at home (and are) in the upper ranges of European or American society. To develop her romance, Morgan could have invested her heroes with any European nationality; that she chose Polish, despite her reluctance to probe the dimensions of Polishness, suggests that by the mid-1830s, the reading audience had already formulated a clear and sympathetic picture of the "typical Pole." The reader has no doubt, for example, that the American Laura's decision to marry her half-Polish count and live with him in Poland is an exemplary choice; or that Grace, Laura's

daughter, attributes some of her charm, breeding, and general attrac-
tiveness to her Polish blood—despite the fact that Morgan drops the
Polish theme as *The Polish Orphan* wears on. For Morgan and her
readers, the suggestion that Laura and Grace have ties to Polish aristocracy is enough to hold them in esteem.

Morgan's Poles remain two-dimensional sketches, composite aristocrats whose ethnicity equals nothing more than the tastes of European
gentry. Similarly, Samuel Knapp in *The Polish Chiefs* is less interested in
depicting character and culture than in offering a general testimony to
Poland through selected cultural traits, not the least of which is service
to those whose freedom is threatened. Morgan, for instance, does not
fail to mention that Poles had fought in the American Revolution;
Baron Laniski's second son perishes at Yorktown. Likewise, Knapp
concentrates almost exclusively on Pulaski and Kosciuszko, the two
Poles most readily recognizable to an American audience. Knapp la-
boriously recounts the political and military exploits of his Polish chiefs
in Poland and in America. Even then, his aim is to create a simplified
but convincing national type. Consequently, he notes that a typical
Polish family tree is a chronicle of freedom's children. At one point he
writes that "Polanders . . . are born to fight; live to fight; and when tired
of life, fight to die" (74). (James Michener in his 1983 novel, *Poland*,
would offer essentially the same national portrait.) Knapp also depicts
the Pole as a highly cultured man of the world, one who has "facility
for acquiring languages and [is] a member of a class whose hospitality
is proverbial" (2:34–35). Bravery and honor, high-mindedness and
breeding receive ample emphasis in Knapp's novel, which offers us
Poles who are sophisticates and scholars, warriors and poets—embodi-
ments of the beau ideal.

Robin Carver's Poles are made of similar cloth—admirable com-
binations of sensitivity, sensibility, and tenacious patriotism. Ostensibly Carver's aim, as he explains it, is to introduce his readers to Poland.
In only three of twenty-one chapters, however, does he look even
superficially at Polish culture, and in those short chapters his remarks
are thin, romantic, and restricted. Of course, Carter limits his remarks
to the life of the gentry, who are "fair, well-proportioned, manly, and
hardy" (16), as generous in victory as they are proud in defeat. When
Carver does talk about manners, music, and gardening, he does so in a
way that makes the Poles indistinguishable from the upper classes of
any other Western country. Polish music and dance reflect the graceful
movements and familiar strains of the European masters; Slavic music
is alluded to only once. Carver also generalizes the religious convictions
of the Poles without identifying the unique role of the Catholic church.
He also limits his remarks to Warsaw and Krakow, the two cultural

centers, and thus ignores rural, peasant Poland. Consequently, the reader receives an impression of cosmopolitan cities filled with Turks, Frenchmen, Russians, and Germans. Carver's Warsaw resembles his native Boston insofar as commerce, manufacturing, and finance are concerned. The people themselves are proud, brave, happy, and honorable despite their loss of nationhood. In most of the book, Carver depicts Polish efforts to maintain independence and cultural integrity against historically difficult neighbors. What emerges from these pages is an image of long-suffering, indomitable, chivalric, romantic Poles, unquenchable in their thirst for the right. What would Europe have done without them, Carver (and America's writers) seems to ask, and what might America do with them?

The Polish crisis soon found its way into American drama. Silas S. Steele's *Emil Plater* (unpublished) and *The Brazen Drum; or the Yankee in Poland* performed in Philadelphia in 1842 and again in Boston in 1846, were among the most popular. Set somewhere in Poland in 1831, *Yankee in Poland* features Calvin Cornwheel, a drum major in the "Varmount" militia and an ordinary frontiersman in the style of Cooper's Leather-stocking. As such, the play reflects dramatic interest in the frontier hero as illustrated in J. K. Paulding's popular play, *The Lion of the West*, and other such works of the period. A blend of melodrama, low comedy, spectacle, patriotism, music, and history, *Yankee in Poland* is more concerned with theatrics than with Poland. Even so, the play, which closely resembles other works about Poland, testifies to continuing interest in the Polish situation. In fact, it serves as a summary of sorts, an end note to America's newly found fascination with Poles in the 1830s.

Despite the vagueness of the setting and the minor parts assigned to the Polish characters, *Yankee in Poland* reinforces the central images of Polishness introduced in the 1830s. First and foremost, Polish means aristocracy. All four Poles who appear in the cast—Count Poloski; Zyrenski and Gabinski, his aides; and Rowina Poloski, the Count's daughter—are educated, mannered, brave, patriotic, and cultured, the stock of Knapp's and Morgan's novels, so to speak. Polishness, Steele indicates, also signifies armed struggle against tyranny, a divided country, and a martyred people. Steele gives a short history lesson to this effect in Act 2, when Count Poloski reviews Poland's three attempts to free itself of foreign domination, the partitions, the exile of Polish leaders to Siberia, and the Russian effacement of the liberal 1791 constitution.

Steele's emotional pitch is most effective when he links Polish and American fortunes in ways designed to touch the heart. First he associates both countries with freedom; then he proceeds to offer brief allusions to, and examples of, their shared role in the historical struggle. His frontier character, Cornwheel, points out that the spunky Rowina reminds him of his grandmother's role in "Our Yankee Revolution." He also compares her "to a gal from down East . . . a regular Liberty-Pole, cap and all" (16). Count Poloski's reference to the Polish constitution, patterned after that of the United States, strikes a similar chord. Later, Steele includes a scene where Polish and American flags wave together, signifying historical ties beginning with Kosciuszko and Pulaski, whose names are invoked alongside that of George Washington. Cornwheel explains his presence in Poland, in fact, as a response to Polish participation in the Revolution: "When the news came over that the brave Poles had struck against the tyrant . . . I thought o' Rusciosko [sic] and Pulaski helpin' us—and thinks I one good turn deserves another, so here goes for Poland" (34). Steele's plot about Americans journeying to aid the Poles is, of course, as fictive as the dreamy plans of Poe. In addition, Steele sees no irony in the rush of ordinary Americans like Cornwheel to assist Polish aristocracy. Nonetheless, the play serves to assuage America's conscience as well as to document its generosity in welcoming exiles to native shores. *Yankee in Poland* ends with the fixed impression of the Pole as exile, waiting for yet "another dawn," on board a ship heading for America, his second home—a notion that still prevails in American literature and in the minds of most Poles.

4. THE BEARERS OF CULTURE

In his introduction to August Jakubowski's *The Remembrances of a Polish Exile* (1836), W. B. Sprague asks, "What American has not felt his heart beat sympathetically to the sad and tragic story of the destinies of Poland?" (1). Sprague's rhetorical question suggests that by the early 1840s American and Polish writers had already succeeded in their intent to create a fraternal bond between peoples and a shared destiny between the nations of Poland and the United States. The writers of the period seized upon an image already alive in the American temper, and fueled that Revolutionary memory into a national enthusiasm and a cultural myth. As their works hoped to suggest, America would always be in Poland's debt; so too would Europe and freedom-seeking peoples everywhere. The Poles were both savior and martyr, and their destiny was the Old World parallel to our own: to point the way to freedom and to sacrifice life and nation, if necessary, in the cause.

So eager were Morgan, Knapp, Carver, and Steele to link the history and the people of Poland and America that the Poles in their works appear to be a version of Jefferson's natural aristocrat or, at the least, interchangeable European aristocrats. By ignoring or understating cultural differences, novelists and poets made it easy for Americans of their generation, and of succeeding generations, to accept Polish immigrants. As their works illustrate, the seeds for symbolic ethnicity were sown much earlier—as Herbert Gans has suggested (211)—than most sociologists have believed. As early as the 1830s, writers created a set of Polish ethnic symbols to which succeeding generations of writers would continually return: patriotism, breeding, courage, democratic instincts, high moral and ethical standards, education, culture, and self-sacrifice. Fortunately, but not surprising, these symbols were perfectly compatible with America's national aspirations and self-image.

After the emotional fervor of the period lapsed, America's literary interest in Poland declined but did not disappear. In his 1846 "Ode Inscribed to W. H. Channing," Ralph Waldo Emerson referred to the Cossack eating Poland "like stolen fruit"; and in Herman Melville's "I and My Chimney," Melville compared his family's assault on him to the three-power partition of "poor Poland." Both examples suggest that the subject of Poland was never far away from the minds of American writers. And although in the last half of the century only a few writers used Poles as characters, their work illustrates both the persistence of the literary image created in the 1830s and the gradual emergence of a new set of symbols—resulting in a somewhat different conception and definition of ethnicity in general and Polishness in particular.

In the latter half of the century, writers continued to draw upon the images and themes of the 1830s to portray the beau ideal of European character. Louisa May Alcott is a case in point. In *Little Women*, Laurie Laurence is undoubtedly the most attractive and the most important male in the novel. Handsome, polite, accomplished, he plays the piano, dances and is, in Franciszek Lyra's words, "the embodiment of Victorian kindliness" (63). Alcott describes him as "a universal favorite, thanks to money, manners, much talent, and the kindest heart that ever got its owner into scrapes by trying to get other people out of them" (qtd. in Lyra 63). He is, in short, the very model of Victorian manliness. Although Laurie is presented in the novel as an American, there is, as Lyra has shown and as Alcott herself has indicated, substantial reason to believe that Alcott's ideal is modeled after a young Pole, Wladyslaw Wisniewski, whom she had met in Vevey, Switzerland, in the autumn of 1865. A participant in the 1863 uprising, he had been imprisoned and came to Vevey for his health. In a letter to a friend, Alcott talks about a second meeting with Wisniewski, this time in Paris, and "the days spent in seeing sights with my Laddie" (qtd. in Cheney 182). Alcott was constantly plagued with questions about Laurie's prototype. At times she gave conflicting responses, but seemingly brought the matter to rest when she confessed that "Laurie is not an American boy, though every lad I ever knew claims the character. He was a Polish boy, met abroad in 1865" (qtd. in Cheney 193).

Alcott's somewhat detached admission does not, however, reveal her emotional attachment to Wisniewski, who corresponded with her and later visited her in America, nor does it reflect the extent of her infatuation with Polishness. During 1868, the year *Little Women* was published, Alcott also published short stories in *Frank Leslie's Chimney Corner* and *The Youth's Companion,* popular magazines of the day. In both pieces a young American girl of Victorian tastes and propriety, traveling in Europe, meets a Polish boy with whom she falls in love. Although "My Polish Boy" appeared a few months after "The Baron's Gloves," it appears to be the source of the longer sketch serialized in *Chimney Corner* over a two-month period. Like Wladyslaw Wisniewski, the model for Laurie, these Poles are political refugees, participants in the 1863 uprising, who, having lost fortune, family, and nation, have come to Western Europe to renew their health and to continue the struggle against tsarist oppression.

Alcott's American travelers—Amy and the unnamed narrator of "My Polish Boy"—are visibly moved by the self-sacrifice of the Poles and the Polish cause in general. In their account, the Polish experience is transformed into myth and legend. Vladimir Prakora still has "hope against hope," even as he remembers his imprisoned friends and the massacre at Varsonie, as Alcott calls it, where 500 were shot while singing a national hymn. Similarly, Casimer Teblinski talks about Poland in chains, and the girls conclude that "Poland loves liberty too well" (78). They all appear familiar with Polish history and express their intense sympathy for "poor Pologne." For them Teblinski and Prakora epitomize all that's best and bright. Alcott praises the Poles' manners, breeding, intelligence, and taste. They speak French fluently, know music, travel widely. Together with their dedication to freedom, these traits represented to Alcott the very stuff of literature and the idealized life. She used her stories as an opportunity for melodrama and sentiment, to be sure, but also as a way to present the best face of ethnicity to her readers and to kindle sympathy for Poland. Helen, for example, is worried about Amy's choice of a Catholic and a foreigner and warns her about the problem of cultural differences. But Alcott makes it clear that neither American women nor the nation should fear Poles; rather they should be attracted to them.

Alcott's brief encounter with Wisniewski and her acquaintance with Poland's misfortunes moved her deeply. She also seemed influenced by a popular romance of the time, *Thaddeus of Warsaw,* which Amy and Casimer read to each other during their courtship. The novel and Wisniewski perfectly suited Alcott's preference for sentimental romance and shaped her image of Polishness. During the period 1865–68, she thought about Poland often enough for us to conclude that Poland indelibly influenced the design of *Little Women,* however difficult to measure, as it did certain of the works of her contemporaries.

E.D.E.N. Southworth's *The Missing Bride* (1886) and Willie Triton's *The Fisher Boy* (1860) resemble Susan Rigby Morgan's novels, *Swiss Heiress* and *The Polish Orphan,* in the sense that the authors appear to have neither a genuine interest in nor an understanding of Poles. In fact, Southworth, one of the most popular writers of her day, rarely refers to Poland and Poles in her novel. Set in antebellum Maryland, the work deals with the fortunes and misfortunes of a "typical" family of the southern aristocracy. Southworth is primarily interested in manners, courtship, and plantation gentility. For reasons that at first appear unexplainable or obtuse, Southworth traces the origins of the Waugh dynasty to a Pole, Alexander Kalouga, who is only passingly referred to in the introductory chapter. For the remainder of the plot, Poles are forgotten even by Kalouga's descendants, who regard themselves simply as southerners. In a novel exuding southern romanticism, the Gothic, and a lament for antebellum life, the introduction of a Pole is somewhat puzzling. Southworth, of course, may be relying on local history or hearsay as the basis for her story. At the same time her decision to root the Waugh family tree in Polish ancestry appears ultimately to be compatible with her intent and with the prevailing image of Poles in literary America.

Although we learn very little about the Pole with the non-Polish sounding name, Alex Kalouga fits the model introduced earlier in the century. Kalouga—a soldier of fortune who was engaged with Guy Fawkes, served as a hired sword in various campaigns, buccaneered in South America, and involved himself with Lord Baltimore's intrigues— brings romance, adventure, worldliness, and bravado to Maryland's shores in 1644. He speaks only a few sentences in the novel, enough to explain that his wife is the heroic Marie Zelenski and that he intends to name his Maryland grant "Luckenough," a corruption of Loekenoff, his wife's village. In her choice of Kalouga, Southworth adds a colorful, exotic, and dashing ancestry to her nineteenth-century southern characters, as she suggests that, in part, southern romanticism and culture grew out of central-European temperament. To her readers who would have known little or nothing about Poles, the implied connection may have been accepted without explanation; at least that appears to be the case with the reviewer from *Godey's* who, without referring to Kalouga or the Polish blood that runs through the characters, notes only that they "live and move before us, and are not merely names" (293).

Willie Triton's *The Fisher Boy* also includes Poles in ways that appear to express America's antitsarist sentiments. Set in Cape Cod and various locations in America and Europe, the novel follows the life of Walter Carl and features melodrama, manners, and mush. Three-quarters of the way into this long work, Walter saves a drowning woman who turns out to be the daughter of a Polish exile seeking a home in the New World. As the plot develops, Walter eventually marries the girl and the couple journey to Count Radesky's estate in Ohio.

Like their literary ancestors, the Poles in *The Fisher Boy* are political exiles, cultivated and cultured aristocrats. From them the American protagonist learns about the amenities of social life, develops a passion for the fine arts and nature, acquires knowledge about literature, and, in general grows into a Renaissance man comparable to his Polish tutors. The Radeskys, Triton explains, are "the focus of culture and intelligence for miles around" (332). Their library contains the great works of civilization, and the Countess Radesky is fluent in many languages. Radesky himself fits the type described in 1830s literature. A patriot, soldier, a great landowner in Poland, he gains instant acclaim with Triton and his readers because of his resistance to Russian oppression. He is, moreover, of high character and exceptional stock, qualities he transfers to his daughter and, through her, to successive American generations. Triton's reason for including Poles in his novel, apart from politics and romance, seems to be cultural genetics. The union of Polish aristocrats and genteel Americans improves America intellectually, socially, culturally, and physically. Although this notion is implied in the literature of the 1830s, Triton is perhaps the first to develop with conviction the idea of cultural fusion. Thus his novel formally introduces into literary history a cultural attitude that would be expressed often in fiction about Poles and Americans, from *The Fisher Boy* to *Our Natupski Neighbors* (1916), to many works published in the 1930s and 40s.

Like Southworth, Triton has little to say about Polish customs, tradition, or history. The Radeskys appear to be a composite European type, an approach that suggests that, for Triton and writers of the period, Polishness in particular and ethnicity in general were uncomplicated matters. Walter's marriage to a Pole and Adelgitha Radesky's marriage to an American are presented as natural and desirable unions. The Poles have much to contribute—a point made clear through Count Radesky, whose industry and acumen result in immediate wealth and a greening effect in the form of his magnificent Ohio estate. Like Susan Rigby Morgan's Poles, the desirability of the Radesky presence in America is obvious.

Although Mary Ives Todd's *Violina: A Romance* (1904) and Rupert

Hughes's *Zal: An International Romance* (1905) appeared in the twentieth century, they are, for all intents and purposes, nineteenth-century works. For one thing, Todd and Hughes write as if the great peasant migration had not yet begun. For another, both writers portray their aristocratic characters in the tradition of nineteenth-century fiction. At the same time, Todd and Hughes broaden and expand Polish literary ethnicity by grafting new symbols onto an already recognizable type.

Both novelists root their Polish protagonists firmly in Polish politics and history, with the result that they emerge as close kinsmen of Kosciuszko and Pulaski. This association was noted by a *New York Times* reviewer, who wrote that in *Violina* "there is a strong infusion of the sentiment for which, when Kosciusko [*sic*] fell, freedom is said to have shrieked" (540). Todd and Rupert review Polish history with that sentiment in mind. In chapter two of *Violina*, Todd surveys Poland's past from Jagiello to Czartoryski. She reminds her readers that the Poles who had saved Europe are now suppressed by those envious of democracy. Polish "destiny" is also emphasized as Todd prophesies that Poland will again play a "romantic and glorious part" in Europe's future (18). Similarly, Rupert Hughes devotes an early chapter to Polish history and reminds his readers of Sobieski's defeat of the Turks, the partitions, subsequent rebellions, individual acts of patriotic heroism, the poverty of the nobles after 1863, and the pitiful conditions of contemporary Poland. The November 1830 uprising, a watershed in Polish and American relations, receives singular attention. In *Violina*, Adam Isartoryski's father and mother perish in that uprising. In *Zal*, Ladislav, the protagonist, writes an opera about Emilia Plater, a young woman who died leading the rebellion (and the heroine of an early play by Silas Steele). The Polish families in these novels are connected to Poland's historical struggle in more immediate ways as well: as a youth, Adam Isartoryski had participated in the 1848 uprisings in Europe; and in *Zal*, Ladislav's father emigrates to the United States after the 1863 rebellion and the subsequent loss of his family fortune to the Russian conquerors.

Both families are literary ancestors of Kosciuszko, Hordynski, Jakubowski—political exiles, cultured aristocrats, indomitable patriots. Ladislav, for example, speaks French with "Slavonic ease" and he is described by Hughes as better bred than American or English aristocrats. Sincere, chivalric, and proud, he belongs to a long line of excessively romantic patriots. At one point Hughes credits him with the "unquenchable pride of the gladiator who lies wounded in the dust, with the heel of the enemy on his throat and the bloody onlookers crying for his life, and who resists with his last strength" (164). Todd's Polish men are characterized similarly. All speak several languages fluently, appreciate music, brood over Poland's fate, and carry within themselves the flame of freedom. Early in the novel, Todd explains that there are "no braver, more liberty-loving people on earth" (10) and applauds the Poles' historical assistance to other oppressed peoples.

Neither author develops the notion of shared national destinies nor makes much of America's historical debt to Poland. Late in her novel, however, Todd does suggest that the relationship is a special one. When Violina's aging mother charges her to "unceasingly watch for opportunities to bring her [Poland's] just cause before Christian nations" (260), Todd leaves no doubt, since Violina is by then thoroughly American, that America must assume this duty.

In these novels, the Poles move freely and easily between Polish and American cultures. The characters face no opposition from native-born Americans and have virtually no adjustment problems, primarily because they have lived elsewhere in Europe before their arrival in America and also because the intent of these authors is to present the Poles as a people easily adaptable and assimilable to American culture. Despite the fact that by 1900, the public voice had been raised often in the press condemning Slavs for their "dangerous" cultural differences, Todd and Hughes see only a natural and easy blend of Polish and American cultural characteristics.

Rupert Hughes does, however, make some attempt to compare the two cultures and in so doing, makes his otherwise inauspicious novel an important socioliterary study. In *Zal,* Hughes makes a comparison that would later find its way into many novels dealing with Poles in America, namely, that Poles possess an energy, vitality, and enthusiasm for life that Americans have misplaced or have lacked. At times Hughes's comparison is explicit. Ladislav, for example, believes that Americans fear beauty, and he compares them to the dog that hides a bone, "afraid to be happy, to enjoy" (143). Hughes's main point is that Americans conceal their selves, restrain their feelings, hide their thoughts. Poles, on the contrary, possess an "ingenious lack of restraint" (115) and endeavor to hunt new tones and new colors, "to make the expression" as Ladislav phrases it (143). Hughes's reviewers agreed heartily with this point. The writer for *Outlook* believed that "the contrast between the Polish and American natures is excellently indicated" (838). Later, American novelists, making much of the contrast between the extroverted Pole and inhibited American, would invest the peasant woman with symbolic life-producing and nurturing powers, calling attention to her proliferate nature and associating her with land, crops, and food.

Even though Hughes and Todd stress similarities between Poles and Americans, Hughes's abbreviated comparison of national character makes it clear that American writers were beginning to explore cultural differences. For both writers ethnicity was itself praiseworthy and they searched out qualities that further romanticized the image of the Pole. The result was an extension of the ethnic character, an enlargement of the Polish portrait, and the discovery of new ways and new symbols to portray ethnicity.

Coincidentally, Hughes seized upon his own infatuation with music (a subject he would treat in other novels) to explain his Poles and, along with Mary Todd, to introduce the first of myriad Polish musicians (usually pianists and violinists) who inhabit American fiction. In *Zal*, Ladislav Moniuszko leads the way. He is an artistic genius whose virtuosity takes him by novel's end to Carnegie Hall and fame. Hughes shows that musical genius is a typically Polish gene that, combined with the Polish zest for life, results in artistic greatness. When Ladislav teaches piano to his young American student, he explains that he must "de-Puritanize" her because her New England heritage has dried up her emotion and therefore constrained her talent and her music. For Ladislav, and for all Poles, music is an indelible part of personality, an expression of the national temper: a blend of patriotism and despair, melancholy and hope. Chopin first demonstrated this blend, Hughes tells us, as would later writers including Jerzy Kosinski, whose 1982 novel *Pinball* resembles *Zal* in significant ways. Ladislav himself cites Chopin's Twelfth Etude as a perfect example of "patriotic despair" (163). In fact, beginning with *Zal*, Polish music will suggest love of country and a tragic sense of lost independence. The Polish word for this mood is *zal*, a "morbid brooding," a "desire for something that is lost and cannot ever be found again" (166). When Moniuszko debuts in New York, the critics praise him precisely because he possesses *zal* and therefore can competently interpret Chopin: "the pianist played Chopin as only a Pole can play him. Like Chopin, a sojourner in a foreign land, he knows how to express the exile's longing for his country" (66). At another point, Hughes adds that *zal* is an element in all Polish music (167).

Without mentioning *zal*, Mary Ives Todd also develops Polish ethnicity through music in *Violina*, a novel that appeared in the same year as Hughes's work. In *Violina*, charmingly described by a reviewer in the *Overland Monthly* as "an abomination . . . a miserable excrescence . . . a public nuisance" (482), Todd develops her plot around Violina's talent with the violin. But music in many forms infuses itself into the novel. Often Todd associates music with Polishness. In fact in a chapter entitled "The Polish Ball," she introduces her American readers to the stately dances of genteel Poland: the krakowiak, mazurek, and polonaise. At one point, Violina and her family discuss a recent biography of Chopin, whom twentieth-century novelists would raise to iconic heights, on a level with Kosciuszko. Violina's talent, we learn, is inherited, a matter of Polish blood. Her father Adam, an excellent violinist in his youth, gave up music to pursue national liberty. But he still owns a Stradivarius, which, like his talent, he passes on to his daughter. And when Violina makes her successful New York debut, she plays a program entirely of Polish music, one part of which, the mournful but stirring "Poland is not lost while we live," implies that she too possesses *zal*.

In effect, both these novels are early depictions of immigrant success. That Todd and Hughes would define success as the pursuit and cultivation of the arts says as much about their own values as it does about the Polish temperament. At the same time, they capture the response of Polish aristocrats to the demands of an essentially materialistic culture. Violina and Ladislav are able to "succeed" because of an Old World culture that gave and shaped their musical genius. By associating Poles with music, Todd and Hughes found a way for aristocratic types to respond to a new environment and yet remain loyal to, and take pride in, their heritage. For these writers, music functions as a symbol of the Pole—his patriotism, genius, melancholy, and exile, characteristics introduced in the 1830s primarily in poetry, exposition, and narrative. They add, moreover, to the notion that the Pole brings necessary and highly desirable cultural traits to the New World. Earlier writers lauded Polish courage, spirit, and enthusiasm for freedom and democracy. These novelists suggest that the Poles also offer high culture and art, just as later twentieth-century writers would praise particular qualities of the peasant that enrich American society. That Todd and Hughes would feature aristocrats during a period when hundreds of thousands of Polish peasants were immigrating to the United States attests to the strength of the images introduced in the 1830s and sustained throughout the nineteenth century and into the next.

FROM DEVIANCY TO DIVERSITY
AND BEYOND

Inventing the Polish Literary Self,
1880–1930

*A Lazarus to raise from a sepulchre, sealed
for a hundred years.* —HELEN O. BRISTOL

I. THE PEASANT AND THE PERIODICAL PRESS

For over a century, America viewed Poland as a martyr among nations,
a European counterpart of America's democratic instincts, and a home
of the European beau ideal. Despite a distance of 10,000 miles and the
fact that few Poles were known to Americans and even fewer Americans ventured to Poland, a kindred spirit developed between the nations, created in large measure through American Polish literary associations. After all, did not literature (and history) demonstrate that
Poles like Kosciuszko, Pulaski, and the heroes of 1831 were beacons of
enlightenment, struggling to bring individualism and human dignity to
a despotic world—and did not America owe them a special debt? Did
not America's greatest historical novelist, James Fenimore Cooper, and
Poland's greatest poet, Adam Mickiewicz, recognize in each other the
nobility of character inherent in their respective nations? Did not
Emerson himself link American and Polish fortunes in his celebrated
"Ode Inscribed to W. H. Channing," and did not America's "darling,"
Louisa May Alcott, become infatuated with a Polish beau ideal? Did
not Poland's most celebrated novelist, Henry Sienkiewicz, and most re-
nowned actress, Helena Modjewska, choose California as the site of
their liberal colony? And did not Joseph Conrad, the brightest Polish star in the turn-of-the-century literary firmament, report that he
learned to write about the sea from the novels of America's first writer
of sea tales, James Fenimore Cooper? Although after mid-century Poles
received only modest attention in American literature, literary and
political relations developed along kindred lines well into the twentieth
century. This was evident in Woodrow Wilson's call for a free and

33

independent Poland as part of his peace proposal, and by the raising of a Polish-American division of volunteers to fight in World War I before the United States entered the war. Surely William James was incorrect when he wrote to his friend Wincenty Lutoslawski that "America and Poland are too far off for either to take a 'pragmatic' interest in the other's fate" (qtd. in Lyra 36).

The rapid growth of post–Civil War America and deteriorating economic conditions in Central-Eastern Europe led to new interests, however "pragmatic," as hundreds of thousands of Polish peasants responded to the demand for labor in American industry, thus joining the greatest influx of immigrants in U.S. history. From the 1880s to 1914, approximately 2 million Poles immigrated to the United States. These Poles, many of whom identified themselves as Austrian, German, or Russian, were quite different from their aristocratic predecessors. They were even different from the land-owning Silesians who in the 1850s found their way to Texas, where they successfully founded permanent settlements and helped tame the Texas frontier. The new Poles were landless, poor, unskilled, ignorant tillers of the soil—peasants who belonged as much to the Middle Ages as to the nineteenth century.

The new Poles were different in other ways as well. They had, as Victor Greene points out, little sense either of national identity or of their own ethnicity (*For God and Country* 3). In fact, their idea of Polishness was local and regional, a particular way of life bound up in the daily routine of village life, and they were more interested in America as an economic ideal than as a political one. They were neither particularly patriotic nor nationalistic. In addition, they arrived not in the hundreds, like the political exiles of the 1830s and 1860s, but in the hundreds of thousands, together with millions of other uneducated, non-northern Europeans whose numbers and "strangeness" frightened and confused many native-born Americans. Their influx precipitated a heated debate in the periodical press about the effect of immigration on American institutions—a debate that spilled over into literature as writers sought new literary models to describe a changing America. What had been a consistent and distinct literary image of the Pole as a mirror to the nation gave way to unfamiliar and often contradictory images in an emerging ethnic literature—one that tended to ignore specific ethnic distinctions in favor of nativist concerns and a preference for the universal aspects of the immigrant experience. The result was a sort of Babylonian ethnic confusion to Americans whose first task was to discover who the Poles were and how they differed from other ethnic groups, particularly their Slavic neighbors. In short, Americans had to rethink, rediscover, and reinvent Polishness, which they did largely through portrayals in the press and in literature.

Thus, the period from 1880 to 1930 was, for the Polish experience in American literature, a time of transition and experimentation. During this time, writers frequently turned to the Pole as material, with the result that over a dozen novels and an equal number of short stories about Poles appeared. Some, such as Edward S. Van Zile (*Kings in Adversity* 1897), Thomas Dixon, Jr. (*Comrades* 1909), and Katherine Metcalf Roof (*The Stranger at the Hearth* 1916), were more interested in Slavic types. Others, such as Willa Cather (*My Antonia* 1918), included Poles only as two-dimensional secondary characters whose brief appearance was intended to add local color and exoticism—for example, the "sort of wild," somewhat comic violin teacher, Ordinsky, in *My Antonia*. Nonetheless, in a number of works, host-culture writers, not always well informed about their ethnic subjects, introduced the themes and literary models that would reinforce and redirect the Polish tradition in American fiction. Frances Allen (*The Invaders* 1913) and Edith Miniter (*Our Natupski Neighbors* 1916) wrote about the immigrant on the land. Isaac K. Friedman (*By Bread Alone* 1901), James Oppenheim (*Pay Envelopes* 1911), Marie Oemler (*Slippy McGee* 1917), and others associated Poles with an emerging literature of protest. And Edward A. Steiner (*The Broken Wall* 1903) and Karl Harriman (*The Homebuilders* 1903) produced realistic accounts of urban immigrant life that foreshadowed Sherwood Anderson's structural innovations in *Winesburg, Ohio* and Abraham Cahan's study of urban Jews in *The Rise of David Levinsky*. Others, not surprisingly, portraying Poles as aristocrats in fact or in sensibility, continued to draw upon nineteenth-century models, although their works also reflect the influence of the new immigration. In all cases, however, literature was greatly influenced by the periodical press, where an extended and determined dialogue established the boundaries of ethnicity.

Between 1880 and 1930, writers consciously and unconsciously created the perceptions, images, and characteristics of ethnicity which continue to influence national attitudes, and which in the case of the Poles, invented an ethnic self quite different from the prevailing nineteenth-century image. The invention of literary Polishness occurred, however, within two, often diametrically opposed but ultimately related lines of thought. Concerned with national issues, journalists tended to blur ethnic distinctions and cultural nuances. For them Polishness was described basically as a deviation from the sociopolitical norm—although they succeeded in providing both a forum for an extended discussion of the role of ethnicity in modern American life and a generalized portrait of the new Poles. Taking their cue from the press, creative writers turned to the Pole as material for fiction, associated ethnicity with particular themes and literary formats, and constructed a fuller view of ethnicity as diversity. To the rough outline forged in the periodical press, these writers added precious details and a cultural perspective, refined to be sure through the eyes of the host-culture. In their works, Poles are usually secondary characters against which Americanness and otherness could be compared and evaluated. But in a few instances, writers looked at Polishness from the inside, recording the evolution of New World ethnic consciousness and the emergence of the ethnic self in transition—a theme that would become basic to immigrant literature from Anzia Yezierska to Eva Hoffman's 1989 autobiography, *Lost in Translation.* Of these, Karl Harriman's 1903 collection of short stories, *The Homebuilders,* is exceptional, in that it is the first full-length literary treatment of the new Poles. His interest in ethnicity as diversity and in the sociopsychological implication of transplant offers a sophisticated insight into otherness and a dimension to Polishness that complement the image available in the periodical press.

The debate in the periodical press over immigration, at times nothing more than the racist protestations of a threatened Wasp establishment, was for the most part an honest and necessary exploration of the effects of immigration on American institutions. It was also the first extended discussion of ethnicity and its role in American life. To a great degree, the periodical press reflected America's ambivalence toward the new immigrants, alternately characterized as a blessing and a plague. Even the most prestigious journals, *The Atlantic, Century, Forum, The Nation,* published articles about the economic, political, and racial threat posed by the immigrants. N. S. Shaler's 1892 essay, "European Peasants as Immigrants," is typical. In a wide-ranging attack, he indicts the European peasant for his lack of individuality of mind, citizenly motives, and socioeconomic aspirations. The immigrant is too easily satisfied with too little. Shaler also voices America's fears about the effect on democracy of hundreds of thousands of people without a democratic heritage. "Centuries of such breeding," he notes, "have, of course, checked the development of all those motives and aspirations which are the foundations of our democracy" (651). Shaler also complains about the peasant's lack of skills and his domination by the Catholic church. Although Shaler does not identify immigrant groups by nationality, his closing praise of Germanic people or "perhaps we had better say the Aryan variety of mankind" (655), makes it clear that his racist comments are directed toward Slavs and Southern Europeans. Shaler's attack on immigrant religion, race, politics, and education represented the tendency of many in the press and in literature to depict ethnicity as deviancy.

Although much periodical literature was concerned with the immigrant question in general, a number of journals featured introductory studies of the Slav, whose national characteristics and identity were a mystery to most Americans. These studies reflect the arduousness and the ardor associated with defining cultural boundaries and the gradual emersion of the Polish self. In this sense, periodical literature served an important sociological function, although the tendency at first was to describe the Slav as a type, a process that blurred ethnic distinctions and, in the case of the Poles, prevented Americans from recognizing and understanding the particulars of ethnicity.

In a 1907 article entitled, "Italian, Slavic, and Hungarian Unskilled Labor," Frank Sheridan not only lumped together those groups but included Hebrews and Rumanians in the discussion. In the *American Journal of Sociology*, A. M. MacLean defined Slavs as Slovaks, Ruthenians, Magyars, Poles, and Bohemians. And Allan McLaughlin in the *Popular Science Monthly Review* assigned Poles to the Balkan division of Slavs. Other writers, more sensitive, tried to unravel the increasingly confusing question of national origins. Mary Buell Sayles explained that Poles, given the partition of their country, sometimes referred to themselves as German or Russian and that people in Jersey City who called themselves Russians and Greeks were actually Poles from the "Austrian province of Galicia" (257). Others, such as Emily Balch— who wrote the first extended, sympathetic descriptions of Slavs—also tried to differentiate one Slavic group from another. In Part III of "Our Slavic Fellow Citizens," Balch provided tables and charts from census reports to show the origin, destination, and numbers of each Slavic group.

Unlike Sayles and Balch, most were satisfied to delineate Slavic character in general, resulting in a stereotypical portrait which came to be associated with all Slavs, especially Poles. Emerging during the 1890s, this portrait, according to Karel D. Bicha, stressed negative features as evidence of deviation from normative host values and customs (20). The concept of ethnicity as deviation persisted until the outbreak of the Great War. In 1914, for example, Edward A. Ross, writing in *Century,* continued to associate the negative aspects of immigrant life in America with ethnic character. He complained about excessive drinking, violent criminal tendencies, brutish family life, and the regard for women as property. He warned his readers about Catholic domination, illiteracy, ignorance, Slavic aversion to cleanliness and fresh air, political apathy, excessive procreation, and "an open contempt for Americans and their principles" (596)—and singled out the Poles as the "worst offenders." Other, more well-meaning journalists tried to inform and to create sympathy. Edward Steiner, in "The Slovak and Pole in America" (1903), charted the growth of Polish parishes and communities in various regions, and Peter Roberts looked at the role of Slavs in heavy industry. Providing necessary information, these works nonetheless reaffirmed the notion that ethnic and national differences were less important than the socioeconomic problems of immigrants in general. What the various studies, conciliatory or critical, reveal is that in the periodical press Americans were creating a collective immigrant identity and a prototypical Slavic character on the basis of deviancy.

At the same time, writers began to study Poles as a distinct cultural group and to isolate and identify particularities of custom, tradition, and temperament. One of the first of these articles appeared in 1883 in *Lippincott's Magazine* which featured "Polanders in Texas," a group that predates the great influx of 1880–1914. R. L. Daniels's essay is a curious combination of misinformation, criticism, and myth-making. He seizes upon surface details as symbols of ethnicity that would become recurring elements in both journalistic and fictional portraits of Poles. Describing the Poles as "homely, rugged, and weather beaten," he notes that they "imbibe enormously," care little for education or American-style politics but love music, dance, and joviality. (Daniels appears unaware that he might be mistaking "holiday" behavior for national character, inasmuch as he drew his observations from a Polish wedding he attended.) He praises Polish industriousness, marital fidelity, and farming ability. More important, he fuses ethnic features and pioneer characteristics. For Daniels, the Poles are genuine pioneers helping to settle the West in the great American tradition. Daniels's characterization of the Pole as half-American and half-European is in the best tradition of nineteenth-century fictional portraits of Poles. What is more, his characterization of Poles as pioneers begins a romantic association of the Pole and the American landscape featured in a number of novels about immigrant farmers.

Most Poles, however (approximately ninety percent), settled in the industrial belt where, as far as America was concerned, they melted into the working-class immigrant poor—interchangeable ethnics so to speak. Writers for the periodical press seemed less able to associate urban Poles with the mainstream, although they did succeed in capturing ethnic surface features and in identifying issues of diversity. One such piece is Laura B. Garrett's "Notes on the Poles in Baltimore," a study typical of America's ambivalent attitudes. On the one hand, Garrett describes her subjects as neat, clean, devout, thrifty, industrious, and docile; on the other, they are resigned, indifferent, coarse, and dull. In the face of the passivity which Garrett sees as a national characteristic, she, without irony or sense of contradiction, is able to praise Polish independence of spirit. In "Jan, the Polish Miner," Walter E. Weyl introduces the Pole as an invader, an outsider displacing English-speaking Americans from traditional occupations. He reviews Jan's unionist tendencies and his involvement in labor problems, strikes, and social protest. Weyl also focuses on alienation and generational conflict when he describes how Jan's hope that his children will achieve socioeconomic mobility conflicts with his family values. Jan knows that soon his children will regard their parents and their ethnicity as evidence of inferiority. "America is a wonderful land," he comments, "but it is a land of forgetfulness. My children are not my children, for my children have forgotten that they are Poles" (715). Frederick Almy in "The Huddled Poles of Buffalo" (1911), introduces the notion that Poles are good, raw material that is being wasted and exploited, an observation that would also surface in proletarian fiction.

In a word, the periodical press, despite the tendency to confuse ethnic groups and to rely on deviancy and diversity as characterizing principles, was a powerful force in conditioning American attitudes toward Polishness and in creating the ethnic character and issues that would be associated with Poles throughout the twentieth century. For some, like Victor Greene, the image that emerged is decidedly negative, a castigation of Poles "for their lowly peasant origins, their intemperance, and their rigid adherence to Catholicism . . . high illiteracy, chronic poverty, their innocence of democratic traditions" (*God and Country* 9). Actually the images produced and the issues raised in the press were more complex, more difficult to summarize in regard to ethnic identity. Attitudes toward Poles tended to be as ambivalent as those expressed toward other immigrant groups, in the sense that all groups, especially Slavs, suffered from composite portraiture—the result both of America's inability to distinguish Poles from other groups and of the Poles' inability to describe themselves. Nonetheless, distinctive recognizably Polish features emerged. In addition to establishing national characteristics, the periodical press also associated the Poles with the land, economic invasion and exploitation, generational conflict, alienation, unionism, and a set of folk symbols, all of which found expression in the literature of the period which resembled that of the 1830s when writers first became interested in Polishness.

A number of scholars have studied this period to discover and describe the broad patterns of mainstream ethnic writing. Their observations help to place the Polish tradition in American literature into its proper context of ethnic literature in the period 1880–1930. Daniel Aaron, for example, describing three stages of "hyphenated literature," notes that the first stage exploits the strangeness of new material for local color to win sympathy from the majority, to humanize stereotypes, and to dissipate prejudice (214). Elwood Lawrence has suggested that early ethnic literature falls into two divisions: the immigrant as subject and the immigrant as device in novels of social purpose. Lawrence adds that the literary treatment of immigrants between 1880 and 1920 is primarily designed to produce humor, local color, sentiment, and political awareness, and that immigrants are portrayed as ignorant troublemakers misled by sinister leaders, as "children" needing guidance, superpatriots eager for deethnicization, and quaint, poor, honest, dignified "folk." In his 1930s study of immigrant bio-autobiographies, Carter Davidson found four recurrent assimilation stories: (1) easy, enthusiastic, successful assimilation, (2) difficult but enthusiastic and eventually successful assimilation, (3) difficult assimilation achieved without notable success, and (4) failure of assimilation and alienation (865–66). David Fine also identifies the conflict of cultures as the major theme of early ethnic fiction and categorizes the conflicts as those between immigrants and natives, rich and poor, capitalists and labor, first and second generation, and older and newer immigrant groups (143). More recently, Robin Elliot, citing virtually the same conflicts as Fine, claims that these are not so much ethnic questions as social criticism of capitalism, provincial America, class structure, and stultifying traditions and institutions. Finally, Werner Sollors, basing his argument in part on that of Aaron and Lawrence, has introduced the concepts of descent and consent to describe the main currents of literary ethnicity.

Needless to say, fiction about Poles from 1880 to 1930 falls into all these categories and patterns, suggesting that those writers were at once the creators and benefactors of mainstream ethnic influences. At the same time, the Polish experience in American literature is necessarily different. For instance, without a literary voice of their own until Monica Krawczyk's short stories appeared in the 1930s, Poles relied on surrogate, host-culture writers to portray what Daniel Aaron calls the first stage of hyphenated literature. Similarly, with the exception of Wiszniewski's *Life Record of an Immigrant,* published in Thomas and Znaniecki's *The Polish Peasant,* and one or two others, American literature does not possess Polish immigrant autobiographies—although some were written in Polish. And, until the appearance of Annette Esty's *The Proud House* in 1932, no novel about alienated Poles appeared—except perhaps for Henry Sienkiewicz's short novel *After Bread,* intended for Polish publication but also published in New York in 1897. Lacking the education and cultural association necessary to the literary life, Polish immigrants concerned themselves with survival, with saving money to purchase land in the United States or in Poland (to which many expected to return), and with "work" (as Pietro di Donato would later say of the Italians in *Christ in Concrete*). Unlike the newly arriving Jews who quickly became masters of their literary fate—though Leslie Fiedler reminds us that as late as 1930, American gentiles were still more effective at representing American Jews (5)—Polish immigrants wrote none of the classic novels that trace the journey from the Old World and that deal with such themes as culture shock, America as the promised land, and assimilation.

A possible exception to this is Sienkiewicz's *After Bread: A Story of Polish Emigrant Life in America*. Interestingly enough, *After Bread* has not found a place in American ethnic fiction despite the fact that it is one of the earliest, though hardly best, examples of the journey-arrival genre. Sienkiewicz traces the difficulties of father and daughter in their New World experience, describing the trials of the journey and the misfortunes of the Poles who, lacking sophistication and English language skills, are overwhelmed by the complexities of a bustling, devious, and anonymous New World. Soon, starvation and homelessness face the immigrants who are befriended only by another Pole. In the latter part of the novel, Sienkiewicz takes his sufferers to Borovina, Arkansas, where they try to join a Polish colony, itself overwhelmed by disaster. After her father is swept away in a flood, the young daughter somehow returns to New York where, destitute and hopeless, she loses her sanity and dies. In this naturalistic novel, Sienkiewicz emphasizes the pressures of urban environment, natural disaster, and human depravity (American depravity in this case) within a context of sentiment and social criticism. Not unlike Stephen Crane's *Maggie,* in this sense, the novel, arguing that the peasant is ill-prepared for the "promised land," stands as an admonition to would-be immigrants, although few Poles seemed to heed Sienkiewicz's warning. Despite its shortcomings as an overly emotional, superficial look at the immigrant experience—one quite contrary to Sienkiewicz's own travels in America—the novel is unique as the only journey novel published in English and written by a Pole. All other portrayals of Poles in American literature were wrought at the hands of host-culture writers who defined ethnicity on their terms. Shaped by the sociopolitical climate of the time and by a set of attitudes already implanted in literary history and in the American temper, their works fall into predictable patterns and limited confines. Influenced by the nineteenth-century tradition, American writers continued to portray the Pole as a prince, a European beau ideal; and, reflecting the new immigration, they wrote about the Poles as working-class proletariat and as peasants on the land. These three categories, at once reductive and inclusive, defined the Polish literary self until post-World War II writers searched out new directions and until Jewish American writers discovered the rich possibilities of "memories of Poland."

2. ANARCHISTS AND OTHER DEVIANTS

The periodical press charged that the new immigrants had brought with them a dangerous political outlook—a combination of socialism, anarchy, Old World decadence, and an antagonism toward democracy itself. At the least, the newcomers—as Henry Rood claimed in "The Mine Laborers in Pennsylvania" (*Forum* 1892)—were apathetic about embracing or even participating in democracy. To be sure, as Joseph Roucek has pointed out, Slav involvement in the railroad strikes of 1885 and the Haymarket Affair, and the assassination of President McKinley by a Polish immigrant lent weight to anxieties about the Slav peril (33) and significantly changed America's attitude toward Poles. In the wake of the 1885 disturbances, *The Nation* voiced these fears bluntly and forcefully:

The riots in Cleveland, Chicago and Milwaukee are producing a rapid change of sentiment in regard to the partition of Poland. It has hitherto been considered . . . as a monstrous crime. . . . But the events of the last few weeks are leading many to condemn the powers for not having partitioned the individual Poles as well as Poland. (qtd. in Brozek 116)

It took little time for some to exploit America's growing concern about the immigrant problem. Owen Wister, Frank Norris, Jack London, Ignatius Donnelly, and others produced racist, antiimmigrant fiction, but Catherine Metcalf Roof's *The Stranger at the Hearth* (1916) is perhaps most representative of the literary treatment of Slavs and Poles as deviants.

Uninterested in ethnic distinctions, Roof avoids national labels in her vicious attack on immigrants, whom she describes as the raw waste of Europe, hoodlums who endanger the ideals of the founding fathers, too ignorant even to wait properly on ladies in New York's Fifth Avenue shops. The Slav is singled out for special criticism. In a scene that can only be described as embarrassing, one of Roof's characters wonders why Slavs, "used to a life as simple as a dog in its kennel," expect to earn much money, to which Monty Smith, one of Roof's nativist spokespersons, responds that he considers the comparison an insult to his dogs who are more civilized than the peasants (154). Ironically, Roof briefly introduces a Polish princess who, as a guest at a socialite dinner, receives only a mild rebuke: she is snubbed by the other ladies. Obviously Roof, conscious of class and enamored of titles, is willing to distinguish between Slavic peasants and princesses. Quickly, however, Roof returns to the attack, associating anarchy with the Slavs and the International Workers of the World which, she concludes, is an insult to America and proof of foreign intrigues.

Roof's portrait of the foreigner as political subversive is not original, of course. David Fine has shown in *The City, The Immigrant, and American Fiction, 1880–1920,* that the characterization of the "foreigner" as political subversive, a tradition of sorts in American literature, occurs frequently during this period in such works as Edward King Smith's *Joseph Zalmonah* (1893), and Isaac Kahn Friedman's *By Bread Alone* (1901) (86). As one might expect, the Pole was also portrayed as a subversive, although historically the peasant was not a political activist either in Poland or in the United States. However, with the publication of Richard Henry Savage's *The Anarchist: A Story of Today* (1894), Edward S. Van Zile's *Kings in Adversity* (1897), and Thomas Dixon, Jr.'s *Comrades* (1909), Poles enter the mainstream of political literature in reactionary novels protesting the rising proletariat and exploiting American fears of radical European politics.

Both Savage and Van Zile attack immigrants as the refuse of Europe, a clear and present danger to the American way of life which is fast becoming a sinkhole for immigrant waste. Patently racist, Savage unexplainedly spares the Irish noting, "Say what you will of the Irish, they are not anarchistic! Sixty percent of our arrests or suspects are Germans, Slavs and Poles" (368). Savage's villain is a Pole, Stanislav Oborski, who immigrates to America because he believes that it offers the best possibility for world revolution. Ostensibly to stir up racial hatred, Savage adds yet another dimension to Oborski, whom he portrays as a violent anti-Semite. At one point Oborski says that "the Jews are a dead weight of the world, bearing no generous burdens of the great social movement" (83). Van Zile's views and approach are similar, although he does not specifically identify the nationalities of his anarchist conspirators. Instead we learn that a band of Old World revolutionaries, exiles from Rexania, has established itself in New York's Lower East Side, where it is "inclined to talk anarchy." Given the names of the anarchists—Posadowski, Rukacs, Ludovics, Smolenski, Posnovitch— it is clear that the fictional Rexania is a composite Slavic nation. Van Zile's particular twist is that the prince of Rexania, a liberal-minded, progressive aristocrat, has come to America to study democratic institutions and, at the same time, to warn the country against unbridled anarchy.

Interestingly enough, the anarchists in these novels are not the peasants who comprised the greatest majority of the immigrants but rather the aristocrats, a testimony to the type of novel that Savage and Van Zile were writing and to America's persistent tendency in the 1890s to romanticize Poles as upper-class characters even in novels that are anti-Slavic and anti-Pole. Savage's Oborski, for example, is a Polish count, a former aide-de-camp to the Austrian emperor, whose mission is to redress Polish grievances after the partition and occupation of Poland by Germany, Austria, and Russia—a resistance that had received enthusiastic and universal support from American writers throughout the nineteenth century. And in *Kings in Adversity,* the anarchist leader Posadowski is a cultured, upper-class, well-bred intellectual. By the 1890s American attitudes toward what had been regarded as a noble and praiseworthy movement toward enlightened democracy had changed. This shift in perspective resulted in a new kind of "ethnic" novel, one which continued to portray Poles simultaneously as European beau ideals dedicated to the overthrow of oppression and as socialists and anarchists whose political views endangered America's status quo. Literary reviewers seemed puzzled by this new kind of ethnic novel. Although the *Saturday Review,* for example, faulted Savage for his ornate style and crude plot, it avoided commenting on his sociopolitical views or his portrayal of Poles.

Thomas Dixon, Jr., as he had done in *The Clansman* (1905), continued the nativist attack on immigrants and minorities. In *Comrades* (1909), he focuses on a utopian socialist colony which collapses under the weight of its own wrongheaded philosophy. Socialism, Dixon contends, runs counter to the American grain, and socialists are traitors to the country that had offered them refuge from Europe's tyrants. What we see in *Comrades* is not only that socialism, on both a practical and philosophical level, cannot work but also that it leads inevitably to state tyranny.

Dixon, however, has something more than a refutation of socialism in mind: his intent, like Savage's and Van Zile's, is to pin the socialist threat on foreigners, particularly on the new Europeans flocking to America's shores. Thus, of the three principals in the novel who carry the socialist standard, two are Polish and the other, Herman Wolf, is tainted by his foreign-sounding name. Dixon's choice of Poles as conspirators can only be explained as an expression of antiimmigrant, anti-Slavic sentiment, and as part of the literary convention that cast Slavs as political subversives. Dixon's characterization of Catherine and Barbara Bozenta bears witness.

Early in the novel he links radical politics with Eastern Europe when he introduces Catherine, the dedicated revolutionary, as Polish-born and German-educated. Known as the "Scarlet Nun," she has already led two great strikes of women workers in New York and has come to California to foment worker unrest there. Although her colleague, Barbara, is American by birth, she too has a foreign background in that she was born at Anaheim in the socialist colony of "Polish dreamers led by Madame Modjeska, Count Bozenta, and Henry Sienkiewicz" (23). By connecting his "villains" with the historical enterprise of Helena

Modjewska, Dixon deliberately misrepresents Modjewska's essentially apolitical California venture in order to suggest that Poles brought the dangers of socialism to the New World. Dixon tells us that Modjewska's colony failed and that Barbara was spirited away to Poland by her "foolish kins-men," where Catherine found her homeless, ragged, and starving in the streets of Warsaw. What Catherine is doing in Warsaw is unexplained. Dixon may be reacting to exigencies of plot or implying that Catherine has returned to sharpen her radical ideas. In any event, Barbara, influenced by her youthful experience in Anaheim and by Catherine's tutelage, soon becomes a fiery orator and leader in the cause.

With that introduction, Dixon refrains from any further description of Polishness or even of ethnicity. The only references to ethnic groups occur when the socialist assembly discusses what to do with "inferior races" and when a former slave compares socialism unfavorably to his former condition. Dixon is quite satisfied to define "Polish" simply as political radical, even as certain writers of the proletarian novel would do in the 1930s. Ironically, at a time when the greatest majority of Polish immigrants were peasants, Dixon characterizes his Polish villains as European beau ideals. Both women are educated, refined, and cultured and possess the charm, manners, and grace ordinarily associated with aristocrats or the upper class. Barbara is also ravishingly beautiful and intelligent enough to eventually see the error of her ways. When all is said and done, Dixon is reluctant to condemn his genteel Polish heroines. He solicits sympathy for Catherine when she is mistreated by Wolf, the colony's dictator, and he portrays Barbara as the innocent victim of sinister forces. These Poles are not evil; they are unfortunately misled. In fact, Barbara and Norman Worth, the rich but naive Anglo protagonist, are poised for marriage—although Dixon cannot bring himself to consummate their courtship because, despite his sympathy for his Polish conspirators and his awe of gentility, Dixon will not violate his essential message: Poles bring radical politics to the American garden. Ethnicity means socialism and this threatens "the noblest dream yet conceived by the mind of man" (5).

At the same time, writers with political sympathies different from Dixon's began to write about the plight of America's immigrant working-class poor. They wrote in the context of social criticism directed against unscrupulous capitalists, unregulated industry, and the accompanying exploitation of the masses. A number of these works feature Poles: I. K. Friedman's *By Bread Alone* (1901), Jack Fletcher Cobb's "Polak Joe's Finish" (1909), James Oppenheim's *Pay Envelopes: Tales of the Mill, the Mine, and the City Street* (1911), Upton Sinclair's *King Coal* (1917), and Marie Conway Oemler's *Slippy McGee* (1917). Although none of these writers is interested in ethnicity or Polishness per se, they do succeed in associating the Pole with the rising labor movement and the moral awakening of America in regard to the need for social reform. What is more, they place the Pole squarely in the midst of an emerging protest literature, a literary association that, finding full expression in the 1930s and 40s, would continue through the century even in the works of descent writers.

The most important is I. K. Friedman's *By Bread Alone,* which introduces the radical tradition into twentieth-century fiction. Friedman draws upon political events of the period—the assassination of a president by a radical immigrant, the fiery intrusions of anarchists like Emma Goldman, and infamous labor crises such as the Homestead strike—all of which find their way into the novel, including Friedman's own transformation from middle-class student to steelworker, socialist, and political activist. In *By Bread Alone,* Friedman argues for a moderate version of socialism as the answer to America's domestic problems and condemns both anarchists and industrialists. He is especially interested in the situation of the new immigrants and calls attention to their presence and their predicament. In fact, except for the major characters, virtually everyone in *By Bread Alone* is ethnic: Sophie Goldstein is a Russian Jew; La Vette is French Italian; the Brodskys are Polish; and various Hungarians, Croats, Slovaks, and others appear in passing. Even the "older" generation of workers is identified by nationality: Bach, the superintendent of the steel mill, is German; McNaughton is a Scot; Wilson is English.

These characters fill out an ethnically diverse landscape, but the Poles play a special role as Friedman's representative ethnics. Only the Brodskys have major speaking parts and only they appear throughout the novel in ways significant to the plot. In effect Friedman is one of the first to provide a three-dimensional portrait of the Polish peasant in American fiction. This portrait reflects the ambivalent feelings of the period toward the Slavic immigrant and certain stylized features already rooted in literary history. At the same time, Friedman moves beyond stereotype and literary convention and in so doing broadens and intensifies literary ethnicity. For example, like Savage and Van Zile before him, he characterizes his Poles as anarchists. The Brodsky brothers attend secret meetings led by Goldstein, a Bakunin disciple. Michael serves on the strike committee; Paul, like Leon Czolgosz (the McKinley murderer), attempts to assassinate the mill owner; and Jan leads an armed force of striking immigrants. "If anarchists are born and not made," Friedman says, "Jan was a natural anarchist" (470). Mrs. Brodsky, without a defined political connection, is perhaps the most radical of all, leading the women of the town in assaults on the police, the Pinkertons, and the militia. The Brodskys, however, are anarchists with a human face. We understand them and like them because we see them in their home as well as at work, at play and in prayer.

What Friedman suggests is that the Poles have been driven to anarchy as a last resort. They are socioeconomic victims of unregulated and insensitive capitalism. They live segregated from the community in "dog town," a hideous world of mud lanes and bleak tenements surrounded by "a few willows black and stunted" (51). Friedman's first reference to the Poles is as sordid as their surroundings. He talks about "dirty, unkempt wretchedly-clad children," "squabby, corsetless, barefooted" women, and stupid, brutal, cruel men, personified by Vorlinski, "the spirit of anarchy," who terrorizes the neighborhood and the mill. Eventually, Friedman softens his portrayal and we see that the Brodskys, despite their primitiveness, are decent, hard-working, caring people twisted more by desperation than by ideology.

Although Friedman lifts the Poles beyond the caricatures offered by Savage and Van Zile, he cannot free himself from popular preconceptions and racial prejudices. Blair Carrhart, for example, refuses to adopt Vorlinski's tactics when they fight, and only the "heredity of a superior race" prevents him from "beating and stamping this monster" (85). Friedman also indicts the Poles for their alleged disinterest in education, their "dull lethargic mind," and their crude behavior. And as Fay M. Blake contends, Friedman, like other novelists of the period, assumes that all foreigners are ashamed of their background and culture (75). At the same time, Friedman moves beyond physical description and surface behavior to define ethnicity as diversity. He tries to penetrate Polish temperament, claiming that dreaminess is a "salient characteristic" of Polishness, as common to Poles as blue eyes. Almost incredulously, given the political fervor of the novel, he dubs a chapter, "Polish Wedding," and spends a number of pages recounting the postmarriage celebration often cited by later writers to explain Polishness to their readers. With awe and envy, Friedman describes the music of the polka, the octogenarian dancers, Mrs. Majewski and Mr. Kuflewski, and the curious custom of breaking plates to collect money for the newlyweds—a custom that also infatuated Karl Harriman who wrote about it at even greater length two years later in *The Homebuilders*.

Friedman is perhaps the first to look at the Polish Catholic church in the context of political unrest and social problems. He successfully captures the church as a powerful and intimidating force in the daily lives of the Poles: the children attend parochial school; the Brodskys regularly attend mass; they decorate their home with icons—lithographs of the Virgin, busts of Christ, crucifixes, religious scenes—and structure their calendar around religious feasts such as "Trzy Krole"—

47

January 1, when Poles use red chalk to inscribe the initials of the three kings on their front doors. More important, Friedman astutely differentiates between religiosity and institution—the peasant devotion to ceremony and aversion to clerical authority. The church, Friedman shows, has little interest in the poor and less in the struggle of the steelworkers and their union. As Father Kozma threatens the strikers with excommunication, it is rumored that the company enriches the church's coffers to insure its assistance. Friedman's brief but penetrating examination stands as one of the few attempts by an American writer to examine one of the most important aspects of Polish American culture—although Jerome Bahr, Russell Janney, and Wanda Kubiak, among others, would later deal with the Polish Catholic church.

Thus, Friedman addressed ethnicity in a variety of ways, although his major interest was in the Pole as proletariat. Drawing upon sketchy literary portraits of Poles as anarchists, and on images of the Pole circulating in the periodical press, Friedman fashioned a notable version of the Polish self that influenced his successors, especially those involved in protest fiction. More than anything, however, he permanently identified the Pole with the proletariat.

Soon after, other writers also used Polish characters in political fiction. In 1909, Jack Fletcher Cobb—in his *Harper's Weekly* short story, "Polak Joe's Finish"—associated the Pole with the proletarian movement. Actually, Cobb's story would work just as well with any kind of working-class protagonist, although his choice of a Pole suggests that by 1909, Americans had come to associate the Pole with heavy industry and had already formed recognizable impressions of the Polish character. Fletcher took advantage of these associations and the conventions of literary naturalism in presenting Polak Joe. In fact, the story in many ways foreshadows Eugene O'Neill's *The Hairy Ape*. Joe has "hulking shoulders, from which dangled long, thick, ape-like arms" (22). He is slow-witted, physical, violent, intemperate, a creature shaped and exploited by an environment described as "silent traps of death in the darkness . . . hot acrid gases from steaming ovens" (22). And like Yank, Joe, a mill worker, strikes out helplessly and pathetically, not at the rich and powerful as Yank does, but at the managerial class which taunts, humiliates, and oppresses him daily. In the end, Joe is consumed by his own environment when he falls into a cupola of molten iron. Cobb's naturalistic lesson follows in the footsteps in Sienkiewicz's *After Bread* as one of the rare examples of failed assimilation and alienation involving Poles. Divorced from any social, community, or family life, Joe is a lonely individual whose solitary journey to America is played out without the benefit of an Old World identity or the prospects of a new one. Cobb's characterization of Joe as brutish, uncultured, slowwitted—fit only for physical work and violent behavior—reflects the stereotype already fastened to the American imagination. In America's eyes, he is nothing more, as the foundry foreman says, than "a damned animal" (23).

Like Cobb, neither James Oppenheim nor Upton Sinclair did much to extend ethnic boundaries. Like their journalistic and literary predecessors, they ignored ethnic distinctions, choosing to describe Slavs as a type. Oppenheim, for example, mirrored prevailing confusion by alternately identifying his characters as Slovaks, Poles, and Hunkies. And in emphasizing Polishness as size, strength, and the capacity to work, he relied upon familiar surface characteristics. Oppenheim's contribution lies in a different direction. Associating his hero, Stiny Bolinsky, with the labor movement, he portrays the Pole as a sleeping sociopolitical giant, ready and able to seize both his own and America's destiny. Having entered the mines at age twelve, Bolinsky inevitably follows the path of his father until the local school teacher, the Anglo Miss Denby, awakens him to the prospects of a better life. Bolinsky recognizes that for him, for his fellow Poles, and for all American workers, those prospects lie most immediately in labor unions and he becomes an advocate of both the United Mine Workers and its leader, John Mitchell. From this point on, there is, Oppenheim writes, "something in the air that tempted him forth; it was a voice hinting of glories on the other side of the mountain" (247).

In *King Coal*, Upton Sinclair also looks at immigrant mining communities. Like Oppenheim, he is more interested in politics than in ethnicity. His Poles are two-dimensional figures whose Slavic names are enough (for Sinclair) to suggest national character. He presents the Pole as a bedraggled, browbeaten, submissive peasant used to being driven and exploited in Europe. Nonetheless, Klowoski and Zamierowski are good-natured, humble, earnest men who live a tired, pathetic existence until they, like Bolinsky in *Pay Envelopes*, sense the prospect of a better life through strength in unions. In the style of Oppenheim, Sinclair shows a Pole leading a protest to support independent weigh-masters to prevent the miners from being cheated. But both Sinclair and Oppenheim regarded the Poles as little more than ammunition for labor reform, lacking any real chance of permanent leadership. Their fiction would serve as fact until a Polish American, Joseph Yablonski, led a reform movement within the United Mine Workers in 1969.

Marie Conway Oemler's curious novel *Slippy McGee*, set in turn-of-the-century rural South Carolina, testifies to how quickly and extensively the Pole found a place in regional literature. The 1910 census shows, for example, only four foreign-born Poles in the entire state of South Carolina, although Oemler gives the impression of having observed Polish immigrants at first hand. Strictly speaking, *Slippy McGee* is not about Poles or immigrants but rather about postbellum rural southern culture. In an oblique but telling manner, Oemler also portrays a changing America, in this case a social awakening toward the difficult lives of white non-Anglo southerners who labor in the canning factories and mills. Oemler's liberal views seem not to include African Americans, who do not appear in the novel, although it is possible that Poles serve as surrogates to mask Oemler's private agenda.

Oemler presents a somewhat colorful, generalized description of Polishness. She tells about "broad-bosomed, patient, cow-like" women and "shock-headed" youngers, and she reminds the reader about immigrant fecundity—a fear already planted by the periodical press. She also touches upon Polish Catholicism through Father Armand De Rancé who, though not a Pole, talks about the prominent statue of St. Stanislaus, the patron saint of Poland "whom my Poles love." And she is perhaps the first to describe a Polish version of the padrone system, where an aggressive and more sophisticated immigrant assumes the responsibility for newcomers, including finding them housing and work for a fee. Oemler's "Padrone," the only Polish character of any consequence, is a villain, however, who embodies many of the traits—intemperance, violence, greed—attributed to the Polish peasant. For the most part, Poles exist only in the background, in thin descriptions of their neighborhood (which "other folks religiously avoided"), children at play, work at the mill, and the daily toil of life. Much is assumed about the Poles, whose culture receives only passing glances as Oemler fails to see the possibilities either of local color or of ethnic fiction. Instead, she seizes upon the symbols of ethnicity—church, family, physical description, the iconic St. Stanislaus—to construct her ethnic parameters and to differentiate between them and us. By integrating the Poles into social and labor reform in the South, however, Oemler suggests that Polish (immigrant) problems may serve as a catalyst for a full-scale moral and social reawakening in American life.

3. TRANSFORMATION AND REORGANIZATION: THE HOMEBUILDERS

Preoccupied with immigrant issues affecting America on a national level, most writers looked at the Pole from Oemler's perspective as strangers at the hearth whose presence forced changes in American attitudes and institutions. Few wrote about the immigrant community from the inside, from the point of view of Poles trying to live a life made doubly difficult by conflicting desires to discard and retain ethnicity and to maintain an ethnic community within New World surroundings.

Two notable exceptions, however, are Karl E. Harriman in *The Home-builders* (1903) and Harold Waldo in *Stash of the Marsh Country* (1921).

Harriman's collection of short stories resembles the naturalistic-realistic fiction of many of his contemporaries. In the style of Stephen Crane's *Maggie,* he looks at the lives of working-class Americans in an urban setting, Detroit, where the environment has hardened their speech as well as behavior. The first words of dialogue, "Would yeh like a beer . . . where d'yeh work?" (13) are reminiscent of the dialogue spoken by the inhabitants of Crane's Rum Alley. Like Crane's, Harriman's intent is to show how America's largely immigrant, urban poor fall victim to nature, the system, and their own limitations. Structurally the work foreshadows *Winesburg, Ohio,* as Harriman unifies his stories through time, place, and the actions of reappearing characters. Although Harriman's work lacks the bone-piercing insights of *Winesburg* or the innovative impressionism of *Maggie,* the collection is a milestone in ethnic literature. In its move beyond the confines of deviancy and diversity, it is the first realistic, credible, and extensive literary portrayal of the Polish American community.

Harriman presents the Poles in their own milieu, without major American characters whose concerns usually dominate plot and theme, and from their own point of view. While his contemporaries were writing about Poles as outsiders who provided local color, or as the fortunate half of melting-pot marriages, Harriman, along with Harold Waldo, introduced three-dimensional characterization and ethnic concerns. He thus broadened the scope of ethnic literature in ways usually credited to such better-known authors as Mary Antin, O. E. Rolvaag, Willa Cather, and Abraham Cahan. A fictional prelude to Thomas and Znaniecki's classic study, *The Polish Peasant in Europe and America,* Harriman's *The Homebuilders* tackles the complex theme of social reorganization and the transformation of an essentially peasant society into an American ethnic community.

On the surface, Harriman's community appears to be a colorful chaos of bewildering and exotic European activity without a carefully defined social organization. Neighbors gossip at the garden gates, fuss with domestic duties, and occupy themselves with the ordinary matters of Old World life: the fish peddler calls to his clients; children gather wood; Felician sisters stroll noiselessly through the streets; Mr. Stefansky is arrested for operating his cart without a license. The Poles work, marry, and die without an awareness of New World institutions and without invoking old ones. Yet Harriman's stories are, in fact, studies of social organization, especially the role of work, church, property, and family in determining status, in regulating behavior, and in shaping identity. In "The Homebuilders," Julia and Henry cannot marry until Mrs. Fernowicz outlines and agrees to the conditions. The Brodsky son in "The Patriots" cannot join the army without parental and church consent; Paula in "The Will of Anton Tschaeche" happily receives the family blessing, sanction, and inheritance of her grandfather; and Jan Adamowsky in "The Day of the Game" chooses family and community over his newly won social status in the Anglo world.

In "The Wages of His Toil," Harriman looks at the plight of the ethnic laborer in a market-driven economy. For the peasant, gifted with a solid physical frame and an eagerness to please his employers, success was often measured by work output and physical prowess, giving rise to the Pole's reputation as a desirable worker in heavy industry. In "The Wages of His Toil," Ladislav Adamowsky perfectly illustrates the relationship of work to status and the consequence of being doomed to a lifetime of suffering once those physical abilities disappear. In the stoveworks where he is employed, Adamowsky's physical feats are legendary. Everyone remembers the day he wheeled a barrow "piled high with pigs of iron ten times around the room at a jog trot" (162) and then added the weight of two of his huskiest coworkers. All this brings him approval at work and in the community, which assigns respect according to physical performance. When Adamowsky is injured and reduced to becoming a sweeper in the mill, he loses his status and self-respect and turns to alcohol.

Harriman is equally perceptive about the role of the Catholic church as a social authority and organizer. In telling about the huge Polish church built by a nationalistic priest who threatened to withdraw his church from the German-dominated diocese, Harriman alludes to the struggle for an independent Polish Catholic church in America and to the church as a symbol of emerging Polish ethnic consciousness, a subject ably explored by Victor Greene in For God and Country. Harriman underscores the parish's influences on the sociomoral behavior of its members. In many of the stories, Father Durowsky's function is to counsel and approve appropriate behavior. When a visiting Polish general addresses the community about the homeland's pressing problems, Durowsky lends credibility to the meeting by introducing the speaker. When Anton Tschaeche's granddaughter runs off, Anton seeks guidance from his priest, just as his granddaughter does while she debates returning home. The Poles turn to the church even in matters of national allegiances. When their son wants to join the U.S. Army, the Brodskys first ask the opinion of Father Durowsky, whose resounding "Go!" indicates the force of his authority.

Harriman's plots depict a peasant society transplanting itself into new surroundings while carefully maintaining, and in some cases revising, a social organization constructed around Old World models. In the title story, Harriman develops the idea of the importance of property to a people unaccustomed to ownership, and whose determination to save money in order to establish permanence through property was often misinterpreted by Americans as niggardliness or thrift. Yet Harriman's real interest lies in the Polish sense of property as status and identity. Henry's passion for saving money is compulsive and unconscious. Although he has been saving for six years, he cannot explain why. "Oh, I d'know . . . couldn't help it I guess," is his only response. Julia's mother knows better. "Yeh got t'have a house" (25), she tells them, aware that marriage without property fails to provide the necessary social base. Consequently, Henry thinks of owning a "great brick house on Jefferson Avenue, the backyard of which was alive with chickens," the front of which was surrounded by a white picket fence (29). Henry's idealized house is a cultural bridge, combining his peasant background (yard with chickens) and his vision of America (broad avenues and picket fences on Jefferson Avenue). To Julia the house is a sign of successful immigration, a combination of ethnic pride and newly achieved American status. In "The Homebuilders," the new Brosczki house represents successful transplant just as Julia's wedding gifts symbolize her dual ancestries. To furnish her home, Julia receives the traditional gift given by a Polish husband—a new stove. From Mrs. Fernowicz she gets an imitation mahogany pedestal, "supporting in tinted plaster, the bust of an American Indian" (63), a token of the young couple's adopted American ancestry.

The Brodsky passion in "The Patriots" also involves saving for and buying a house, which precipitates a temporary crisis in loyalty. For the Brodskys the dilemma is whether to give their savings to the cause of a free Poland or to use the money to purchase an American house. Resisting her husband's inclination, Mrs. Brodsky generously contributes to the fund-raising commission but secretly withholds enough to pay for their own home. The Brodskys have thus remained Polish even while becoming American. Conflicting loyalty, often expressed as the persistence of Old World memories and identities, is Harriman's overriding theme. For most of his characters, memories of Poland are a constant point of reference. These memories were unacknowledged even by sympathetic writers until Annette Esty's portrait of a lonely Polish woman in *The Proud House*. Harriman, however, shows how first-generation Poles made decisions with an eye toward Old World identities. In Mrs. Brodsky's mind, for example, she is forever a "fresh-cheeked girl" watching from the roadside "the soldier that she loved marching away" (105). And her decision to allow her son to enlist in the U.S. Army is a response to her husband's having served in the Old

Country. Likewise, in "The Wages of His Toil," Ladislav Adamowsky solves his American problem by remembering peasant skills learned in his youth. Having lost his job in the mill, he decides, "I kin milk. I guess I ain't forgot, I did once, a long time ago—over there" (176). For others the prospect of eventual return to Poland shapes their future.

Harriman makes it painfully clear that dual ancestry does not come easily and that conflicting allegiances disrupt social organization and fragment the ethnic self. Hardship, sorrow, and dislocation accompany transplantation. Anton Tschaeche cannot accept the fact that his daughter would go to Buffalo with a bookkeeper who has changed his Polish name and "forgotten his people." He dies of loneliness, a victim of reorganized family relationships quite different from European models. Similarly, Ladislav Adamowsky is destroyed because he believed that physical skill and vigor, highly esteemed in the peasant community, would be enough in America. Max in "The Artist" hopes to succeed in America only so that he can "go back across the ocean—back home" (293). Harriman's best example of the high cost of immigration—the loss of identity and cultural isolation—occurs in "The Day of the Game," a story that deals with Michigan's victory over the Cornell football club, John Adams's starring role in the game, and his confrontation with his American girlfriend. Seemingly suave, educated, and admired, Adams is unsure of himself, visibly bothered by an anonymous drunk who tries to participate in "his" great day. Eventually Harriman reveals that Adams is really Jan Adamowsky, son of Ladislav, the now half-crippled sweeper in the stove works, and the protagonist in "The Wage of His Toil." In his new identity as university student and football hero, Adams, foreshadowing the protagonist of Millard Lampell's 1949 novel *The Hero,* has shed his ethnic skin and "passed" as an Anglo in what is thus the first "passing story" involving Poles. The victory celebration juxtaposed against the sight of his drunken father precipitates an examination of conscience and the subsequent revelation of his past to his girlfriend. To her he confesses his guilt at having rejected his name, traditions, religion, and family that "sent me here to college to study, to learn, to make something of myself" (274). Ironically, America's gift—an education—has caused him to feel ashamed of his ethnicity. When Jan tells his friend about his Catholicism, Polish heritage, and working-class status, her shock and denial suggest that ethnicity in America is a social barrier impossible to transcend. With melodramatic suddenness, Adams gives up his newly won acceptance and returns to his family to resume his place in the stove works alongside his father. Even so, a significant event has occurred. Jan has become aware of ethnicity in ways different from his parents, and his altered consciousness suggests the transformation from Pole to Polish

American, from first to second generation. At the same time, Harriman offers no easy answers to Adamowsky's future. What we are left with is two generations of alienated Poles whose social and psychological well-being reside, they think, within the confines of ethnic community.

The Homebuilders looks backward to Sienkiewicz's *After Bread* and forward to Harold Waldo's *Stash of the Marsh Country* (1921), Annette Esty's *The Proud House* (1932), Millard Lampell's *The Hero* (1949), and Darryl Poniscan's *Andoshen* (1973)—to a sequence of works about the unsuccessful search for place, the troubling legacy of ethnicity, and the continuing problem of homebuilding. Harriman's reviewers chose to overlook his darker truths, however. The *New York Times* preferred to notice the colorful customs of the peasants, their love of country, loyalty to America, and poetic character (71). The peasant was still a prince to the *New York Times*.

During this period, the only other writer to look at the Pole as an individual struggling within the ethnic community to make a life is Harold Waldo whose 1921 novel, *Stash of the Marsh Country,* is dedicated to Rupert Hughes, "a friend of Poles where any are living." Like *The Homebuilders*, *Stash* blends realism with romance, hope with despair, Old with New World tensions. Set in turn-of-the-century Detroit and the environs of Lake Michigan, the novel covers the adolescence and young manhood of Stash Plazarski, whose family disintegrates soon after arriving in the United States. He suffers through his father's imprisonment, his mother's desertion, and his uncle's suicide. He passes his adolescence in wanderings between Detroit and the marsh country. Cut off from his ethnic roots despite his continued presence within the Slavic community, he tries to find a place in America. He is an early version of the modern hero who, like Stanley Kowalski, retains only enough traces of ethnicity to isolate him from the mainstream.

Although the novel shares many characteristics of the "immigrant" genre, Waldo avoids displays of ethnic color and the usual conflict of native and ethnic characters that mark much ethnic fiction. Instead he concentrates on a young man's search for maturity and identity in the context of an immigrant world dissolving and an ethnic one waiting to be born. Except for the ethnic dimension, Waldo's novel parallels the spirit of Thomas Wolfe—although without Wolfe's lyricism. And Stash's journey resembles the personal and universal aspects of Eugene Gant's search for meaning and self—although without Gant's power of penetration. Unfortunately, Stash has acquired an American thirst for wealth and fame which, unfulfilled, leaves him embittered and alienated. Neither his American dream nor his Old World self serves him very well and he ultimately rejects both, hoping to "leave all that I know . . . behind" (316). At the outbreak of the war he enlists in the Canadian army and with the help of time and distance comes to believe that there are two Americas—the one that destroyed his family and the other that offers him a new life—and that he will try to accept both. Waldo is a bit fuzzy about all this, and Stash's abrupt decision to "accept" America goes unexplained. Consequently, the problems of social disorganization and alienation yield to Waldo's apparent desire to supply a happy American ending.

4. THE PRINCE IN THE PEASANT

Despite the fact that by the early 1900s, immigration had completely changed the make-up of the Polish community in America, and that virtually all arriving Poles were peasants, writers of sentimental romances continued to show a preference for Polish aristocrats. In the 1920s, a period of restricted immigration and hostility to ethnics personified in the Sacco-Vanzetti incident, writers avoided the Polish peasant almost entirely, choosing instead nineteenth-century models which, with some alteration, offered a way to transcend an unpleasant reality. Turning their backs on the huddled masses of Buffalo and the mine laborers of Pennsylvania, Rupert Hughes, Mary Ives Todd, Dorothy Richardson, Charles J. Phillips, John N. Greeley, and others wrote romantic versions of immigrant history more compatible with mainstream ideology. Their novels linked nineteenth-century literary forms and attitudes with a rejuvenated myth of New World success. They continued to insist that the Poles (even as peasants in Greeley's case) were a mirror to the nation, the standard-bearers of a European cultural tradition that could only enrich American life.

In *Violina: A Romance* (1904) and *Zal: An International Romance* (1905), Mary Ives Todd and Rupert Hughes bridged the centuries with works distinctly nineteenth-century in flavor. Their stories of cultured, courteous, and melancholy patriots focused on individual, upper-class Poles, avoiding even a passing glance at the realities of Polish immigration. In *Violina* and *Zal*, Todd and Hughes carried their readers back to the days of Kosciuszko and the 1863 uprising, to a century of self-sacrifice and aspirations of freedom. Dorothy Richardson in *The Book of Blanche* (1924) and Charles J. Phillips in *The Doctor's Wooing* (1926) built upon this tradition. Strictly speaking, their Poles are neither princes nor peasants but rather second-generation Americans without direct connections to Poland or to the Polish-American community. Blanche Wolska, orphaned at an early age and raised by her Hungarian foster father and Rhoda Palisy (Palackowski), grows up in rural Wisconsin. Nonetheless, Richardson and Phillips provide for their protagonists a genteel background connected to a cultural-historical past already familiar to American readers. We learn that Blanche Wolska is the daughter of Countess Markiewitska and that her great-grandfather was exiled to Siberia for his patriotic activities. Rhoda Palisy, the daughter of an ordinary, backwoods Wisconsin farmer, has an even more illustrious heritage. Her grandfather was cut down by Cossack sabers in the 1863 uprising and her father, who also fought in the rebellion against the tsar, fled to Canada in the 1890s, exiled for his subsequent efforts to liberate Poland. He is, Phillips writes, one of thousands of Polish emigrés "scattered over the face of the earth" as a consequence of their "fight for freedom" (22). Not themselves aristocrats or political refugees, both Blanche and Rhoda embody a popular tradition attractive to 1920s readers eager to reattach a romantic image to the Slav.

Toward this end, Richardson and Phillips ignore the ethnic traits, characteristics, and customs that had been criticized in the periodical press and exploited (and explored) in political fiction and the realistic works of Harriman and Waldo. For example, except for her ancestry, Blanche hardly seems Polish. Richardson avoids references to the Polish language, Catholicism, customs, and traditions, suggesting instead that ethnicity resides in Blanche's character—her high-mindedness, nobility of spirit, and artistry. Blanche herself epitomizes romanticism. She believes that "poetry is a shortcut to all knowledge" (69) and that music is the passionate expression of that knowledge. The plot of the novel develops around Blanche's violin virtuosity as Richardson, like Todd and Hughes before her, uses music to emphasize and represent the genius of Polish culture.

In *The Doctor's Wooing*, Phillips focuses more explicitly on Polish history to define ethnicity and to delineate character. He devotes a substantial part of the novel to a history of Poland, particularly to its nineteenth-century uprisings. Phillips tries to explain nineteenth-century Polish history by comparing it with American history, thus linking the destinies of the two nations as other American writers had done before him. He explains that Rhoda's family fought alongside Kosciuszko and describes the 1792 revolt through comparisons with the American Revolution. He additionally describes the 1863 rebellion as a concurrent expression of America's own noble efforts to free the slaves. "Your freedom and ours," he reminds us, was the rallying cry of the Polish aristocrats to the peasants, a rather confusing and inaccurate analogy of Polish and American political aims.

Like Richardson, Phillips also relies on standard devices—symbols, icons, art—to define ethnicity. Rhoda's temperament, similar to Blanche Wolska's, is rooted in high culture and romanticism, more

particularly in a mysterious, Byronic posture. She is a blend of speculation, surmise, canniness, childlike faith and joy—a play of light and
shadow, generated, according to Phillips, by a thousand years of forest
existence. "There is," he writes, "something mystic, something clair-
voyant in the Slavic nature. All Poles have it" (23). Rhoda is another in
a line of Polish musical geniuses, as the image of the ethnic political
exile gives way to that of the musician-artist (Kosinski's Slavic protagonist in *Pinball*, 1982, is a composer). Her father is a beau ideal in the
broadest sense. He knows languages, painting, music, Greek mythology, Norse and Slavonic sagas. A devotee of opera, he purchases a
piano for his rural Wisconsin house.

In both novels, the duty of the protagonists is to preserve genteel
Polish values at the expense of their own safety and happiness in
America. Blanche lives up to her obligations when she rededicates
herself to her music and, at the cost of her health and eventually her life,
plays at Carnegie Hall. And Rhoda rejects her attractive, wealthy
American suitor to search for her mother, just as she had previously
spurned another offer of marriage because of a disagreement over her
father's burial place. Excessively sentimental and romantic, Blanche
and Rhoda place family and art before personal pleasure in these
nonassimilationist novels which illustrate how Americans of genteel
Polish ancestry triumph over adversity—an object lesson consistent
with the American mythos.

Thus, by the mid-1920s, writers had successfully transferred the
qualities and themes formerly associated with the nineteenth-century
beau ideal to second-generation American Poles. In *War Breaks Down
Doors* (1929), John Greeley takes this process one step further, suggesting that the peasant also carries the seeds of a vigorous cultural stock
which, under the right climate, would produce the type of American
who bears witness to the essential rightness of the immigration period.
In the spirit of Horatio Alger, Greeley records the rise of such a peasant
from his humble beginnings as a child laborer in the mines of Shamo-
kin, Pennsylvania, to his life as a business tycoon and social beau ideal
in the roaring twenties.

Yet, Greeley's novel does not celebrate the triumph of ethnicity. His
depiction of a "typical" Polish family is decidedly negative. The Sin-
cowiezs appear to be without redeeming qualities. The sulky violent
father cuffs his children regularly, prefers the saloon to church, and
lacks the cultural interests attributed to the Wolska and Palisy families.
Similarly, Jan's mother, thick and dark, is more interested in food than
in art. And Jan himself, barely literate, reacts physically to problems
just like his father and neighbors whose lives reflect the oppressive
environment of the mining camp. *War Breaks Down Doors* is about the

flight from ethnicity; the greater the distance Jan puts between himself and his ethnic background, the greater his chances to succeed.

Jan glimpses the opportunities available to Anglo army officers and quickly seeks to Americanize himself, although he is not consciously ashamed of his past; he does not change his name, for instance. Rapidly, he discovers the force of the printed page, the power of money, and the advantages of sophistication, much of which he learns from his commanding officer. Greeley also credits Jan's rise to his own abilities, which he ably demonstrates in combat: he is intelligent, ambitious, observant, fearless, quick to seize the day.

Greeley's novel is a straightforward commentary on the American dream: the immigrant makes good, capitalism avails its benefits to the working class; natural ability is rewarded. Through shrewd investments in the bull market, Jan rises high enough to marry into the family that owns the mills and mines of his childhood, and Jan's separation from his ethnic origins is absolute. He returns to his Pennsylvania hometown only once and observes that "his family belonged still to a world he had left forever" (179). As far as Greeley is concerned, ethnicity has had its time and has served its purpose. In the second half of the novel, he concentrates on Jan's integration into the establishment. To Greeley, the Flower family is not an enemy of the working class, and Jan himself has no intention to "free the serfs" once he becomes a Flower in this distinctly nonproletarian novel. We do see, however, that the Anglo world, in the person of Dev Flower, has grown sterile and lethargic, in need of a robust transfusion by the Polish Jan. Greeley thus includes a regeneration theme, more fully developed in novels about the peasant on the land.

In the novel, the ethnic Jan transforms the Anglo Flowers from a lifeless to a life-producing family. Ellen is an austere, withdrawn, bloodless beauty who changes, after her marriage to Jan, into a woman of humor, exuberance, and fecundity. In return she smooths Jan's rough ethnic edges and supplies him with an American social identity. Their child (Ellen had been childless in her former marriage) testifies to Jan's regenerative power and to the successful grafting of Slavic and Anglo stock, especially since the child shows no physical signs of his Slavic blood. So much the better, Greeley seems to say in his response to the racial implications of the debate over immigration. Like writers such as Edna Ferber, Greeley is eager to prove that assimilation and intermarriage can only improve the native stock which, in these novels, seems happily to dominate genetically.

With the publication of *War Breaks Down Doors*, American literature had completed the transformation of a European aristocrat into an American beau ideal—a happy and content Jay Gatsby. Avoiding peasant culture, an unpopular topic in the 20s, Richardson and Phillips substituted art for social realities in their portraits of Poles. And Greeley turned to the Alger theme to praise the ability of the natural aristocrat in immigrant dress to adapt himself to an American style with beneficial results for melting-pot America. Even peasants, Greeley's novel shows, could be princes in America.

5. ARCHETYPAL AND EXOTIC FARMERS

The period from 1880 to 1930 gave rise to yet another kind of ethnic novel: fictional treatments of the immigrant on the land. Usually thought of in connection with Willa Cather's *My Antonia* (1918) or O. E. Rolvaag's *Giants in the Earth* (1927), peasant farmers were actually introduced earlier in Frances Allen's *The Invaders* (1913) and Edith Miniter's *Our Natupski Neighbors* (1916). These novels about Poles in New England seized upon the historical association of the Polish peasant and the land and took as their subject the contemporary crisis in American agriculture precipitated and worsened, as some claimed, by unrestricted immigration. Interest in the Pole as farmer dates back to a congressional proposal to set aside a large tract of land for the refugees of the 1831 uprising and to the first Polish settlements in Texas, as reported in *Lippincott's* in 1883. In that article and succeeding ones, journalists placed the Pole into the pioneer tradition and thus helped to create a personality and typology that novelists would refine in the twentieth century. In 1910, William N. Morse described the unending patience, capacity for ceaseless toil, great vigor, honesty, and optimism of immigrant farmers in New England and suggested that the Polish characteristics of integrity and simplicity, productivity and frugality were not unlike those of earlier New England pioneers (*Outlook* 86). Similar articles appeared in *Survey* ("Slav Farmers on the Abandoned Farm Area of Connecticut," Oct. 7, 1911) and *Charities* ("Slavs as Farmers," July 1907), with the result that by the 1920s in the press and in fiction, the Pole had come to represent a redemptive force, a regenerating agent for American agriculture complete with the qualities and outlook of the Jeffersonian small farmer.

As a sort of fictional response to the agricultural crisis in New England, *The Invaders* and *Our Natupski Neighbors* record America's ambivalence to the immigrant on the land. Both novels are set in New England, both deal with the "invasion" of the Polish peasant, the ensuing cultural conflict, and the resulting accommodations and changes, and both look at the subject through the eyes of native protagonists. The Poles are secondary characters—objects of study and catalysts of change. Apparently unable to decide who the Poles are, Allen and

Miniter characterize them as both aristocrats and peasants, archetypes and objects of local color, invaders and saviors of New England culture. Yet despite their indecisiveness, Allen and Miniter place the peasant in congenial surroundings that are sympathetic to most Americans. Thus ethnicity in their novels takes on an earthy humanness and an American flavor lacking in novels about the urban life of proletariat and princes.

Allen's *The Invaders,* a transitional novel in many ways, reflects both her own ambivalence and that of the region. She is torn between equally strong desires to criticize and praise, to accept and reject the new immigrants. And she appears afraid to offer the public a novel about Polish peasants without including an aristocrat as a character. In either case, her major interest lies not with the Polish and Irish invaders but with a changing New England. Even so, the novel furnishes some of the first glimpses of peasant culture, of "cheerful red roofs around the little church with the yellow dome," of the pictures of St. Stanislaus and John Sobieski hanging on the cottage walls, of the odors of cooking onions and cabbage, and of the temperament and style of the peasant woman. Allen is clearly intrigued by the barefooted Mrs. Wienaski and singles out the woman for gentle criticism because she keeps a littered kitchen with shoes stuffed under the stove and because chickens march through the front hall as Mrs. Wienaski mutters in "untutored" Polish between bites of bread and lebenwurst. Apart from generalizing the peasant character as industrious, undereducated, and socially backward, Allen chooses not to look carefully at peasant behavior and customs.

As it turns out, Allen is more interested in Stefan Posadowski, an unlikely lodger in the Wienaski household since he is upper class. Her portrait of Posadowski suggests that she prefers the aristocrat to the peasant and believes that the American public better understands the Polish self as it had been presented through the beau ideal. Posadowski falls in that tradition. He has dark, tragic eyes (which allude to the Polish past) and a stately formality. His manners and breeding stand in marked contrast to the Polish and American villagers. We are told that he is the son of a great Polish singer and Prince Nicholas Posadowski of St. Petersburg. Like his counterparts in *Zal, The Book of Blanche,* and *The Doctor's Wooing,* he is characterized through music, patriotism, and melancholy. When he performs Chopin's C Minor prelude, he uses the occasion to instruct the town about the "real Poland" (genteel Poland, of course). "Now you shall hear the ring of swords, the laughter of beautiful women, the tap of high heels and spurs on ballroom floors," he tells them. "Now you shall know how we love and woo and suffer—and die—die we Poles whom you know only as onion-weeders and tobacco settlers" (185). What the Wienaskis think about Posadow-ski's "real Poland," Allen, unfortunately, does not think to tell us. Clearly, she has decided where Polish ethnicity lies and what images are best suited to American tastes. By juxtaposing Posadowski and the Wienaskis, Allen gives her readers doses of two very different Poles, but her heart seems to side clearly with America's continuing love affair with the Polish beau ideal. Nonetheless, Allen gives a new design to ethnicity by associating the peasant and the land.

Appearing three years later, Edith Miniter's *Our Natupski Neighbors* has been generally ignored even by ethnic specialists, although it is one of the most important ethnic novels of the period. Miniter also writes from the viewpoint of the host culture, in the voice of a sympathetic but distant narrator. She treats the peasant more broadly and more succinctly, if not with more depth of characterization, and probes questions of assimilation and ethnicity new to the Polish tradition in American literature. Miniter's method is to concentrate on one family, the Natupskis, while alluding to the presence of other Poles in the immediate area. This pattern, favored by most host-culture writers, results in the image of Poles as solitary individuals when, in fact, the tendency was to live within large Polish American communities. For her, as for Allen and writers to follow, the attraction of ethnicity lay primarily in the contrast of the immigrant and the native American. Such is the case in this novel.

Miniter's major contribution resides in her analysis of the peasant character and, to a greater degree, in her portrait of the Polish family, a literary study that predates Thomas and Znaniecki and Theodore F. Abel's seminal study, "Sunderland" (1929). The Natupskis are a tightly knit, patriarchal unit. Everyone works in the fields—children, husband, and wife sharing equally in the labor—and everyone shares responsibility for the well-being of the family. As head, Kania, the father, makes all decisions and enforces his authority vigorously. He treats the children roughly and even beats his wife, an action she regards as a sign of his masculinity and love. Kania's family, even as it tries to maintain itself, is disintegrating, a victim of social reorganization in America and of generational conflict. Once grown, the children are reluctant to accept Kania's leadership. In a remarkably short time, their acquired taste for socioeconomic mobility displaces patriarchal authority. Statia, aping the ways of Anglo Americans, changes her name and refuses to marry her father's choice—a fellow Pole. Marika also wants to marry outside her ethnicity and breaks away from the family altogether. Kazia, educated in a normal school, moves to East-field to pursue a teaching career. Only Stanislarni remains loyal to the family, but with a radically different perspective toward work, family loyalty, and the distribution of responsibilities. By novel's end, he represents the reconstituted immigrant family which only slightly resembles the original Natupski clan.

Within this context, Miniter looks at peasant character with mixed emotions. In general, the peasant is a primitive sort: slovenly, ignorant, naive. Mr. Natupski, without any sense of aesthetics or appreciation of beauty, cuts down all the lilac, woodbine, and wysteria that grace the old house. His stubbornness reaches legendary proportions among his neighbors and his reluctance to add to the material comforts of his family becomes something of a local scandal. Even so, Abner Slocum, a neighbor and spokesperson for the community, eventually comes to regard peasant character as worthy—without pride, covetousness, wrath, gluttony, envy, or sloth and characterized by prudence, justice, temperance, and fortitude.

Miniter is determined to show that the Polish family will make a positive contribution to American life and that Poles and Americans share a common cultural tradition. Toward this end, she turns to a familiar technique: a comparison of cultures designed to connect the history and ideology of both. At one point, Stanislarni, awakening to these similarities, compares Sobieski with Washington and Mickiewicz with Stowe as evidence of the democratic spirit of both nations. Later, in a school program, Poles and Americans exchange history lessons and literary history. Abner Slocum, who becomes enamored of Mickiewicz's poetry, recites the poet's "The Father's Return." Kasia and her mother sing "Jeszcze Polska Nie Zginela," the Polish national anthem; and each group departs believing that common traditions transcend cultural differences. In *Our Natupski Neighbors,* the Polish family successfully integrates into American life in ways, as Harriman showed earlier, that deethnicize and disorganize the peasant culture. Miniter, however, assumed the task of portraying the Poles in ways attractive to Americans and, in the process, designed an archetypal model, to be discussed later.

By the late 1920s, the general direction of the literary treatment of Poles was fairly well established, even though Polish American writers had not yet emerged and no important American writers had produced works about Poles. From Savage to Greeley, writers reflected America's ambivalence toward its new citizens, albeit with an increased understanding of Polish culture and character and with a greater sensitivity to the problems of assimilation, the reorganization of a peasant culture, and the rise of ethnic consciousness. Some sought to politicize the Pole, either in proletarian fiction as the victim of unchecked capitalism or in reactionary literature as a dangerous threat to the social order. Others portrayed the peasant realistically within an urban or rural setting. At the same time, writers continued to stress Polish and American cultural connections largely through nineteenth-century models of patriotism, iconic history, and aristocrats who embodied the "real" Polish cultural and historical tradition. Even in works about peasants, such as *The Invaders* and *War Breaks Down Doors*, American writers reflected the public's preference to think of the Pole as a European beau ideal. Throughout the period the literary self stumbled along, expanding through folk symbols, archetypes, and historical analogies and contracting into stereotypical portraiture. Throughout, the Slavic character remained alien to most Americans who, like the authors whose books they read, tended to be interested mainly in the immigrant's impact on America's institutions. Although to the sophisticated reader these efforts may appear to be reductive and simplistic, they were, in fact, outreaching—a fundamental and necessary stage in literary ethnicity which, as Werner Sollors reminds us, is continually "reinvented and reinterpreted in each generation by each individual" (*Invention* xi) and, as Sollors implies, by each generation of writers. This process continued into the 1930s and 1940s when the Great Depression and World War II produced an altered consciousness about ethnicity and offered new opportunities to ethnic writers.

3

THE IMMIGRANT ON THE LAND

A man without land is like a man without legs; he crawls
about and cannot get anywhere. —REYMONT

I. TYPOLOGY AND ETHNICITY

In the few novels written about Poles during the 1920s, writers observed ethnicity at a distance, trying—as it were—to suggest that Poles, and by extension all ethnics, were "just like us." Rupert Hughes (*She Goes to War,* 1929) and John Greeley (*War Breaks Down Doors,* 1929) record the contribution of America's Poles in the Great War. Dorothy Richardson in *The Book of Blanche* (1924) praises the artistic abilities and achievements of the immigrant. And Harold Waldo (*Stash of the Marsh Country,* 1921) and Charles Phillips (*The Doctor's Wooing,* 1926) show that Polish-born Americans responded to the frustrations of day-to-day life in much the same fashion as their native-born neighbors. In a decade of hostility to ethnics that resulted in the National Origins Quota Act of 1924, the few who wrote about ethnic Poles turned away from the cultural-historical traditions that characterize Polishness in order to make ethnicity more respectable.

This determination to soften the edges of ethnicity continued into the 1930s where, prompted by the abrupt socioeconomic changes wrought by the depression, it collided with a radical shift in literary attitudes toward ethnicity. During this decade, writers identified the Pole with the proletarian tradition, rooting him to the land in a series of novels about immigrant farmers. These associations, as we have seen, date from the early 1900s. But the fullest expression of America's interest in the immigrant on the land occurred in the early 1930s, and illustrated what can only be described as a disproportionate and puzzling literary phenomenon. According to Edward Pinkowski's estimate, by 1920 almost 200,000 Poles lived in rural America—although not all were directly engaged in agriculture (*Poles in America* 303–70). In Panna Marie, Texas, Radom, Illinois, Poznan, Nebraska, and elsewhere, Poles founded agricultural communities. But given the fact that approximately 2 million Poles immigrated to America between 1880 and 1914, 80 percent of whom settled in urban areas, the numbers of Polish farmers in America never reached significant numbers, except perhaps in the Connecticut River Valley.

New England Polish farmers found themselves at the center of controversy and debate about the agricultural crisis facing America, particularly New England, which had suffered from neglect and from the emigration West. As some would have it, the crisis was exacerbated by the new immigrants themselves. The crisis prompted official inquiry such as L. H. Bailey's *Report of the Commission on Country Life* (1911) and led to other studies and responses which identified the immigrant as part of the problem. In 1926 Carl C. Taylor argued that immigrants compounded the farm problem because they, like the American farmers, wanted to own land rather than to work as much-needed farm laborers. E. R. Eastman, editor of the influential weekly, *American Agriculturist,* took another tack, condemning the mostly Slavic farmers for corrupting rural life with their inferior intelligence and low standards of living. They are, he asserted, "a serious menace to the people of fine, old country communities" (223).

Racial attitudes such as Eastman's were especially pronounced in New England. As Barbara Solomon has shown, the tolerant views of Emerson and Lowell at mid-century soon gave way to the prejudiced views of Senator Henry Cabot Lodge, R. Mayo Smith, and Francis A. Walker, president of M.I.T. and superintendent of the census, who warned his fellow New Englanders against committing Anglo Saxon racial suicide (*Ancestors* 82). Popular magazines echoed these fears. Edward Kirk Titus, writing in the *New England Magazine* in 1903, attacked the morals, religion, and customs of Polish farmers and observed that in the Poles, "one sees little hope for a helpful social or political influence" (166). In "Two Glimpses of the New England Pole," Harry Shipman Brown presented Poles as "animals [who] work under the sun and in the dirt; with stolid, stupid faces" (286). Such disparaging comments stood firm against the more balanced, informed views of Konrad Bercovici (*On New Shores,* 1925) and Theodore Abel, whose short work "Sunderland" is among the first studies of a Polish-American farming community.

Almost immediately, American writers, beginning with Frances Allen's *The Invaders* (1913), responded to this controversy with a sensitivity that was lacking in official reports and magazine articles. In a dozen or so novels they document the interaction of Poles and Americans, usually in New England, and introduce the Pole in ways quite different from earlier depictions. The Poles in these works are peasants. They have no patriotic mission or cultural-historical tradition attributed to the nineteenth-century Polish beau ideal. They do not possess the democratic instincts and social attitudes that Americans had admired and identified with in works about Kosciuszko and his fictional counterparts. Written over a sixty-year period from Allen's 1913 novel to Mary Ellen Chase's *A Journey to Boston* (1965), they instead provide a minihistory of the Polish American agricultural experience and serve an equally important sociological function as documents of cultural assimilation and the resulting acculturation of America. Thus, by drawing upon romantic images of ethnicity and the immigrant experience and grafting them onto American ideological stock, this group of novels illustrates how writers fused American and immigrant concerns and thereby fashioned a new portrait of Polishness and a revised version of the American mythos.

To introduce the Poles and to dramatize their impact on American culture and vice versa, writers turned to what Sacvan Bercovitch describes as the Puritan rhetorical forms that permeate American literature and to a set of fixed models that, according to Ursula Brumm, have guided American writing since the seventeenth century (199). In short, the Polish experience was presented in terms of a familiar format: the biblical drama of a chosen people seeking a new life and identity, searching for a new Eden, which they find and cultivate as the American garden. Although this model finds its way into almost all novels about the peasant farmer, postwar writers such as William Castle, Maurice Hindus, and Mary Ellen Chase moved toward greater realism and psychological depth in examining the relationship of the ethnic to his world. Motivated in part by postwar concerns, they emphasized the loss of Old World identity and the failure of Poles to find a home in the American garden. Thus, the literary treatment of the peasant on the land is divided into modernist and postmodernist phases influenced by social realities and by a reevaluation of ethnic identity.

Before World War II, those who wrote about Polish farmers—Frances Allen; Edith Miniter, *Our Natupski Neighbors,* 1916; Cornelia Cannon, *Heirs,* 1930; Edna Ferber, *American Beauty,* 1931; Annette Esty, *The Proud House,* 1932; Gladys Hasty Carroll, *As the Earth Turns,* 1933—produced strikingly similar novels, a response of sorts to the New England agricultural crisis. All are set in the Northeast, most often the Connecticut River Valley, where Poles settled in sizable numbers; and, Ferber excepted, all are written by women with New England connections, none of whom are immigrants or Polish Americans. These writers grieve the passing of traditional values usually associated with rural America and feature female protagonists struggling to maintain those values. The Polish newcomers, secondary characters for the most part, act out their own struggle against the background of a deteriorating agricultural society.

America in these novels, while still a promised land, is now in ruins.

Poverty, despair, and sterility have settled over the land and the people; New England is a blighted garden—a physical and spiritual wasteland. Cornelia Cannon's landscape is dotted with cellar holes, all that remains of "houses which, long since deserted . . . had crumbled and disappeared" (59). In *The Proud House,* Annette Esty features a countryside so forlorn that nothing "could bring success from these stony acres" (57). By the turn of the century, even the successful farms had retreated into the wilderness. In *American Beauty* Edna Ferber writes that the early settlers had fished the rivers clean and left the land barren; now the land had taken "revenge upon a people who had taken it without love" (15).

If the land appears to be cursed, so too does the native American stock. In her 1913 novel, Frances Allen presents a culture in which "the old families have petered out." Later, Cornelia Cannon attributes this decline to centuries of repression which have left only a "crippled inheritance." The New Englander, "crystallized and finished like the rocks . . . had ceased to be interested in appearing well before his neighbors" and "disregarded the sound economy of keeping his buildings well painted and shingled, and his garden and fields free from noxious and encroaching plants" (97). Ferber's portrait is equally damning: her New England men are "stringy of withers, lean shanked, of vinegar blood and hard wrung" (69); the best blood had gone west, "leaving behind the old, the incompetent, the sick, the unadventurous, and the contented" (63).

What these novels offer is a representation of typological declension: America is an Eden in ruins, and the inability of its distressed people to make the land flourish testifies to their fallen state. Into this fictional wasteland come the Poles who, on one level, appear to add little more to the narrative than local color. Each novel describes Polish weddings and feast days, refers to familiar national figures such as Mickiewicz or Chopin, and introduces Polish folk art and foodstuffs. In other words, Polish culture is presented through devices that would later be described by Herbert Gans as the "symbols of ethnicity" (204). The Poles themselves are portrayed as naive, backward, and culturally eccentric but ultimately, and more important, as nonthreatening ethnic newcomers. Such benign and charming representations, in meeting the requirements of local color, also serve to fashion a social shield that protects the group from a potentially aggressive majority; the Poles' involvement in typological patterns familiar to all Americans serves this purpose even better.

The Poles are portrayed, for example, as a type of chosen people whose New World experiences resemble those described in the literature of Winthrop, Mather, Crevecoeur, and others. Unlike their seventeenth-century predecessors, however, the Poles enter New England as redemptive agents whose mission is to reclaim a lost America. Frances Allen sets the tone in her 1913 novel when one of her characters, a minister named Dr. Britten, helps his suspicious neighbors understand that the Poles are "a chosen people [sent] to work out our destiny" (223). They bring to us, another character adds, "what we ourselves are in need of—and just when we need it" (123). In 1930 Cornelia Cannon voices essentially the same theme in *Heirs,* whose readers are told that the Poles "are bringing youth and energy to these worked-over lands— and they're bringing beauty, too" (74).

In stark contrast to the withered and withdrawn Yankees who populate these novels, the Poles are robust, vigorous, prolific. Ferber's "very male" Polish men have strong angles, red blood, sinews rippling, pulses pounding (69). Edith Miniter makes a similar comparison as she notes, "It would have killed an American baby . . . to sleep on the ground in May after a shower, but it would not injure Zinzic Natupski" (233). Kids scuffle, men fiddle, women dance. Everywhere the Poles exude vitality, freshness, and spirit. "It seems as if they've never learned to hold themselves in the way we do," Marilla Lamprey exclaims in *Heirs;* they are the "abundant promise for the future" (88).

Nowhere is the restorative power of the Poles more visible than in a comparison of Polish and Yankee women. Most of the New England women are portrayed as either unmarried or childless. Not adhering to the usual image of farm girls, they teach school, manage run-down estates, care for their parents, cultivate the arts, intellectualize their experiences. Polish women, generally considered unattractive and unladylike by our female writers and their spokeswomen, are associated most often with the soil and with children. Earth mothers all, they burst forth with life, naturally and without effort. Mrs. Janowski, in *As the Earth Turns,* is typical: "I eat so much wit' not'in to do . . . t'em kids, t'ey just come" (190). We learn that there are, in fact, some "fifteen or twenty little Janowskis." Similarly, Mrs. Natupski (in Miniter's novel) produces children with the enthusiasm of a missionary among the heathen. The novel ends with her giving birth again, this time to twins.

Cornelia Cannon offers the best extended comparison of Yankee and Polish women through the characters of Marilla Lamprey and Ewa Zabka. An old maid of twenty-eight, Marilla is too thin, too plain, too severe. Her day-to-day existence has been one of austerity and self-control, a life without hope. Eventually Marilla marries Seth Watson, only to be told by their Boston doctor that they will never have children. Many of the old New England strains have become sterile, the doctor explains. Ewa Zabka, Marilla's pupil, is sensual and attractive. In contrast to Marilla, Ewa lives for pleasure, self-abandonment, and materialism. The difference between them is obvious, as Marilla makes clear when she compares her own "fastidious" courtship to the "robust" one that Ewa enjoys, and when she considers the prospects of Ewa's many childbearing years to the childless ones she faces.

If Polish women are life giving, Polish men might best be described, in the words of Marcus Lee Hansen, as "spontaneous puritan immigrants"; that is, they resemble the rural American New Englander who exists mostly in the American cultural imagination (119). Jeffersonian small farmers, they are industrious and thrifty, efficient and neat, self-sacrificing and self-reliant. They recognize the value of education and the need for progress, for investing in the future and repaying their debt to the community and the nation. They are made, in effect, to look like Yankees in Polish clothing. Annette Esty cites their "willingness to labor like serfs" (51); Edith Miniter gives us Kani Natupski, who lives by the code that working late and eating little "gets you somewhere." Although Miniter seldom comments on Kani's farming techniques, she heartily approves of the fact that he reinvests his earnings in his New England farm and that he sacrifices the comforts of a home so that the barn could be "efficiently patched with new boards . . . and shingled with cedar shingles at an extraordinary price per thousand" (94).

Like Miniter, Carroll praises the improvements the Poles bring to the farm economy: they lay culverts, repair bridges, fix roads, and mend fences. With enthusiasm and earnestness, Polish children adapt easily to American schools. Olivia's school in *The Invaders* is full of ambitious, eager, intelligent, attentive Poles. Edith Miniter documents the educational success of the second generation: Kazia Natupski finishes normal school; her brother Stan graduates from Harvard. Old World farmers using Old World methods, the Poles are quickly attracted to farm technology because they see, with typical Yankee shrewdness and foresight, that a combination of industry, education, and technology represents America's agricultural future. Orrange Olszak, in *American Beauty*, enrolls in the state agricultural college and soon understands, "We're not getting anywhere with the farm. You can't go sticking things in the ground and hoping they'll come up all right. Farming is going to be as technical as manufacturing" (276).

The Polish immigrant's relationship with the land is portrayed as consistent with the biblical mission so often evoked in American literature. For the Poles an Old World view of agriculture—originating in folklore, pagan superstition, and historical necessity—combines with a view of America as the promised land. In *The Proud House*, Adam and Jozefa Zalinski, on their hands and knees weeding onion rows, believe that "no harm can come to this land. . . . It is a land God loves with his heart" (49). Much as she would later describe the romantic feelings of

Texas ranchers in *Giant,* Edna Ferber alludes to the Poles' almost mystical attitudes: "Their passion went into it," she writes. "They felt about it as men feel about women. It was their pastime, their emotional life, their dream of passion, their dream of possession. Money they did not covet. They were land lovers" (69). Later, William Castle in *Hero's Oak* (1945) and Maurice Hindus in *Magda* (1951) would try to capture the Poles' mystical understanding of nature by structuring their novels around Polish folklore. Among the earlier novelists—driven by a depression mentality, less aware of Polish culture, and motivated by regional concerns—only Edna Ferber recognizes these aspects of peasant culture. She briefly notes how Old World myths regulated New World planting, sowing, and reaping, how sick heifers were made well by plant spirits, and how the water spirits (*boginki*) and the cloud beings (*planetniki*) influenced crops.

Infusing the promised land with their own blend of industry, passion, and faith, the Poles rejuvenate the region and the people. In their hands, the garden blossoms forth once more. Carroll praises the Polish barns where the cows were "fat and round and curried clean" and "the mows were full of good sweet hay" (308). Cannon notes how, almost as if by magic, the Pole "grew the biggest cabbages and cauliflowers and raised the earliest sweet corn in the region. . . . His hens seemed to outdo themselves in laying eggs, his broilers fetched the top prices in Boston" (97, 75). Edna Ferber makes a similar point, but in her panoramic view of the Still and Housatonic River Valley, she emphasizes the transformation that has occurred throughout the region: "The Polish farmers spread over the valley, and the region bloomed like a garden. . . . Fields thick with tobacco, barns bursting with hay, siloes oozing, cattle in the meadows; children and chickens and geese and dogs shouting, cackling, barking, squawking in the yard—that was a Polish farm" (244). And such prosperity will be turned back into the land to the benefit of all. If the Poles will be satisfied enough to stay by the land, Cornelia Cannon states in *Heirs,* "New Hampshire will blossom again."

Like the land, the native New England stock is also infused with new vigor, purpose, and quite literally, new blood. Assimilation and acculturation are, in fact, the major but subtle themes of all these novels, which feature the courtship and marriage of Yankee and Pole as a plot device. Through their union, a new type emerges, a new man who foreshadows an America of the future. In most of these novels, the new American Pole is decidedly more Yankee than Pole. Even as his characteristics are designed to ease fears of ethnic fusion, they are also meant to exemplify the inevitability of Anglo-Saxon racial dominance. Cornelia Cannon describes the process this way: the New Englanders are like potters who mould and shape the immigrants into "new forms to fit new uses" (274). Gladys Carroll shares Cannon's view. In her novel, Stan Janowski rapidly becomes Yankee enough to be acceptable even to the most New England of families, the Shaws. Eventually replacing Mark Shaw as head of the family, Stan accepts Congregationalism, attends Harvard, melts completely into the majority culture, and serves as breeding stock for future generations who will undoubtedly be more Shaw than Janowski. This point is made even more dramatically by Edna Ferber, whose heroine, Temmie Oakes, possessed by the fear that her 200-year-old ancestry nears extinction, produces through Ondy Olszak a son whom she names after the founder of *her* New England clan. In the son, Orrange Oakes, Polishness almost completely disappears. With his "New England head and aquiline nose," Orrange is the reincarnation of his maternal great-grandfather. He is, as Temmie proudly announces, "an Oakes from head to foot." Even Orrange understands, as Ferber hopes the reader will, how the melting pot really works. At one point he tells his mother that after 200 years, "there wasn't any blood left. A good job, your marrying Pa" (280).

By and large, everyone wins in these novels: Poles gain the promised land; rural New England prospers; the stable social order is perpetuated; good Yankee families are made better; the immigrant threat is absorbed. All that remains is to emphasize the immigrants' awareness of their debt to their "new family" and to rally hopes of America's prospects. Stan Janowski hangs an American flag in his kitchen, where "the children can look at it every day" (280); Stepan Natupski leads his mother to the schoolyard so that he can show her the American flag that flies there. Writing during World War I, a time in which immigrant loyalty was suspect, Edith Miniter labors to combine patriotism, service to country, and the rising glory of America. The Harvard-educated Stan Natupski returns home to a modest job as a conservation agent and protector of New England's forests. "I don't think I want to spend my life buying something and selling it again," he explains. "Too many of us do that.... It's up to us to make better use of what America offers" (239).

Thus, what initially seemed to be the random appearance of a few novels celebrating the virtues of rural culture and eulogizing a vanishing way of life turned out to be a literary response to the agricultural crisis facing America, particularly New England, at the beginning of the twentieth century. At the same time, such novels collectively eased the transition of a new ethnic group into the American mainstream by humanizing the stereotype lodged in the popular imagination. Ethnic characters, who at first appeared simply as a colorful way to enliven the novelist's tale, are, in the end, converted into New England's heroes— the people who would preserve its land and fight its battles. In writers like Allen, Miniter, Cannon, Ferber, Esty, and Carroll, then, we find local color—a literary approach often derided for its preciousness and limited compass—being used in the service of social ends to present not just a sentimental view of the past but a dynamic and myth-reinforcing vision of the future.

2. OLD WORLD ROOTS IN THE NEW WORLD GARDEN

The intense, even remarkable, interest in the Polish farmer in 1930s fiction marked a particular stage in the literary treatment of the immigrant on the land. With restrictions on immigration, fewer Poles came to the United States and even fewer took up farming. Nonetheless, postwar authors, enamored of the romantic association of the peasant and the soil, continued to write about Polish farmers. With some variation, they used the typological format introduced earlier but with quite different intentions and with decidedly different results. If 30s writers seemed quick to embrace the popular idea—expressed as early as 1912 by Alexander Cance—that assimilation occurs more rapidly and easily in rural areas (69), the next generation saw that life on the farm offered ethnic groups neither a promising socioeconomic future nor a resolution to ethnic tensions. Wherever they looked, they saw social disorganization, failed attempts at assimilation, and personal tragedy. The dilemma of the Poles in these novels is that the peasant can neither transplant his world to American soil nor leave it quite behind.

On the one hand, writers such as Joseph Wedda (*Jasna Polana* 1945), William Castle (*Hero's Oak* 1945), Maurice Hindus (*Magda* 1951), and Mary Ellen Chase (*A Journey to Boston* 1965) rely heavily on the typology employed by Allen, Ferber, and the rest. On the other, they infuse the pattern with postwar sensibility and adapt it to changing perceptions of ethnics and an evolving sense of ethnic identity. They understand that for many Poles the problem of transplant, what Erik Erikson calls "the interval of being suspended between past and present," overwhelms questions of assimilation and emerges as an aspect of ethnic identity itself. In other words, the struggle to define the ethnic self—a major concern of postwar literature about Poles, perhaps best observed in Jerzy Kosinski's fiction—becomes synonymous with ethnicity, even as it had with Jewish American writers in both pre- and postwar America. The characters in these works simultaneously look to an American future and a Polish past. The tension resulting from the pull of Old World roots and New World aspirations, from the paradox of accepting and rejecting both the past and the present, produces an ironic portrait of an alienated yet hopeful group confined within an often sentimental plot that emphasizes romantic desires in the face of perceived reality.

Such is the case with Joseph Wedda's *Jasna Polana* (*Bright Meadow*), a work that defies genre categorization and that strains typology and reality to the break point. Part essay, part novel, this curious work, set in the Quincy River Valley, portrays an idyllic farming community of good fellowship, love of God and country, and an appreciation for philosophic inquiry. Wedda's "peasants" are more philosopher-gardeners than farmers, given more to universalizing experiences in Platonic-like dialogues than to defining the Polish self. Even so, their ethnicity, always close at hand, governs their thought and behavior. Wedda re-creates his garden on a level that transcends nationality and ethnicity. His Poles in their bright meadow have moved beyond the physical and the temporal, beyond assimilation and acculturation—beyond ethnicity. His American garden is free from the conflict of Yankee and Pole, New and Old World rivalries, and the issues of the divided self. His philosopher-farmers and their spiritual garden are reminiscent of Thoreau at Walden Pond.

For all his intentions, however, Wedda does little to present the immigrant on the land or to define ethnicity, and his novel has little in common with those of his colleagues who, at least on the surface, follow the New England model. For example, although only Mary Ellen Chase has New England roots, all of the novelists "New England-ize" their works according to ready-made comparisons existing in the Yankee-Pole formula—traceable not only to prewar fiction but to the nineteenth-century tradition exemplified in Silas Steele's *Yankee in Poland*. Chase's book is set in the Connecticut River Valley of Western Massachusetts and Castle's takes place in Vermont. But even in Hindus's upstate New York and in Kubiak's Wisconsin, the atmosphere, the people, and their rural concerns are more New England than mid-Atlantic or midwestern. Hindus populates his novel with descendants of New England settlers, named Baxter and Titus, whose speech and values seem indistinguishable from the characters of Cannon, Carroll, and Ferber. Even Mike Koziol, the Polish immigrant, recognizes their New England characteristics when he refers to their "Yankee inge-nuity" (54).

More important, the resemblance between these writers and their New England predecessors extends to the details of the typology employed. Once again, writers focus on the Polish love affair with the new Eden, the regenerative potential of the immigrant, and the accultura-tion of America. For example, the historical relationship of the Pole and the land, a relationship perhaps more fictional than real as Thomas and Znaniecki argue, is transferred to the American landscape which the Poles infuse with their own mystical traditions. Maurice Hindus opens *Magda* by quoting from Ladislaw Reymont's *The Peasants:* "A man without land is like a man without legs; he crawls about and cannot get anywhere" (4). Hindus wastes no time transferring Polish affection for the homeland to the American landscape. His protagonist, Mike Koziol, remembers his uncle's advice to "go out to the land my dear nephew in free America . . . and plant yourself in it as though you were a tree and in time the good Lord will bless you with the sweetest fruit you have ever tasted" (4). William Castle in *Hero's Oak* also describes the union of Pole and land in mystical terms. "On my farm," Alex Krupa explains, "I know every blade of grass, every stone, every grain of soil as if it were the hair on my own head. When I breathe, the air breathes. When I feel sick my Freeplace moans in pain. Brothers we are . . . brothers" (285).

Like their Adamic predecessors in the 1930s novels, the Poles rejuvenate the American garden wherever they settle. In her opening chapter, "The Bright Land," Mary Ellen Chase suggests that the clear sunsets, sparkling waters, brilliant autumns, and flowering hillsides owe something to the presence of immigrants. "Perhaps the very fact that many of them are Polish does its share . . . in adding to the brightness of the valley" (15–16). In *Magda*, Mike Koziol sets to work immediately to invigorate his employer's farm. He plants new crops, breeds new stock, and employs modern farming methods learned at the local agricultural college. In *Hero's Oak*, a corner of Vermont flourishes as never before. Alex Krupa's trees, Castle tells us, "had the biggest apples in America and his brook [was] alive with trout" (147).

Once again, writers show that the greening of America has an equally important biological aspect, implied in comparisons of austere Yankees and earthy Poles who reenergize the native stock by example and through marriage. One of Hindus's characters humorously notes that Polish girls are prettier than Americans because "they have no appetite, these American girls, for food that puts flesh on the bones, sends blood to the cheeks" (148). Hindus carefully illustrates this difference when he compares Magda to her American husband, Dan, who believes that "Polish folks have got so much life in them, always know how to have a good time among themselves" (93). Throughout the novel, Magda displays her life force through her sensuality and her love of dance, music, and art. She thus undercuts her withdrawn and emotionless Yankee husband who commits suicide because he cannot match Magda's enthusiasm for life.

In plots that occasionally feature melting-pot romances between immigrant and native-born Americans, novelists pay lip service to the popular theory of painless and inevitable assimilation, made easier in rural America. In addition, they stress cultural similarities to counteract the inherent differences between Yankee and Pole and to re-establish ties of kinship introduced a century earlier. In truth, the fictional mission of the Poles to reclaim the land and regenerate a worn-out native stock is less convincing than in prewar fiction. The novels do not portray a decaying American Eden nor a people in desperate need of genetic transfusion. Consequently, the Poles are not the powerful redemptive agents depicted in such works as Frances Allen's *The Invaders.* In addition, by the late 1940s, American writers felt no need to propagandize the potential contribution of the Polish immigrant to the American melting pot. They offer no substantial mixing of central European and American blood through marriage, nor do they suggest the emergence of a new and better American in the next generation. Quite the contrary, Poles marry Poles in *A Journey to Boston,* and the courtship of Poles and Americans ends unsuccessfully in *Magda* and *Hero's Oak.* In effect, the naive but hopeful notion that the immigrant would easily gain cultural acceptance on the farm is replaced by the sobering understanding that the American garden, so apparently suited to the peasant, offers no easy solutions to the problems of transplant, a situation documented as early as 1929 in Theodore Abel's pioneering study of Poles in a New England farming community.

Despite appearances and the persistence of a typological formula, the novels are more concerned with questions of identity than they are with American mythology. The Poles are caught between a desire to assume an American identity and an equally strong desire to remain ethnic. They exist midway between two worlds, at home in neither. In this sense, postwar novelists explore the immigrant on the land in the context of what Werner Sollors describes as the standard theme of ethnic literature: the relationship of Old and New Worlds in the struggle for identity ("Literature" 660).

The Poles are ambivalent toward their own ethnicity. Some are desperate to remain Polish. Alex Krupa in *Hero's Oak* embraces both cultures, but Poland is his touchstone in his brightest and darkest moments. He refers often to Polish history and culture and even comes to identify the large oak tree on his Vermont farm with the one in his Polish village, where King Sobieski is said to have rested on his way to defend the country from invaders. In *Magda,* Mike Koziol's return to New York State after a thirty-year absence is a symbolic return to ethnicity. On the outside he looks American and Texan, but ultimately his inner Polish self shines through. As he ceremoniously dances with Magda, "the gallantry of the old Pole" flashes once again (305), and his thoughts turn to his former village, to the "ever dreaming, ever joyful, ever defiant people of his native land" (310). Hindus leaves no doubt that, at least for the moment, Koziol has rediscovered his old self. Yet, even as he thinks lovingly of his village, dances the elegant oberek, and compares the American orchestra unfavorably to Polish musicians; even as he feels more Polish than perhaps at any time since his arrival in the United States, Koziol feels compelled to announce that the America he loves best is a deethnicized one where no one is labeled "Yankee or Pole, Irish or Slovak, farmer or mill hand" (306).

Mary Ellen Chase's Polish Americans still look to Poland and to their ethnicity for their values and traditions. They equate Poland with stability and order. Stanley explains it this way: old country habits and customs "made the past stable and dependable, gave one an odd sense of safety in the present" (73). As much as any of the characters in these novels, Stanley, an uneducated farmer, is aware of the balancing art required of all immigrants and the place of ethnicity in the lives of Poles. Others, such as Castle's Jan Krupa, are perfect examples of second-generation antipathy and the resulting loss of the ethnic self. Although Jan at first claims to believe that "the good Polish earth is always in us" (50), he actually dreams of lifting himself out of the "dull plodding life of a Polish-American farmer" because as he sees it, "this land offers me nothing" (75). His rise, we soon learn, is also his fall. Educated as a doctor, he has no patients because the townspeople will not forget that he, a Polish doctor, made a serious medical mistake early in his career. Isolated from native Americans partly because of his ethnic background ("In this little town we are never permitted to forget our Polish birth" 53), Jan also distances himself from the Poles, his "inferiors." When he takes Marja to the ice rink, he feels ashamed of her Polish appearance and clothing; and when he sits with Poles on a train, he views them as shabby, stupid, beaten people with thick accents. He complains that Polish American families live "colorless, unimaginative, useless lives" (51).

The past thus haunts the present for postwar generations. For some, often the second generation, the issue is simple: ethnicity is an embarrassment, a yoke to be discarded. Mary Ellen Chase's second-generation characters are representative. A little boy tells Stanley, "I don't pass for Polish. . . . We don't call ourselves Polish any longer" (79). And Mrs. Waskiewicz explains that her daughter Yadwiga "isn't Polish any longer . . . and the worst of it is she doesn't *want* to be Polish either" (37). Others, including Mrs. Waskiewicz, reject not only ethnicity but Poland as well. After a brief visit to her native land, Waskiewicz tells her friends that she would never again return to the old country, "not for all of Poland" (57).

In between the lines of these stories of the "wonderfully warm, rich texture of American rural life and of its meanings as democracy," as one reviewer put it (Fuller 253), lurks the notion that in fundamental ways the exchange of old for new has not necessarily benefited the immigrant generation or their children. What they have received, however worthy and appreciated, cannot replace the loss of ethnic identity, as isolation and alienation quickly undermine the stability and dependability of the Polish past so warmly referred to by Stanley in *A Journey to Boston*. Mrs. Waskiewicz's complete denial of Poland, for example, her insistence that she would never again visit, springs from her implicit, but conscious, recognition that she has lost her Old World self. "It's the price you pay when you leave an old country for a new," she comments (355). And for those who still have a foot in both worlds, they will always, as Mike Koziol offers, be "in search of a past" (268).

In *Magda*, Koziol confesses that he had reached the point where he hated himself and "hated life" (241). Koziol's glimpse into the tragic merger of Pole and American, the fiery Rusalka and her good-intentioned, naive husband, has taken the glow from his eyes. In America, he is only "a stranger who was overstaying his time . . . desolate and alone" (253). In *A Journey to Boston*, Mr. Tarnowski talks about his mother who stares out the window crying. To his wife's explanation that "old folks don't transplant any too good," Stan acknowledges that they might have been happier in Poland (72). Actually Stan speaks for most of the first- and second-generation Poles in these novels who sense that they belong to the lost world of Polonaise Nevermore. Ironically, the socioeconomic mobility that attracted the immigrant to America in the first place contributes to his alienation and ultimate separation from the soil he loves. Even while he happily tills the fertile soil of New York, Mike Koziol dreams of managing a large estate and studying at the agricultural college. When he returns to Pineville some thirty years later as the owner of 8,000 Texas acres, we see, however, that his heart has remained in the simple rural life of the Northeast. Similarly Magda, afraid of having to marry a fellow Pole and forever remain a peasant, leaves the Baxter farm to become a successful innkeeper. When we see her later, however, she seems to be only a shell of her former brash, alluring, and mysterious self.

William Castle pursues this irony to a greater extent in *Hero's Oak*. Alex Krupa is the model of a successful immigrant farmer, but his son, Jan, is driven to become something more. After medical school, he proudly hangs his shingle, but his selfless efforts are misunderstood and his neighbors regard him as that "son of a bitch Polish butcher" (137). The desolate, unhappy life that ensues, his wife Marja's breakdown and tragic end, the miserable poverty that afflicts the once prosperous farm—all appear to be a curse born of Jan's divorce from the land and his New World ambition. At least twice, Castle issues a warning to this effect. Juljusz, a family friend, questions how "a man could turn his back on the land which gave him his daily bread" (79). Later in the novel the Anglo community also suggests that mobility has its price. All of this happened, they seem to believe, because Krupa had "high-falutin" ideas about making his son a doctor.

Ultimately, the Polish farmer in these novels is displaced from the land, and the marriage of the peasant to his new Eden ends in separation or divorce. Fictional romance and historical myth making, the literary motivation of 1930s novelists, give way to a realistic reevaluation of the peasant family and the American garden. Mike Koziol, a successful Texas rancher-businessman, looks with longing to his best days as a farm laborer in New York. After decades of travail, Jan Tarnowski and Stan Malekski perish in a highway accident on their way to market. The family farm dies with them, and Helena Malekski turns to house cleaning to support herself at the conclusion of *A Journey to Boston*.

One way or another, these writers seem to mock the naive conviction, expressed by Alex Krupa, that "the land would be good to him as long as he lived" (334). What William Castle shows is that hard work is no guarantee and that Anglo American hostility—together with the Poles' own misguided understanding of their place in the New World—work to destroy the Polish American Eden. Consequently, images of the bountiful promised land are reversed in these novels, which move from garden to wasteland imagery. With the death of Alex Krupa in *Hero's Oak*, the family farm goes to pieces: "The barn needed repairing, the house needed paint and shingles, the hay had rotted and mildewed where the rain leaked through" (284). Maurice Hindus also ends his novel with a picture of an Eden in distress. When Koziol returns to the landscape of his youth, he finds Titus's pristine pine forest cut down, the house burned to the ground, the land fallow. The new owner tells him, "all it's good for is reforestation and someday I'll sell it to the state" (277).

Thus it is that the dozen or so novels that deal with Polish farmers come full circle. By mid-century, American novelists, retaining to some degree the spirit of futurism inherent in the Biblical typology which infuses their works, had, nonetheless, grown more cynical about the immigrant experience. With changes in immigration patterns and the ethnic mix of American society, they had less reason to turn to Poles as material for local color or to offer two-dimensional supporting characters whose fictional mission was to enlarge the American experience. In the hands of Castle, Hindus, and Chase, the Poles became primary characters, protagonists whose individual lives and inner selves are important in themselves. And what we see between the lines of romantic enthusiasm for Poles and Poland are people who are neither completely at home in the host culture nor successful in maintaining their own ethnic boundaries as a community or as individuals. In effect, the theme of assimilation and acculturation that dominates prewar fiction gives way to cynicism and alienation by mid-century. Whereas prewar writers lamented a vanishing rural America, postwar novelists mourned the slow erosion of ethnicity and the exile in the kingdom.

4

PROLETARIAT AND PROTESTER

In this life, Benedict, the poor are doomed always to lose,
the worker always to fall in defeat. —BONOSKY

I. RADICALS AND UNDERDOGS

Over the first half of the century, writers persisted in trying to offer pastoral visions of American rural life imprinted with ethnicity and reenergized by Polish immigrants. Yet, they never quite succeeded in remodeling the peasant into an American farmer in the style of John Dickinson and Hector St. John de Crevecoeur or even in the image of Willa Cather's European pioneers. They did, however, succeed in hewing the rough outlines of the ethnic self by describing certain characteristics that represented Polishness to them and, they hoped, to their readers, and by identifying once again the aligned destinies of Poles and Americans. Nonetheless, one might observe that the whole of ethnicity in these works seems less than the sum of its parts. More concerned with the mythology of agrarian America and the more immediate deflowering of New England than with ethnic perspectives and cultural realities, writers Americanized ethnicity by transforming the Pole into the Puritan. The Polish self became an American shadow cut off from Polish institutions, community, and the historical past. Ethnic identity served the demands of romantic fiction.

In addition, novels about the immigrant on the land rubbed against the grain of a social reality which overnight turned the vast majority of Poles from Grodno, Nowy Targ, and Katowice, into industrial laborers in Scranton, Buffalo, and Omaha. Tillers of the soil throughout the centuries suddenly became miners, steelworkers, and assembly-line "robotniks," as the Polish population had by the mid-1920s settled not in the Connecticut River Valley but in the urban clusters of the Northeast and Midwest. The novels of Miniter, Hindus, Chase, and the rest also ran counter to a major literary shift beginning early in the century.

While Edith Miniter was thinking of uniting Pole and New Englander in *Our Natupski Neighbors* (1916), others were developing ethnicity along political lines. As early as 1901, Isaac Friedman had introduced the peasant as proletariat in *By Bread Alone*. And in the

81

works of Cobb, Oppenheim, Sinclair, and others, the Polish peasant entered into American political fiction, portrayed variously as the enemy within, the innocent victim, and the worker hero in the class struggle. In this sense, the literary history of Poles in America records the shift in America's attitudes toward workers between 1870 and the 1930s. In *The Strike in the American Novel,* for example, Fay M. Blake describes the literature of 1870–1895 as antagonistic to workers, as suggesting that any form of working-class organization was dangerous and abhorrent. According to Blake, the period from 1895 to 1929 saw some softening in antagonism toward workers, although fiction continued to view foreigners with distrust and virulence (34–74). As for the Poles, one need only compare the works of Richard Savage and Edward Van Zile with that of Friedman to see how closely the representation of Poles corresponds to Blake's observations.

By the 1930s, with the onset of the Great Depression, literary portrayals of workers shifted radically as proletarian writers came out of the closet, so to speak. For the first time, an entire generation of writers—as Daniel Aaron reminds us in *Writers on the Left*—explored social themes usually ignored (152). In addition, almost all major writers, except for those described by Leslie Fiedler as the "unreconstructed writers of the south" (qtd. in Madden xvii), published proletarian art or sympathized with its aims. For the Pole this was an auspicious time in literary history. For one thing, the eyes of proletarian writers were focused on that part of the population of which the Poles comprised a significant percentage. For another, proletarian artistic theory—first introduced by Michael Gold in the *Liberator* ("Towards Proletarian Art" 1920) and by V. F. Calverton ("Proletarian Art" 1924)—insured the kind of literary interest that the urban Pole might not have otherwise received. In 1930, Gold, writing in *The New Masses,* outlined the aims of proletarian fiction. He called for works about "the struggle of the workers," "real conflicts of men and women," "literature with a social function," "swift action, clear form, the direct line," honesty alone, no "straining or melodrama, or other effects" (3–5).

Interestingly, Gold, whose major work, *Jews without Money,* is heralded as both a proletarian and an ethnic piece, does not specifically identify minority or ethnic culture as a primary target for proletarian art. In fact, like Gold, virtually all those who tried to define proletarian art—from Clarence Darrow ("Realism in Art" 1899) to V. J. Jerome (*New Masses*) to Joseph Freeman (*Proletarian Literature in the United States* 1935)—ignored ethnicity in their discussions, although the subject is, at times, implicit. Not until the Second World Plenum of the International Bureau of Revolutionary Literature had criticized the

John Reed clubs for neglecting "cultural activity among the Negro masses," and had recommended that *The New Masses* organize national federations "of all cultural groups in all languages" (qtd. in Aaron 221), did ethnicity become a visible concern of the movement. Even so, the place of ethnicity in the minds of proletarian literary theorists remains a mystery, even as it does in scholarly treatments of that literature by Blake, Aaron, Madden, Rideout, Howe (*Politics and the Novel*), Blotner (*The Modern American Political Novel*), and others.

What perhaps Michael Gold and the rest only assumed turned into reality as writers, taking their cue from Friedman and other turn-of-the-century literary activists, produced fiction that was decidedly ethnic. The working-class characters in their novels are more often than not ethnic minority workers: Jews, Blacks, Irish, Italians, and Slavs, dispossessed and victimized by the system. Ethnicity and the proletariat become almost synonymous, as even a brief survey of that era's novels makes clear. In works such as Gold's *Jews without Money,* Farrell's *Studs Lonigan,* Wright's *Uncle Tom's Children,* Fast's *The Proud and the Free,* and Mailer's *The Naked and the Dead,* writers radicalized and extended literary ethnicity, altering once again America's image of its ethnic-racial minorities.

The Polish "presence" in this literary movement amounts to a minor renaissance of sorts, more than equal to the burst of interest in the immigrant on the land that occurred in the early 1930s. Between 1935 and 1955, approximately twenty-five pieces of "proletarian" or political fiction were published, featuring Poles directly or in passing. What is more, almost all those writers who achieved popular or critical success in this genre—Joseph Vogel, Betty Smith, Norman Mailer, Nelson Algren, Willard Motley, James T. Farrell, Howard Fast—wrote about the Pole in America. From the point of view of numbers alone, proletarian writers paid more attention to Poles than had any group of writers at any time since the 1830s. And for the first time, major writers, producing serious works, wrote about Poles not to introduce aliens to American audiences or to capture local color but rather to examine the relationship of a large ethnic group to an even broader populist movement. The immediate result was literary visibility and the emergence of the Pole as a representative of the oppressed urban worker whose future, if he had any at all, rested in the collectivized movement of the working class. That proletarian writers would have paid so much attention to America's Poles is not surprising given the intent of populist fiction and the numbers of Poles employed as industrial workers.

In addition, the image of the Pole as political, radical, and social victim had already been planted in literary tradition. Proletarian novelists needed to look no further for literary models than to nineteenth- and early twentieth-century examples. In works about Kosciuszko and the 1831 exiles, the Pole was identified with politics, insurrection, revolution. So long as the United States viewed itself as a culture in revolution—even Emersonian revolution—this image was sympathetically received and cultivated. For their part, the Poles reinforced this image in a major uprising against the tsar in 1863 (and in 1905); but this time America, occupied with its own rebellion and social dilemma, virtually ignored the Polish uprising. No flags in Faneuil Hall, no free land in Illinois, no Cooper to write a letter to his countrymen. Instead, an increasingly fearful America, worried about social agitation in the South, labor unrest in the East, and Indian uprisings in the West, had had enough of rebels in any cloth. Furthermore, as everyone believed they knew, postwar economic protests among workers in Cleveland, Chicago, and Milwaukee were inspired by foreign radicals or radical immigrants—threats to stability and the nature of government itself.

Perhaps America had some reason to suspect the politics of the second wave of Polish immigrants. Persecuted during the 1790s partitions and mercilessly crushed by the tsar in 1831 and 1863, some Poles, a small number to be sure, were naturally attracted to the new political philosophies of the day: socialism, anarchy, Zionism, political fragmentation of all sorts. This surge in political consciousness in late nineteenth-century Poland, not entirely coherent and not especially pronounced among the peasants, naturally carried over to America in the form of the peasant instinct to band together to gain a measure of self-respect, self-government, and prosperity. This made the Pole, as it did other immigrant groups, the natural ally of those forces in post-Civil War America that protested the excesses of capitalism and industry. Poles became active in the labor movements in particular regions and industries. In the coal industry, for example, union strikes and slowdowns did not begin to succeed until Poles began to cooperate in large numbers (Greene 213). These situations and the media blitz which indicted the Slavs as political subversives had a direct bearing on the literary history of the Pole. By the end of the nineteenth century— although some writers would continue to portray the Pole as a patriotic prince—the Pole was identified with political unrest.

At the turn of the century, as we have seen, writers addressed the Pole from a variety of political perspectives. Richard Savage and Edward Van Zile associated anarchy—a clear and present danger—with the Polish immigrant. Karl Harriman and Harold Waldo studied the urban life of Poles, implicating, however indirectly, a system unresponsive to immigrant needs. In "Polack Joe's Finish," Jack Fletcher Cobb pitted

Pole against Anglo, worker against owner, the individual against the system with fatal results for the immigrant. Although none of these writers produced what might be called political literature, they integrated the Pole into a context of social realism and politics in the same way that Samuel Knapp and other nineteenth-century romantics had supplied a patriotic framework for their characterization of the exiled aristocrat. Isaac Friedman did more. With the 1901 publication of his novel, *By Bread Alone,* he catapulted the Pole directly into the major political crisis of the twentieth century: the rise of socialism. His novel focuses on the uphill struggle of the Pole for economic and social parity, a constant theme in ethnic literature. It stands at the center of the social protest literature of the period, as seen in the works of Oppenheim, Oemler, Steiner, and Sinclair, all of whom on occasion associated the Pole with political radicalism and social discontent. In addition, Friedman outlines the ways in which proletarian writers would employ Polish characters in the 1930s and after.

On the one hand, the socioeconomic fiction of the period is far removed from the nineteenth-century tradition of cosmopolitan Polish princesses and urbane, patriotic aristocrats. On the other, it reinforced certain cultural and national characteristics that the nineteenth century cultivated and applauded. Once again, Poles are involved in a struggle against long odds—although in the twentieth century, faceless mine and mill owners, economic forces, and a profit-driven socioeconomic system replace tsarist armies as the enemy. As they were to Cooper and Emerson, the Poles in these works are sympathetic underdogs engaged in a symbolic struggle far beyond the considerations of plot. And as they did at the hands of Russian oppressors, they end up bloody but unbowed.

With the advent of World War I, the subsequent return to normalcy, and the boom years of the 1920s, the Polish part in American political literature came temporarily to a halt. In the Palmer raids, radicals were hunted down and deported, socialist assemblymen were "unseated," the leaders of the Industrial Workers of the World were arrested, and strikers in Centralia, Washington, were massacred. Union membership fell from 5 million to 3.5 million from 1920 to 1925. Not much political fiction was published during the period. In fact, according to Rideout's bibliography, only ten political novels appeared in the 1920s, half of them by one author—Upton Sinclair.

Flush times for the Polish worker as a literary hero occurred shortly after the appearance of proletariat fiction in the 1930s. Beginning with Evelyn Scott's short story "Kalicz" (1929), a half-dozen works appeared, linking the Pole to this literary-political genre and focusing on the Polish American as a representative ethnic/worker: novels by Michael Musmanno (*Black Fury* 1935), and Joseph Vogel (*Man's Courage* 1936), shorter pieces by James T. Farrell and William Carlos Williams, and a collection of stories by Jerome Bahr (*All Good Americans* 1937). Not all have a socialist political bias; the fiction of Williams, Farrell, and Bahr might best be described as depression realism with a populist flavor. Actually, the works represent a fairly diverse range of views, but all share a concern for the struggles of the working class, and all indict a system that appears to have neglected or exploited its ordinary citizens.

For the most part, the fiction deals with microcosmic, melting-pot communities in which everyone has two national identities: ethnic and American. The best friend of Musmanno's Polish protagonist is a Russian, and his female interest is born in Italy; and the miners themselves, with names like Ernest Morrison, Paul Enkovitch, Vincent Moran, Tony Velag, and Steve Gunthers, come from most major ethnic groups. Jerome Bahr alternates between Norwegians, Poles, Germans, and Anglos in his tales of upstate Wisconsin. William Carlos Williams's Passaic is a conglomeration of ethnic America: Poles, Cockneys, Irish, Jews, Italians, Russians, Germans. But for Williams, as for the rest of these writers, the Pole serves as representative ethnic. Describing the Dundee section of Passaic in "Life Along the Passaic River," he moves about from smiling African Americans to Jewish merchants to wonderstruck Poles and zeroes in on the Poles, deciding that "they'll do for the whole bunch" (111). Williams's reflection aptly serves to identify the motivation for all these writers who, themselves ethnically linked (Williams's West Indies connection, the Irish Farrell, the Anglo-German Vogel, Bahr, Scott), turn to the Pole to dramatize the crisis of the ethnic outsider. In so doing they continue the tradition introduced by Friedman and others of reconstructing the literary identity of the Pole as proletarian.

Reminiscent of the urban realism of Crane, Dreiser, and Anderson, Evelyn Scott's "Kalicz" is a transition story with ties to the romantic portrayal of Poles in the tradition of the nineteenth century, but with an eye toward the social themes that dominate the period in which she writes. Set during the Civil War, Scott's sparse story of the immigrant Kalicz is actually about industrial, urban America and the fate of innocence. Her protagonist, Kalicz, finds a job in a foundry, described in hellish terms, part of an America that believes only in machines to make armaments. Her references to godlessness, blackness, grime, dust, smoke, flames, and gasses reinforce her metaphor and contrast sharply with her depiction of the simple Kalicz, whose piousness and integrity offer a counterpoint to materialism and false values. Kalicz's mother recognizes the fate of the immigrant when she observes that there is "no joy in America." And Kalicz, in his own simplistic way, becomes an activist by setting fire to the factory which has become the enemy of both the immigrants and the nation. Scott suggests that Kalicz is Christ-like, a redemptive agent who fuses moral conscience with political activism in the old Polish tradition. New York itself is inflamed with draft riots, the protest of ethnics and nonethnics alike against bureaucracy and exploitation; and Scott parallels this uprising to Poland's rebellions against tsarist oppression. Once again Poland's and America's histories intertwine as Scott fuses Polish uprisings, Civil War demonstrations, and the fictional protest of the lone immigrant in ways that foreshadow the militancy of the 1930s. Americans had "always been the friends of Poland," Scott tells us, drawing upon historical and literary associations already fixed in the American psyche and connecting Polish and American kinship, values, and the protest tradition.

Scott's little gem, buried in a collection of short works entitled *The Wave,* is a harbinger of what is to come. Published in 1929, the year of "the great swing leftward" (Aaron *Writers* 110), "Kalicz" ushers in a period in which American realists would draw upon ethnicity not to present information about the colorful "other," as their romantic counterparts had done, but to draw attention to vast social issues. Even so, Scott's definition of ethnicity is as distinctive (some might say reductive) as her protagonist's decision to set fire to the arms foundry. She describes Polishness as poverty and protest, romance and redemption, alienation and Americanness. Her association of ethnicity and the liberal tradition (activism and integrity) characterizes 1930s' fiction about the working class. At the same time, she illustrates the tendency to see ethnicity through "American" eyes and to select ethnic symbols, aspects of character, folk culture, and peasant behavior to represent ethnicity. Day-to-day life in the Polish-American community and the subtle transformation of Old World identities give way to yet another kind of typology intended to serve the immediate concerns of the new political fiction. Ethnicity is once again reduced to representative action and image. Kalicz, the naive but moral factory worker, is not too far removed from Kosciuszko and the patriotic rebels of nineteenth-century literature. Like Polack Joe in Cobb's story, he is an Americanized version of the Polish patriot victimized by Polish landowners and Russian aristocracy. In this case, the Polish peasant and the American working man replace nineteenth-century models in order for writers to add a new chapter to an ongoing story.

Scott offers no specific political agenda in "Kalicz." Rather she works through symbolic action and analogy to tie together Polish and American, immigrant and activist, and to define literary ethnicity. In other cases, however, writers often relied on conventional approaches to portray the ethnic Pole. In "A Casual Incident," Farrell features physical description: stolid, giant, ox eyes, heavy-planed faces. About Polish-ness, Farrell has little else to say. Musmanno refers to animal joy and brute strength. Joseph Vogel emphasizes Adam Wolak's "brawn." Qual-ities originally associated with Slavic peasants surface everywhere: Poles have too many children; they are stoical, nonverbal, overly pas-sive, undereducated, lost in America (as Singer would later phrase it). And like some of their predecessors, writers show occasional irritation with the peasant temperament. Even sympathetic writers cannot, as Fay Blake phrases it, "grant full equality" to their ethnic characters (108). Musmanno criticizes his Poles for shortsightedness, for having "no window on national or international affairs," for longing only for sen-sory happiness together with physical and emotional gratification" (11). Williams chides the Poles for their lack of spontaneity, ambition, and initiative. That the closing of the factories in depression-ridden Passaic has forced the Poles to consider change—the future—is perhaps a good thing, Williams muses. "It's what they need . . . they've needed it a long time. You can see that too on their faces" (111). Jerome Bahr singles out the social backwardness of the immigrant who hides when visitors come because she does not feel at ease, and he acquaints us once again with foreigners "who don't believe in education," with mate-rialistic and egotistical priests, and with Poles jealously guarding a status quo that yields little in return.

Apart from these familiar tableaux, ethnicity gains little except for the emergence of the worker-figure. Yet even in this case, literary ethnicity takes second place to political dogma. The irony of literary ethnicity, as far as proletarian fiction is concerned, lies in the nature of proletarian fiction itself. For by insistently melding minorities and ethnics into a multiracial, multiethnic class movement, proletarian writers found that, to be true to their convictions, individual and minority identity had to be sacrificed, replaced by a larger and necessar-ily more anonymous image of the transethnic worker. Consequently, ethnicity is friend and foe in these works, but more often than not it is a hurtle to be transcended before the purified and fortified American-international worker emerges.

In order for populism-socialism to succeed, these writers seem to say that ethnicity itself must be defeated. The populist writer, Jerome Bahr, epitomizes this dilemma in *All Good Americans*, a collection of short pieces motivated by the depression and Bahr's interest in the American who is ethnically rooted in Europe. Bahr is perhaps the only author within this genre to observe the Pole from inside the community, to ex-amine first- and second-generation antagonism, the attraction of the church, and social stratification within the ethnic group. In addition, Bahr is moved to celebrate a collective spirit, strength in unity, the hope of the NRA and the New Deal, and ethnic participation in these efforts. All is well until Bahr brings together his dual themes—appreciation of ethnic diversity and melting-pot populism—in "NRA Day." In this story, Bahr's spokesman, speaking at a post-parade rally, identifies Bahr's dilemma—and indeed that of the proletarian writer of the 1930s. He urges his listeners, whose ethnicity had been intriguing, colorful, and valuable in the other stories, to bury old country customs, traditions, and outlooks, and "to unite as hundred-percent Americans."

The message is clear: ethnicity and populism are strange, even incompatible bedfellows. Michael Musmanno's *Black Fury* is another case in point. His is a transformation novel, the shedding of the uninformed, browbeaten peasant self and the unleashing of the worldly, clever, American activist eager to assume his place in the rank and file. Musmanno, later to become a Pennsylvania Supreme Court judge, situates his tale in the western Pennsylvania coal fields of the 1920s—at the time a microcosm of European peasant society—and uses a Pole, Jan Volkanik, as protagonist. Despite the potential of this setting, Musmanno does little to capture the ethnic flavor of mining communities—unlike Peter Roberts whose 1904 study of anthracite coal communities focuses on the ethnic world. In *Black Fury,* the action occurs in an ethnic void; nothing is said about Polish organizations, institutions, or customs. Musmanno shows little interest in Jan as a Pole or as an immigrant. Instead he concentrates on unionism, populism, and the transformation of the hero into a deethnicized ethnic. Whatever Polishness exists inside Jan is squeezed from him when he spends a year in prison because of his union activities. When Musmanno points with pride to the fact that Jan has read *Black Beauty, Treasure Island,* and *Huck Finn;* when he notes that Jan "had been purified of all dross and slab"; when he insists that Jan is not "the same man he had been when he arrived here" (132), Musmanno, in effect, praises the loss of ethnicity. Jan's friendly, open, trusting, and generous ways—the peasant nature he had grown up with—are neither effective nor desirable in a setting that values intellect above character. In the tradition of transformation fiction, *Black Fury* shows that even in a proletarian world ethnicity has no home.

Transformation is, in fact, implicit throughout this fiction, as it is in 1930s stories dealing with the immigrant on the land—except that class struggle takes the place of Anglo-Slavic courtship, and "ethnic" comes to mean economic victimization and political protest. William Carlos Williams refers to the textile strikes in New Jersey and police brutality: "The Poles paid for it all" (114). Jerome Bahr gives us a glimpse of Fred Dunla and Ted Karlan, radicals who want to "tear down the whole rotten system." James T. Farrell introduces Comrade

Gumowski, paraded as the party's representative worker, and Stanley Gradek, who leads a strike against landlords in his Chicago neighborhood. Adam Wolak supports the union movement in Joseph Vogel's *Man's Courage* because, as his colleague Mike Zamorski explains, "It's a lousy world we're living in. And it's not the fault of working people" (240). Wolak's death by police gunfire justifies Zamorski's remarks. Vogel also draws parallels to the 1934 Vienna workers' revolt and the role of Wolak's brother in the struggle against fascism. "Somebody's got to put up a fight and break into the rich racket. It can't always be the same guys," William Carlos Williams insists (114).

By the late 1930s in American fiction, the Pole was poised to become that somebody, the representative American, the common man in pain and in revolt. In 1938 Joseph Vogel, a contributor to Jack Conroy's *The Anvil* and a member of the "first Proletarian school of forgotten writers" (Aaron, *Writers* 210), wrote a classic tale of the worker in revolt, *Man's Courage,* and identified the cause as an ethnic one. For his protagonists, Vogel chose Poles—the Wolak family, which had immigrated to America a generation before the plot action. The Wolaks live in a Polish neighborhood in Genessee, New York, but Vogel provides no sociocultural or historical context. For him, Polishness appears to be nothing more than the peasant temperament, a passive, weary, listless attitude toward events that seem to just happen. Ironically, Vogel is careful to associate the Wolaks with political activism by referring to their brother who was killed in the Vienna workers' revolt of 1934. For the most part, however, Vogel's Poles are the humiliated, the poor, the dispossessed, the workers whose lives have been undercut by the depression and the economic system. He develops his thesis by leading us through examples of institutional arrogance toward the working class. Relief agencies treat the Wolaks as second-class citizens; doctors refuse medical aid without prior payment; the schools humiliate ethnic children; social workers pompously preach against socialism and un-American behavior.

The only escape for the Polish worker appears to be a return to the land, as Vogel draws upon a familiar 1930s theme. Wolak remembers a lost opportunity, a chance to buy a farm and, trying to recapture the past, he moves to a shack outside of town amidst the hills where "the dream came back to him" (292). Vogel debunks the agrarian myth quickly and decisively. Adam Wolak meets a farmer who explains how he lost his farm, "Poof!" and how there's no future in farming. Wolak associates the foreclosures with the situation in Poland where the landowners drove people from their homes. Nothing much has changed after all, Vogel implies, as he comments that, even in America, it is the poor man who "suffers most from our laws" (75). Although Vogel could have expressed this idea through any social or minority group, the fact that he chose Poles suggests that in his eyes the Pole and the proletariat had become indistinguishable.

2. THE WORKER IN POSTWAR AMERICA

The Pole as proletarian is also featured in the fiction of Nelson Algren. In a number of short stories and two novels, *Never Come Morning* (1942) and *The Man with the Golden Arm* (1949), Algren enlarged upon themes introduced earlier without the pointed political agenda of his colleague Joseph Vogel and with literary intentions (and talents) that elevate his fiction into a somewhat different category. Except in Algren's case, the war brought about a brief hiatus in the romance of the Pole and the proletarian writer. But the postwar years soon produced a new crop—the second phase so to speak—of politically inspired protest fiction that continued to attack the evils of the capitalist-industrial system and to champion the working class and its representative hero—the ethnic American. More than a dozen of these novels featured Poles and Polish Americans usually juxtaposed with other racial and minority groups: Lester Cohen's *Coming Home* (1945); Antoni Gronowicz's *Four from Old Town* (1944); Josiah Greene's *Not in Our Stars* (1947) and *The Man with One Talent* (1951); Jean Karsavina's *Reunion in Poland* (1945) and *Tree by the Waters* (1948); Russell Janney's *The Miracle of the Bells* (1946); Willard Motley's *Knock on Any Door* (1947) and *We Fished All Night* (1951); Betty Smith's *Tomorrow Will Be Better* (1948); Norman Mailer's *The Naked and the Dead* (1948); Dan Levin's *Mask of Glory* (1949); Millard Lampell's *The Hero* (1949); Howard Fast's *The Proud and the Free* (1950); V. J. Jerome's *A Lantern for Jeremy* (1952); Jack Karney's *Work of Darkness* (1956).

To be sure, not all these works fit the rubric of proletarian fiction, not all direct their energy toward class struggle in a revolutionary context, nor do all sympathize with socialism or radical platforms. Yet all share a liberal bias, a concern for the plight of working-class Americans unable to grasp the gold ring—although in a few novels that prospect appears to be possible. Those most closely identified with politics and the proletarian novel (Cohen, Karsavina, Motley, Greene, Jerome) still focus on the radical edge of change: on unionism, labor unrest, strikes, demonstrations, political corruption and response. Others treat the subject more indirectly, if not more subtly, by moving the campaign away from the battlefields of the industrial Northeast into new geographical, social, and historical zones. The realistic depression settings of Bahr and Williams turn into historical fiction as Norman Mailer and

Dan Levin write about the war in the Pacific and as Howard Fast looks at the political ideology of the American Revolution. Antoni Gronowicz, Jean Karsavina, and V. J. Jerome move even farther away, to Poland to be exact, to drive home their decidedly left-wing perspective. Jerome even situates his novel during the 1905 uprising against the tsar.

In every case, ethnic and proletariat are fused if not synonymous, and political impulses and ethnic interests vie for position in ways that reveal the dilemma of the proletarian writer. On the one hand, writers rushed to embrace a wide range of ethnic and racial minorities to demonstrate the attractive vision of the new left. Some dramatized the need for tolerance and acceptance; they celebrated cultural differences as a desirable and necessary part of the workers' utopia; they even in some cases featured the recognition of an emerging sense of ethnicity in their characters. On the other hand, the politics within the fiction, the ideology itself, and the fictional strategies often employed conspired to deemphasize the ethnic self, to reduce ethnicity to vague and harmless stereotyped associations, to damn it through silence, or, ironically, to bury the ethnicity they had come to praise. What the movement needed most, some thought, was discipline and unity, not individualization and cultural pluralism. As a result, writers were at odds with themselves in their desire to create a new postwar vision. With the right hand, they sought to preserve ethnic diversity; with the left, they reduced it to a mere technique in the service of the cause. Through it all Polishness both expanded and contracted into singular hard images devoid of cultural, historical contexts.

The trouble began, as Mark Twain was fond of saying, in conception; that is, in the nature of a movement that tried to unite workers from radically different cultural backgrounds. Faithful to this principle, writers often included as many ethnic types as possible. For example, Russell Janney in *The Miracle of the Bells* divides his attention among his Irish protagonist, the Slavic miners of Coaltown, and a Jewish philanthropist. V. J. Jerome deals with Russians, Poles, and Jews. Lester Cohen features Jews, Poles, and Anglos in conflict in wartime Pittsburgh. And Betty Smith's Irish family lives among Poles and Italians. In both of his novels about union and management, Josiah Greene offers a wide cast of barely identifiable ethnics. Even when Poles appear as major characters, they share the stage with other ethnic groups: Willard Motley juxtaposes Aaron Levin, Don Kosinski, and Jim Norris in *We Fished All Night;* Jack Karney divides his novel into separate sections dealing with Joe Kusack, a Pole, Lenny Kramer, a Jew, and Juan Rivera, a Puerto Rican; and Dan Levin's Polish protagonist, Glen Manson, serves in an infantry platoon next to Mancini, Lewicki, Elbrus, Powalski, O'Bradovich, Hunter, Berkowitz, and Carrington.

As the names of Levin's characters suggest, a number of writers featured a microcosmic America representing the broad spectrum of regional, cultural, and ethnic diversity. In addition to Levin, Howard Fast and Norman Mailer turned to this device. In their hands and in those of others writing about the war—Leon Uris, James Jones, Herman Wouk, and Irwin Shaw—the microcosmic approach would become not only a popular convention but also a particular dilemma for literary ethnicity. Consumed with the demands of plot and polemics, writers simply had too many characters to develop and resorted to stereotypical associations, a surface feature or two, or suggestive names. The ethnic characters themselves often had little to say or do and little time to display whatever ethnic culture they possessed. Being there, in the case of some writers, seems to be enough to provide an illusion of pluralism and internationality.

Mailer's *The Naked and the Dead* typifies this approach. Reflecting in part the realities of a conscripted armed force, his platoon includes Red Valsen, a Swede from Montana; Goldstein and Roth, "eastern" Jews; Brown, a rich kid from Kansas; Wilson, a southerner; Martinez, a Texas Chicano; Gallagher from Boston; the Italian Minetta; and an urban Pole named Casimir Czienwicz. Apart from introducing his "Americans" one at a time in separate chapters, Mailer spends most of his time on the liberal-conservative confrontation of Hearn and Cummings. The rest, with the possible exception of Roth and Goldstein, receive only scant attention. Czienwicz, with the "unpronounceable name," for example, stalks the plot waiting for his brief profile, which comes 600 or so pages into the novel. Only then do we even learn his full name or anything about his brutal childhood in Chicago. We do know that he is a cynic, con man, and social misfit who believes that the system exists to be exploited. His view is that "it's all a lousy racket," although he has no chance to conceptualize his own attitudes within a larger sociopolitical context. Mailer includes him because he needs a Slav and an urban guerilla whom only a mother could love to complete his ethnic diorama. What makes Czienwicz Polish, or Gallagher Irish, or Martinez a Chicano, we never learn. Mailer counts on popular preconceptions, a detail or two, and unstated assumptions to suggest ethnicity. He seems content to elicit a programmed response to ethnic names which, as it turns out, don't seem to matter very much in *The Naked and the Dead*. Ethnicity simply means working class, the lower social levels who are drafted, shot at, bombed, and killed so that the reactionary Cummings and his kind can inherit the earth.

Howard Fast employs a similar model with more or less equal results in *The Proud and the Free*, his third novel in a series about the American Revolution. Fast relies on the traditional form of the historical

novel to serve his radical politics. He interprets the American Revolution as class struggle, a view he supports by recounting a supposed
historical incident in which a Pennsylvania unit mutinied against its
officers (see Rideout 281). Fast's brigade, like Mailer's, is an ethnic-
racial cross section of "the people": the black Kabanka, the Jewish
Levy, the Polish Prukish. Like Mailer, Fast also wants a Pole in his novel
but shows no interest in describing Polishness. All we know is that
Prukish has a thick accent which the narrator "cannot reproduce,"
although he is adept at other times in mimicking Irish speech patterns.
He also tells us that he is aware of the "haunting Slavic rhythms of the
Polish men," a line designed to penetrate the supposed melancholic
history of Poland or the Byronic nature of Polish characters expressed
in a number of American novels. Other Poles pop up from time to time:
a soldier named Krakower, otherwise unidentified, and a Piotr Lusky,
broad shouldered, quiet, blond, flat-faced, slow of speech, hungry for
his own land. Whatever Fast knows about Poles seems to come from
popular presentations about the Polish peasant. That Prukish is ex-
ecuted for his role in the mutiny, serves, however, to place him in the
tradition of Polish patriots, rebels, and democrats who parade through
American fiction, although the peasant as revolutionary hero runs
counter to literary and historical tradition. Fast, it seems, exchanges
princes and peasants to serve his own interests; nonetheless, the martyred Prukish takes his place in the proletarian pantheon as he would in
other protest novels of the period. In effect, Fast draws upon the
popular perception of Polish hostility to tyranny and to class oppression.

Dan Levin's *Mask of Glory* also features the microcosmic infantry
unit in what Chester Eisinger describes as the "rhetorical war novel,"
an unblushingly patriotic, rather "simple-minded" genre that touts the
American as the "standard-bearer of liberty" (45–47). Like Mailer and
Fast, Levin records the struggle of the common man against the system,
calls for tolerance toward all minorities, and offers a vision of America
based on brotherhood, harmony, and change. Levin spends more time
than the others, however, on his ethnic theme, structuring the plot
around the recognition and acceptance of ethnicity by Glenn Manson,
the Polish American protagonist. The rest of the platoon serves, as it
does in other works of this type, as a proletarian chorus, sometimes
praising and sometimes chastising their country. In either case, they
have no chance to express the ethnic self. Mancini, Berkowitz, Hunter,
O'Bradovich, and the rest function as a brotherhood of one.

Consequently, cultural differences are usually minimized and in
some cases completely ignored in these transethnic novels. The resounding theme is union, equality, oneness: "Let us unite—Poles, Jews,

and Russians, and make a republic in our land," Yanek and his com-
patriots sing in *A Lantern for Jeremy* as Jerome's Jews, Poles, and
Russians put aside ethnic differences to form a transcultural solidarity.
In his departing glimpse of Poland, on his way to London, Jeremy sees
Poles and Jews playing, smiling, marching together as wrongs are
corrected, history rewritten, the future made bright. In order to dis-
solve social classes, group prejudices, and ethnic rivalries, Jerome and
other writers emphasized universals, the shared condition of the working class and of all men. Explicitly and implicitly the characters or
narrator remind us that ethnicity is the enemy, a barrier to a common
goal, a factor that must be transcended or at least put aside. As one of
Jack Karney's characters explains it, "We were kids, Irish, Jew, it was
nothing but a means of identification" (98). And Betty Smith's Irish
spokesperson senses that ethnicity may be part of the working-class
antagonism: "All day I'm shoved around, you get shoved around too.
Brother, do we have to shove each other around?" (23). Implicit in his
plea for human decency and brotherhood is, of course, the notion that
the working class must set aside its Old World prejudices. Similarly
Don Lockwood in *We Fished All Night* feels best when he leaves his
Polish self behind and merges with the masses. When he joins the union,
he is exhilarated. "He belonged to the people, to something big, the
people" (294). In *Mask of Glory,* Dan Levin also offers the joy and
camaraderie of the group. Because he selects his characters to represent
the ethnic spectrum, Levin feels obliged to pay tribute and praise to
their "diverse ways . . . their quaint and differing accents" (34). In the
end, however, it is ethnic anonymity that is most valued as the "diverse" platoon members solidify into a soldier-worker unit whose
members belong more to internationality than to America. Elbrus, the
platoon spokesman for this point of view, helps his buddies understand
this: "This is for the workers," he tells them about war, heroism, and
sacrifice. "It isn't for nothing . . . it is for them, in some way, and
someday we will all know . . . it is all for the working people" (215). In
the same breath Elbrus recites the ethnic-sounding names of his buddies as Levin tries desperately to associate ethnicity and the working
class, although by this time he has already demonstrated otherwise.

Lester Cohen displays a similar bias in *Coming Home,* an antifascist
work in the style of Lawrence Lipton's *In Secret Battle* (1944) and
Arthur Miller's *All My Sons* (1947). From all appearances, Cohen has
great hopes for the union of Jews, Poles, and Anglos in the common
cause of class struggle and a reformed postwar America. Beneath it all,
he makes it clear, as far as his Polish characters are concerned, that the
necessary consequence of victory is the defeat of Old World rivalries,
thought, and behavior. In Cohen's postwar America, ethnicity has no

real place. His sympathetic portrayal of the injustices endured by the Witowskis is more than countered by his trivialization of their culture and his charge of anti-Semitism. His closing illustrates this contradiction perfectly: he offers the marriage of Stella Witowski and Joe Drew as a sign of ethnic assimilation and Anglo acceptance, but when the Witowskis plan a Polish wedding—a continuation of their cultural heritage—Drew dismisses the idea and Cohen gives him the last word on ethnicity in America: "Oh for Chrissake," he shouts at Stella, "are we going to have that old stuff forever? Good God, men have fought and died about that kind of stuff" (308). Ironically for the Witowskis, Cohen's last chapter is titled, "Life Begins."

Two of Cohen's contemporaries, Jean Karsavina and Russell Janney, employ similar techniques—an ethnic cast of characters, group euphoria, melting-pot relationships—and both pay lip service to ethnicity while transforming American diversity into a vision of solidarity that proves the rightness of the Allied cause, their own political sentiments, and the power of populism. Karsavina's *Tree by the Waters,* like her *Reunion in Poland* written three years earlier, is inflamed by left-wing sentiments, except that the setting is in Connecticut rather than in Warsaw. She pits rich against poor, reactionaries against liberals, and Anglos versus Poles as Abby Bemis, a rich kid unaware of racial, political, or class differences, is transformed into an energetic participant in the proletarian cause. Karsavina intends to sensitize her readers to her political platform unoffensively and to awaken America to its ethnic minorities and their rightful place in the scheme.

As a consequence, Karsavina includes obligatory scenes which document the heroine's introduction to a world completely alien to her—a world by and large Polish. Abby's awakening is two-dimensional. She claims that she had never thought of people as ethnics and is amazed that people still do. In truth she had not thought of "the people" at all. She realizes, for example, that, despite the fact that she had gone to school with Polish kids, she had never joined in activities with them or stepped inside a Polish house. When Mac Kowalski invites her home for dinner, all she can say about Polishness is that the food was "simply different from what she was used to" (121). Karsavina pushes hard for appreciation of ethnicity without necessarily bringing any understanding of the Polish American community to Abby or to us. It's all rhetoric after all. Nonetheless, recognition, appreciation, and mutual respect are the game rules in *Tree by the Waters.* One of the characters, offering help to his Polish neighbors during an emergency, discovers that New Englanders and Poles are "kind of like kin to each other." The Polish Americans come to recognize this kinship as well. "The real Americans and our kind—they all found out they were just people" (61), Karsavina cryptically reports. In like fashion, Abby's family, sweeping away its resentment toward ethnics, joins in mutual admiration and in marriage with their Polish counterparts.

Unfortunately, Karsavina doesn't explain the basis for the kinship theme that runs through the novel and seems unaware of nineteenth-century literary and historical references to Polish and American kinship. She does, however, turn back to the nineteenth century for the catalytic event in Abby's transformation. Abby discovers her grandmother's diary in which she has recounted her own transformation from a smug racist socialite to a compassionate political activist. She had joined, Abby learns, an 1830s strike of immigrant Irish laborers, an act that precipitates Abby's own conversion, which in turn motivates others in the community to examine their own attitudes. History shows, Karsavina argues, that relationships must be adjusted to the realities of class struggle. And so they are as the novel closes with a grand vision of futurism and unity, not unlike American literature about Poland written in the 1830s. And like New England novelists of the 1930s, Karsavina rewards her Poles by arranging a multicultural marriage for the union activist and socialist, Mac Kowalski. "It's good to belong together," Anglo tells Pole, but neither Abby nor Karsavina really expect that "together" will include ethnicity.

Actually, the doctrinaire Karsavina gives mixed signals about the fate of ethnicity in the proletariat paradise to come. The whole community awakens to the existence of its Polish citizens and all join hands in dancing the Mazurka at Abby and Mac's engagement. Mrs. Chapin and Mrs. Kowalski, an unlikely twosome at any party, even raise their voices in unison, singing, "We'll rise and fight together / we shall not be moved," echoing Yanek's pitch for solidarity in *A Lantern for Jeremy*. Ironically, ethnicity is doomed in Karsavina's well-meaning novel and in her hoped for utopia. She reveals the fate of ethnicity even as she praises the elimination of ethnic-racial prejudice. "This year, for the first time," she writes, "Poles and Yankees are celebrating together . . . the words, *Polack, ski* had been washed away . . . with them had gone a state of mind" (181). Unintentionally ambiguous to be sure, Karsavina's prophecy nonetheless suggests that the loss of ethnic culture is a precondition toward assimilation into a socialist world.

Russell Janney's *The Miracle of the Bells* is yet another novel that captures the spirit of postwar optimism and the promise of a reconstituted America. Set in the late 1930s (but without historical references), the novel points to a morally and socially regenerated America where Poles, Jews, Irish, rich and poor, workers and owners, live and work in mutual respect. Not a political writer in the mold of Karsavina, Janney pushes soft politics, liberalism, and religious mysticism, although his populist sympathies are evident throughout. For example, he opens by describing the coal breaker, a symbol for a system that crushes Coaltown and the region. The breaker, "chewing and separating and digesting . . . devoured men also," Janney warns (4) as he leads the conflict between absentee owners and Polish miners. The owners are unenlightened capitalists, who believe that "the working classes are getting entirely out of hand. . . . It comes from government coddling" (409). They and virtually all the American-born characters—including the governor of Pennsylvania and his entourage—harbor strong prejudices toward ethnic groups, especially the Poles.

Janney has an even greater problem with ethnicity than does Karsavina. He brings together Bill Dunigan, son of an Irish washerwoman; Marcus Harris, a Jewish tailor turned Hollywood producer; Father Paul, the Polish pastor of the impoverished parish of St. Michael; a cast of ethnic miners, mostly Polish; and a dead Polish American movie star Olga Trocki whose spiritual presence motivates the entire action. All conspire to reawaken the community, the region, and the nation into a new era of love, faith, brotherhood, and equality. Apart from a passing glance at Bill Dunigan's Irish heritage, however, Janney pays little attention to the ethnic make-up of his cast. All we learn about ethnicity is poverty, religion, and work. Even then the portraits are ambivalent or shallow. The Poles are suckers for religious mystery (they believe that the movement of the statues in St. Michael's is divinely inspired) and easily cowed into submission. Olga Trocki is a woman of industry, ambition, and integrity, but her Hollywood success seems more accidental than self-directed, more a testament to American opportunity than to cultural diversity.

Janney is happier offering symbols of ethnic solidarity than he is in examining the ethnic profile. At one point he labels his characters (Bill, Olga, Marcus, Father Paul, and St. Michael) the "Five Musketeers" and the whole country joins in their cause. Harris, dismissing the anti-Semitism that had bothered him, contributes funds to build a new St. Michael's. The Pennsylvania governor decides not to veto the mass transit bill. The mine owners pay for a new public hospital. And all Hollywood turns out for Olga's funeral. For a brief moment at least, a miracle spreads through the lives of individuals and the nation, and this miracle includes the transcendence of ethnicity. Janney's characters, as it turns out, are "the people" first and ethnics second; in fact, ethnicity steps aside ultimately to let the populist force pass through. The new dawn that "must follow as bright day succeeds the night" (334) begins with a puzzle. Janney closes the novel with a vigorous statement about ethnic solidarity, people power, and political renewal. A thousand miners, mostly Polish, march à la Cecil B. De Mille through the streets of Coaltown to express union and unity. They sing, moreover, the Polish "Sons of Poland, on to Battle" and "Onward Christian Soldiers." What more could anyone ask?, Janney seems to say.

3. SOCIAL SPOKESPERSONS AND THE MULTIFACED ETHNIC

The ethnic message of proletarian fiction is that minorities have arrived and that Poles, in particular, have achieved literary parity and equal literary status with those still outside the mainstream of power. The obligatory Pole, as well as the obligatory Jew, Italian, or Irishman, is a constant with which many writers felt at ease, so much so that they discontinued the practice of introducing the "Slav" to the reading public. What is more, associating the Pole with populist, union activities also seemed perfectly natural. While it is true that the ethnic self often dissolved into the anonymity of the working class, writers continued to reshape the face of ethnicity by calling upon techniques and symbols already rooted in the popular imagination and literary tradition. As might be expected, they did not include the model of the nineteenth-century Polish beau ideal. The Poles in these books are peasants or from peasant stock, possessing a familiar outlook and set of cultural associations.

For example, by the late 1940s Polish catholicity was not a revelation to American readers. In fact, the catholicity of the new immigrants had been a sore spot to many who warned about the effect of immigrant dependence on Rome. At the same time, writers tended to ignore the unique nature of Polish historical Catholicism, referring only obliquely to religious or to feast day celebrations. Somewhat surprisingly, proletarian writers often defined Polish ethnicity in religious terms, sensing what most sociologists perceive as one of the principal determinants of ethnicity in America (Greeley 15). For one thing, we are given a sense of the priest's role in Polish-American culture as "the natural leader of the community" (Napierkowski "Priests" 168). Jerome Bahr's portrait of Father Patko, including his mission to transplant the Polish Catholic church to America and his influence in all matters, is perhaps the most sustained look at the subject in this subgenre. Priests roam through postwar proletarian fiction as well: Father Tadeusz in *Coming Home*, Fathers Paul and Spinski in *The Miracle of the Bells*, and Father Dymek in Frank Riley's novels about street people and revolutionary clergy in Los Angeles (*The Kocska Formula* and *Jesus II*). In these and other works, Poles seek advice and consent from the church. Even the most unlikely characters, including the misfit Joe Kusack in *Work of Darkness*, have a childhood association with Polish Catholic schools. Russell

Janney also cites the prominence of the church, church rivalries, and even a bit of Polish mysticism. Father Paul is proud that the statues in St. Michael's have come from Poland; when they move because of a mine upheaval, all are willing to trust in the miracle. To the Poles, the saints are "potent and alive." Willard Motley shows the importance of religious ritual in everyday life from the formal openings in letters (Praise Be Jesus Christus), to the Panna Maria medals exchanged as gifts, to the annual visit of the parish priest to bless the house. In Motley's novel, Don Lockwood's grandfather pinpoints the religiosity of Polish ethnicity when he tells his grandson that a good Pole is always a good Catholic (70). Yet, the tremendous role of the church as a socializing institution within the Polish American community is not adequately attended to by writers who often tread warily because of the ambiguity of religion's role within a political, populist movement. (Polish Catholicism is more fully developed in Edwin O'Connor's *The Edge of Sadness* [1961], Wanda Kubiak's *Polonaise Nevermore* [1962], John Abucewicz's *Fool's White* [1969], and the novels of Richard Bankowsky.)

The strategy is to provide sufficient signs of ethnicity but not enough to blur the political thrust of the fiction. Writers quickly established religion, customs, and physical appearance, then moved into sociopolitical issues. Cohen notes the sunken noses and earthy skin of Polish women. Mailer points out Czienwicz's beady eyes and missing front teeth. Greene tells us that Wojcik is a "burly, pigeon-breasted, peasant type." Karsavina emphasizes Mac Kowalski's massive strength, blue eyes, and high cheekbones. And Willard Motley introduces Don Lockwood with his blond hair and broad forehead. The composite portrait is perfect; enough to differentiate Poles but not severe enough to isolate them or reduce them to comic caricature. The same might be said of Polish customs. Most writers mention just enough to establish the flavor of Polishness without resorting to using ethnicity as local color. Karsavina, for example, spends a moment on cabbage soup, baked groats, and sour cream. She also feels confident enough to refer to the mazurka without any words of explanation. Likewise, Levin makes quick reference to George Manson's skill in playing Chopin, but Levin's allusion to an iconic figure from Polish history stands almost alone in proletarian literature. Only Willard Motley goes beyond the obligatory mention of Polish culture. But even his comments, confined to peasant Poland, emphasize the simplicity of the peasant who brings a package of soil to be placed under the head at burial, who kisses hands and shoulders as signs of respect, who believes in "Wil," a folk demon, while simultaneously observing "Swieconka," the blessing of the Easter food.

In fact, the humility of the peasant, his introverted social life, and his stoical outlook are vexing problems for the proletariat writer. On the one hand, peasant character lends itself to the fictional formula which tends to show political awakening and the social conscience regenerated. On the other, these same qualities stand in opposition to the emergence of the active, energetic, and visionary worker, the real hero in most of these works. Consequently, the Poles are symbols of the recalcitrant, sleepy-headed laborer who needs to be pushed, pulled, and prodded into action. Lester Cohen, for example, is furious that the Poles are so willing "to take it." He complains about their Old World mentality, their view of justice as a personal gift of petty officials. He accuses them of lacking ambition, vision, or drive toward self-improvement and he shows that ultimately it will take an outside agent to motivate and lead them. Russell Janney has a similar attitude toward his Poles. When they march ten abreast singing "Onward Christian Soldiers," Janney is proud. At other times, he lashes out because they cling unnecessarily to the home land, drink too much, avoid school, breed too frequently, and resist healthy and sensible diets (they fry with lard, Janney reveals). In short, Janney appears almost ashamed to offer the Pole as a model for his social utopia.

Although these portraits are the kind that incite Polish American fraternal, civil, and religious organizations to pass resolutions of protest or compose defensive monographs praising the achievements of America's Polish heritage, not all Poles in these novels are etched in darkness. Olga Trocki, Mac Kowalski, Glen Manson, Father Paul, Don Lockwood (to some extent), and others are decent people who have tested their ethnicity with good effect. In this sense, they signal a more active literary role for Poles in the 1940s, one that would identify them with social causes and social problems. In these works, the Pole sheds his old skin as farmer, patriot, aristocrat, bearer of Old World culture and romance, and docile war refugee, and emerges as a sociopolitical symbol with a variety of faces: victim, scapegoat, misfit, activist, worker hero, urban guerilla. Not all are complimentary, but all direct attention to the problem of American's ethnic and minority groups and to the working class.

Some writers, in the tradition of Isaac Friedman (the Brodskys), James Oppenheim (Stiny Bolinsky), and Michael Musmanno (Jan Volkanik), portrayed the Poles as political activists involved with unionism and even revolution, although for the most part they are secondary characters rather than protagonists. Howard Fast's Prukish, for example, dies for his conviction that the American Revolution ought to be a class revolution, but he is one among many of Fast's ethnic soldiers without a significant speaking part in *The Proud and the Free*. Similarly Phillip Bonosky, praised by Michael Gold in "The Writer in America," includes Poles as background characters in *Burning Valley* (1953), a sister novel of sorts to Jerome's *A Lantern for Jeremy*. Bonosky, writing about millworkers in the West Virginia hills in the 1920s, features Lithuanian immigrants. But it is clear that Poles make up a sizable percentage of the aggrieved and suffering workers who unionize and revolt against their industrial masters. Josiah Greene in *Not in Our Stars* and *The Man with One Talent,* assigns the major roles in his novels about union activity to non-Poles, although Poles appear as people of action and conviction in the movement.

Jean Karsavina, however, develops Mac Kowalski as the primary advocate for the worker movement and the rights of the ethnic community in *Tree by the Waters.* Kowalski, a catalyst for change and the social conscience of the community, also stirs the thinking of the non-Polish community which, thanks to Mac's persistence and eloquence, comes to see that the class struggle is a just one and that workers and ethnics deserve a fair share of America's prosperity. "We want a share of the money," he tells them pointedly. "By what right? We say it's because as American citizens we want to live by our country's standards—in homes we can be proud of—giving our children a good life, a good education—good food to grow on. It's because we're not robots, but men" (177). That Karsavina would assign a Pole such a role not only illustrates the change in attitudes that had formerly condemned Polish activists as anarchists in turn-of-the-century fiction, but also the improved literary position of the ethnic in postwar fiction.

In *A Lantern for Jeremy,* V. J. Jerome takes the image of the Pole as political activist one step further by elevating Yanek to a major position in the novel and by characterizing him as a red-blooded revolutionary. Given the fact that the novel was published during the heyday of McCarthyism and within earshot of Tennessee Williams's whipping of the Pole in *A Streetcar Named Desire,* Jerome's decision to portray the Pole as radical is either doubly courageous or doubly foolish. He does blunt some of the sting, however, by writing a "historical novel" set in Poland during the 1905 uprising against the tsar. Yanek (we never learn his surname) is a literary double of Dobrik in Bonosky's *Burning Valley,* another *Masses and Mainstream* publication of the early 1950s. Like Dobrik (suggesting "good" in Polish), he teaches the adolescent protagonist about class oppression and helps to awaken in him the conscience of the worker-hero. Young, courageous, selfless, Yanek defends the Polish Jews against pogroms instigated by the Russian police, rouses the community to rise up, to unite, and to strike, and then dies for the rights of "the people." A proletariat martyr, he is "always on the side of those that get whipped" (189). Assuming a larger-than-life stance in the novel, Yanek's insistence on the rightness of the people's cause and the wrongness of the tsarist system buoys both Christian and Jewish villagers alike. And his battle song, "Let us unite . . . and make a republic in our land," stands as a hymn to Polish nationalism, trans-ethnic unity, and the proletarian revolution. For Jerome, what makes Yanek Polish is his patriotism, his social conscience, and his moral vision—nothing else matters. Consequently we learn little about other dimensions of ethnicity except that once again Poland and America, Jerome implies, have a shared destiny in a novel that has obvious analogies to the worker movement in the United States to which Je-rome, a party member since his youth, remained forever committed.

Unlike Yanek, Mac, and a few others, Poles in protest fiction are usually passive voices—the victims of social ills, economic injustice, and a system for which, as it turns out, they are ill prepared. Often a blend of politics and sociology, the literature bears witness to the dire predictions of sociologists such as Emily Balch, who issued repeated warnings about the consequences of immigrant conditions in the cities. Ground down by poverty, ignorance, and the environment, they appear either as social misfits in rebellion or advanced stages of deterioration, or as honest, hard-working, blue-collar Americans. The former, as in Karney's *Work of Darkness* and Algren's fiction, have few redeeming qualities except that they stand as hostile reminders of national failure. Most Poles, however, are church-going, family-centered, honest, and frugal, a mi-nority integrated enough to share equally in whatever fate has in store for the working class, but near the bottom of the socioeconomic ladder by structural design. For the Anglo American writer (and Willard Motley too), they parallel the fictional roles that urban African Ameri-cans would be assigned more frequently beginning in the 1950s.

Lester Cohen's Poles, for example, are models of the ethnic citizen who has supported his new country more than it has supported him. At the outbreak of war, Mr. Witowski responds patriotically, doubling his efforts at the mill as a way of "getting even with Hitler." All he wants is to work hard, be a good citizen, and "help Poland and the United States" (42). Against this backdrop, Cohen looks at life in the Polish American community. Mother scrubs floors to earn the family bread; father opens a "crummy little grocery" which fails; Stella, without education and without prospects, is beaten and raped by a local official elected to defend her rights. The family lives in an ethnic ghetto. Nothing good happens to the Witowskis. Mr. Witowski is victimized by the company, the union, and the courts. The Poles understand that they are helpless against such odds and they "take it." Although Cohen criticizes the Poles for their submissiveness, this peasant quality iron-ically may serve the Witowskis and all Slavs well in a world Cohen admits is "always going to be this way" (305).

Russell Janney does not individualize many of his Polish characters in *The Miracle of the Bells,* and those he does, Father Paul and Olga Trocki, do not represent the mass of mining families leading lives of quiet desperation in Coaltown. But Russell makes it clear that little has changed for the Poles over the half century of their new life in America. They still live in ethnic ghettos and their lives are still controlled from the cradle to the grave by absentee owners. Cultural diversion, hope, ambition, and the chance to break the poverty cycle are as absent from Coaltown as the mine owners. The Poles have only to await the next mining catastrophe. Life as bondage is Janney's way of presenting the ethnic dilemma, and Olga Trocki's brief moment in the Hollywood sun serves only to remind us that there is no real escape from Coaltown, as her return in death shows.

The Poles in Willard Motley's Chicago fare little better than their coal-mining kin. They too dwell in economic darkness without expectations of real change except, as Don Lockwood does, to maneuver within a corrupt system. Their neighborhood is a slum, and Motley's Poles, in the spirit of Algren to whom Motley is sometimes compared, are among the urban poor whom the benefits of the American way have eluded. They, like all of Motley's ethnics, encompass the "myriad frustrations, dislocations, alienations, and defeats which Motley sees young Americans subjected to in . . . [the] aftermath of World War II" (Rideout 261). The Kosinski family includes nine people, a mother, grandmother, and seven children, all of whom live in one room, dirty inside and out. Fifteen-year-old Ewa has been sentenced to the factory and Helcia to an obscure clerical job. Don (Chet) quits school in the fifth grade and grows up learning the code of the streets. He expresses the outrage of his people when he complains, "Life played a dirty trick on me. Life made me a Pole and put me in the slums and gave me a prostitute for a mother" (407). Despite his association with the Progressive Party and his leftist orientation, Motley does not openly engage in political polemics, but his portrait of the Pole as victim in the class struggle is as unmistakable as that offered in more radical novels.

What we see in Cohen's Pittsburgh, Janney's Coaltown, and Motley's Chicago is that the prospects of middle-class America are beyond the grasp of the ethnic community, despite the fact that the Poles have remained faithful to a system that ignores them. Other writers show, however, how Poles have dropped out of the system and in their rebellion have become social misfits even further removed from the edge of social stability. Norman Mailer suggests this in his portrait of Casimir Czienwicz who, like Chet Kosinski, is also a Chicago kid from a broken home. He is a street tough without moral vision or principle except the belief that "gimme a gimmick and I'll move the world" (619). Of course, Czienwicz does not move the world. With no redeeming qualities, he is perhaps the most despicable member of a platoon composed of men like himself. Mailer doesn't like him; neither do Czienwicz's buddies, nor does the reader. Although Mailer does not investigate Czienwicz's background or supply him with character motivation, he is content to offer him as one who, at a young age, has been irremediably warped by his environment. Motley offers essentially the same kind of character in *Knock on Any Door,* the first volume in his saga of Chicago ghetto life. Although most of the characters including the protagonist are of Italian descent, Motley's Poles stand out. Nick's friend Stash, a bashful, self-conscious but tough Polack Kid, lives with a father who drinks and gambles away his weekly paycheck. Squint Zinski, another of Nick's cohorts, is a petty thief and con man who eventually rats on Nick, his best friend, and testifies against him. Permanently disfigured by their environment, these social misfits represent the Polish American community-at-large, since Motley introduces no other Poles to balance this picture.

In other works, the Pole as social misfit makes only brief appearances as two-dimensional characters in novels not particularly concerned with Poles. The most fully developed characterization occurs in Jack Karney's *Work of Darkness.* This 1956 novel is a somber, realistic, literary equivalent of Leonard Bernstein's *West Side Story* which, opening just a year later, has a faint but noticeable Slavic dimension. Like the musical, *Work of Darkness* deals with East Side groups of mixed cultural heritage in the early 1950s. Dividing his novel into three sections, Karney examines the interlocked lives of three young hoodlums: Lenny Kramer, a Jew; Juan Rivera, a Puerto Rican; and Joe Kusack, a Pole. To a degree, Kramer and Rivera are sympathetically portrayed. We see, at least, that Lenny's family offers an alternative to street life and that Juan has some conscience and compassion. Kusack is another matter altogether. Bitter, violent, vulgar, Kusack's vision is as dark as his home life, dominated by an alcoholic father who beats Joe regularly. Dumb, amoral, psychotic, Kusack is a study of the results of social disintegration, although Karney demonstrates this primarily through implication. When Kusack and Kramer are shot to death by a rival gang, few tears are shed. Kusack gets only what he deserves and the reader gets a clear image of the Pole as outcast, misfit, hoodlum.

From Stella Witowski to Casimir Czienwicz, from Squint Zinski to Joe Kusack, the pattern runs deep. By the 1950s, even as proletarian fiction had dissolved into protest realism, the literary identity of the Pole had assumed another dimension: socioeconomic victim and misfit.

The emerging image was that of the literary heavy, not fully victim or villain or blameless, decidedly ethnic but not especially the bearer of Polish culture, second-generation toughs eager to reject the values of their parents. What Polish literary selves gained in being identified with the proletariat struggle, they lost in their association with a deteriorating urban America. This shift paralleled the movement of first- and second-generation Americans of Polish descent away from their heritage, an ethnic phenomenon documented in numerous studies.

The conflict of ethnic and American identities and the subsequent rediscovery of ethnicity—the subject of Lampell's *The Hero*—is ignored by writers concerned with only political issues and social landscapes. The exceptions are Dan Levin and Willard Motley, two non-Polish writers without any direct connection to Poland. As we have seen, Levin's primary interest is the impact of the war on the future of America and the working class. Motley realistically records urban corruption and decadence. Within these frameworks, however, both focus on a more personal struggle as their protagonists learn to deal with their own ethnicity. The contradictory impulse to destroy and yet to preserve ethnicity is not new to these works. Karl Harriman, Monica Krawczyk, Annette Esty, and Millard Lampell had all touched upon this theme. In addition, the loss of ethnicity surfaces briefly in other works of the period. Betty Smith writes about Dr. Paolski who, in the fashion of Abraham Cahan and Irving Fineman's protagonists, gains success only to lose self. Paolski, a Brooklyn medical doctor, lives a drab, penurious life. His heritage means nothing to him except for its absence. He appears in *Tomorrow Will Be Better* only briefly, but his aloneness speaks for itself in a powerful way that reaches out into the ethnic community. Stella Witowski in *Coming Home* dislikes her environment precisely because her family is Old World, immigrant, and outcast. She decides that she will never marry a Polish millworker, while simultaneously insisting that she wants to live always in the old neighborhood. Olga Trocki rejects her name and her family in her pursuit of Hollywood fame, although she "wills" herself to return in death. Other characters experience similar tensions even in the happy valleys of the Connecticut River novels about Polish farmers.

For Dan Levin, the conflict of ethnicity has national ramifications in the sense that the war is a turning point for ethnic recognition, a point also made by Paul Driscoll, Ruth Tabrah, Katherine Burt, and others. Whereas Driscoll, Tabrah, and Burt deal primarily with the transformation of attitudes in the host culture, Levin pays attention to the internal conflict of his Polish American protagonist. *Mask of Glory* follows Glen Manson's fortunes from his enlistment in the Marines to his first landing in the Pacific, where he is killed. Levin's ambitious novel works on many fronts: as a vindication of democracy and the war, as an homage to the common man, as a redemption of the lost self, as a protest novel, and as a drama of ethnic rediscovery.

Levin initially portrays Manson as just another American soldier, but Manson's Polish heritage hovers about, following him through boot camp and confronting him finally on a Pacific island. Even as he trains, he thinks of his parents who are apparently peasants, although Levin gives few clues about their background. He does tell us at one point that Manson pictures his mother sitting at the window remembering bright kerchiefs, trinkets, and old Poland. Later he remembers his brother George playing Chopin on the violin and occasional scenes from his Polish neighborhood in Cleveland. But to Manson, Polishness is not culture, it's class. More specifically, it is the hopelessness and misery of a class in exile, of a sooty house on Railroad Street and of failed ambitions. A high school dropout, he explains, "I used to read everything . . . then I thought what the hell, what for, where I'm going, what's the percentage" (120). Manson knows that he, like his father, is doomed to a life in the mills, primarily because he's Polish and poor. Consequently, he turns away from his family and from himself. He hates his mother's ways and his father's words. To Glen, his family is rootless and ashamed of who they are. He recalls how his mother enrolled him in school as "Glen" instead of Casimir and how the family changed its name from Minkiewicz to Manson. He sees all this as futility. "They knew nothing had changed. You can't change it with a name" (236).

Glen's rejection of the ethnic self is only superficially developed. We really don't know much about growing up as a Pole in Cleveland, but we know enough to prepare us for Levin's rhetoric about the war as a catalyst to change. Elbrus, the populist voice, awakens Glen to the dignity of the people and the working class and the need to vindicate otherness; and Glen seemingly conquers his ethnic inferiority and his view of himself as a second-class American. "I've broken through," he whispers to himself, as Levin cryptically adds that the war was "where Americans were made" (238–39).

Through Manson, Levin offers the standard notion that ethnicity is secured only when it disappears into melting-pot America. The acceptance of the ethnic self in Manson's case comes from believing that war gives Polish Americans the opportunity to pay their dues to their adopted country. All of this is more clearly explained later when the Mansons receive notice of Glen's death. Patriotic sacrifice erases class distinctions, the Mansons believe. They were, Levin explains, "no longer fearful of memories of the hurtful past; with their son, their new history began" (278). Levin doesn't challenge the view of blood-rite citizenship; in fact, he reinforces the idea through the comments of Glen's brother George. "If you had a kid brother that got killed for the goddamn country, it means you're here to stay—you start from scratch with everybody else—doesn't it?" (275). George's rhetorical question is Levin's unambiguous response to the conflict of ethnicity: ethnicity equals fear, shame, and secondary status; only through sacrificial death can the Poles "look the goddamn thing in the face" (277). For Levin, Polishness is secondary to ethnicity and populism, and Manson's discovery of his ethnic self amounts to little in the way of history and culture. Instead, Polishness is a sign of social paralysis.

Willard Motley also deals with the conflict of ethnicity in *We Fished All Night,* a novel about the seamy side of tenement Chicago and the slow rise of the ethnic into the corrupt and petty world of local politics. Like Manson, Don Lockwood is a second-generation American who has put aside his ethnic self in order to blend more easily into a culture that still regards the Slav with suspicion. Motley is no sentimentalist, however, nor does he offer patriotic gore as a substitute for realism. There is much about Lockwood that is difficult to like. His hard outlook and scheming desires to rise in the world render him less than sympathetic no matter what his ethnic-identity problems. His rejection of his heritage is brutal and self-serving. He has learned that to succeed he must become Anglo and drops his real name, Chet Kosinski, for one that sounds more Hollywood.

The "new" Chet Kosinski is much more critical and bitter toward the ethnic community than Manson is. Motley establishes Lockwood's aggression early when Lockwood takes a satiric look at himself and sees "just an ordinary Pole-Polack. He should marry a rather dumb Polish girl, work in a factory, get drunk on a weekend, bring kids like himself in the world" (22). Lockwood chooses instead to renounce his cultural identity and to pass for an Anglo, an unusual occurrence in novels about Poles in America. "I'm no goddamn Polack," he tells one of his union acquaintances. When another union official asks him to work with the Polish population, he replies, "they're too dumb to help themselves. I believed in them once. I tried to help them" (546). And when McCarren, a political boss, asks him to join the Polish National Alliance in order to influence votes, Don indignantly responds, "But I'm not Polish" (305).

Motley contrasts Lockwood's cynical denunciations with his half-hearted attempts to come to terms with his ethnicity. Don's grandfather, having immigrated in 1887, expresses a fondness for Poland and has nostalgic memories of thatched roofs and a barefoot people with strong feet. He knows little, however, about Polish history or culture and has failed to pass on his traditions or his national spirit. Nonetheless, grandfather Kosinski, who speaks Polish to Don, admonishes him to "remember the old country, always remember Poland, always remember home. That way luck lies" (17). Quite impossible for Don who has no image of life in Poland, these urgings draw Don homeward. When he reads the family letters written back and forth from America to Poland, he feels pride in Polish humanity and history. "These were his people," he admits (123). And at a time of crisis, he returns home to his mother and senses his ethnic roots when he remembers the proverb: "natura ciagnie wilka do lasa—what's bred in the bone, can never be out of the flesh" (446). Lockwood's brushes with the ethnic self are not permanent—no Manson-like transformation for him—although he never fully escapes his roots. Despite Motley's refusal to bow to sentimentality or to supply a romantic conclusion to the conflict of the ethnic self, Polishness comes to the same end as in *Mask of Glory:* it disappears. Lockwood manages to reject his ethnicity enough to satisfy his own needs. The Mansons are content to sacrifice their culture to gain social acceptance. Motley doesn't approve, Levin doesn't mind.

The efforts of Willard Motley and David Levin notwithstanding, proletarian writers never tried very hard to supply more than a one-dimensional view of Polishness; and by the mid-1950s even this effort dwindled to a trickle. One of the last of the radical writers, Howard Fast, wondered where all the great ones had gone, "the whole school of talented progressive writers who arose out of the unemployed struggles led by the Communist Party" (*Intellectuals* 14). As for the Poles, Fast's "great ones" left mixed literary blessings. The protest-proletariat tradition brought, as Walter Rideout points out, a heightened consciousness toward the underprivileged, a respect for common experience, a democratization of the American writer, and the entrance of new characters and their experiences into literature (278). In addition, the tradition stirred up controversies, discovered new writers, broke down barriers, and as Daniel Aaron reminds us, opened up neglected areas of American life to literary treatment (*Writers* 396).

To be sure, the Polish experience in urban America received modest attention by radical writers. In many cases, the Poles are the new characters, the underprivileged, and the neglected culture noted by Rideout and Aaron. The protest tradition succeeded in introducing the urban Pole to American readers in sympathetic and often controversial ways. More specifically, writers often turned to Poles as representative proletariats—part victim, part rebel—in order to dramatize the worker struggle. As a consequence, they also defined Polishness for generations of Americans. The Poles, we find out in this fiction, were part and parcel of the American experience, with drives and failures that corresponded to those of the average citizen. At the same time, "otherness" is usually minimized, as Poles are often separated from their cultural and historical heritage by writers uninformed and disinterested in "otherness" and yet obliged philosophically to pay attention to ethnic groups. The result is that ethnicity both gains and loses in these works. Protest writers succeeded in mainstreaming Polishness by identifying Poles with familiar events, while at the same time further isolating Poles by associating them with radical causes. Similarly, they transplanted to American soil an international political movement without necessarily deepening or broadening the Polish cultural-historical context either in the Old World or the New. Committed to a single agenda, protest writers reduced ethnicity to a set of signs and symbols with the result that Polish ethnicity, in their hands, is "like gold to airy thinness beat."

5

WORLD WAR II AND AFTER

Strangers and Other Neighbors

*Look, we're Poles, but we aren't like the Poles
you used to know.* —KARSAVINA

I. VICTIMS AND REFUGEES

In "Poland in the Second World War," Norman Davies reminds us that
the legends of the campaign are "better known than the facts," and
points, as an example, to the oft-repeated stories of the Polish cavalry
charging German tanks. Considering the bitterness and humiliation of
the war, it is not surprising, Davies concludes, that the Poles "should
propagate a legend which showed how they lost with a gesture of
glamorous defiance. It is entirely natural that people in the West and in
Russia, unwilling to recognize the unworthy parts played by their own
governments in 1939, should also want to believe it" (II 439). The
propagation of legends Davies refers to helps characterize the whole of
Polish history. Moreover, it is consistent with the romantic portrait of
Poland which Americans first rushed to embrace and then to promote
from the late eighteenth century onward. It is not surprising that
American fiction relating to Poland during World War II and the postwar period would carry on this romantic idealization, especially since
writers with direct links to Poland authored much of the fiction. Yet, the
actual war in Poland—as gruesome, destructive, and ambiguous as that
fought anywhere—was not the direct subject of fiction until John
Hersey and Leon Uris wrote about the Warsaw Ghetto uprising and the
concentration camps, and until the exiled novelist W. S. Kuniczak
described the more emotional (and romantic) aspects of the military
campaign in his trilogy, *The Thousand-Hour Day, The March,* and
Valedictory.

Instead writers concentrated on Polish refugees, on a trapped population trying to survive the opening weeks of the war, or—as in Rulka
Langer's *The Mermaid and the Messerschmitt* and Antoni Gronowicz's
Bolek—on those fortunate enough to escape to America. As one might
expect, these writers used fiction as a forum to familiarize the nation

with events, to dramatize Poland's plight, to plead for tolerance toward a new group of immigrant-refugees, and to prepare Americans for the rise of People's Poland. Information, sympathy, and propaganda were thus the aims of largely two-dimensional works that glossed over cultural nuances and historical complexities. Similarly, the literary development of Polish ethnicity in America was temporarily shelved by many who turned to familiar images in times that required, so they thought, direct and dramatic, trusted and tried literary methods.

In a half dozen or so novels, Poland as a nation became the subject of fiction for the first time since Eric Kelly's celebrated historical novels about the Polish legendary past. America's conceptions of its far-off neighbor were thus supplemented by the particulars of a Polish landscape usually referred to only in passing by previous writers, but which in these novels received more detailed attention. More incidental than purposeful even in these works, this information, nonetheless, may have added as much knowledge about Poland as all the previous fiction written about Poles in America.

A number of works were produced by Polish Americans or recent arrivals whose books were published in the United States after they had themselves undergone an immigrant experience. Thus, the novels represent the collective viewpoint of "international" writers, American, Polish, and others who fashioned America's literary image of wartime Poland. That image centers on a homogeneous and unified nation without political and religious friction, social classes, or ethnic, racial, and religious minorities. Most writers look at the gentry or the upper middle class, characterizing it once again as the standard-bearer of European culture. They also praise the richness of Poland's past and stress the interconnectedness of Polish and American history and culture. Jona Konopka's *Dust of Our Brother's Blood* (1941) comprises the recollections of a young girl growing up in the Carpathian region around Nowy Sacz. As such it is a unique, fictional glimpse of upper-middle-class Poland in the 1930s, a world that would permanently disappear with the advent of the postwar people's republic. Rulka Langer in *The Mermaid and the Messerschmitt* (1942) also provides a view of an upper-middle-class family with aristocratic connections. In *While Still We Live* (1944), Helen MacInnes follows the opening days of the war and the developing resistance movement from the point of view of a young English girl caught by events. MacInnes's characters are urban, educated, and wealthy—the privileged class of Warsaw. Similarly, Catherine Hutter in *On Some Fair Morning* (1946) writes about the landed class of Silesia, and records German-Polish relations from the 1860s to the 1940s from the perspective of a wealthy German/Pole of American descent. Only Antoni Gronowicz sets his novel in the rural countryside, but even the characters in *Bolek* (1942) are not peasants.

With the possible exception of Langer, who provides extensive commentary on the siege of Warsaw, none of these novelists concentrates directly on the military aspect. These are not war novels in the style of *Guadacanal Diary, The Naked and the Dead,* or even *The Young Lions.* The central issue is the sweep of history as it has affected Poland in the past and as it overruns Poland again. Within this context, writers turned to moments of past glory, of victory in defeat, of the nation's triumphs even as it fell time and again to invaders. Konopka reviews highlights from Polish history: the liberal constitution of 1791, Sobieski's victory at Vienna, Poland's 1,000-year defense of Western civilization. MacInnes, sprinkling similar symbolic events throughout her narration, calls attention to the 1920 war with the Soviet Union as an example of Poland's defense of the West, this time from the specter of Communist tyranny. Gronowicz cites the battle of Grunwald, the Polish conquest of the Teutonic knights, and the rise of sixteenth-century Warsaw. Hutter calls attention to Poland's tragic fate during World War I, Pilsudski's victory over the Soviets, and the Phoenix-like emergence of an independent Poland as an example of the historical cycle of Polish triumph amidst apparent disaster.

Likewise, the Poles in these novels are carefully drawn to illustrate culture and breeding as the upper middle class replaces the aristocrat as a European beau ideal. Langer's protagonist talks about guest bathrooms with scented soaps and embroidered towels, about eccentric aunts versed in the esoterics of Swedish history, and about student days at Vassar as if this were the life of a typical Pole. As for the peasants and Jews who comprise the majority of the population, Langer admits that they are "completely foreign" to her, referring at one point to Warsaw's Jewish neighborhood as a Polish version of New York's Chinatown or Harlem. Jona Konopka's Poland gives us courageous, dignified, patriotic, upper-class Christian Poles, a romantic picture of folk culture, and a landscape of colorful and emotional religious icons and ceremonies. MacInnes points to the "music and poetry . . . rooted and growing in every Polish heart" (314), and presents a group of gentlemanly partisans, led by Wisniewski, a man of breeding and resourcefulness. MacInnes is, in fact, especially given to romanticizing partisan activities and to showing, as all these writers do in one way or another, how much more clever the Poles are than their German oppressors—a dubious claim in the face of the September campaign. Antoni Gronowicz's Poles embody the artistic tradition. Bolek, the young protagonist, is a violin virtuoso in the tradition of characters created by Rupert Hughes, Mary Ives Todd, and Dorothy Richardson. As for Bolek him-

self, he carries forward the art of Chopin, Szymanowski, and Paderewski, who are conjured up in the novel to give substance to Polish
character. Gronowicz's "typical" Poles fly in airplanes, eat in good
restaurants, and hustle about Warsaw in the roar of traffic. When
Gronowicz does mention rural life, he favors the nationalistic elements
of folk culture—peasant dances and festivals.

In Catherine Hutter's *On Some Fair Morning,* the internal rivalries
of ethnic groups in independent Poland receive some attention, notably
the Silesian question. Otherwise, neither Hutter nor any of the writers
trying to describe prewar Poland looks at economic and industrial
issues, shifting borders, the political right and left, or the dark side of
Polish nationalism. They regard the 1939 invasion by Germany and the
Soviet Union as yet another example of how Polish history has been
shaped by external forces and events. They responded as previous
American writers had learned to respond, as the Poles themselves had
learned: by transforming the event into a symbol. A martyred nation
once again assumes a Christ-like role as defender of Christian values
and Western enlightenment. Little boys enter the army with a smile,
women fight in the forest alongside their husbands, old men defiantly
refuse to submit. All of Poland in these novels stands its ground.

One of Helen MacInnes's characters associates Poland's role in 1939
with Sobieski's defense of Christian Europe in the seventeenth century.
He explains, "By taking the first blow from the German fist when it was
strongest, we may have helped preserve buildings and lives in other
countries. So in the end we will win, for Poland will live in the hearts of
men" (141). The idea of history as self-sacrifice, martyrdom, and transcendence appears again in *Dust of Our Brothers' Blood.* In various
ways, Konopka asserts the nation's "long heritage of hope and un-
daunted determination to thrive and survive" (168), but her novel ends
with a symbolic scene which says it best. An aged Polish count and a
villainous Nazi general engage in a sabre duel. After Count Michael
triumphs according to the rules, he is savagely struck down by the Nazi
onlookers, sadistically murdered as centuries of Polish-German antagonism is telescoped into a single event. Michael is buried in a tenth-
century vault where he joins other nobles, warriors, and defenders of
Polish integrity. That Poland suffers for all is the theme of these novels.
In fact, the American journalist in *While Still We Live* suggests that
Warsaw's fate could easily be New York's.

Konopka's oblique analogy between Poland and America is, in this
case, a legitimate reference to the universality of war and the fate of
nations. In other cases, however, Poland and America are more closely
linked as once again American writers, even those without a Polish
connection, found it perfectly natural to associate the United States and

this distant neighbor. Some of the connections serve plot interests; others originate outside the text, in the perception of a shared history, destiny, and national character. Langer's Polish heroine is married to an American so that her frequent references and eventual journey to the United States are natural and even predictable. By the 1940s, kinship between Poles and Americans needed no explanation—at least not in fiction. Catherine Hutter's Silesian heroine is an American, Elsa Crewe, who in the nineteenth century married a German and made Silesia her home. She prefers, however, the ethnic Poles, praises their progress in the interwar period, and even bequeaths her estate not to her German (by this time Nazi) children but to her Polish servant Josefa, whose decision to emigrate to the States is a consequence of the "American" Crewes's affinity with her Polish neighbors. In *While Still We Live,* MacInnes emphasizes similarities in Polish and American temperament. Her hero, the partisan leader Adam Wisniewski, bold, clever, forceful, is admirable precisely because he possesses qualities that "made America, after all."

The fullest expression of Polish and American kinship occurs in *Bolek* by Antoni Gronowicz, an immigrant writer whose publications were often directly influenced by his politics. Gronowicz emphasizes the fact that the two nations and cultures are mutual admirers. At one point a little American girl in the novel tells her Polish friends that Szymanowski and Paderewski are known in America. At another point, Bolek's father, who worked for a time in Chicago and Pittsburgh, familiarizes his neighbors with the "mischief and privileges" of America's cities. For Gronowicz Polish and American connections are not without hazard, however. Poles, he implies, have sometimes become prisoners of American industry or distracted by the meaninglessness of sports. Even so, Gronowicz leaves no doubt that America still represents the promised land: golden, lovely, "a happy world" where people can "buy a house and garden in the country" and "live like millionaires" (236). In a novel about a war-ravaged country and its refugees, these comments seem a bit out of place, but Gronowicz draws upon century-old attitudes about America still current in Poland, as any visitor can attest.

Others turned directly to the newly arrived refugees themselves to raise America's consciousness and to fashion a sympathetic atmosphere. In the process, writers—such as Flannery O'Connor in "The Displaced Person"—frequently characterized their refugees as "Poles," reflecting the turn-of-the-century practice of regarding the Pole as the representative Slav or East European.

Consequently, ethnicity in these works resides primarily at the edges of personality and in the assumed "otherness" of the refugees. Polishness is itself rounded off, reduced to symbolic historical reference or friendly semiotics: names, hand-kissing, and peasant shawls in Ida Wylie's *Strangers Are Coming,* and St. Casimir, Krakow, and Slavic blondness in Robert Nathan's *The Sea-Gull Cry.* Through her heroine, Wylie exploits the myth of Polish musical genius and emphasizes the equally mythic passion for land through John Pusak who, though college educated, still dreams of a farm where he can live a simple, independent life. Wylie also seizes upon the familiar qualities of the peasant—vigor, solidity, plodding earnestness, integrity—with an eye toward showing how these qualities combine with American charac-teristics in the second generation in ways beneficial to America. By and large the Poles in all these novels are streamlined ethnics without distinct cultural markings or "dangerous differences." Writers instead offered educated, well-bred bearers of culture—a twentieth-century version of the aristocratic beau ideal hardly objectionable to critics of immigration. In Annie B. Kerr's "The Picture," Anna Kowalska is a princess despite the working-class origin of her surname, and Wanda Dombrowska is a countess. Wylie's Poles are a mixed bag: a Jew, an orphan child, a worker, and a princess. Of these, the princess interests Wylie most and she devotes a good part of the plot to reconstructing the girl's amnesia-bound memory. Even in memory loss, however, "anyone could see she was not a peasant" (68). In *The Sea-Gull Cry,* Louisa and Jeri are nobility, a "picture of beauty and wonder." In *Without Passport,* Jean Coon's Poles are gentry in peasants' cloth; that is, Coons does her best to attribute "aristocratic expressions" to peas-ant stock, not a new development in American fiction.

By the mid-1940s, those writing about Poles no longer felt it neces-sary to introduce the cultural landscape to American readers. Instead, they relied on symbols and an established literary tradition, however misleading and incomplete, to identify the "other" and his problems. Their oblique characterization of Poles and Poland suggests that Ameri-cans had accumulated a set of sufficiently developed symbols through which to recognize ethnicity and that Poles were no longer either a major novelty or socioeconomic threat. It seems enough for Nathan and Wylie to mention "Pole" to produce the reader response they desired, although in actuality Americans in the 1940s knew little more about Polish culture and history than they did in the 1890s. For the time being, explorations of Polish culture and American ethnicity were set aside for the larger issues of the war and its consequences.

For now, according to these writers, the immediate problems were political refugees and the threat of a reactionary response by Ameri-cans. Thus the theme of these novels is the familiar good *them* versus

the good and bad *us*. Nathan's Americans worry that too many foreigners would "crowd us out" (107) and Coons's believe that immigrants are "usurpers." Needless to say these tensions are resolved to the
benefit of all. In fact the Poles, once again, serve as models and even as
an inspiration for their host-culture acquaintances. In *The Sea-Gull
Cry*, the Czarnowitzs exude courage, determination, innocence, and
integrity; they are a moral constant in an ever-darkening world. Their
sacrifice and their behavior motivate Richard Smith, a middle-aged
college professor, to deepen his understanding of love and paradoxically to commit himself physically and mentally to an American victory. Similarly, Ida Wylie in *Strangers Are Coming*, while hardly mentioning Poland before or during the war, uses her refugees to teach
Americans about themselves. "We've been un-American—just plain
mean and bigoted and snobbish," one of her characters concludes
(223). Another comes to understand, "It's no use dying for something if
you won't live for it" (81). As these statements show, liberal attitudes
and a spirit of national self-examination dominate in these novels.
Wylie's plea for the acceptance of otherness is nothing less than a call
for a more tolerant and pluralistic America. In the end, her divided
fictional family—a metaphor for the nation—puts aside its prejudices
for a new sociomoral vision that cuts across both cultural pluralism
and the class structure.

In these fictional appeals for charity and acceptance, Poles, through
their temperament and behavior, ease their own entry into society and
reveal themselves to be the type of ethnic group most appreciated by
Americans. Kerr's ethnic community is nonthreatening: a microcosm of
industry, neighborliness, and patriotism, with a cultural heritage frozen
in time and descended from Sobieski, Kosciuszko, Mickiewicz, Chopin,
and Paderewski. In an *Atlantic Monthly* story, Alice Berezowski adds
that Polish refugees are a blessing in disguise. Fiercely freedom-loving,
they quickly transfer their allegiance to their adopted country and dive
into the war effort. "I am helping America win the war," Pavel announces without a second glance toward occupied Poland.

As for the Poles themselves, their problems receive only secondary
treatment as a corollary of sorts to a postwar changing America.
Without establishing Old World identity, writers allude to the loss of
identity as the central problem facing the immigrants. Wylie's nameless
princess laments, "We are all lost, poor people. What we have been is
gone. What we are to be we do not know" (72); and after years in
America, Lena Brodinski in Joan Coons's *Without Passport*, still sees
herself "wandering between two worlds" (110). The threshold theme (a
foot in each world) appears rather casually and without a historical

context, but nonetheless points to the works of I. B. Singer and Jerzy Kosinski. For now, most were satisfied to refer in passing to the loss of cultural identity to win sympathy for their characters.

2. THE NEW POLAND

In what was probably his first major television interview, in August 1990, the new Polish ambassador to the United States, Kazimierz Dziewanowski, was asked if he thought Poland's future was bright. Mr. Dziewanowski hesitated, then replied that first Poland would need to confront the problems of organizing a "new state," "new institutions," "new rules of public and political life," and a new "all," as he phrased it, which had not existed for many years. As he concluded, Dziewanowski turned once more to the idea of a new Poland to explain that Americans need to believe that this is a "new embassy and a new Polish state," embarking on a "new set of relations. . . . We have all possibilities," he added, "to create new and friendly fruitful relationships." In the last two minutes of the conversation, Dziewanowski used the word "new" ten times as a conceptual notion designed to accommodate a vision of Poland's past and future and as a construct intuitively understood by an American audience. What Ambassador Dziewanowski meant by "new" necessarily includes the euphoria and doubt, direction and misdirection of the present, as well as a reflective awareness of repeated instances in the last two centuries of Polish attempts to throw off oppression and occupation and to reemerge as a "new old" member of the European community of nations.

This latest transformation and Dziewanowski's reliance on the idea of newness calls to mind events of fifty years ago when Poland last experienced a dramatic and wrenching socioeconomic political transformation. As it had in the Solidarity-dominated eighties, the American press then offered full coverage of events. Hundreds of articles appeared across the periodical spectrum, in scholarly journals, such as *Current History,* in popular and populist magazines, such as *The Saturday Evening Post, The New Republic,* and *Nation,* and in special interest journals, such as *Catholic World.* As one might expect, history dictated content. In late 1943 and early 1944, American periodicals reported on the drive to liberate Poland from the East. In 1944, attention shifted to the rival claims of the London government-in-exile and the provisional Lublin government. With the end of the war, American magazines featured stories on the destruction and reconstruction of Poland, along with political factionalism in the context of growing East-West tensions. By the late 1940s, journalists increasingly portrayed Poland as an innocent victim of Stalinism, and as a Cold War enemy of the United States. In six years, the perception of Poland in the periodical press changed from that of a martyred champion of Western ideals to a willing accomplice of totalitarianism.

The interpretation of events by the periodical press is illustrative. Beginning in mid-1944, stories focused on the Eastern front and the conflict between the London and Lublin governments. More to the point, journals sympathetic to the Soviet-inspired Lublin group employed America's predilection for newness as a way to discredit the government-in-exile. Complaining that this was the same group of landowners and reactionaries who leaned toward fascism and militarism in the 1930s, *The Nation* observed that the situation "demands a new and different government . . . prepared to find a basis for good-neighborly relations with Russia" (653). Similarly, *The New Republic* argued that the exiles in London "are not the leadership material out of which a new and healthy Europe can grow" (623). These periodicals and others succeeded in linking the legitimate government with the failures of old Europe. A number of articles about wartime destruction and rebuilding employed a similar approach. Photo displays made it clear that old Poland, defined as buildings and property, was gone forever and that the demands of tomorrow took precedence over the traditions of a thousand-year-old culture. Like the London government and the rubble of war, old ways had no place in Poland, these articles implied. In a score of stories between 1944 and 1949, newness was the cry as periodicals sang out America's acceptance of an *inevitably* new society in articles such as "Poland's New Phase," "Enigma of a New Poland," "New Poland," "Proud Poles Create a New Warsaw," and "New Blows in an Age of Insult." Largely undefined, newness itself *is* the story in these articles. As early as July 1945, *Newsweek* was quick to announce that "old Poland has gone" (51) and that, as *The New Republic* phrased it, the old government is in "the process of being liquidated" (59). *Life* and others documented the new Poland in pictorials showing recently constructed nurseries, churches, schools, and factories, with only a passing nod given to the new political order. In a full-page photo in *Life,* a Pole identified only as a former partisan marches alone toward newly annexed territory, a striking visual symbol of the new Poland (117). By 1947, the word "new" took on another, more ironic dimension. Surveying political events from 1939 to 1947, S. Harrison Thomson, editor of the *Journal of Central European Affairs,* concluded in "The New Poland" that the die was cast. Poland was already "them" and the future irreconcilably fixed. Similarly, Lawrence King writing in *Catholic World,* described Poland's struggle as the conflict between the eternal forces of darkness and light, yesterday and tomorrow. Even after Poland's painful disappearance behind the Iron Curtain, journalists continued to emphasize newness.

During this same period, American novelists offered their own version of Poland's postwar transformation. Antoni Gronowicz's *Four from the Old Town* (1944), set in Lwow, covers the years from 1939 to 1944, and his young protagonist's experience with conquest, resistance, and triumph. Jean Karsavina in *Reunion in Poland* (1945) focuses on the Soviet liberation and the formation of a provisional government, while V. J. Jerome in *A Lantern for Jeremy* (1951) offers historical justification for contemporary events in Poland and in Eastern Europe. All three of these writers have a singular and shared purpose: to soften and acquaint the American public with the prospect of a radically different Poland. (Jerome's link with *Masses and Mainstream,* where he was an influential editor, and Karsavina's willingness to follow the socialist version of events, underscore their intentions.) What is more, they point the way to the renewal, rebirth, and reemergence of a new and better socialist Poland, the real victor and hero in the novels.

For the Polish-born Gronowicz, the enemy in *Four from the Old Town* is the past, particularly the cultural animosities that plagued Christian, Jewish, and Ukrainian Poles in the prewar period. As such, Gronowicz sets out to heal old wounds and to create cultural bonds necessary for the success of the new Poland. This is nowhere more obvious than in his choice of protagonists: Izio Katz, a Jewish Pole; Kazik Ziomkowicz, a Christian Pole; and Maruska Szewczenko, a Ukrainian Pole; all set aside their differences to defeat a common enemy and rebuild the nation. Gronowicz avoids references to historical unpleasantries, preferring emotional rhetoric instead, such as Maruska's reminder that the German army is "as much my enemy as it is the enemy of Poland" (44). On other occasions, history serves Gronowicz's purpose. He has King Jagiello declare that Lwow "for all eternity . . . shall belong to the Polish kingdom" (56), and he reminds his readers frequently of Polish-Ukrainian unity in the face of past tsarist oppression.

Gronowicz, without full knowledge of the Holocaust at the time of his writing, tries even harder to heal Christian-Jewish wounds. For example, Izio—the best student in his school class—explains that "King Kazimierz invited the persecuted Jews from Spain, France, and Germany to come to Poland" (25), and later notes that he had "generations of Polish ancestors behind him" (47). Even the landscape affirms Izio's Polishness. He hears the sun whisper, "This is your land, where you and your great-grandparents were born, this is your forest, your clean air, and your home" (94). Not surprisingly, Izio saves Kazik's life in the Lwow uprising, and Kazik's family in turn helps to shelter the fleeing Katz family. In short, Polish-Jewish relations in *Four from the Old Town* could not be better.

All of this points toward Gronowicz's central concern: the emergence of a new Poland connected to the romantic past of Jagiello, Kilinsky, Mickiewicz, Konopnicka, and the other Polish icons he mentions, and the visionary Poland of tomorrow, radically, if inexplicably, different. As the Germans are driven westward, Gronowicz begins to invoke the future as Kazik reads from Maria Konopnicka's poetry:

> The sun will lean from the morning skies,
> Sun of the morning.
> And drink the dew on the meadows rise,
> Daylight is dawning. (96)

Similarly, the Jewish Katz family believes that "tomorrow would be a new and bright day . . . a new life is coming" (96), even as Mr. Ziomkowicz, pointing to the Polish landscape, tells Kazik that "a new spring is dawning." The novel closes with a hopeful, if opaque, look toward the future as Kazik tells Maruska, "We must work and build a new and better Poland" (149). Just what kind of future to expect Gronowicz does not say, just as he fails to distinguish between rival underground groups or to comment on the likelihood of Soviet control. In the dark days of 1944, Gronowicz was satisfied with a sufficiently vague but comfortable image easy enough for all to interpret as they saw fit.

If Gronowicz hesitates and obfuscates, Jean Karsavina rushes headlong into political intricacies without blinking. Consequently, *Reunion in Poland,* also addressed to a youthful audience, reads like a primer on contemporary Polish politics. That Karsavina would include so many references to specific issues and events suggests that she regarded her mission as immediate, specific, and purposeful. As such Karsavina sets out to discredit the past, to explain the present, and to create a future. Early and often she indicts Polish prewar society and its wartime government. The old regime did not educate the masses, modernize agriculture, or practice democracy. In addition, Poland's minorities suffered; the Ukrainians were "little better off than serfs in the middle ages," and anti-Semitism was rampant. In Karsavina's view, prewar Poland was little more than a collection of fiefdoms, designed as always to secure power for rich landowners.

Consequently, she presents many of her characters as critics of a prewar class system which some desperately wish to preserve at the war's end. Maciej Biruta, for example, is introduced as a political activist formerly jailed because he dared "to demand that the government give the peasants land grants" (16). And Dr. Stefan's fictional role is designed to explain that "winning the war is only half the job. Wait till we start dividing up the land," he says. "The great princes will scream for their manors back. They'll try to start a civil war" (26). Reconstruction is similarly politicized and the past discredited. All opposition to reform and progress is attributed to the London government which waits "for the day when they can start bleeding us again" (43). Karsavina goes so far as to attribute prewar anti-Semitism and a betrayal of the Warsaw underground to the opponents of the Lublin government. The old guard is labeled a group of traitors who "didn't stop at murder and did the enemy's work" (89).

Simultaneously, Karsavina praises the postwar order, comprised of new political and social alliances. Like Gronowicz, she addresses longstanding rivalries and problems by explaining that all this will change in the new Poland. One of the characters tells his Ukrainian and Jewish colleagues: "Look, we're Poles, but we aren't like the Poles you used to know" (56). Karsavina, apologizing for Polish treatment of its Jewish citizens, makes it clear through such characters as the Rosenthals that Jews will play a central role in the new Poland. Internally, the new alliance is composed of the peasants, the army, and (ironically, considering her emphasis on Jewish centrality) the church. Externally, Poland's future lies with the Soviet Union. Karsavina wastes no time celebrating this alliance. The story opens in Moscow among Polish refugees generously taken in by the Russians, who treat them like brothers allowing "real Polish schools" and rebuilding a "new Polish army." Wanda Gorska speaks for all Poles when she tells her Russian friend Vania, "You're our best friends. It's pretty wonderful" (21).

These new alliances prepare and point the way toward Poland's future. From beginning to end, *Reunion in Poland,* is structured and directed toward a sufficiently abstract but attractive image of futurism, loosely defined as renewal, rebirth, and redemption from past errors. Karsavina opens her novel by citing a "letter to Julian Tuwim by Lucjan Szenwald written on the Eastern Front, May 1944." The poem begins:

> Already beyond the horizon, cradled in a deep red mist.
> The new day is born.

Moreover, the action begins on the eve of a new year, 1944, and the final drive to recapture Polish territory from the East.

Similarly, Karsavina closes the novel in a crescendo of symbols, icons, and rhetoric designed to emotionalize Poland's prospects. Everything bespeaks harmony and regeneration. Karsavina describes the advent of spring and points to the erupting earth, "pale and young and tender . . . the color of new life" (102). The characters then attend a joyous marriage in Lowicz and contemplate their own imminent marriage, symbolic of rebuilding the nation. Wanda, Bolek, and their fellow patriots (never identified as Marxists or Socialists) are securing "the foundations of the future." Thus, Karsavina brings her futuristic theme full circle from the opening reference to Szenwald's "new day" to the title of the last chapter, "Faces toward the Future."

Published six years later, V. J. Jerome's *A Lantern for Jeremy* appears on the surface to be unrelated to Karsavina's novel. Set in 1905 during yet another insurrection against an occupying force, the novel makes no direct references to postwar events. Instead, Jerome concentrates on the life and times of poor, oppressed Polish Jews and their Christian counterparts who rise toward human dignity in a collective response to socioeconomic injustice. As in the novels of Gronowicz and Karsavina, *A Lantern for Jeremy* employs a youthful protagonist who witnesses events that transform him from a naive innocent to a politically astute activist. Interspersed with these chapters about a Jewish Pole's maturation are others dealing with a Christian Pole, Yanek Matuszewski, a fiery idealist eventually murdered by anti-Semitic ruffians egged on by landowners and officials of the regime.

The subject matter of Jerome's 1951 novel appears both anachronistic and irrelevant to the new Poland. By 1950, as the periodical press had made clear, the idea of Poland as a fully Sovietized puppet of Moscow and a suffering example of world socialism was fixed in the American imagination. Jerome obviously had no need to prepare Americans for the advent of a people's republic or to urge them to choose sides in a Lublin versus London confrontation. That he would turn to events in Poland of fifty years before suggests a change in party strategy more than a loss of interest in contemporary Polish affairs. In an era of heightened Cold War tension, Jerome turned to history as a way to influence American attitudes, and as a way to justify the turn of events in Eastern Europe in the late 1940s. In other words, *A Lantern for Jeremy* is as much about postwar Poland as it is about proletarian revolution in tsarist Russia.

Jerome's methods bear resemblance to his predecessors, Gronowicz and Karsavina. Once again, simple and singular images predominate: an oppressed people needing to break with the old order, a kinship of culturally diverse groups, the harmony implicit in a unified response to injustice, a generalized vision of a future and better world. Jerome includes enough examples of class oppression, anti-Semitism, and political violence to make the case for world revolution; and he does so by bonding Christian and Jewish Poles in ways that defy history but reflect the make-up of socialism in Eastern Europe. Yanek voices the call for social, cultural, and political unity as a prelude to a new Poland—the focal point of Jerome's novel—when he sings: "Let us unite—Poles, Jews, and Russians / And make a republic in our land" (145). By the end of the novel, Jerome has made his case that history is on the march toward a new, more humane, more just social order—the kind ostensibly in place in Poland by the late 1940s. As the young Jeremy leaves for London, he has a dream vision of the new Poland: Christians and Jews playing, smiling, marching; old wrongs transcended, history corrected, the future secured. All are "talking and laughing and singing," anticipating "a republic in our land" (288).

Substituting one historical period for a politically analogous one, Jerome looks beyond 1940s Poland, as do Antoni Gronowicz and Jean Karsavina. In all three cases, American writers transcended the immediate, avoiding thorny questions and a history of Polish complexities, just as Ambassador Dziewanowski looked beyond a disappointing historical relationship between Poland and Americans of Polish descent in his call for unity and harmony between the two. Dziewanowski's call to think "new," draws upon a literary tradition dating from the 1830s, and upon an ideology perfectly suited to introduce to Americans a set of diverse and complex values rooted not in the new but in the old Poland.

3. THE LIMITS OF ETHNICITY

In the 1940s, fiction about war-torn Poland, political refugees, and the emergence of People's Poland added new literary dimensions to ethnicity. The decade was also the most prolific in regard to works about Polishness. Over thirty novels, a dozen or more short stories, and Tennessee Williams's fateful play about Stella and Stanley Kowalski appeared. These numbers alone indicate that Polish Americans, whose population now reached into the millions, had become a significant, although still silent, presence in ethnic literature and American life. In the postwar years, this heightened literary interest continued amidst the euphoria of an America happy to be at peace and eager to achieve the promises of its cultural ideology. The decade produced a number of congratulatory works about Polish American war heroics and sacrifices: Frederick Bell's "The Shipmate Spirit," Elizabeth MacDonald's *The Way and the Life,* Peter Mankowski's "The Holy Basket," J. P. Sheldon's *Miss Bronska,* Paul Gallico's "Welcome Home," and others. For the ethnic self, the war offered opportunities to win self-respect and material rewards. According to Joseph Wytrwal, these were flush times:

The era after World War II was one of continued progress and prosperity for the Americans of Polish descent. The lush years had brought new wealth and affluence to members of the older generation who were solidly entrenched in business and the various professions. Polish names became more and more identified with charitable, educational, and community projects. Thousands of immigrants' sons returned from the battlefield to continue their education or resume careers. . . . (414–15)

Eager to find evidence of success, Wytrwal—typical of some writing about Poles in America—ignores the darker truths. Others did not. Instead of progress and prosperity, they saw that America's ethnics remained invisible, as Ralph Ellison would say, and that they grew more estranged and dispirited, dissatisfied both in their struggle for full assimilation and their contrary wish to remain hyphenated. As Americans would better understand after the riots and civil rights protests of the 1960s and 1970s, ethnicity was still a label that targeted large groups of citizens as undesirable others. For most of those writing about Poles in postwar America, assimilation, success, and pluralism were more dream than reality. Contrasting sharply with fiction about refugees or the war effort, their works feature returning veterans disillusioned by a cynical world forgetful of heroics but mindful of self-interests. Otto Schrag's *Sons of the Morning* (1945) criticizes an America unable to understand the global consequences of the war and unwilling to adapt to change. Ironically, one of the most reactionary of Schrag's characters is a Polish woman who, half-crazed by her son's war death, acts as a spokesperson for a smug and hypocritical citizenry. The bitterness in *Sons of Morning* is matched by Lester Cohen in *Coming Home*. Other writers—Paul Driscoll (*My Felicia* 1945), Ruth Tabrah (*Pulaski Place* 1949), Millard Lampell (*The Hero* 1949), Katherine Burt (*Strong Citadel* 1949), and Alfred Slote (*Denham Proper* 1953)—share Schrag's and Cohen's cynicism, if not their anger and despair. Employing ethnic protagonists, Driscoll, Tabrah, and Lampell write about assimilation and the promises of democracy, although they do not advocate pluralism in their new America. Burt and Slote worry about moral and social rigidity in middle-class America. All, however, probe ethnic life actively and seriously. Their realistic and sensitive novels dramatize the continuing crisis of ethnic minorities and the often solitary and fruitless socioeconomic struggles of Americans of Polish descent. Neither stylistically or thematically innovative nor exceptional as thinkers, these novelists nonetheless push ethnic literature one step forward, toward the respectability and world-class recognition that would be won by African American, Jewish, and feminist writers beginning in the 1950s. For the first time, Polish characters are able to survey the kingdom and evaluate host-culture perceptions and attitudes. What is more, Tabrah and Lampell relate ethnic problems to national concerns, moving ethnic literature about Poles closer to mainstream literature as Saul Bellow and Bernard Malamud would do for Jewish American literature.

All the major ethnic characters in these novels are outsiders, though most labor toward harmony and reconciliation and tend to wear a smile on one side of their faces. The other side, however, shows the accumulating effects of economic misery and social inferiority as Polish Americans grew increasingly uneasy with their heritage. In *My Felicia,* Paul Driscoll captures these tensions in his story of the second-generation American, Felicia Zielinski. Felicia, the outsider, eventually marries the Anglo Mark Standler, thus seeming to end her exile based on ethnicity. But Felicia moves inside without any real conviction on Driscoll's part or in the mind of the reader. Driscoll's ethnics have problems too deep-seated to be swept aside by the kind of melting-pot marriage introduced by earlier novelists and offered once again by Driscoll as a quick and certain way to an American ancestry.

For the sons and daughters of immigrants, ethnicity had itself become as much of a problem as ethnic-Anglo confrontation. Generational differences between fathers and sons and constant reminders of cultural inferiority combined to produce psychological anxieties and a desire to break free from a "non-American" heritage. As it is for Lampell's and Tabrah's protagonists, the task for Felicia is to be free from the shadows of her Polish self, not necessarily because she envies middle-class America but rather because her ethnicity has become too heavy a burden. Her parents have remained "too Polish," we are told; but Driscoll has difficulty explaining just what this means. He is able to define Polishness (Felicia's problem) only in terms of weddings, polkas, pierogies, and the remnants of a folk culture. He also recalls the legendary Polish passion for land and country. At the outbreak of the war, the Polish National Alliance meets in Kosciuszko Hall (where else?), buys bonds, makes speeches, sings "Jeszcze Polska Nie Zginyla." Additionally Driscoll defines Polishness in the exclusivity of Felicia's mother who clings desperately to her Old World identity, who wants Felicia to marry a Polish boy, who regards herself as alien, and who sees her identity slipping away: "Always in this country we will be a little lost," she explains. "Soon there will be no more Polish people" (67).

Ironically, the characteristics that writers had celebrated earlier in the century are now the qualities that continue to mark Poles as outsiders and from which the second and third generation flee. The Anglo community adds to Felicia's inferiority complex through unfavorable comparisons of family ancestry and heritage. Mark Standler's mother eagerly directs Felicia to her "family paintings," reminding her in the process that "my mother could trace her ancestry back to Captain Goodwin of the *Mayflower*" (128). Felicia senses that Mrs. Standler smiles at her in the way one does when speaking to underprivileged children. Felicia knows that ethnicity equals less and nonethnicity equals more without knowing exactly why. The same might be said of Driscoll, whose use of surface characteristics to describe otherness is largely unsuccessful precisely because those signs continued to deflect Americans away from any deep understanding of cultural differences.

Felicia Zielinski may be the first Pole in American literature to recognize that Polish immigrants and postimmigrant generations have failed either to maintain their own tradition or to melt into the mainstream. The *Mayflower* and the mazurka appear to be irreconcilable. Consequently, Felicia comes to regard herself as strange, as one who "doesn't celebrate American Thanksgiving" but who is too ignorant and ashamed to celebrate Polish feast days. She has, she believes, no traditions at all to contribute to a marriage with the Mayflower-bedecked Standlers. American literature itself certifies her status as an outsider. Melville's *Moby-Dick,* she judges, is "not of my people."

Despite her mother's "lostness," Felicia's "otherness," and the Standler's pilgrim pride, Driscoll forces reconciliation in the marriage of peasant and pilgrim. He suggests that if you can't sink Melville, swim with him; but he also gives credence to the mother's lament that soon there will be no more Polishness in America. Driscoll's contrived ending, his refusal to confront the exigencies of the outsider, overshadows his introduction of this theme about Poles in America. Two of his contemporaries, Millard Lampell and Ruth Tabrah, more aggressively pursued the ethnic as outsider in their postwar novels.

Both published in 1949, Lampell's *The Hero* and Tabrah's *Pulaski Place* have much in common conceptually and thematically. Both employ protagonists of Polish descent living in ethnic communities; both view events from the ethnic perspective; and both deal with the social problems of returning veterans and their families. Moreover, Lampell and Tabrah each offer a cynical appraisal of working-class prospects and the ethnic environment. In fact, these authors are among the first to deromanticize the Polish experience and to evaluate that experience in objective and even critical terms. These sociologically valuable novels reflect the postwar expectations and disappointments of ethnic Americans who, after having been assimilated in military units and after having listened to promises about a new postwar world, felt thwarted in their economic ambitions and social aspirations. At the same time, both ethnic and nonethnic veterans faced similar problems in housing, jobs, education, and general adjustment. In this sense, the limits of ethnicity reflected those of America at mid-century. Thus the protagonists of *The Hero* and *Pulaski Place,* representing ethnic and national interests, emerge as a new kind of postwar American literary hero. A consequence of war more than of literary innovation, the integration of ethnic and national concerns served to Americanize the ethnic protagonist more successfully than the melting-pot marriage which, despite obvious symbolic value, produced only illusory solutions. Together with Tennessee Williams, Tabrah and Lampell revolutionized the literary portrayal of the ethnic Pole. Their characters were neither the subdued peasants of 1930s novels nor the impoverished workers, genteel artists, or daring patriots of earlier times. Instead their heroes are realistic second-generation ethnic Americans whose problems are the essence of America, as other postmodernist writers would soon make clear.

Events in both novels parallel the historical situation of returning veterans seeking and expecting individual recognition, reward, and a changed nation. Lampell and Tabrah emphasize the disillusionment and hostile behavior that result when returning ethnic GIs fail to find even modest improvements in their communities or in majority attitudes toward ethnicity. In *The Hero,* Lampell offers two variations on this theme. In one plot, Joe Novak returns home to an America that cannot offer him even a nonskilled job. Brooding and uncommunicative, he misses the comradeship of his combat buddies, and becomes angry with himself and his family. His future is in doubt as he unsuccessfully searches for work. The novel's major plot follows Joe's younger brother Steve, who is awarded a football scholarship by a prestigious southern university. In *Pulaski Place,* Steve Kowalski has a modest ambition to join the town's police department, a higher socioeconomic rung than he, his family, and his fellow Poles occupy in the mills where they have labored for a half century. When Kowalski's appointment is repeatedly postponed, Ben, his younger brother, declares with disgust that "the war is over and everything is the way it was again; we're just a bunch of goddamned Polacks" (148).

The status of these largely Polish communities decades after immigration is a comment on the state of the nation. The bleak descriptions of the towns reflect the mindset of their inhabitants and the social position to which ethnics have been assigned because of their own short-sightedness and host-culture prejudices. Pulaski Place, the Polish section of Milltown, is literally on the other side of the tracks. Tabrah's neonaturalistic description emphasizes monotony and confinement: "The houses were all of one pattern—narrow, wooden, set close together and all painted a deep unpleasant yellow that was long since dulled and streaked by the seasons" (3). Millard Lampell's White Falls,

New Jersey (nothing is white, there are no falls), is a sister city to Milltown. A mixed ethnic community, the town is encircled by railroad tracks that resemble "a long black scar." Similar to Milltown, the houses of the dye workers stretch in lines, each house the same, with peeling brown and tan paint and small, untidy yards. "In White Falls," Lampell explains, "the seasons come without poetry . . . a kind of second-hand spring and summer riding in on the stale wind across the Jersey marshes" (2).

The dreary landscape of these novels parallels the bleakness of individual lives, especially in the mills. Anton Kowalski has been conquered by his job, ruined by his "ceaseless struggle to make a living" (9); and the Novaks' prematurely old father faces "endless days in a narrowing world." When the Novaks and Kowalskis try to improve their lot and gain socioeconomic mobility, they are met with old prejudices as confining as the railroad tracks that encircle their neighborhoods. Steve Kowalski's appointment to the police force meets with interminable, unexplained delays. When he assumes his post, the first Pole ever to be selected, the other officers ignore and abuse the rookie cop. Younger brother Ben meets with a similar response when he tries to date Mavis Waverly whose father, greeting Ben with, "Kowalski, sounds like a Polack," refuses to allow his daughter to date him. Waverly also refuses to rent a vacant apartment to Steve, a returning veteran, and his new bride. "The nerve of them Polacks," Waverly tells his family. In *The Hero*, Steve Novak has an even greater fall. "I don't want to work my guts out in a dye shop and wind up on a twelve-dollar pension" (10), he tells a football recruiter, and goes off to make his fortune as an athlete at a football-mill in Virginia. A star even as a freshman, a willing student, and a decent young man, Novak abruptly learns about host-culture attitudes toward minorities. He is denied membership in a fraternity because he is a Polish Catholic; and, when an injury prematurely ends his athletic career, he discovers that his sponsors regard him only as "another dumb Polack" (241).

What Lampell and Tabrah aim to show in these novels is that postwar America has not fulfilled its promises to ethnic minorities, although it continues to wave the American dream in front of ethnic noses. Even so, it is this vision of a mythic America that drives the Novaks and Kowalskis forward. "I want to learn something," Steve Novak announces as he sets off for Geneva, Virginia, his idea of "real America." Geneva is an idyllic place, previously available to him only in book titles, grammar school songs, and history classes—a country of tradition, gentility, wealth, and manners, "the heroic tradition of the nation," Novak calls it (47). Conversely, Steve Kowalski is considerably less romantic about his prospects now that his wartime talents are no longer valuable. For him, the American dream is modest and immediate: a decent job, marriage, an apartment outside the ghetto. His bid for a place on the Milltown police force represents a realization of success in America, an end to the cycle of working-class poverty and ethnic enclosure.

Perhaps the most striking aspect of these novels is the authors' attitudes toward the ethnic self. Unlike those, such as Paul Driscoll, who turn to folk culture to depict Polishness, Tabrah and Lampell avoid folksy traditions and the standard icons of Polish history and culture. They concentrate instead on the character of working-class descendants of peasants, hardened by a half century in the mills of America's urban centers. By the late 1940s, however, Polish peasant character had become largely indistinguishable from working-class urban behavior, with the result that American writers found it difficult to define ethnicity and to capture "ethnic" behavior. Lampell, for example, almost reluctantly admits that there seems nothing particularly Polish about his protagonist "except the cheekbones." And in *The Hero,* there is no viable, active Polish American community except for the multiethnic neighborhood tavern where the local men follow their hero's exploits on the football field. And our only glimpse of Polish traditions is through Novak's father, who maintains certain old-country habits. A nonverbal, simple man who remembers his peasant past, he eats barley soup, black bread, and cabbage. He regards physical labor with pride, supports the labor movement, and stands in awe of his son's apparent success and university education. The reader accepts the Novaks as Polish principally because the Novaks refer to themselves as Polish. For Lampell, ethnicity lies in the desire to transcend the past, to succeed in America, and yet to maintain ties to a murky and rapidly receding cultural past. Folk symbols, aristocrats, and genteel artists have given way to the family community, parish ties, and a "yet unidentifiable" longing to create a self at once American, ethnic, and secure.

As much as anything, to be Polish means to be an outsider, insecure in the host-culture world, uncertain about the worthiness of heritage, unable to feel comfortable outside the boundaries of ethnicity. Ben's benediction in *Pulaski Place*—that "we're just a bunch of goddamned Polacks"—is not unlike young Novak's realization in *The Hero* that America is an "alien and hostile world [where] . . . he would never be one of them" (231). Novak speaks, of course, for all ethnics and all outsiders. All his young life, he explains late in the novel, he wanted to be "accepted and secure, to be free of the humiliations of adolescence, the embarrassment of being Polish or poor or Italian, or Jewish, or the son of a grandfather who came over from the old country" (257). Once Novak is rejected by middle-class America after his football days have ended, he turns automatically toward ethnicity and "home"—synonymous in this case—even though he has permission to stay on at the university. Like Novak, Kowalski's young wife in *Pulaski Place* comes to believe that security and identity reside only in place, which for them is Polish. She refuses to leave the old neighborhood when Steve finds an apartment. She remembers Mrs. Kabala's admonition, "The only place Poles are welcome is among their own people. . . . To leave your own people is to court unhappiness and trouble" (76). But even Steve is pleased that his son is born in Pulaski Place.

Novak's return to ethnicity is more dramatic—even tragic—but consistent with Lampell's proletarian point of view. His brother Joey, the returning veteran, after a period of desperation and hopelessness, had learned from his immigrant father about the integrity of work, the sacrifice and nobility of the working class, and the brotherhood that comes with a common cause. While neither Mr. Novak nor Joey is political, Lampell implies that pride in work and labor unions are aspects of ethnicity; and Steve sees in his father and brother the ethnic self at rest. At novel's end, Steve returns to White Falls, New Jersey, to a job in the mill next to his family, and to the comfort of an ethnic self more "intensely alive and healthy and solid" (284) than the host culture he desired so much to imitate.

Lampell appears to suggest that ethnicity is a safe haven for the Pole. Unlike Ruth Tabrah, however, he does this without seeing that for the Pole at least, ethnicity is part of the problem. Cynical where Lampell is romantic, Tabrah is among the first postwar writers to note that the Pole at mid-century is not the beau ideal of nineteenth-century Europe. In fact, for the most part, her Poles lack redeeming qualities. They have limited horizons, crude manners, a we-they selfishness, brutal domestic lives, and no sense of nation or world existing outside their daily rounds through the foundry, kitchen, saloon. Their superstitious nature (they believe in hexes and "witch-doctors") suggests a primitive culture. *Pulaski Place* opens with what appears to be round four of an endless battle in the Laznewski household, and the sequence of events that follows complements the opening. For Tabrah, Polish American youth is an especially hopeless lot. Twelve-year-old Veronica is seduced by her music teacher and, in a state of near madness, jumps from the roof of her house; Tessy Urbanowicz thrives on wicked gossip; young Sobiewski heads a gang of thieves; Rosy Coznyar takes Ben Novak for all his money and lands in a whorehouse where she enjoys her new prosperity and status; Ben, Steve's younger brother, steals from his mother, robs his neighbors, and dies the violent death of a criminal.

One might think that Tabrah is building a case for genetic degeneration or is portraying, like Nelson Algren, the fatal consequences of urban life. However, Tabrah's naturalism is flavored by ethnicity which itself functions as an enemy. Measuring Polish success three generations after immigration, Tabrah finds it to be without distinction. For this, her protagonist blames the Poles: "I'm the only one from South Mill-town who ever tried to take it [the police exam]. Most of them would rather go to work at the plant or the Bolt Works for big money now, and then push a broom for ten bucks a week when they're fifty" (82). He adds derisively, "I can't forget that a lot of us were like that. . . . I made up my mind that the only way you can stop people from calling you a dumb Polack is to stop being one" (83). With this, Tabrah seems to agree with the late-nineteenth-century assertion that Poles were willing to settle for too little.

Neither Tabrah nor Lampell is able to solve the plight of the Polish American at mid-century. Novak's dramatic return to the mill after his glory days in Virginia condemns him, and by extension his fellow ethnics, to another generation as working-class fodder. Ruth Tabrah leaves her protagonist, Steve Kowalski, with a foot in two equally precarious worlds. His success as an officer implies better days ahead, except that Tabrah has already shown that the world is what it is, and that Kowalski's willingness to remain partly in the Polish American community runs counter to his ambition if not his experience. Despite the limitations of *The Hero* and *Pulaski Place*, American writers for the first time grappled realistically with the sociological problems of ethnicity from the Polish point of view. In these works, writers freed themselves from the condescending attitude of the local colorists and the one-sided perspective of urban naturalists. By mid-century, the Pole in American fiction had taken on many of the problems and issues associated with postwar America, without any of the solutions.

If Lampell and Tabrah were concerned primarily with interior issues—that is, identity and success within the ethnic community—other postwar writers explored somewhat broader political concerns during a time of increasing immigration and political conservatism. Katherine Burt's *Strong Citadel* (1949) and Alfred Slote's *Denham Proper* (1953) view the ethnic Pole within this context. Unfortunately, the force of their argument is muted by the constraints of the popular romance. Poles linger in the background, safely deethnicized, as Burt and Slote concentrate on manner and courtship in a period of change precipitated by cold war politics. "It is an age," one of Burt's characters comments, "of great confusion, of profound change . . . [of] traditions on the skids" (27). Both writers imply that this age is also a time of increased awareness of ethnicity in America and an opportunity to cast off cultural provincialism and invigorate America with a new burst of melting-pot energy. In the liberal tradition, Burt and Slote take as their theme the adjustment of Anglo-Saxon America to its non-Anglo citizens, especially the newly arriving war refugees from Eastern Europe.

The novels capture America's cold war mentality with the tendency to regard all foreigners, especially East Europeans, with suspicion. In *Strong Citadel,* Katia Polenov's father is a long-standing but harmless Trotskyite who serves as a catalyst for an abbreviated presentation of socialism. In *Denham Proper,* Maida Polanski is a liberal political activist who writes about the effects of the depression on the working class. Neither is a major character, but their presence and ultimately their rejection reflect America's continuing association of Slavs with anarchy and a heightened fear of postwar socialism. Either is enough, both writers show, to frighten establishment America. Jan Lane in *Strong Citadel* voices the sentiment that "we are the people that matter [in America]" (73) as the Philadelphia Lanes oppose their son's courtship of the Slavic Katia. Likewise, in *Denham Proper,* the ethnic is rejected out of hand by Robert Denham Manning, the product of a private school for "white protestant boys of wholesome family" (126). Mrs. Manning wonders whether her son's friend, Maida, can "fit into our pattern" and reminds him that their town is lovely because "it stays the same"; and Uncle Will chides Robert's father by asking if he would like his son "to marry a name like Polansky" (262).

Both Burt and Slote are critical of America's cold war mentality as represented by the Lanes and Mannings, whose provincialism has resulted in a frightened, tentative, and withered America. Slote sees an America unable to break a cycle of racial and religious bigotry. We learn that in his youth, Robert Manning's father had also forsaken the love of a Polish girl because of family and community pressure. He tells his son with a mixture of regret and satisfaction that he chose to fulfill the obligations of his "ancestry" and that he realized that the union of Anglo and other could not fit his kind of life. In her novel, Burt forces the issue in the marriage of Katia and Harold Lane and argues, as writers of the 1930s had, that a cultural transfusion could only benefit America. Even Harold admits that his family hasn't "lifted a finger to create anything since they left England in 1700" (76) and that his marriage to the life-giving Katia could rejuvenate the family stock. Reminiscent of Edna Ferber and Gladys Hasty Carroll, Burt's Polish heroine gives birth to a son who lacks any signs of his Slavic ancestry. Instead Katia sees the features and spirit of grandfather Lane. "He has come back," she exclaims. "And see, it is my body he has used" (281).

As Katia makes clear, ethnicity in these novels is pressed into the background and rendered into familiar and conventional characteristics. Although the major Polish characters are not aristocrats, they bear the carriage and deportment of nineteenth-century types. Katia Polenov, a servant on Prince Yusserpenski's estate, has been raised in genteel surroundings, educated, and refined. Her manners, awareness of high culture, and attitudes resemble the princess more than the peasant. Similarly, although Maida Polanski in *Denham Proper* is the daughter of a factory worker, she is an intelligent, educated journalist, a liberal activist, and political idealist. Both authors seize upon the democratic instincts associated with Poles—particularly Slote, whose Maida believes that romantic idealism can "conquer worlds." Neither of these women possesses the brutish qualities traditionally attributed to Polish women of the peasant class, nor do they embody a folk culture or, in fact, any of the obvious characteristics of ethnicity. Ethnicity takes the high road in these novels: Maida, the spirit of ethnic liberalism, is an example for all Americans, and Katia, completely selfless, represents romantic love stripped of all social pretensions.

Both authors also speak to the complexities of transplant as they affect the community and the individual. Not a primary theme in these works, the issue of ethnic identity seems directed more toward arousing sympathy than toward sociological analysis. Nonetheless, in the style of Ida Wylie's *Strangers Are Coming* (1941) and Joan Coons's *Without Passport* (1943), both touch upon identity loss as a consequence of ethnicity, a major theme in postwar American fiction. Katherine Burt best illustrates this in the Polenov family subplot. Isolated politically, socially, and physically, Katia's father, Fydor, experiences cultural confusion at all levels. At the same time, he sees that for his son and, of course, for millions of others, this phenomenon will soon reach a crisis. He says of his son, "He lives indeed in a no man's land—not free, not rooted, not democratic, neither proletarian nor socialist, nor capitalist. . . . He is nobody's son" (124). For the Polenovs, America offers little to replace their Old World heritage, and Katia's rapid assimilation, as her marriage and new "American" son indicate, leaves the Poles without a world to remember.

The war and its aftermath significantly affected the literary history of the Pole in American literature. For the first time, thoughtful works incorporated a Polish setting that allowed insights into prewar and wartime Poland. These works supplied the rough outline of a cultural landscape for a large ethnic group whose "history" had previously been recorded by non-descent writers. In addition, new concerns began to replace the issue of peasants adjusting to rural America and to a hostile and ignorant populace. Sociopolitical issues were temporarily set aside for the more immediate concerns of war and refugees and for an America trying to accommodate itself to rapid political and cultural changes—akin to those presented in Lester Cohen's *Coming Home,* Millard Lampell's *The Hero,* and Norman Mailer's *The Naked and the*

Dead. Although Nelson Algren and others continued to write realistic fiction about urban Polish Americans, the period was marked by another wave of romanticism about Poles and Poland and another stereotype—"the displaced person," as Flannery O'Connor would phase it. This time, however, the effort was shared by Polish American writers like Antoni Gronowicz, and by liberals (such as Jean Karsavina) who were directly linked to the homeland.

The problems of Poland and its refugees were not, however, the significant salient in 1940s fiction. Political writers (Cohen, Mailer, Karsavina) and nonpolitical writers alike (Lampell, Tabrah, Janney) moved ethnic concerns closer to those of middle America. Steve Kowalski's ambitions were barely distinguishable from those of countless other veterans grappling with socioeconomic security, and Stan Novak's defeat is similar to that experienced by Ralph Ellison's invisible man and Saul Bellow's Tommy Wilhelm. As ethnic literature moved closer to mainstream literature, Poles were no longer identified as immigrants or aliens in the traditional sense. Rather they emerged as outsiders, rebels, and working-class stiffs—an ethnic group poised to assume a major and, as it turns out, curious place in American ethnic fiction of the 1950s and 1960s.

6

DESCENT AND DISSENT

Major Writers and Turf Warfare

*I protest against further publishing of this book, for it fosters
national disunity and should have no place in our libraries
and homes.* —PRESIDENT OF POLISH ROMAN CATHOLIC UNION

*Mindless jackass bray from rear-echelon patriots and
Sunday-morning Forgive-Me-Lords.* —NELSON ALGREN

I. WHOSE ETHNICITY IS IT?

Although before the postwar period well over a hundred literary works
about Poles were published, these works reached only limited audiences. Those treating Poles extensively and intensely—Harriman's
The Homebuilders, Hughes's *Zal,* Esty's *The Proud House,* Vogel's
Man's Courage, Tabrah's *Pulaski Place*—never achieved popular or
critical success, were never adapted into Hollywood films, and never
found their way into college classrooms. Almost none remained in
print. In addition, few major American writers had turned their attention to the Polish self, although some of the leading names in American
letters (Emerson, Alcott, Hemingway, Flannery O'Connor) had added
a brush stroke or two to the Polish tradition in American literature.

Since World War II, however, well-known writers have achieved
popular and critical success with works that explore the Polish experience and that alter the evolving ethnic literary self. Over a forty-year
period, Nelson Algren, Tennessee Williams, William Styron, James
Michener, and Jerzy Kosinski have confronted ethnicity head-on in
works that have thrust the Pole into the cultural spotlight. Algren's *The
Man with the Golden Arm* received the first National Book Award.
Williams's *A Streetcar Named Desire,* has—with the possible exception of *Death of a Salesman*—been seen and read by more people than
any other American play. Styron's critically acclaimed *Sophie's Choice*
boasts of more than 5 million copies sold. Michener's 1983 novel, *Poland,* headed best-seller lists for months. And the much-discussed Kosinski retains an eminent position in American letters. These works
reached additional millions in popular film adaptations. Otto Premin-

ger's controversial version of *The Man with the Golden Arm* launched the film industry into uncharted territory with his frank depiction of the drug culture; the film version of *A Streetcar Named Desire* made Marlon Brando and Stanley Kowalski into household names; and the film of *Sophie's Choice* won numerous awards and Oscar nominations.

The critical reception, the vast circulation, and the film versions of these works have had a substantial impact upon popular notions of ethnicity and of Polishness in particular. Each of these writers has further defined the Polish literary self and altered America's sense of ethnicity. They have made permanent what previous writers labored to create and have succeeded in joining marginal types with the mainstream. (In their works ethnicity becomes mainstream.) They reflect America's continuing fascination with Poles, as underscored by the national infatuation with a Polish Pope and a Polish labor movement while paradoxically reinforcing America's negative perceptions of Polish character. At the same time, they have reinvented for postwar generations the identity of a substantial group of ethnic Americans who have largely cast aside their own ethnicity in their drive for assimilation.

It is not surprising that controversy, especially protests by the Polish American community, surrounds each of these works in proportion, so it seems, to its prominence in American letters. Ethnic commentators have voiced their disapproval and disappointment with the representations of Poles. In part, the debate has concerned nonliterary matters. But in all cases, ethnic critics have axiomatically objected to works written about them by outsiders while praising less deserving works, such as the short fiction of Monica Krawczyk, written by those within the group. Algren documented one such attack. Soon after the publication of his *Never Come Morning,* the president of the Polish Roman Catholic Union wrote to Harpers and Company: "I protest against further publishing of this book for it fosters national disunity and should have no place in our libraries and homes" (qtd. in *Never Come Morning,* 1963 ed. ix). *Zgoda,* a Polish daily in Chicago, described Algren as a writer with a "distorted mentality . . . on a narcotic jag" and his novel as a "Pole-baiting tale . . . anti-Polish propaganda . . . directed by Nazi money" (*NCM* ix). A letter to *Zgoda,* also sent to Harpers, attacked the novel for smearing "Chicago voters" and for using the word *Polack* forty-one times, "an average of more than once every seven pages" (*NCM* ix).

In a preface written for the 1963 edition, Algren responded. He characterized the criticism as "mindless jackass bray" from "rear-echelon patriots and Sunday morning Forgive-Me-Lords," complaining, in addition, that his book was still unavailable at the Chicago

Public Library twenty years after its publication (xii). Algren explained that the novel is a "thinly fictionalized report on a tough neighborhood" and that he drew from people he grew up with and from the news reports about the trial of Knifey Sawicki. Recalling Whitman's defense of convicts and prostitutes, Algren claimed that he wrote about the American outcast in the style of James Baldwin, and that *Zgoda's* "failure to feel" represents the failure of the nation (xiii). In his rebuttal, Algren says nothing about Poles or ethnicity, makes no attempt to understand the ethnic perspective, shows no sensitivity to his critics. He prefers instead to talk about his work as if it were not really about Poles, or any other identifiable group, but rather a portrait of America's deethnicized outsiders. Algren's dismissal of ethnicity is perfectly consistent with his denial of his own ethnic background. "My father and mother were neither gentiles nor Jews," he announced once during an interview (Donahue 14). "I wrote the books," he insisted, "because, because I was living in the middle of those books" (93), a rather typical response of the writer who resists being labeled or associated with ethnicity. Critics have universally accepted Algren's self-proclaimed rejection of ethnicity, with the result that studies of Algren's ethnic dimension have yet to appear. One might, in fact, explain the total absence of interest in Algren in Poland (his books are unavailable and he is unfamiliar even to Polish intellectuals) to his dismissal by the Polish American community and the critical failure to "read" Algren as an "ethnic" writer. Oddly enough, many continue to believe that the Scandinavian Jewish Algren is actually of Polish descent.

Like Algren, Williams is regarded as one whose interest in Poles is incidental. Most reviewers of *Streetcar* emphasized the gothic strains of the southern romance or the aggressiveness of the blue-collar male. The rare instances of comment on Stanley's Polishness have been occasions for condemning Williams's ethnic insensitivity. Examining Hollywood and American ethnic groups, Caroline Golab claims that Slavs have always been portrayed in films as stereotypes: physically strong, hard working, brutal, crude, sexual, inarticulate, stubborn, amoral, clannish, violent, intemperate—a fairly good description of Kowalski. She refers to 1970s films such as *F.I.S.T., Blue Collar,* and *The Deer Hunter* to show how recent film makers have drawn upon the popular image in 1930s films and especially upon the film version of *Streetcar.* "It was Williams, more than anyone else," she observes, "who perfected the use of a Slavic stereotype as a metaphor for the working class" (150). Although Golab could have more accurately credited the proletarian literary tradition in this regard, her apparent unhappiness with the metaphor has foundation, given Williams's self-described message in *Streetcar:* "If we don't watch out, the apes will take over" (148). Golab stays clear of openly accusing Williams of prejudice, although her essay and its title, "Stellaaaaaa...!!!: The Slavic Stereotype in American Film," point in that direction. Thomas Napierkowski is not so subtle. He reads the play as little more than a weapon for bigots to translate their views into societal realities and as yet another host-culture statement on Polish inferiority ("Image" 18).

Compared to criticism of Williams and Algren, the ethnic backlash from Styron's *Sophie's Choice* has been nothing short of volcanic. Widely read and discussed in Poland, the novel has been condemned by academics as an untrustworthy and malicious fabrication of Polishness. Jerzy Strzetelski bitterly complains about Styron's mean comments on "this gentle country" and lists scores of inaccuracies that call into question not only Styron's knowledge but also his intentions. For Strzetelski and others, Styron has misapplied the facts to produce a novel that maligns Poles and distorts the historical relationship of Poles and Jews, especially during the war years.

In the United States, *Sophie's Choice* appears to have satisfied no one interested in literary ethnicity. Jules Chametzky worries that Styron has appropriated mainstream material to create the false image that "regional" writing stands at the center of American literature (433–41), while David Baldwin accuses Styron of "stealing ethnic and other territory" to cater to the demands of the marketplace (474). Critics who are of Polish descent have blistered the novel for its defamation of Poles. In 1983, *Polish American Studies* published a group of essays that underscored Styron's ignorance and distortion of Polish culture and that attempted to set the record straight. The essayists examined the novel from the following assumptions: that Styron's work is a "history" and must be judged as such; and that they, through descent, have a truer understanding of ethnicity. Jerzy Krzyzanowski challenges Styron's characterization of Poles as anti-Semites. Thomas Napierkowski, pointing to certain inexcusable errors of fact, documents Styron's ignorance. And Thaddeus Radzialowski attacks the historical weakness of a novel that offers a "strained analogy between the American South and Poland" (61). In addition to these cultural and historical distortions, Styron, his detractors continue, misrepresents Polish character. Krzyzanowski objects to Sophie's overly sexed nature, heavy drinking, and filthy vocabulary. For Radzialowski, Sophie seems hardly plausible as a Pole, particularly her facial features and the fact that a woman of her education would be ignorant about Polish "haute cuisine" (61–62). "Only in America," Napierkowski contends, "could such a characterization be taken seriously" (65).

While it is true that Styron is often careless with facts and tends toward romantic oversimplification or popular renditions of complex cultural-historical issues, it is equally true that he captures the spirit of Poland and Polishness with a degree of skill matched by few others. That his work, like Algren's and Williams's before him, would precipitate such a vitriolic response says perhaps less about his novel than it does about the self-consciousness of Polonia, the contemporary reputation of Poland, and the preference of some for presentations of Polish ethnicity more compatible with the nineteenth-century beau ideal or with heart-warming tales of peasants with princely attributes busying themselves with folk art, ubiquitous weddings, and Americanization.

Within a few years of the publication of *Sophie's Choice* and the release of the equally acclaimed film, James Michener penned what is without question the most deferential, sympathetic, and extended portrait of Poles ever to appear on American bookshelves. Like *Sophie's Choice, Poland* ran into the millions of copies, remained on bestseller lists for months, and introduced Poles to countless readers who would have difficulty locating Poland on a map. Capitalizing on contemporary events in Poland (Solidarity, martial law, economic crisis), Michener produced an empathy for Poland unmatched in American literary history. At the same time, the book stirred familiar passions and objections. Justifiably, reviewers and critics upbraided Michener for all but ignoring the rich legacy of Polish Jewry. Polish scholars and ethnic commentators in the United States labeled the work as a simple-minded and even dangerous fiction about a country yet to be understood by American writers. For them, Michener's novel is too far removed from reality to be taken seriously. In contrast to American reviewers who applauded Michener's popularization of Polish history, their judgments were seasoned by the cold war mentality dominating the Polish perspective and by the long-standing ethnocentric notion that few outside Poland are qualified to write about that country. In his review, Nikita Roedkowski suggested that, since the Poles have historically been better off than the Russians, Michener's empathy for Poland is exaggerated and perhaps unmerited. Immediately Sergius Wroblewski replied by challenging both Roedkowski's qualifications and Michener's understanding of history. "My hope," he wrote to the editor of *America,* "is that you will choose experts in Polish history to review Polish matters." Wroblewski goes on to charge that Michener is an unwitting tool of the communist regime and that he has swallowed the dialectical view of Polish history as a class struggle culminating in the overthrow of the aristocracy and the postwar establishment of a people's republic (440). Writing in *The National Review,* Wladyslaw Pleszczynski describes Michener as "an unabashed Polonophile," a member of the Kosciuszko-Walesa view of Poland: heroic, defiant, noble, romantic. More to the point, he cites the "countless errors and distortions" and complains about Michener's limited understanding of Polish history, particularly as it relates to Russia as the historical catalyst for Polish misfortunes (1418–20).

In the case of Jerzy Kosinski, the ethnic turf war becomes even more complicated (and more emotional) because of Kosinski's Polish roots, his ambivalent attitude toward the country of his birth, and his sustained denial of his own ethnicity. From the outset, Kosinski's fiction has produced emotional and often contradictory responses. *The Painted Bird* and *Steps* were praised highly; the latter, like Algren's *The Man with the Golden Arm,* won the National Book Award. Kosinski's novels, however, have never been translated into Polish or made available in English editions in Poland where he has been severely criticized as a non-Polish writer who has only derogatory comments to make about Poland and who has nothing to say about the Polish experience at home or abroad. In Warsaw, *Polytika* denounced *The Painted Bird* and Kosinski in general. For years, in fact, the official Polish view has been that Kosinski's novels are politically inspired, perhaps even funded by the United States government. Outside Poland, Kosinski has met with similar opposition. Polish language newspapers in London criticized him for his "communist admiration"; *Ameryka-Echo,* a Chicago Polish language weekly, complained that Kosinski portrayed Poland as a nation of "perverts" (Corry 1). In 1982, *The Village Voice* charged that Kosinski had considerable assistance in writing his novels and repeated Wieslaw Gornicki's 1969 claim that Kosinski may have used a ghostwriter, supported by the CIA (Lilly 158–59). Soon others, John Corry in the *New York Times,* Charles Kaiser in *Newsweek,* Calvin Trillin in *Nation,* and Kosinski himself entered the debate without necessarily exonerating Kosinski or mollifying his detractors. Charges of duplicity, self-aggrandizement, and national betrayal notwithstanding, Kosinski's problems were, to a great degree, rooted in ethnicity—in his reluctance to identify himself as a Jew and a Pole and in his portrayal of Eastern Europe and the literary ethnic self. It is no surprise that Poles and Polonia have rejected his works or that he would rush to reattach himself, as he did in *The Hermit of 69th Street,* to his ethnic origins and to the Polish literary tradition.

One might conclude from the controversy that surrounds these writers that the success of their works naturally demanded a response from ethnic and Polish scholars and that this response followed legitimate and predictable lines. In the case of Algren and Williams, what also emerges is an apparent resistance to writers who have forced ethnicity into dark corners, typecast Polish Americans as representatives of working-class America or as cultural outsiders, and reminded Polonia that the transition from Poles to Americans has not been without pain and failure. A similar sensitivity to Poland's postwar economic and political difficulties and its inability to come to terms with its own past colors appraisals of those who in fiction (Styron and Michener) and in history (Davies) have sought to reexamine "the heart of Europe." Had the novels of Hindus, Castle, Chase, and others who write about ethnic failure in the promised land reached best-seller status, they doubtlessly would have been subject to the same harsh scrutiny.

Disappointment with postwar portrayals of the Polish identity originates, to some degree, in a suspicion of history, since for centuries outsiders (occupiers and invaders) have acted as the chroniclers and interpreters of Polish culture. The critical reaction of those of Polish descent is a reflexive resistance to this historical dilemma. What many readers accept in Algren, Williams, and Styron as expressions of the universals of the human condition, those of Polish descent see as an exposure of failed dreams, cultural primitiveness, and national shame. Styron, Michener, and Kosinski have become entangled in postwar politics, in the national neuroses that paralyze contemporary Poland, in cold war sensibilities, and in a Holocaust backlash against Poles. These readers have a penchant to deconstruct texts and to flush out the painful realities lying beneath the surface.

From a literary perspective, the works under discussion do not depart radically from established conventions. One might even say that they return to techniques and themes already in place by 1930. Working-class, urban Poles had been written about long before either Algren turned to Division Street and Chicago's Polonia or Williams discovered Stanley Kowalski in the Elysian fields of New Orleans. And the idea that the Slav was a threat to the cultural-political fabric had been voiced energetically at the turn of the century in the press and in fiction. At the other extreme, from the 1830s on, many writers had created a vision of Polishness emphasizing values compatible with America's and including an image of an ethnic group harmlessly colorful, politically docile, and eager to be adopted into the extended American family.

Apart from their artistry, what differentiates these works from those less widely known is the willingness of writers like Algren and Williams to take chances, to strip away sentimentality, the preciousness of local color, and the pleasing prospects of acculturation and assimilation, and to look at the rawness of postimmigrant ethnicity, the erosion of New World hope, and the restrictions of ethnicity itself. Algren's and Williams's protagonists have neither Old World memories nor New World appreciation except for the mercantile and the immediate. Bicek, Kowalski, Zawistowski, all angry, disillusioned, and alienated, are comfortable neither in America nor in their past. With their appearance, the Polish self is reinvented once again—this time as a problematic rebel, a social outcast, a dispossessed European, and an emblem of literary modernism and postwar alienation.

2. ALGREN'S POLISH CHICAGO

In most ways, Nelson Algren's fiction stands squarely in the middle of the literary movements of the 1930s and 1940s. Chester Eisinger refers to Algren as a determinist and notes the radical political impulse in his works. Maxwell Geismar sees Algren as a representative of the extreme phase of American realism. And Richard Wright ties him to the proletarian movement and to social issues that "periodically push their way into the arena of history in times of crisis, war, civil war, and revolution" (intro *NCM* ix). In the face of this consensus, Algren's examination of poverty, ignorance, the urban jungle, and man's bestiality—the reality of those living on the cultural fringe—is not unusual. Neither are his Chicago settings.

Yet none of this satisfactorily explains the extent of Algren's familiarity with minority culture, his decision to fashion so many of his characters as Poles, or the ethnic dimension in his works. Algren has never been considered an "ethnic writer," despite the fact that his collective works offer one of the most probing examinations of ethnicity. The world of immigrants depicted in Algren's fiction is not a pretty one. He portrays social disorganization, the conflict of Old and New World aspirations that lead to defeat and disintegration, and the hostility between generations that marks, for many, the immigrant experience. He equates Polishness with alienation and hopelessness, with the betrayal of dreams, and the inadequacies of a hybrid culture no longer Polish and not yet American. The Polish cultural tradition, Algren also implies, is too ineffective and antipodal to American interests to insure a place for the peasant in the New World.

Algren's work is thus an important chapter in ethnic representations and the literary history of Poles. His stories resemble many of those who wrote before him, not because Algren consciously imitated or even knew these works but because, like his predecessors, he felt that Poles represented larger sociopolitical concerns. His studies of urban life have antecedents in Waldo's *Stash of the Marsh Country* and Cobb's "Polack Joe," two works that questioned the prospects of immigrant urban life. In *Never Come Morning* and *The Neon Wilderness*, Algren's portrait of the Pole as proletarian builds upon such 1930s works as Michael Musmanno's *Black Fury* and Joseph Vogel's *Man's Courage*, and points toward other postwar radicalizations of the Pole by V. J. Jerome and Jean Karsavina. One story in *Neon Wilderness* recounts the adventures of an ordinary worker from East St. Louis who travels to

Spain to fight against the fascist Black Arrows and Falangistas and who, after being injured, lives a dissolute, lonely, but proud life. In another piece, Algren looks at the lives of poor women who, in the face of a society that oppresses and deprives its working class, can turn only—and absurdly, according to Algren—to prayer.

Unlike typical proletarian fiction, however, Algren's stories end in defeat; the future never belongs to workers or minorities. His works usher in a decade of novels that call attention to the dilemma of otherness and the fragile nature of ethnicity. William Castle, Lester Cohen, Millard Lampell, William Motley, though perhaps not as cynical as Algren, followed with graphic accounts of the ethnic tragedy, featuring Poles as outsiders, innocents, and victims of a postwar society still moved by racial prejudices, a fear of strangeness, and a reluctance to disturb the status quo. These writers clamored for tolerance, change, opportunity, and ethnic invisibility. Moreover, they used Poles to identify America's failure to accommodate multiculturalism. In their novels and in Algren's, Poles occupy a position similar to oppressed characters in the works of African American writers contemporary to Algren: Richard Wright, James Baldwin, Ralph Ellison.

Like everyone else, Algren faced the problem of establishing ethnicity within the text, of creating a literary culture that would satisfactorily define characters without intruding on the plot. In this regard, Algren's invention lags. He relies mainly on surface characteristics that were already timid and tired even in his day. In *Never Come Morning,* for example, Polishness means physicalness: "the wholesome, placid, sallow Polish face with cheekbones set high and widely" (13). On occasion, he alludes to familiar Americans of Polish descent (Stanley Ketchel, a 1920s boxer). Here and there he sprinkles a Polish word or a folk proverb: "Better a good peasant than a bad priest" (*NCM* 228). He associates Poles with Catholicism through random references to prayer, church attendance, and clerical presence and, again, by trying to explain their mystical Catholicism and religious nationalism through folk sayings: "Every mass you go to goes with you" (*NCM* 45). He also pays lip service, as other prewar writers had done, to the tenuous relations of Christian and Jewish Poles, explored earlier by Irving Fineman and Henry Roth in more sophisticated and sensitive fashion. Algren is content to mention Polish anti-Semitism without providing a cultural-historical context, suggesting instead that bigotry accompanies ignorance and social depravity. In this case, he again speaks through a proverb: "When the thunder kills a devil then a devil kills a Jew" (*NCM* 3). Seldom, if ever, does Algren write about Polish history or culture, or appear even knowledgeable about these subjects. Algren's shadowy outline of Polish character and culture has prompted one critic to say that "virtually none of the traits, characteristics, or nuances of Polish life is present to reveal the ethnicity of these figures" (Napierkowski "Images" 17). What we mainly have is Algren's insistence that culture is a name, a proverb, a facial feature.

One might conclude from the paucity of cultural detail in his work and the absence of dialogue about ethnicity in his published interviews and conversations that Algren knows next to nothing about the minority that figures so prominently in his fiction. At best, Poles are synonymous with the working class and the neon wilderness. Actually, he tries to combine working class and ethnic in the same image. In "Stickman's Daughter," for example, his protagonist decides "to take the old woman to the little Pulaski triple horror feature with blue enamel ovenware to the ladies and community singing" (NW 65). At worse, Polish means deviant, a community inhabited by pimps, derelicts, and morons.

In his study of Algren, Napierkowski points out that Algren's minor characters are indeed graphic examples of deviancy ("Image" 14). Old Stash, whose greatest joy in life is tearing pages off the calendar, is an imbecile. The equally idiotic Meter Reader coaches The Endless Leather and Belt Invincibles, "an aggregation that hadn't won a game since Meter Reader had taken it over." Old Doc Dominowski is a quack and Zygmunt is a disbarred ambulance chaser. As for the community in general, a passage from *The Man with the Golden Arm* best describes Polish Chicago:

There were only boys with bad teeth, wives with faces still dented from last night's blows and girls whose hair was set so stiffly it looked metallic. There were only drooling lushbrims with faces like emptied gaboons. There was only a long line of faces that had passed straight from the noseless embryo into the running nose of senility. (248)

Frequently Algren uses "Polish" as an adjective to connote bad taste and low standards. A stray mongrel becomes "a Polish Airedale." Frankie Majcinek says his wife needs "a good Polish beating," and Sophie refers to her brief stint in high school as "a good Polish education." That these cynical labels are applied by the Polish characters themselves, not without a touch of irony, suggests the contempt with which they have come to view their ethnic selves.

Ironically, Algren's most popular short story, the oft-anthologized "The Devil Came Down Division Street," exemplifies his limitations as an ethnic writer. The piece is an extended Polish cliché, a compendium of surface characteristics and ethnic symbols widely used by less talented writers. The story opens in the Polonia bar, safe-haven for all the drunks in the Polish neighborhood: Symanobi, Oljiec, Koncel, Czechowski, Orlov. Algren, who explains how Roman Orlov wins the dubious honor of "biggest drunk," inserts truncated examples of Polishness once removed from peasantry: alcohol, food, music, religion, poverty, ignorance, and resignation. Father and son are both afflicted with the "natural" peasant fondness for drink, and the attitudes of the entire family are shaped by a half-superstitious, half-mystical reverence for religion. They attend Mass regularly, read their catechism, seek the approval of priests, and interpret events as spiritual manifestations to which they respond with prayer and devotion that transform the household, temporarily, into a pious model. Unfortunately all this cannot save Roman, who becomes the Devil's next victim. Not all the Orlovs' accordion-playing, pierogi-baking, and prayers to St. Kowalski can alter the pattern of decay for this ethnic family. Tenement life and the poverty of Division Street grind down one Orlov after another, leaving the reader with the impression that ethnicity is a synonym for human misery.

In Algren's case, this misery is rooted as much inside ethnicity as outside. If his image of Poles is sometimes insensitive, exaggerated, and restricted to conventional cultural symbols, his fiction is nevertheless the first sustained, penetrating, and nonsentimental study of social disintegration. All three of his ethnic works, *Never Come Morning, The Neon Wilderness,* and *The Man with the Golden Arm,* can be read as a realization of Thomas and Znaniecki's worst fears about the transplanted family. In these works family life is a shadowy frame of reference for all that has ceased to be, a vehicle for brutality and disintegration. Frankie Majcinek is raised by a foster mother in what he describes as a "scrumblebug family." The fatherless Bruno Bicek has no extended family at all. He is reared by a worn-down elderly mother whose infrequent appearances testify to their distant relationship. In "It's a Barnum and Bailey World" (*NW*), the Polish protagonist visits an Anglo friend's "clean and bright" home and remembers it as "the first [and last] memory I have of being happy" (*NW* 114). And in "A Lot You Got to Holler," Augie gives up on his quarreling parents. "That was their business," he decides, "so long as they stayed in the kitchen" (*NW* 117).

With few exceptions Algren's ethnic families are divided by conflicting loyalties and values, exacerbated by the knowledge that New World promises are not meant for them. To some degree, the peasant women, as Cox and Chatterton point out, are repositories of "domestic mores and folkways of the old country" (98); but this is more felt than textually demonstrated. Actually we learn little about the operation of mores and folkways in shaping behavior except to conclude, given the social problems of the children, that Old World culture is relatively powerless and unattractive in a New World setting. Virtually all the descendants of immigrants have embraced the values of young America. The immigrant generation still speaks Polish, embraces Old World perspectives, and comes to believe that it has been betrayed by false promises and by the New World code of deceit. The widow Rosenkowski regards everything American as "crooked business." The barber Bonifacy adds that "they were always trying to cheat him in this country" (*NCM* 10). Mama Bicek blames America for her own winter of discontent and for the problems that beset family and neighbors: "If they had stayed in the old world, she felt, her son would have been a good son" (*NCM* 16).

Unlike their immigrant parents who quickly adopt the conniving style of the New World even as they resist it, the next generation grows up thinking that deceit, petty crime, and the subterranean life are perfectly natural. The title of Algren's short piece, "It's a Barnum and Bailey World Just as Phoney As It Can Be," perfectly captures the outlook of the Poles. The protagonist boasts about his jail record and a childhood spent conning the unsuspecting. Success to him is leaving the suckers "waiting in front." Lefty Bicek, the young hero of *Never Come Morning* behaves similarly. His rapid decline into mayhem and murder is as directly connected to his ethnic background as it is to socioeconomic conditions. While he too has come to believe "everything's a fake," he also senses that his problems stem from his ethnicity. "It's best for a Polack who ain't got much," he says, "not to think too much about getting more" (37). Bicek's resentment toward his ethnic self extends to his fellow Poles whom he treats with disdain, especially the foreign-born whom he charmingly refers to as "boobatch" (37).

The antagonism of Algren's ethnics to the world around them and to the heritage they reject is enhanced by their situation as cultural halfbreeds. They occupy, as Jerzy Kosinski would later show, a shadowy borderland "spawned of the old but not yet chartered to the new" (Cox 90). Their hybrid culture is evident in their American nicknames and Polish surnames: Lefty Bicek, Fireball Kodadek, Catfoot Nowogrodsky, Finger Idzikowski. For them, ethnicity, turned in on itself, has become the sport of the Anglo-American. In *The Neon Wilderness,* Algren exposes this confused identity through an Italian character who ironically believes it would improve his lot if he had a different ethnic ancestry. "If he just wasn't a wop," he thinks to himself, "if he were a Polack . . . that would fix everything" (72). The ending to *Never Come Morning* exposes the lunacy (and the pity) of such thinking with a boxing match between the sons of a Polish baker and a "mulatto pigsticker," "a white man's evening" according to Algren. This scene, occurring also in Ellison's *Invisible Man,* implies that all minorities share the same fate without the capacity to verbalize their feelings, to intellectualize a response except to fight for their self-respect. For the Poles, ethnicity is as much a prison as the Chicago tenements they inhabit. Sophie, Lefty Bicek's girlfriend, confronts her dreadful vision even as she admits her own fall from grace: "God has forgotten us all. He has even forgotten our names" (215).

Although only a few years separate *The Man with the Golden Arm* (1949) from Algren's other works about Poles, the novel illustrates Algren's deepening understanding of ethnicity, even though he continues to rely on conventional techniques and similar subject matter. Once more the characters are second-generation Poles, who share a tenement on Division Street, trapped within a cycle of poverty, crime, and ignorance. And once again, Algren resorts to semiotic shorthand to outline ethnicity. Frankie Majcinek's paralyzed wife sports a babushka, his friends drink wisniowa, and Frankie kisses his rosary for luck when he gambles. As he had before, Algren uses Polish proverbs in English translation and alludes to Polish anti-Semitism, although this occurs as an indicator of interethnic suspicion more than as a national characteristic. Like their fictional predecessors, Majcinek and his neighbors resent all ethnic groups, particularly the foreign-born. As their names indicate, they belong to a hybrid culture, marked by alienation from the past and the present. They lay no claim to Polish or Polish American culture, observe no customs, carry on no traditions. In *The Man with the Golden Arm,* names and memories are all that is left of Polishness.

In this sense, Algren's later novel, different from *Never Come Morning* and *The Neon Wilderness,* resembles Jewish American fiction in which New World Jews move through the corridors of time, the Lower East Side, and the Polish countryside. As in the stories of Kaplan, Liben, Ozick, and Paley, Algren's Poles touch upon their heritage only in distant memories recalled during moments of desperation and loneliness. Frankie's wife, confined to her apartment by psychological paralysis—a metaphor for her hopelessness—recalls better times and better places. She remembers the lost paradise of her ethnic youth peopled with those who knew who they were, tucked safely inside a culture rooted in the Old World. Whereas the Poles in Algren's other works speak bitterly of childhood, Sophie idealizes the past through rose-colored ethnic lenses. She remembers celebrating "Boze Narodzenie," the years of "soft and wild ancestral songs, 'Chlopek' sung in the evergreen's light. . . . Feasts of epiphany when she and Frankie together have marked neighbors' doorways with the letters that remembered ancestral kings" (62). Echoing the view of contemporary writers of Polish descent, Sophie regards ethnicity as order, stability, and moral certainty, constants within the chaos that surrounds her. "These," she continues, were "years when everything was so well arranged, when people who did right were rewarded and those who did wrong were punished. . . . God weighed virtue and sin then to the fraction of an ounce, like Majurcek the grocer weighing sugar" (62). A remarkable passage in Algren's Polish profile, Sophie's internalization is one of a few instances when his characters think beyond the immediate and measure their world in moral-ethical terms framed in ethnicity, a technique common in the work of descent writers from Pellowski to Poniscan to Bukoski.

Algren develops the theme of lost ethnicity and faded vision in other less poignant but equally telling scenes. Frankie, less verbal than his wife, shares her sense of loss, although his sentiment gives way to a cynicism that ethnicity cannot be regained. Frankie makes this clear in the finality of his abrupt response to his friend who wonders if "I got somebody left in the old country." "There ain't no one left in the old country," he answers. And in a recognition scene evocative of Sophie's, Frankie realizes that the true Frank Majcinek had never quite lived, that the Frankie "who was straight with himself as he was with the world" exists only in a lost tradition and in an ethnic self snuffed out early in his life (144).

For a century and a half, American writers had constructed a model of Polish and American kinship, one that thrived and evolved as the image of the Pole changed from patriot to farmer, from proletarian to refugee, from myth to memory. In the streets of Algren's Chicago, this kinship is again declared with terrifying results for ethnics and Anglos alike. "All had gone stale for these disinherited," Algren writes. "On skid row even the native-born no longer felt they had been born in America" (17). The title of Sophie's "scrapbook of Fatal Accidence" serves as bitter comment on the kinship theme and as an epitaph for Algren's portrait of ethnicity at mid-century.

3. STANLEY "SNOPES" KOWALSKI

When *A Streetcar Named Desire* opened on Broadway, reviewers said little about the play's ethnic dimension other than to note that Stanley Kowalski is a Polish American. Some ignored Kowalski's heritage completely. Similarly, except for Caroline Golab who discusses Williams's use of the Slavic stereotype ("an ironic distortion" 150), scholars have limited their interest in ethnicity and culture to explorations of "southernness," personified largely in Blanche and less so in Stella. But as Vivienne Dickson has shown in her study of the *Streetcar* manuscripts, Williams, from the first, had thought about the play in ethnic terms. In successive versions, he characterized his male lead as an Italian (Lucio), an Irishman (Ralph Stanley), and a Pole (Stanley Landowski, then Stanley Kowalski). In a manuscript version entitled "Electric Avenue," Mitch is named Eddie Zawadski. Only in "The Poker Night" (the sixth revision?) does the male lead emerge in the identity familiar to theater-goers and modern readers. Dickson observes that the change from Italian to Irish to Polish parallels Stanley's evolution as an aggressive figure (154–74). When Williams fixed upon the characterization of the sisters as relics of a decaying southern aristocracy and the Pole as a Snopesian newcomer, he created a "new dimension with the addition of cultural differences" (159). Unfortunately, Dickson does not elaborate on the cultural conflict, and Kenneth Barnard, who ably discusses the play in a cultural context, does so without examining ethnicity. Conse-quently, Williams's treatment of ethnicity, which explains Kowalski's aggressiveness and the Blanche-Stanley antagonism, invites review.

There is ample textual support to regard Kowalski's aggression not as a manifestation of Williams's naturalism (the beast in the man) but rather as the product of Williams's own ethnic nightmares and Stanley's own cultural predicament. A second- or third-generation Polish Ameri-can, Stanley is completely cut off from his heritage. He has no past, no family, no link to his ethnicity. He is an example of ethnic dislocation and isolation. His presence in New Orleans—a sociological curiosity in terms of Polish demographics—testifies to his separation from his cultural roots. In fact, by its absence, Kowalski's ethnicity assumes significance. That he has consciously rejected his ethnic self is implied when he tells Blanche that he is "one hundred per-cent American" without ties to Poland or to Polonia. Kowalski may publicly claim to be "one hundred per-cent American," but his irritation with Blanche's ethnic references, his resistance to being identified as ethnic, and his self-imposed distance from his roots suggest that he has an inner conflict not unlike that of the protagonists of Levin's *Mask of Glory,* Lampell's *The Hero,* Tabrah's *Pulaski Place,* and other works in which a Polish protagonist tries to divorce himself from his past. In short, he protests too much.

Early in *Streetcar,* Williams draws attention to the cultural differ-ences of his characters. In a stage direction he notes that Stella is from a "background quite different from her husband's" (10). And Blanche's first reference to her sister, "I'm looking for my sister, Stella Dubois. I mean—Mrs. Stanley Kowalski" (12), reveals that something remark-able has occurred in the life of the Dubois sisters, something to which neither of them has quite adjusted. These comments amount to little until the first conversation between Blanche and Stella in which Wil-liams, through an abrupt transition, links them to the ethnic issue hovering over the action. To Blanche's question about the sleeping arrangements in the small apartment, Stella replies, "Stanley is Polish, you know" (21), revealing her anxiety about Stanley's ethnicity and her need to bring this to the forefront. Clearly Stella is not presenting new information to Blanche, who in her reply and demeanor shows that she already "knows" about Kowalski.

In the same conversation, Williams establishes the Dubois sense of cultural superiority and their antiethnic attitudes. "Oh yes," Blanche knowingly comments on Kowalski's cultural heritage, "they're something like Irish, aren't they?" (21). This provokes a "well" from Stella followed by Blanche's "only not so highbrow?" and then laughter of intimacy between the two who are now more comfortable with each other, having asserted their disdain for the Kowalskis and having established their own social superiority. Moments later, Blanche asks, "Is he so different?" and Stella answers, "Yes, a different species" (22). Although most critics tend to read this as evidence of Williams's naturalism, the dialogue, in the context of previous statements, seems to refer more to ethnic differences between the characters. The conversation includes other buried references to ethnic tension. Stella, for example, confides that there were adjustments to make in her marriage to Stanley. What exactly these adjustments are Williams doesn't say; but, when Blanche refers to Stanley's "civilian background" as probable cause and hints that Stanley's friends might be "Polacks," we have some reason to believe that Stella's adjustment is related to Stanley's Polish background. "They're a mixed lot," she tells her sister.

Blanche's aversion to Kowalski is epitomized in an oft-quoted passage in which she describes him as "an animal . . . survivor of the stone age . . . swelling and gnawing and hulking," a pure sign that America has indeed become the planet of the apes (80–81). Blanche's bitter denunciation, rooted in her own frustration, is motivated also by cultural biases and America's parochial fears of ethnics. When Blanche is angry, she lashes out at Stanley's Polishness, which she rarely mentions otherwise. "Where were you?" she accuses Stella. "In bed with your Polack!" (26). On other occasions, she labels Stanley "a healthy Polack," "a Polack," and so on. Additionally, Blanche's sexual dance with Stanley is accompanied by background music which Williams and the others refer to as Varsouviana (misspelled by Williams and erroneously identified as a polka), a stately French dance with Polish overtones suggested by the French word for "Warsaw" and patterned after the mazurka. The Varsoviana (correct spelling) is heard intermittently in the background during and preceding Blanche and Stanley's love-making. The grace and elegance of the Varsoviana stands in stark contrast to Stanley's less than genteel encounter with Blanche. What is more, by employing music ordinarily associated with the Polish beau ideal, Williams makes a cynical comment about Stanley's fall from high culture.

Stanley, as we learn, is equally aware of cultural-ethnic tension. He tells Stella that "the Kowalskis and the Dubois have different notions" (38); and he lashes out bitterly at one point when Blanche calls him a Polack: "I'm not a Polack. People from Poland are Poles, not Polacks. But what I am is a one hundred per-cent American, born and raised in the greatest country on earth and proud as hell of it, so don't ever call me a Polack" (126–27). We also learn that ethnic slurs are not the sole province of Blanche, nor limited to those instances reproduced in the dialogue. To Stella, he says, "Don't ever talk that way to me! Pig-Polack-disgusting . . . them kind of words have been on your tongue and your sister's too much around here" (124). Kowalski's anger with the sisters' ethnic slurs and his quickness to correct Blanche regarding Poles and Polacks show that his description of himself as "American" is a provoked response to a string of defamations that Stanley has likely heard many times.

Williams's cryptic references to ethnicity, Kowalski's sensitivity about his Polish roots, and Blanche and Stella's slurs all point to two different Americas on a collision course—or rather on a postcollision rebound. Blanche's world is an America in decline, one associated with land, property, gentility. The Dubois sisters carry the remnants of class, culture, and the agrarian tradition. Kowalski, on the other hand, is everything they are not. As a worker, foot soldier, ethnic, and materialist, he stands far removed from the Dubois tradition. Like Ichabod Crane, he regards property as cash because, having lost his peasant past, he has no other value context. He carries the seeds of radical postwar change, if not proletarian revolution, and is bent on the destruction of social classes and the ancient regime, as witnessed by his shedding of his ethnic self and successfully transforming Stella from a Dubois to a Kowalski. Near the end of the play, he reveals his conscious motivations to Stella, who appears aware of the large issues involved. "When we first met, me and you, you thought I was common. How right you was, baby. I was common as dirt. You showed me the snapshot of the place with the columns. I pulled you down off them columns" (129).

The Kowalskis have indeed pulled the Dubois sisters "down off them columns" as Williams's reactionary play demonstrates, a point not unnoticed by Henry Taylor who reviewed the play for *Masses and Mainstream*. Taylor accuses Williams of lacking a sociohistorical context and of writing a social drama without "the aura of large reality and of moral conviction" (55). Perhaps what Taylor really means is that Williams withholds his approval from the ethnic Kowalski and the social forces at work in postwar America. Nonetheless, the Kowalskis are on the rise. Stanley, for example, as a traveling representative of his factory, has already transcended class expectations, an accomplishment proudly noted by Stella who tells her sister, "Stanley's the only one of his crowd that's likely to get anywhere" (54). Stella is dependent on a man who in former days might have been employed at Belle Reve. Appropriately, the family legacy, or what's left of it, is now in Stanley's hands figuratively and literally. Blanche herself sees the irony of shifting cultural dominance: "I think it's wonderfully fitting," she tells him, "that Belle Reve should finally be this bunch of old papers in your big capable hands" (45). Blanche's collapse and her turn to madness result, one might say, from cultural dispossession and her awareness that history is itself the problem. She recognizes the enemy from the first, as she explains to Mitch, "The first time I laid eyes on him I thought to myself, that man is my executioner! That man will destroy me" (106). Stanley is equally aware of the inevitability of their personal conflict and the cultural metaphor it represents. "We've had this date with each other from the beginning," he tells her in their climactic scene (151). By play's end, the Kowalskis and the Dubois have permanently exchanged power positions, a shift that greatly troubled Williams, who said that the message of *Streetcar* is "if we don't watch out, the apes will take over" (qtd. in Golab 148). Unfortunately for pluralistic America, Williams had an ethnic/minority ape in mind, one that was best represented, he thought, as Polish.

4. WILLIAM STYRON: THE ACCIDENTAL ETHNIC

Almost three decades would pass before a nonethnic, major American writer would produce another popular and critically successful work dealing with Poles. In an interview given the year before *Sophie's Choice* was published, William Styron explained his motivation for the novel: "What I'm trying to do here is to take something that's on the rim of people's consciousness," the notion that the Holocaust was a "universal thing in which Jews were the chief victims, but not the only victims," without "reducing Jewish suffering at all" (Arms 9). In choosing the Holocaust as subject and a Pole, Sophie Zawistowski, as heroine, Styron made himself vulnerable to a broadside of criticism from Polish American critics, as we have seen, and from Jewish Americans who challenged Styron's infiltration of "Jewish" topics. Irving Saposnik suggested that Styron's work illustrates his desire to join "the hottest thing around," if only as "an adopted son," and that the presence of Jewish characters in his fiction can be explained only by his "unconscious urge to be among Jews" (323). Others fretted about the "usurpation of ethnic and other territory" (Baldwin 474). Who, the question was asked, is really entitled to write about ethnic and minority groups? In the case of Styron, a southern writer without familial or cultural ties to Poland and without Algren's immediate and extensive observations of the Polish community, the question is not without legitimacy.

In many ways, *Sophie's Choice* fits rather neatly into America's literary history of Poles. For one thing, the novel is related to a large group of works dealing with World War II and its aftermath. Like *The Sea-Gull Cry* and *Strangers Are Coming*, *Sophie's Choice* is about a displaced person, a war refugee who, having wandered through various camps in Europe, finally arrives in America where she must, with difficulty, begin a new life. Sophie is yet another Polish immigrant learning the mysteries of English, Coney Island, and American literature, which she appreciates with almost fawning approval, considering that she never mentions the Polish literary works that she surely must have read. Her passion for Wolfe, Whitman, and Dickinson illustrates, Styron seems to suggest, the superiority of American writers. The novel also provides a brief look at the war in Poland. Styron reconstructs the long-standing antagonism between German and Pole in much the same way that Jona Konopka and Helen MacInnes do. As for actual events, he includes the familiar, romantic example of the Polish cavalry charging German tanks ("foolish and gallant and futile"), the equally overworked, though tragic, arrest and execution of the university faculty in Krakow, and the machinations of the underground. These three strikingly romantic images serve as a metaphor for the nation. In truth, we learn little about the actual war in Poland other than through emblematic incidents intended to provide insight into the national temperament in the style of Antoni Gronowicz or, for that matter, the nineteenth-century tributes of Samuel Knapp and Silas Steele, who introduced the Pole as a romantic warrior and defender of Western civilization.

Except for her fatal lack of patriotism, Sophie herself is a descendant of the tradition of the Polish beau ideal introduced in the 1830s. She is, after all, no peasant. Her father and husband lecture at Jagiellonian University and her mother teaches music. She reads classic literature, speaks languages, and has considerable knowledge of other cultures. Her attraction to poetry and classical music defines her sensitivity and cultural depth. She talks easily about Italian and French opera (Verdi, Rossini, Gounod) and refers offhandedly to Scarlatti and Bach. While Styron's characterization of Sophie stems partly from his need to contrast the extremes of human behavior (within Sophie as well as with the Holocaust perpetrators) and his need for a protagonist capable of verbalizing this irony, his portrayal of Sophie as a feminine version of the beau ideal owes much to the image of the Pole already fashioned in the American literary imagination.

Similarly, his depiction of Polishness also depends on literary convention and historical precedent. More than once, he defines ethnicity through physical traits. Sophie's father's face is "classically Polish, high wide cheekbones, blue eyes, rather full lips, the broad nose tilting up . . . light fine hair swept back evenly" (290). Sophie has "straw-colored hair" and the "broad lovely swerve of Slavic cheekbone" (55). Poles are "somber," given to "intimation of strife and doom" (225), Stingo observes, as he gradually learns the meaning of the phrase "Slavic melancholy" (441). Styron also makes much of traditional depictions of the hard-drinking Pole and seems to enjoy exaggerating this cultural stereotype. Of Sophie he says, "she had the capacity of a Polish hussar" (377) and "she puts it away like some female riveter at a Polish bar in Gary, Indiana" (431).

To his credit, Styron uses European settings to legitimize Sophie's ethnic nature, unlike most American writers who have filled in their Polish landscapes with memory scenes and allusions to people, places, and events. Even so, Styron's Poland is little more than an accidental tourist's guide to the Krakow region which he visited during the preparation of the novel. The Auschwitz scenes notwithstanding, the Polish episodes focus on the culturally exotic in the tradition of Robin Carver's stories of the 1830s and Eric Kelly's adolescent novels a century later. Styron comments on the poor quality of Krakow's drinking water, the cobbled streets, the Jewish ghettos, and the storks nesting in crooked chimneys—all of which have been dismissed by Jerzy Strzetelski as cultural fabrication. He walks the reader through the market square, past St. Mary's Cathedral, the Sukiennice, and the clock tower and pauses, as all tourists do, to listen to the legend of the trumpeter of Krakow (around which Kelly develops one of his novels). He makes a few references to Jagiellonian University and to Polish cuisine, which oddly enough is more German than Polish, and he tosses in capsule comments about Lodz, Lublin, and a few other locales.

Styron's insights into national character are likewise colored by the kind of historical romanticism prevalent in nineteenth-century works and carried to an extreme by James Michener. He talks about "pride and the recollection of vanished glories. Pride in ancestry in family name . . . a frenzied nationalism . . . a melancholy heart" (301). Jews, peasants, the middle class, and the day-to-day life of ordinary people take a back seat to high romance. If David Baldwin is correct in his judgment that Sophie is not a character but rather an "image, a vehicle," his observation applies even more so to Styron's Poland and to his story of star-crossed lovers, the Christian Sophie and the Jewish

Nathan. Following on the heels of Jewish American writers from Roth
to Malamud, from Weidman to Uris, he associates Polishness with
anti-Semitism and makes a case, through Sophie and her family, that
Poles did little to stem the horrors of the Holocaust. This "feature,"
which dominates Styron's ethnic portrait, rankles many of his readers
because it reinforces historical biases that ignore a thousand-year
phenomenon of relative peace and goodwill between Polish Christians
and Jews. By focusing on the late 1930s, perhaps the most sorrowful
decade in the history of that relationship, and by isolating Poland from
the rest of Europe where indifference, legislation, and violence toward
Jews occurred in equal measure, Styron inadvertently identifies the
Polish connection with the Holocaust as uniquely and singularly abhorrent.

The tragic story of Sophie and Nathan, their bizarre love-hate relationship, must be seen as a symbol of the ill-fated history of Poles and
Jews, played out this time in a surrealistic New World landscape of pink
rooming houses, Coney Island, and make-believe dress-up parties.
Sophie's willingness (her psychological need) to suffer Nathan's abuse
can only be regarded as atonement for her own and the nation's moral
cowardice and anti-Semitism. Similarly, Nathan's own racial and religious bigotry, explained away by Styron as the ravings of schizo-
phrenia, is rather a cultural response to the perceived historical enemy
of the Jews. His abuse of Sophie, for example, often takes the form of
cultural slander. Sophie is a "dumb fucking Polack" (55), "a sloppy
Pole," "a dirty Polack," "a filthy Polish pig, crummy Nafka, Kurvey," to
which Nathan adds, "filthy Polish pigs have always killed the Jews"
(97). Nathan's initial attraction to Sophie stems as much from her
ethnicity as from his compassion, almost as if he senses a potential
victim/partner in his mad dash to rectify history. Upon first meeting
Sophie, Nathan explains that he "divined" that she was of "Polish
extraction."

Nathan's anger and bigotry, the legacy of history, are paralleled (and
even justified) by the racial attitude of Sophie and her father—Styron's
"representative" Poles. At various times, Sophie portrays herself as
someone ashamed of her father's fascist sympathies, including his prejudice against Jews, but in the end Sophie makes it clear that she too has
always hated Jews. She condemns Jewish Americans with their "psy-
choanalysis, always picking their sores, worrying about their little
brilliant brains" (429), but her hatred extends to Jews in general as we
learn in her confession to Stingo. Everything she had told him about
Krakow, she admits, was a lie: "All my childhood, all my life I really
hated Jews. They deserved it, this hate. I hate them, dirty Jewish

cochons" (430). Whatever sympathy we have for Sophie and Poland as victims is thus undercut by Styron's powerful indictment of Polish anti-Semitism and Sophie's duplicity, resembling in its naked intensity that of Adam Kelno in Leon Uris's *QB VII.* The same might even be said of Nathan, who has made the Holocaust his passion and Sophie his revenge.

Styron's characters serve more as the repository of history than as realistic people. And Poland embodies the paradoxical capacity for extreme evil and high culture: classical music clashes with ghetto life; nobility of spirit with meanness; democratic instincts with intolerance; Judaism with Christianity. Polishness in *Sophie's Choice* represents the potential for self-sacrifice (Wanda and Joseph) and for deception and the unspeakable (Sophie and her father). It is the contradiction of humanness, the paradox of civilization, a microcosm of human behavior and a radical departure from the nineteenth-century beau ideal. Whatever Poland was, Styron seems to say, has been obliterated by the ravages of war and the fires of the Holocaust. Only caricature and memory remain. Sophie lives without family, Old World connections, or any tangible link to the past. "There is nothing at all that remains from Poland," she tells Stingo. "Everything you see in this room is American, new books, my clothes, everything. . . . I don't even have a picture from that time" (171). She, Nathan, and even Stingo try to piece together history through memory, myth, and memorabilia. Nathan gathers photographs, documents, papers to correct the fact that, as Stingo phrases it, he "has no sense of history at all" (25). Stingo himself tries to turn his back on history as he decides never to live again in the South, although he suspects he will visit history in his fiction. And Sophie's past consists only of the memories of "anguish, confusion, self-deception, and above all, guilt" (228).

Ultimately, Stingo, who bears the burden of southern history, comes to identify with Sophie, who carries the Polish past inside her. Stingo admits in the end that "I felt Polish, with Europe's putrid blood rushing through my arteries and veins" (599). Stingo's identification with Poland, which in this instance is little more than a mea culpa for the horror of history, hardly resembles the bond of Polish and American kinship that writers had invented over the years. Stingo himself has no real interest in Polish history and culture, no particular curiosity about everyday life except for the abnormality of the war years and his quest to "understand Auschwitz." Stingo's Poland is actually an extension of the southern nightmare, a historical correspondence to America's own tragic past, a crazy quilt of moral compromise and daring deeds, a darkling plain where ignorant armies clash by night.

5. THE DEMOCRATIC BEAU IDEAL

Despite their importance as works that bring "Poles" to the literary mainstage, Algren's fiction, Williams's *Streetcar,* and Styron's *Sophie* have never been regarded as ethnic literature. Their place in the canon has been secured more by their concern with universal and distinctly American issues of urban decay, social reorganization, and regional eccentricities. In this sense, James Michener's *Poland* (1983), at least at first glance, stands apart. Not only does *Poland* take place far from the familiar confines of the American landscape, but also it deals with the details and complexities of a culture with which few readers even within the Polish American community are familiar, with names, places, and events too foreign for most to mark or name an experience by.

Poland's popularity might be explained as the consequence of America's sustained love affair with the historical novel, or due to Michener's cumulative reputation, or the merits of the novel itself, which reviewers greeted enthusiastically for its "epic sweep," "deft panorama," "total immersion," and "masterful blend of fictional and historical characters." More likely, it is history itself—the juxtaposition of eye-catching improbabilities—that guaranteed *Poland*'s timely success: the election of a much-beloved Pole to the papacy; the rise of Polish-born Zbigniew Brzezinski to the post of assistant for National Security Affairs in the Carter administration; the appeal of Solidarity, whose every move was reported on the evening news; the awarding of a Nobel Peace Prize to a charismatic electrician from Gdansk. One might justifiably claim that politics also played a part, in that Solidarity, martial law, and Poland's economic woes assured Reaganite America of the rightness of the American way. Even more, *Poland* caught America's fancy because it offered a vision of a country that mirrored America's own ideological sympathies. This appeal is prominently featured on the book jacket advertisement for *Poland,* described as "the inspirational saga of a people who not only survived catastrophe but [who] were capable of building on that very destruction." In effect, Michener draws upon the images, icons, and traits of national character most appealing to and "felt" by Americans, including America's own pathway to democracy, its resiliency, and the historical antecedents for Polish and American kinship.

There seems little doubt that Michener had a teaching function in mind and that *Poland* is his lesson for America. His employment of Polish scholars to furnish historical background, his encyclopedic introduction and glossary, and his authorial intrusion substantiate this intention. The whole of *Poland* is, of course, a readable, popular history lesson; but within the text Michener interrupts plot to provide lectures on language designed to familiarize the reader with Polish sounds and names. On one occasion he spends almost a full page on the intricacies of pronouncing Przemysl (the name of a city), extends his comments to the Polish alphabet, and concludes with a pronunciation table labeled "Always Remember Polish Is Easy." Other cultural and historical allusions seem designed less to advance plot than to reacquaint America with familiar cultural anecdotes. While he describes at length peasant wedding customs, decorating eggs at Eastertime, and the trumpeter of Krakow legend, the novel's Polish cultural landscape, particularly Jewish life, remains unevenly developed.

What Michener seems most intent on proving is that the course of Polish history is not unlike America's own, that Poland has stood as a bulwark against oppressive, expansionist nations, and that the nation's political ideas are a European equivalent of America's. In short, Michener's Poland and his version of ethnicity perfectly match the portrait introduced by American writers of the 1830s; as such his novel is a fitting contemporary parallel to earlier works and an example of the sustained and consistent view of Polishness in American literature. Once again Poland appears as a beau ideal among nations, a bastion of Christendom, an outpost of democracy, a bearer of enlightenment, and the embodiment of the genteel tradition. Michener's selections from Polish history consistently portray the Poles in this light. In chapter after chapter, Poland resists invasion by Tartars, Mongols, Turks, godless Nazis, and atheistic Communists; and in all cases the invaders are morally and culturally inferior. His explanation of Sobieski's defense of Vienna in the seventeenth century is representative. Poland, he writes, had always "volunteered to stand forth as the champion of Christian Europe" (158). And he has Sobieski repeat, "It has always been our duty to defend the Christianity of Europe from the threat of its barbarian enemies" (177). His dialogue echoes the poetry of the 1830s in which Poland was hailed as a nation whose

> . . . spirits walk abroad. Though years
> Elapse and others share as dank a doom,
> They but augment the deep and sweeping thoughts
> Which overpowered all others and conduct
> The world at last to freedom.   (qtd. in Coleman 59)

Similarly his celebration of Poland's passion for freedom, democracy, and individual rights restates familiar testimonials occurring in American periodicals a century and a half earlier. Lines such as "there was no nation on earth which prized freedom more," and "personal freedom was the lifeblood of freedom" (53) are the literary grandchildren of those first penned to support the November Uprising. In addition, the notion that Poland is a creature of destiny, common in 1830s literature, recurs often in the novel. In the opening to Chapter 6, "The Golden Freedom," Michener, for example, explains how Mars and Venus influence Poland's fate.

Likewise, Michener's vision of history as the inexorable march of democracy resembles that of the romantic historians of the first half of the nineteenth century—Bancroft, Prescott, Parkman, and Motley. The juxtaposition of princes and peasants throughout the plot is best understood in this context, rather than by the claim of those who assert that Michener presents the official party view of history as class struggle (Wrobleski 440). To be sure, he champions the peasant and indicts the aristocrat, but he does so with the ambivalency that characterizes America's historical fondness for the genteel tradition tempered by an egalitarian commitment. Typically, Michener lauds the gentry for their bravery in the face of awesome odds and laments the unequal division of spoils among princes and peasants. After the defeat of the Teutonic knights, Pawel, a petty noble, is rewarded with knighthood, a second village, and new horses. The peasant Janko, forced by starvation to eat one of Pawel's rabbits, "was dragged to the public square, where a rope was suspended from a limb and he was hanged" (104). Summarizing Sobieski's victory, Michener notes that Count Lubonski won a hero's death; "Lukasz Bukowski came home with a name, eighteen Arabian horses, and a room full of treasure . . . and the peasant Janko, as always, received nothing" (203). In his chapters on the period of partition, Michener again indicts the class system, as Janko Buk visualizes a world in which every man owned his land and cottage, but "he could imagine no system which would permit him to acquire his" (353).

Simply put, Michener's Polish beau ideal is both hero and villain, responsible for Poland's triumphs and its tribulations. His fierce protection of individual rights and privileges led ultimately, Michener charges, to Poland's darkest hours. "With rot at the core," he says of the seventeenth-century magnates, Polish politics became the most corrupt in Europe. And with that Poland was doomed. At the same time, the aristocrats are usually the only Poles who escape Michener's two-dimensional characterization and who capture the imagination of the reader and Michener's fervor. Princess Lubomirska, the proprietress of Lancut, is described as the "grandest woman in the world today," the constant companion of Franklin and Jefferson who "adored her and brought their problems to her almost daily" (256). Andrez Lubonski, perhaps Michener's most notable character, is a far-sighted statesman who, having risen to high position in the Austrian government, applies himself with dignity, enthusiasm, and competence to the cause of independent Poland in 1918. His son, Walerian, leads the resistance against the Nazis and plays a key role in the London government.

Wiktor Bukowski is perhaps the best example of Michener's ambivalence toward the aristocratic beau ideal. A member of the gentry whose family dates back hundreds of years through the best and worst of times, Bukowski has a quixotic position in the novel. He leads the life of an aimless aristocrat, "tramping his estate, kicking a clod of earth now and then, and accomplishing nothing.... He has only the vaguest understanding of who was ruling the country or what was happening in the surrounding countries" (400–401). He spends his time with his horses, two Packard cars, and the music of Chopin. But when the Soviet invasion of 1919 threatens again to erase Poland's independence, Bukowski shows his mettle. Once again, the beau ideal's love of country, pride in its heritage, and his inherent nobility of character surface. Bukowski rushes off to defend Poland's freedom and, as Polish history has it, the freedom of people everywhere. His transformation is complete; the wasted ne'er-do-well becomes Major Bukowski, "rather debonair," rallying his men, galloping "with terrible force right at the heart of the Russian position" (436). He seemed "immortal," Michener observes, as he attaches Bukowski to the tradition of Krzysztof who fought the Tartars, Sobieski who battled the Turks, Kosciuszko who rose against the tsar. Ultimately, Michener's respect for the Polish beau ideal and the romantic tradition surrounding him carries the day as his modern aristocrats, Bukowski, and the Lubonskis play havoc with the egalitarian sentiments which guide the novel.

If Michener has difficulty deciding whether "true" Polishness resides in princes or in peasants, he has no such problem in portraying the family as the heart of ethnicity. His extended history of the Buks and Bukowskis over an 800-year period structures the novel and appeals to popularly perceived notions of the ethnic family. Thomas J. Ferraro, writing about Mario Puzo's *The Godfather,* attributes its phenomenal success to the fact that it feeds upon the "myth of the natural ethnic family" (192). *Poland*'s emotional appeal rests likewise in the struggle of two families to retain their identity and their existence in the face of external and internal disasters. Through it all, the families endure. Michener does more. He brings together the estranged national family divided by class and politics, with the symbolic marriage of Szymon Bukowski, scion of the government and heir to the gentry, and Biruta Buk, patriot and peasant. "I am proud to have him join my family," Jan Buk says at the close as Solidarity and the government try to reconcile their differences and Poland's problems.

Whereas Puzo, according to Ferraro, joins Italians and Americans by fusing corporate America to familial, clannish Europe, Michener binds Poles and Americans through the literary convention of marriage which reinforces the notion of the two nations as an extended family with a shared destiny, aspiration, and character. The 1895 marriage of Wiktor Bukowski and Marjorie Trilling, daughter of the American ambassador to Austria, occupies most of Michener's history of Poland from 1895 to 1945, a long section which ironically and unfortunately ignores the immigration of vast numbers of Poles to the United States. Michener, however, anticipates this union by citing previous examples of Polish and American kinship. Earlier he had associated Princess Lubomirska, the grand dame of eighteenth-century Europe, with the mythic figures of the American Revolution, Jefferson, and Franklin "whom she loved . . . and might marry" (256). In regard to the Kosciuszko rebellion, Michener announces that, almost miraculously, "America had come to Poland" (294) and equates Kosciuszko's promise to free the peasants with his release of his American slaves. Thus the union of a Chicago industrialist's daughter to a Polish landowner occurs not without historical antecedents. The marriage in many ways is Jamesian: American innocence, vitality, commerce, and new money in contrast with tradition, high-culture, the land, and breeding. Unlike James, however, Michener successfully reconnects Old and New World cultures through marriage. The wedding of Marjorie and Wiktor and their dual-ancestry offspring suggest an extended natural family and the natural attraction between Poles and Americans. With American money and vision, the thousand-year-old Bukowski palace—the embodiment of Polishness so to speak—is restored to former splendor. Marjorie, in turn, learns about European culture and this "amazing land" (365). She is taken with the landscape, Polish nationalism, and the national character and becomes Polonized, an ardent defender of Polish culture even in the dark days of Nazi oppression during which she dies, an old woman defying Poland's enemies in the tradition of Krzysztof with whom the novel begins. Poland and America are so closely linked, Michener seems to say, that Marjorie's adoption of Poland as her native land and her easy transformation from Chicago millionairess to female Polish beau ideal seem perfectly natural, devoid of either painful transplant or the ambiguities found in James's novels.

Michener updates the kinship theme in his account of Janko Buk, the leader of rural Solidarity. In the last chapter, he reverses Trilling's journey of a century ago by bringing Buk to America to explain Solidarity's program. Buk is shocked (and delighted) to discover that Poland thrives in America. Touring the Polish community in Detroit (which Karl Harriman described in his 1903 work, *The Homebuilders*), Buk finds excellent Polish restaurants and a host of sights and sounds that remind him of Krakow. He listens to Polish-language radio programs, visits with Polish American farmers, and witnesses the extent of Polish culture in America. He cannot believe that the ethnic Poles of Detroit equal in number the population of some Polish cities. He confers with labor leaders and meets President Reagan. His warm reception is that of a distant but like-minded relative, and he, correspondingly, is amazed to meet "so many men who know my country so intimately" (569). Michener extends his portrait of Polish and American solidarity by having Buk visit the Pope as the alliance of Christianity, democracy, and Western ideals broadens into an international eternal triangle. The novel closes with multiple unions of old and new kinships: Poland and the church, Buks and Bukowskis, Poland and the United States—a hopeful vision of yet another new dawn in Poland's history and a transcendence, but not a denial, of nationality and ethnicity.

Believing that history moves inexorably toward democracy, Michener, with some reluctance, topples princes in order to elevate peasants who, given "equal status" in the government-Solidarity negotiations, emerge as the new beau ideal. Earlier Wiktor Bukowski resisted legitimizing his bastard son, arguing that the classes "have never mixed, there have been two Polands, one for the gentry, one for the peasants" (422). When Miroslawa gives Seweryn Buk the Bukowski name he is entitled to, she reminds Wiktor that "a new day is dawning in Poland" (422), a point of view echoed later by Szymon Bukowski and a fitting epitaph for Michener's *Poland*.

6. THE NONETHNIC ETHNIC NOVELS OF JERZY KOSINSKI

In a *Paris Review* interview, George Plimpton asked Jerzy Kosinski, "Could you see yourself starting all over again—new country, new language?" to which Kosinski replied, "It's a nightmare, but . . . yes, I could" (185). Starting over characterizes all phases of Kosinski's life and art—from his youth in Poland to his residency in the United States, from sociologist to novelist, from an East European writing in Polish to an American writing in English. Starting over aptly describes his protagonists as well from the Jewish Pole of *The Painted Bird* to the universal selves of the subsequent novels—the everyman who "begins again" in a strange new world. Kosinski's major fictional interest, the survival of the self in the postwar world, dramatizes the point that Kosinski also transcends geographic, ethnic, and cultural boundaries as he starts over. In this sense he joins the family of twentieth-century Slavic writers (Conrad, Nabokov, Milosz) who, starting anew, earned their literary reputations in a language and cultural setting other than their own and who created characters and themes native to all grounds.

Kosinski's international status makes it difficult, however, to categorize his fiction in strictly ethnic terms. He is not regarded as a Polish writer in Poland, where his works remained unavailable until recently; and, of course, his European background denies him the host-culture status of his American contemporaries. Moreover, neither Polish nor Jewish American scholars have claimed him as one of their own, principally because he seemingly ignores the essentials of the traditional Polish-Jewish experience in Poland or in America and because he never actively identified himself with or wrote about transplanted cultural communities. Kosinski complicated the issue by refusing publicly to think of himself as a Pole, a Jew, or an ethnic writer (except as a gesture of self-defense in *Hermit*) and by deliberately distorting the facts of his life. His attempts to make a life from his fiction and a fiction from his life have resulted in a web of autobiographical fictions and fictional selves so tangled that Kosinski the man is thought of as "a kind of Polish James Bond" (Gelb 45).

Few casual readers are even aware of Kosinski's Polish roots, and most serious readers have overlooked this aspect of his work. For the few who have not, Kosinski's "Europeanness" has been noted merely as an influence on his early novels (Corwin, Raymont) or "a source of contextual information" (Tepa 53). By and large, Kosinski's critics regard him as one whose "Americanization" was so complete that he could be described simply as "among the more widely honored American" writers (Klinkowitz 82). For good reasons, critics have concentrated on the deracinated self, cut off from time and place, divorced from a cultural context and native tradition, trying, as it were, to protect and defend itself against the threatening forces that exist in the postwar world (Coale, Furbank, Hutchinson, Sanders).

Describing his novels as portrayals of men "desperate to find out who they are" (qtd. in Sheehy 55), Kosinski had himself reinforced this reading. As early as 1968 he outlined in *The Art of the Self* what would become the pattern of his novels when he wrote that "the self must constantly get clear from its past in order to live fully in the present" (21). Unfortunately, this approach has to this point effectively neutralized the ethnic dimension in his fiction.

Despite their international settings and universalized protagonists, the novels are unmistakably ethnic. They deal invariably with the cold war immigrant self, adjusting—simultaneously, in Kosinski's case—to a new American culture and to an old Polish one which lies beneath surface events and in the repressed consciousness of the narrator. Seven of the nine protagonists, for example, have East European backgrounds;

most are political refugees from socialist Poland. Four of the novels include scenes in Eastern Europe, usually Poland, and a fifth, *The Painted Bird,* is set entirely in Poland. With the possible exception of *The Devil Tree,* all of the novels include Slavic characters—Poles, Russians, Ruthenians. In addition, the works are laced with frequent references to Polish customs, place names, institutions, and history, many of which remain obscure to the general reader. Taken together, these seemingly random and often disjointed references offer significant insight into contemporary East European politics, the Polish temperament, and Polish culture, including Polish Jewish relations. Kosinski's Polish roots have shaped his fiction in even more important ways. His themes, his eccentric protagonists, his thematic coherence, and even his development as a writer are directly related to his own struggle to come to terms with his Polish past—a struggle which, as a common thread in all the novels, offers a way to understand Kosinski's growth as a "nonethnic" ethnic writer and his unique version of the Polish self.

Kosinski's obsession with the problem of the self originates in his own ethnic past, in the process of "growing up in Poland and the USSR, societies so ravaged by war that between 1939 and 1944, Poland, for instance, had lost one-fifth of its entire population" (qtd. in Sheehy 55). Kosinski specifically traces the loss of self back to the Holocaust and to the concentration camps of wartime Poland. In *Steps* (1968), he explains that the purpose of the camps was "hygiene," in the sense that their function was to eliminate disease and disease carriers. That process denied the self, in that "the victims never remained individuals, they became as identical as rats" (64). In his 1976 preface to a new edition of *The Painted Bird,* he elaborates on this point when he quotes a letter written by a camp inmate: "They tattoo the newcomers. Everyone gets his number. From that moment on you have lost your 'self' and have become transformed into a number. You are no longer what you were before, but a worthless moving number" (xii). In *Pinball* (1982), Kosinski returns to that letter, reproducing it exactly as he had in the preface but crediting the remarks to Gerald Osten, one of his characters, who keeps the letter under the glass top of his office desk. Thus it is that Kosinski's novels are framed with bold announcements that the destruction of the self begins in East Europe, specifically in a Polish memory.

Given the horrors of wartime Poland and the civil strife and political oppression that followed, it is no surprise that Kosinski's first two novels reject everything associated with Poland. In both novels, the singular aim of the protagonists is to slough off the old skin and "to get clear of the past." Kosinski's portrait of Poland is devastating. Reminiscent of Isaac Singer's *The Slave, The Painted Bird* (1965) portrays Poles

as sadistic animals. Superstition, anti-Semitism, violence, and ignorance characterize daily life. Ultimately what emerges is a nation indicted for its part in the Holocaust. Victimized because he looks like a
Jew or a gypsy, the narrator suggests at one point that the peasants
transformed the Holocaust into a religious experience by believing that
"the smoke from the crematories went straight to heaven laying a soft
carpet at God's feet without even soiling them" (101). At war's end, the
Poles, quick to consort with their Russian liberators, behave no better,
as the narrator closes his tale with images of a nation consumed with
profiteering, corruption, and fear. So alienated is Kosinski's young
narrator that he will not identify his own cultural-religious background, refer to his ethnic traditions, or even mention the name of the
country despite the obvious Polish setting. The narrator's state of mind
mirrors that of Kosinski who tells us that having left Poland, he was
determined "never again to set foot in the country where I had spent the
war years" (*The Painted Bird* xi).

Although not formally a sequel, *Steps* (1968) functions that way:
The Painted Bird describes physical torture, whereas *Steps* documents
mental torture; the former condemns wartime Poland, while the latter
denounces postwar Polish socialism. Even then Kosinski returns to the
brutality and coarseness of the Polish peasant. The narrator includes a
tale about a Polish woman imprisoned in a cage strung to a barn roof
where for five years she is raped and tortured by the villagers. Aware of
the woman's plight, the local priest excuses the affair as the natural expression of peasant temperament. Kosinski also indicts the subtle anti-
Semitism of the new regime. The narrator visits the cemetery of a
"religious minority who for a long time had not been allowed to bury
their dead within the city limits" (65). Looked after by a former camp
inmate, the cemetery whose "stones had sunk drunkenly into the
ground" recalls for the knowledgeable reader the many abandoned and
desecrated Jewish cemeteries in present-day Poland.

Kosinski emphasizes the destruction of the self begun by the Nazis in
the concentration camps, and continued in postwar Eastern Europe
through "unspecified" policies which resulted in mental collectiviza-
tion or, as Czeslaw Milosz expresses it, "the captive mind." Trapped by
a mindless bureaucracy, the narrator must join a paramilitary organization at his university, conduct "self-evaluations," attend obligatory
party meetings, and live on a collective farm as a punishment for
political dissent. Eventually he flees Poland by inventing fictitious identities, other selves, if you will, who recommend him for study abroad.
Although the final third of *Steps* records the narrator's "first steps" in
his newly adopted country, the novel is thematically finished much
earlier. Leaving his European self behind, the narrator reflects on his

departure from Poland and presents himself as one waiting to be reborn. Like Whitman, he is "timeless unmeasured . . . suspended forever between my past and my future" (108). Later Kosinski would comment that, had he stayed in Poland, "preserving the self in a total-itarian society would have been his aim" (Sheehy 55).

Having ostensibly shed his Old World skin, Kosinski's next two novels, *Being There* (1971) and *The Devil Tree* (1973), offer us new selves in the form of typically American protagonists without any roots at all. Outside of time and place, suspended between the past and the future, Chance and Whalen are true successors to the nameless pro-tagonists of *The Painted Bird* and *Steps*, who must discard their Old World selves before discovering genuinely new ones. Frank Chance, for example, "moves in his own time" as he invents, with the help of the media, the self he comes to believe in. That self, as Jerome Klinkowitz points out, is ironically nothing less than the American collective self (95). In *Being There,* one of the characters succinctly comments, "A man's past cripples him, his background turns into a swamp" (116). As if to prove this point, Kosinski subjects Chance to an exhaustive inves-tigation of his vocabulary, syntax, accent, even his facial features. The investigators, ironically Soviet agents, conclude that they cannot "de-termine in any way whatsoever his ethnic background" (106).

Despite Kosinski's attempt to stay free of "the swamp," Eastern Eu-rope intrudes itself into both novels in seemingly incidental ways. Chance meets, of all people, the Soviet ambassador who, mistakenly believing that Chance speaks Russian, discusses Russian literature with him. Kosinski also describes Soviet methods of gathering information through their foreign ministry, recalling the intimidating atmosphere of *Steps.* A similar pattern runs through *The Devil Tree.* Like Chance, Jonathan Whalen exists without a cultural past. At various points, however, Kosinski shows Whalen's concealed self trying to burst free. For no apparent reason, Whalen's mother discovers that the manager of her favorite Venetian hotel is a Russian communist who subscribes to *Pravda.* Later Kosinski introduces a minor character who has a conver-sation with a grocery manager, "an older Jewish man . . . with a heavy European accent" (62). Richard wants to know why the insecticides are kept so near the vegetables. When the grocer calls Richard a nut for suggesting that someone would poison vegetables, Richard responds, "You are a Jew. Millions of your people died poisoned by gas. Why would anyone kill Jews?" (63). Richard, we learn, witnessed Nazi mas-sacres in White Russia even before "the gas chambers were established" (63). What these incidents make clear, of course, is that the Holocaust, Jewishness, the Soviets, and Poland are never out of Kosinski's mind nor far away even from his seemingly American protagonists.

After *The Devil Tree,* Kosinski returns to an East European-born protagonist whose ongoing struggle with the self occurs within the background that Kosinski knows best: a Polish landscape, Soviet-style politics, the war in Europe, and ethnic subterfuge. Although *Cockpit* (1975) and *Blind Date* (1977) feature Kosinski's familiar theme and ever-present rootless wanderers about whom we know little or nothing (they even use aliases), the novels represent a shift in Kosinski's treatment of Poland and thus mark a major step in his long journey home. For one thing, the presence of Poland is more intense in these novels than in *Being There* or *The Devil Tree.* For another, Kosinski reveals an impulse toward accommodation with his native land.

In both novels, the survival of the self is directly related to the past which, Kosinski seems to conclude, re-creates itself even as it is destroyed. In *Cockpit,* Tarden believes that he exists in a "curious time warp," "completely cut off from my past" (247). His life depends on his ability "to instantly create a new person and slip out of the past" (129). Juxtaposed against this rational formulation is Tarden's rambling monologue in which a single memory picture evokes another so that unconsciously, "the montage of a past self will emerge" (13). Tarden's compulsion is to disguise the past as he desperately tries to reveal it. His behavior is analogous to Kosinski's hide-and-tell method of giving partial information about Poland to a reader who must then identify the specifics for himself.

As a result, Tarden's Polish roots emerge haphazardly, even reluctantly. At the outset, he talks about his former life in Poland, emphasizing the faceless nature of postwar Polish socialism. Curiously Tarden refers to Warsaw landmarks (such as Plac DeFilad, Palac Kultury i Nauki, and the office of Lot, the national airline) without naming them, as if to create a private bond between himself and those readers who might also know Warsaw. This seems to be the case in Tarden's extended description of Warsaw's tallest building where he worked. Although Tarden spends considerable time describing the building inside and out, he does not reveal what virtually all Poles tell visitors (and each other): that the building is a "gift" of the Soviets.

Although the Polish setting occupies only the very beginning of *Cockpit,* Kosinski refers constantly to Poland to provide a context for Tarden's aimless movements from assignment to assignment, woman to woman, phobia to xenophobia. Even then, Kosinski's allusions to Poland are oblique. Without explanation we learn that Tarden may be Ruthenian. He speaks the language of this former eastern province of Poland and even seeks out a Ruthenian doctor in a medical emergency. He also refers, without explanation, to the RUH, a Polish name for the wet winds from warm lakes and to a ski resort which strongly suggests

Zakopane in the Polish Tatras. When he explains that "the new government uprooted hundreds of thousands of families, my own included, and resettled them in recently annexed territories" (111), we know that Tarden must be referring to the massive resettlement and exchange of territory that occurred among Germany, Poland, and the Soviet Union at the end of World War II. Through Tarden's brief meeting with one of his former professors, Kosinski also reopens the subject of Polish anti-Semitism and even suggests that Tarden may be Jewish.

Tarden never fully comes to understand the relationship of the past to his present state of anxiety, nor does Kosinski succeed in coherently developing this theme. Nonetheless, Kosinski's decision to balance Tarden's American adventures with Polish memory pictures and allusions suggests a willingness, however cautious, to come to terms with the past. Even as the novel closes, Tarden's last memory evokes not an incident from his New World life but a grim image of war-torn Europe, "an old army tank . . . sunken in a shallow lagoon . . . rusted open . . . long buried in the sands of a deserted beach" (248).

This impulse continues in *Blind Date,* the further adventures of the deracinated hero. Like Tarden, Levanter is a transplanted Slav who uses his position as an intelligence agency operative to revenge himself on the totalitarian regimes of Eastern Europe. Despite the fact that Levanter hides as much as he reveals and that the reader must once again piece together Levanter's history, we learn, as we do in *Cockpit,* that the struggle features Old and New World selves.

Although he is not specific about Levanter's birthplace, nationality, or religion, Kosinski, for the first time since *The Painted Bird,* strongly implies that his hero may be a Jewish Pole. Levanter explains that his parents emigrated from Russia to somewhere in Eastern Europe before he was born. He also talks about his experience in a Soviet-style army where he was abused because he was thought to be Jewish. On another occasion he recalls a boyhood game called "Name the Jew" and how he was ordered to play by a gang of neighborhood toughs. More important, Levanter is the first Kosinski hero to recognize that his European past cannot and will not disappear and that he must reconcile his ethnic past and amorphous present—his Eastern roots and Western inclinations. Despite his efforts to leave his self behind when he journeys to the United States, the past follows him. Moving to Princeton, he is shocked to learn that Svetlana Stalin is his neighbor. In New York City, he hails a cab whose driver actually delivered groceries in Levanter's boyhood village and who even remembers Levanter as a child. A host of East Europeans, old friends and new acquaintances, pop up wherever he goes: a Russian actress, a former professor from Poland, a "legendary socialist athlete," and a close Polish friend named Woytek.

For the first time, Kosinski's protagonist is somewhat comfortable with his East European roots. He admits to being pleased by "the influence of his European upbringing" (93). Compared to the brutal portraits of Poland in earlier novels, *Blind Date* betrays a touch of sentiment for the homeland as Levanter fondly remembers boyhood escapades with good friends, skiing in the Tatras, and Chopin's Nocturnes. In contrast to the negative characterization of Poles in his other novels, Kosinski presents a more moderate, even conciliatory portrait. To a friend's question, "Have you found that people are good in the West? Are they better than where you and I come from?", Levanter replies, "I have found people to be good everywhere. They turn bad only when they fall for little bits of power" (83). Similar to Tarden, a dying Levanter evokes a series of memory pictures. He too remembers the war—"Dead German soldiers . . . their teeth flashing through the holes in their frostbitten cheeks" (233)—as Kosinski sustains his attempts to connect the war with the alienation of the self.

Another exile whose childhood was "spent in the stony rural life of one of those marginal old countries" (127), Fabian, the protagonist of *Passion Play* (1979), harbors the usual resentment toward his past in Eastern Europe, where his playmates often "turned on him in the bond and unity of their family kinship" (128). And he still festers at the socialist collective that "diminished one's achievements," although he seems unaware of the irony inherent in his empty new American identity: a mobile home and a series of anonymous roadside rests. What differentiates Fabian from his predecessors, however, is his ability to reflect upon his alienation. Through Fabian, Kosinski examines his own ambivalent feelings about the Old World and, like his protagonist, moves one step closer to reconciliation.

Still an outsider, this Kosinski hero surprisingly thinks of himself as an immigrant, one of many to whom dual identities have been a natural, even desirable, condition. He senses that he is not necessarily trapped between two worlds, that he is not unique, and that, instead, he shares "a dual past with many Americans of his generation" (127). Whereas Kosinski's earlier protagonists actively conceal their multiple selves even from themselves, Fabian recognizes that all "the skins that he shed, phases of the body and the mind" (182) were alive in memory—that his quest, in effect, is a search for the buried past. The itinerant polo player, Fabian thus rides toward a knowable, although unknown, destiny.

The striking new turn in Kosinski's journey is reflected in the images used to develop the second half of the novel. Alluding to what can only be understood as the Holocaust, Fabian tells a friend that all his relatives died in "one of the biggest fires ever. . . . It was arson" (205). Formerly,

Kosinski associated the Holocaust with the death of the self. In this work the Holocaust ironically suggests an opportunity for renewal. This new dimension in the history of the self is equally discernible as Fabian rides into a forest clearing where he pauses to wonder why he had not "searched himself as he had searched the clearing" (268). Contrary to the enclosures—the hiding places of the self—that dominate former novels, the clearing in *Passion Play* functions, like the fire, as a cleansing agent. In the clearing, Fabian discovers the "inexorability of the past" and man's inability to "thwart its cycle of repetition" (268).

Kosinski closes his novel accordingly. Typically, his protagonists are either frozen in time between two worlds or perish in the winter of their New World discontent and the memory of the frozen landscape of wartime Poland. *Passion Play* ends with man not in stasis but in motion, with a bizarre image of the inexorable past trying to keep pace with an equally relentless future. Astride his polo pony, lance at the ready, Fabian resembles a medieval knight jousting with a formidable foe—a jet plane taxiing for take-off. Fabian's opponent, the pilot, regards him as an anachronism, hopelessly out of step with the technological now with which he races. "You don't see many of those anymore," he comments (271), as Kosinski, seemingly at rest with his European roots, focuses on the emerging self.

If the impulse toward reconciliation is a faint but constant glow in *Blind Date* and *Passion Play,* that impulse becomes a bright star in *Pinball.* At first glance, the novel follows the familiar Kosinski pattern. Predictably, the hero, who grew up in Eastern Europe and studied in Warsaw, still bears the scars of World War II; and predictably he represents the alienated self in conflict with the threatening modern world. Within this formulaic pattern, Kosinski makes crucial changes. Although Domostroy is another example of the deracinated self, Kosinski blunts Domostroy's alienation by dividing this theme between the Slavic Domostroy and the American rock musician, Jimmy Osten, who retreats into an anonymous private world after each performance. Kosinski still traces the problem of the self to the Holocaust, but he associates this not with his Slavic protagonist but with a minor character, a German Jew who keeps a copy of the inmate's letter—previously cited in *The Painted Bird*—near at hand. Kosinski still makes a few references to the oppressive nature of the socialist system but no longer includes extensive, detailed examples. He even omits the flashbacks and memory pictures about growing up in socialist Poland that appear in virtually all of the novels. Slavs still appear as minor characters, but the portrait of Vala Stavrova, a Russian emigré, is hardly ominous, and the picture of "a group of beefy East European bureaucrats" (254) at an airport is more comical than sinister.

Although Patrick Domostroy is in many ways a typical Kosinski hero, he is not associated with politics. He is neither a spy nor a self-appointed avenger; he hardly refers to his days in Eastern Europe. Quiet and retiring, he is Fabian without a mobile home, a middle-aged cultural exile looking for roots. Kosinski makes this point early when Domostroy talks about a car he had bought fifteen years earlier, now a worn-out "symbol of his own mobility and affluence" (7). Putting aside the urge to keep moving, he moves into "The Old Glory," once the South Bronx's largest ballroom and banquet center which had formerly hosted a mostly Jewish clientele, and serves as the guard and custodian of this symbol of his assimilated ethnic, Jewish, Old World self and his newly adopted American identity.

Although the struggle with self is the major concern in *Pinball*, Kosinski develops this theme differently, by creating two protagonists whose contrasting views toward music illustrate the self in turmoil and the self in harmony. To illustrate, Kosinski turns ironically, but not surprisingly, to Eastern Europe, specifically to Poland's most mythopoetic native son, Frederick Chopin. As artist, political refugee, transplanted Pole, and romantic rebel, Chopin bears certain similarities to Kosinski. At the very least he represents the best of a cultural tradition from which Domostroy (and Kosinski) had so desperately fled. In *Pinball*, Chopin is a bridge back to that world. The difference between the angry Osten and the more forgiving Domostroy is immediately evident in their attitudes toward Chopin. For Osten, Chopin is a failure. He scorns his private life and dismisses his art as "evanescent, fragile music [that] was not universal [and] could never inspire the masses" (127). Domostroy explains Osten's antagonism this way: "Chopin once said that nothing is more odious than music without hidden meaning. But Goddard [Osten's alias] has no meaning to hide. Instead he has cleverly hidden himself in his music" (67).

Domostroy's condemnation of the hidden self sets him apart from his fictional predecessors; his tendency to identify with a Pole distinguishes him even more. What attracts Domostroy is Chopin's Zal, "a spiritual enigma—pain and rage, smothered by melancholy—an emotional trademark of Poles or any people oppressed for long periods of time" (109). Zal afflicts all of Kosinski's adult protagonists. Domostroy has Zal; so does Donna, a protegé of his. Domostroy believes, in fact, that Donna is a potentially great pianist precisely because she manages to capture Chopin's Zal. Kosinski also suggests, as William Styron does in *Sophie's Choice*, that African Americans and Poles share a similar fate: persecution, cultural exile, and ambivalent feelings about their cultural tradition. For Kosinski, the Polish exile who can't go home again, Donna becomes a surrogate. At Domostroy's insistence, she journeys to

Poland to compete in the prestigious Chopin competition held in Warsaw. Domostroy follows Donna's triumph on television. He listens and approves as she plays Chopin's Seventh Étude in C-sharp Minor, one of his "most nostalgic works." He is "profoundly touched by her brief mention of Zal" which, as she notes in her triumphant acceptance speech, she shares "with all the people of Poland" (284). Thus through Donna, Domostroy is reunited with his past.

For the first time in his fiction, Kosinski compliments his native land whose name he could not bring himself to mention in preceding novels. And for the first time he seems at ease with his cultural past and with himself. Now he can even joke about Poland. A law firm that represents musicians is named "Mahler, Strauss, Handel, and Penderecki," associating the avant-garde, contemporary Polish composer with the more recognizable masters. Kosinski's more relaxed posture is especially evident in the conclusion which, in previous novels, had been typically foreboding or, at best, problematic. Snug in his new home, aptly named "The Old Glory," Domostroy plays pinball as "Game Over" gives way to a flashing "Begin Game." Although he cannot decide if he will "start over," we are led to believe he will. Similarly, *Pinball* leads us to believe that Kosinski, having at least partially reconciled Old and New World selves, like his surrogate protagonists, may also be ready for a new game.

Kosinski's private life footnotes his fiction. In 1980 he participated in a tribute to the Polish union, Solidarity, and in 1987 he returned for the first time to Poland where he was warmly welcomed as an exiled native son. Concurrently, in *The Hermit of 69th Street*, Kosinski came out of the closet, so to speak, embracing his Jewish Polish ancestry, although not without the usual hedging. Like his fictional predecessors, Norbert Kosky bears marked resemblances to Kosinski; he is an exiled Polish writer living in the United States confronting the perils of rootlessness and alienation. Whereas the typical Kosinski hero is a man without a country, Kosky has three, culturally if not geographically: the United States, Poland (Kosinski still insists on calling it Ruthenia), and Israel. In direct contrast to a long line of protagonists who deny and repress their ethnicity, Kosky is proud, defensive, and knowledgeable about his cultural past. Correspondingly, Poland and Polishness take on a new face and a new fullness. To be ethnically Polish, as Kosky is, is suddenly to possess a rich cultural heritage quite different from that traditionally ascribed to Poles in Kosinski's previous works, and different, for that matter, from the image of Poles in the literary works of Algren, Williams, Styron, and Michener.

Kosky/Kosinski is the bearer of that tradition. In fact, many of his notes come directly from Polish historians, philosophers, poets, sociologists, and writers, from contemporary thinkers such as Kirly Sosn-kowski, Jan Szczepanski, and Roman Ingarden to classic authors such as Sienkiewicz, Wyspianski, Tuwim, and Conrad. Kosinski proudly parades his familiarity. At one point, when asked how he knows about Jan Lechon, "a well-known Polish poet known only to well-read Poles," Kosky replies, "Poetry belongs to everyone" (105). More important, perhaps, is that in Lechon (Leszek Serafinowicz), Kosinski sees an analogy between a fellow emigré and himself. Kosinski pursues this analogy in frequent and extended references to Joseph Conrad, introduced in the first four pages as a writer who (like Kosinski) had mastered written English without the equivalent mastery of sounds or idiomatic structures. Kosinski suggests that he too chose exile and a foreign language to further his art and, by extension, the Polish literary tradition. Had Conrad written in Polish, Kosky asks, "who would have read him either in Poland or in his neo-native England?" (305). Kosinski's comparisons with Conrad assume the form of patriotism at a distance, when he self-servingly quotes Conrad as saying that wherever he traveled over the seas, he was "never far away from his country . . . the leading principle of my life was to help Poland" (523).

Kosinski's reconstituted definition of Polishness includes Slavs and Jews in equal measure. He explains and defends the important place of Jews in Polish history and, surprisingly and tolerantly, sees Christian and Jewish cultural associations as integral to that history. On one occasion he cites Julian Tuwim, Alexander Wat, and Bruno Schulz as literary giants who *chose* the Polish language even though each of them could easily write in at least one other European language. Kosinski sees himself squarely within that literary tradition. "After all," he writes, "isn't Kosky, like Bruno Schulz, a direct descendant of the Ruthenian Polish Jewish relations with the word," signifying "a traditional narrative as well as narrative tradition?" (253). Kosinski additionally traces the success of American Jews to their Polish backgrounds and legacy. In short, the exiled, anonymous self becomes in *Hermit* the ethnically Polish Jewish writer and the standard-bearer of a multicultural literature.

Much effort and time in *Hermit* are also spent exonerating Poles from charges of historical anti-Semitism. Mending personal as well as cultural fences, Kosinski reminds his readers of "the unbroken chain of Polish-Jewish relations" (401), that Jews lived in Poland "longer than anywhere else except in Israel," that "for a thousand years they mixed freely with their non-Jewish fellow Ruthenians" (46), and that instances of hostility stemmed from "proximity not distance" and from "foreign-made" provocations (46). Quite unlike his frenzied accusations in *The Painted Bird,* Kosinski also defends Poland from charges of complicity in the Holocaust. Early in the novel, he reviews at length the general orders of the Nazis directed exclusively at Poles and notes that only in Poland was the sheltering and protecting of a Jew punishable by death: "And yet in spite of such dangers, thousands upon thousands of Jews like me survived the Holocaust thanks to their fellow Ruthenians" (46). He also documents the vast numbers of non-Jewish Poles tortured, enslaved, and murdered during the occupation, and he attacks versions of history which suggest that the Holocaust is a singularly Jewish event and that it could have occurred only in Poland, as Uris claims in *QB VII*. He cites by example Claude Lanzmann, "who by discrediting my entire nation is no longer a *lanzmann* to me" (526). In *Hermit*, Poland emerges as the prophetic, rightful resting place of the Jews during their exile, which ended with the transfer of Jews from Poland to "Eretz Yisroel. How else could it be?" (525).

Among other things, not the least of which is Kosinski's long-awaited reaction to the *Village Voice* controversy, *The Hermit of 69th Street* is ethnicity revisited and found good. Poland looks much better to Kosinski from the perspective of time and distance, although he remains sensitive to his portrayal of Poles in *The Painted Bird* and the early novels. As to the Polish perception that "you did your native country harm" (112), Kosinski suggests that this is a situation confronting many misunderstood writers. "It's been said before about Cooper and Wolfe, about Conrad and Tolstoy. About Ibsen and Pasternak" (112). Once again, Kosinski turns to Joseph Conrad in self-defense. Conrad was also maligned in Poland, Kosinski reminds us, only because he chose the English language "in order to best express what was inexpressible in his Polish soul" (306)—an interesting approach for one who could not bring himself to utter the word "Poland" in his fiction.

In *Pinball*, Kosinski took a giant step in the extended journey of the divided self in the form of Patrick Domostroy's vicarious return to Poland; and in *Hermit*, he continues this journey, this time through a dialogue about the necessary but perilous acknowledgment of Polishness as a prerequisite to the final step in the long journey home. For Kosinski this is no easy matter. He cites his thirty-year separation, the absence of any family, and the provocative nature of his fiction (the "escape motif" is his description) as barriers to his "return" to Poland and the ultimate integration of his cultural selves. How about going back to Ruthenia, "the spiritual country you and Conrad never left," Jay Kay asks himself near the end of the novel (529). In response, Kosinski notes practical difficulties: language, moving, employment, reputation. He also explains that he is exhausted both as a writer and a self. But when Kosinski quotes Sholem Asch's notion that Poland is named from the Hebrew Poh Lin, "Here shalt thou lodge," he gives good reason to believe that his own thirty-year's war with his native land is over and that his Polish, Jewish, and American selves are close to accommodation. When Kosinski, a recent chair of the American Foundation for Polish Jewish Studies, traveled through Warsaw, Lodz, and Krakow in the spring of 1988, *Hermit* had not yet appeared in print. Nonetheless, the reception he received, the willingness of the Poles to welcome him back into the national family and Kosinski's obvious pleasure in being there are mirrored in *Hermit*.

For Kosinski, as for Jerome Rothenberg, Poland is a state of mind, and ethnicity is a complex metaphor that includes socialist intimidation, war, the Holocaust, and exile, the cruelties of history, the problematics of a thousand years of shared Christian and Jewish community, and the personal vicissitudes of art, immigration, and cultural displacement. In many ways Kosinski's troubled protagonists are not unlike the American Jews of Isaac Singer or the Duluth-Superior Poles of Anthony Bukoski. What makes Kosinski's ethnic heroes so different and so difficult to assess is not so much the distance that separates them from home but rather the trepidations and terror of their own ethnicity. They have no connections with transplanted ethnic communities, no dialogue with their native country, no context in which to evaluate or understand their cultural past. Outside the usual framework of religion (Catholic or Jewish), peasant culture, traditional rituals of village practice and belief, Kosinski's Poles hardly look Polish at all. His only alternative is to draw upon the Polish literary-cultural tradition and the present, tragic circumstances of socialist, Jew-less, cold war Poland, a cruel mockery of its former self. Yet for the hundreds of thousand of Jewish and Christian Poles who have immigrated to the United States since World War II, Kosinski's experience in fact and in fiction represent the immediacy of contemporary Polishness in America. In addition, Kosinski's fiction, focusing on the slow, painful emergence of a displaced person who "becomes" a Pole, a Jew, and an American, places him in a pivotal position in contemporary representations of ethnicity in the works of Jewish, Polish, and other "American" writers. Given the direction of his work and the particular renunciation of the nonethnic self in *Hermit*, Kosinski, had he lived to write more, would have stretched ethnicity into yet different shapes.

7

THE GATES OF HEAVEN AND THE PAINS OF HELL

Jewish American Writers and Memories of Poland

*The Jews from the Kingdom of Poland do not forget whence they have come
and where lies the bones of their forefathers.* —SINKIEWICZ

*Even though there were pogroms and all kinds of trouble,
still I see the Polish side.* —I. B. SINGER

I. CULTURAL KINSHIP AND LITERARY GOODWILL

For almost one thousand years, Poland, today a relatively homogeneous society, contained sizable religious and racial minorities. One of the largest of these was Jews, whose numbers increased dramatically when King Casimir offered safe haven to Europe's Jews in the fourteenth century. Throughout the succeeding years, the relationship between Poles and Jews remained uncomfortable, as that in an estranged family where kin-ness and kindness are often mutually exclusive. Even now, when for the first time in modern history Jews and Poles no longer live side by side, the shadow of each lies fitfully upon the other.

After decades of relative silence, scholars and artists of various nationalities have begun to produce a full range of works on the Polish-Jewish experience—from the Memorial Book project, to Claude Lanzmann's *Shoah,* to Malgorzata Niezabitowska's *National Geographic* pictorial, "Remnants: The Last Jews of Poland," to Eva Hoffman's 1989 autobiography, *Lost in Translation,* to Iwona Irwin Zarecka's *Neutralizing Memory: The Jew in Contemporary Poland* (1989). In Poland, since the early 1980s and the heady rise of Solidarity, the silence has been broken by serious and seemingly urgent discussions of the Polish-Jewish experience. In 1983, for example, *Znak,* a leading Catholic journal published in Krakow, featured the topic, "The Jews in Poland and in the World: Catholicism-Judaism." A corresponding change in official policy has resulted in vigorous public discussion and the publication of such works as the fiction of Isaac Singer and Tadeusz

Sroka's *Israeli Diary.* Polish and Jewish scholars have also begun serious dialogue, as witnessed by the publication of *Polin: A Journal of Polish-Jewish Studies,* and by other initiatives in and outside of Poland. In her study, Irwin Zarecka characterized the postwar period in Poland as a "struggle for memory" from an official silence, to more recent efforts "to create a permanent space for the Jews in Poland's collective memory" (36). Irwin Zarecka's insights are effective not only in viewing the entire range of commentary on postwar Polish-Jewish relations but also in understanding the diverse yet persistent efforts of Jewish American writers to deal with Polish-Jewish connections.

Yiddish literature written in Poland before the war often reflects upon the multifaceted and yet hidden fabric of Polish-Jewish relations. In so doing, it introduces a theme that would later become the main concern of Jewish American writers: the obsession with identity in a non-Jewish world. Thus it is to Yiddish literature that we must briefly turn in order to understand the attitudes, images, and frame of reference toward Poles that would later surface, almost unconsciously, in American fiction in the works of Leon Uris, Saul Bellow, Philip Roth, Jerzy Kosinski, and others. This is not to suggest that Yiddish writers concerned themselves primarily with Slavic Christian culture, but as Chone Shmeruk points out, even in texts which have no Polish characters, "the attachment to the natural and human landscape of Poland is very tangible" (*Polin* 178). Tangible but not necessarily pleasant, the landscape of Poland is peopled with Slavs who represent the accumulation of years of bitterness and resentment. Typically, writers include a "maciek figure," a clumsy and stupid peasant who, as Shmeruk reminds us, "was commonly an object of contempt in Jewish society" (178). Other writers offered portraits of the porets (gentry) who, like the peasants from whom they are carefully distinguished, are also treated with wariness and scorn. Both Rashkin and Burshtin introduce oppressive "porets" who mistreat Jews and waste their own property. A number of writers document the routine mistreatment of Polish Jews by their Christian neighbors often in the form of the stereotypic "phenomenon" of stone-throwing children. Others, such as Isaac Joshua Singer, relied on what appear to be traditional narrative models that illustrate the dangers that await Jews, especially young women, who come into contact with Poles. Singer's short story "Blut" tells about the offspring of Jewish-Christian parents who ultimately meets a tragic death attributable to his mixed blood. Stereotypes of Poles, Jewish attitudes toward Slavic Christians, traditional prohibitions between Poles and Jews, instances of assimilation, and the transcendence of racial and religious bigotry—all would pass into the mainstream of American literature through the writings of Isaac B. Singer, himself a member of the Yiddish school of literature in prewar Poland.

Since World War II, Jews in Poland have continued to write about the life of a Jew in a Slavic Christian culture. These socialist writers, Brandys, Stryjkowski, Sandauer, and Rudnicki, deal primarily with the dilemma of the assimilated Polish-Jewish intellectual for whom the tragic memory of a lost culture and a realization of his own Jewishness collides with his commitment to the new Poland. As a result of their novels, the Jew, as Jan Blonski points out, has become more conspicuous in Polish literature than ever before (198). This irony, the appearance of Jews in the literature of a country rather satisfied to have lost its Jews, corresponds to a similar phenomenon in American literature where Poles, despite their disappearance as a distinct, recognizable ethnic minority, have become prominent in postwar Jewish American fiction.

Whether they are writing in Yiddish, Polish, or English, writers have recognized that the problem of Jewish identity, in Krakow or the Bronx, in Short Hills or Chicago, in inextricably linked to Poland, with the result that memories of Poland, Polish-Jewish relations, and the shadows of the Holocaust in Poland make up an important and substantial part of twentieth-century Jewish American fiction. Despite the wealth of excellent criticism on this latter topic, even the most careful and noted scholars—such as Leslie Fiedler in his study of *The Jew in American Literature* and Irving Howe in his penetrating introduction to the Jewish American short story—have overlooked the Polish-Jewish link. Howe's essay is especially interesting in this regard. At one point, he quotes from Eudora Welty's notable essay, "Place in Fiction," reminding us that "fiction depends for its life on place" (7), without considering that for some of the writers he discusses, that sense of place was—and to a degree still is—Poland. Such writers as Bernard Malamud, Cynthia Ozick, and Jerome Weidman have recognized that the claim of memory, the loneliness of the "outsider," and the crisis of Jewish cultural identity originate, to a great degree, in Polish villages and cities and in a thousand years of shared history.

Over a fifty-year period, Jewish American writers have employed Poles and the Polish landscape in ways that are both surprising and predictable, subtle and heavy-handed, compassionate and cruel, understandable and puzzling. At the same time, their literary treatment of Poles evolves through three fairly distinct periods—pre-Holocaust, Holocaust, and after—from generally sympathetic to overtly hostile to conciliatory. Oddly enough, as many writers turned their attention to "new" minorities—Chicanos, Native Americans, and women—Jewish

American writers kept alive the image of this older ethnic group. In their works, however, Poles were neither princes, peasants, nor proletarian whose mission was to regenerate the American landscape and alter national character. Instead, Poles became literary heavies: anti-Semites, symbols of darkness, social and moral inferiors—the enemy within in the works of Uris, Bellow, Roth, Singer, and Kosinski.

Prior to the 1930s, Jewish American writers rarely explored the Polish connection, although Isaac Friedman had dealt with Poles as early as 1901 in *By Bread Alone*. Interested in politics rather than in cultural history, Friedman paid little attention to the shared history of Poles and Jews or to the congruities of the Polish-Jewish experience. But in what amounts to a decade of renaissance for Polish literary ethnicity, four strikingly different novels appeared in the 1930s to set the direction of the Polish-Jewish literary relationship and to add yet another dimension to Polish literary selves: Edna Ferber's *American Beauty* (1931), Anzia Yezierska's *All I Could Never Be* (1932), Irving Fineman's *Hear Ye Sons* (1933), and Henry Roth's *Call It Sleep* (1934). In some ways these novels resist association. In the tradition of Abraham Cahan, Fineman writes about the crisis of Jewish identity, except that Fineman concerns himself much more with his life in eastern Europe. Anzia Yezierska also writes a transformation novel but defines her own ethnicity in Polish terms. Fineman turns back to the Old World; Yezierska rushes toward the New. *Call It Sleep* is seldom thought of as an "ethnic novel" despite the fact that the young protagonist must penetrate and reconcile the dual worlds of Judaism and Christianity in a novel in which everyone is ethnic and the catalyst is a young Polish American. Edna Ferber's novel, as we have already seen in the context of the immigrant on the land, is radically different from the others. It is a Jewish novel without Jews, an intra-ethnic work in which Polish-Jewish relations exist outside the text in the writer's attitude toward her material.

Despite their apparent diversity, all four must be regarded as essentially ethnic novels whose basic motivation is to reconcile European and American selves and to introduce and define ethnicity, primarily in the contrast of Jew and Pole. That four novelists of varying ability and somewhat different intentions would all write about Poles testifies to the important role that Jewish American writers play in the literary history of Poles and to a cultural instinct that has linked Poles and Jews during the last fifty years of American fiction. For one thing, they introduce the basic images, conventions, and attitudes toward Poles which would find their way into the works of more important postwar Jewish American writers, all of whom wrote about Poles in one way or another. For another, the rather liberal spirit of these 1930s works contrasts sharply with the treatment of Poles by some Jewish American writers at mid-century, suggesting that the Holocaust did much to alter the cultural balance of Poles and Jews in American literature as it did in American cultural life. None of these writers neglects the historical tension between Poles and Jews; yet all exhibit a sympathy and sense of kinship with their immigrant counterparts that marks the decade as one of curiosity, common cultural heritage, and relative goodwill.

For the most part, Irving Fineman is interested in the crisis of Jewish identity after transplant. To develop this theme, he contrasts the present-day circumstances of his aging narrator with the narrator's former life in Russian Poland. In the epilogue, Joseph, a sixty-eight-year-old, wealthy, New York lawyer, recites proudly his New World successes. His eldest daughter has a son at Harvard and a daughter at Smith. One son, Jacob, graduated from Columbia; another, Avrom, is a concert pianist; a third, David, was killed at San Mihiel; a fourth, Daniel, teaches at Princeton and marries a gentile. Here, Fineman tells his readers, is the promise of America fulfilled. Even so, like David Levinsky who cannot forget the "young Hassid of my youth," Fineman's narrator exists simultaneously in two cultures unable to forsake either. Like Levinsky, he turns more and more to the world of memory, to his Old World self, and to his days in eastern Poland. In this fictional autobiography, therefore, we learn much about life in the Pale and something about Russian Poland in the last half of the nineteenth century. In contrast to Yezierska and Levinsky, Fineman provides insights into the day-to-day relations of Poles and Jews. Consequently, *Hear Ye Sons,* rich in background information about two of America's largest minorities, is an especially important "ethnic" novel.

With one exception, Poles appear only in the background, yet they are as much a part of Fineman's landscape as the Vistula. He emphasizes the shared tragic history of Polish Jews when he talks about Russian oppression in Poland and cites specific acts of discrimination against Jew and Catholic alike. He is careful to associate anti-Semitism with the Russians and with the official policy of Tsar Alexander III, whose pogroms forced so many Jews to leave for America. Moreover, with a sense of sadness, he points out that Russian behavior toward Jews has succeeded in influencing Poles. On one occasion he explains that "the Poles with whom the Jews had lived for centuries in peace were learning from the hated Russians to despise them [the Jews]" (42).

Hear Ye Sons shares certain of the characteristics of Yiddish literature of the period, especially in regard to Slavs. Concerned primarily with Jewish daily life, Fineman's characters are in many ways isolated, cut off from the Slavic world. They seem unaware of either Polish culture or nationhood or even the fact that they live in a country called

Poland. In addition, their posture toward the Poles is one of superiority. In a chapter called "The Peasants," the narrator introduces his neighbors as backward, poor, coarse, ignorant people. They are "slow moving," "calm," "stolid," "phlegmatic," "seldom stirred to passion." He sees them as children who accept life without speculation, with a faith that "all that is, must be so" (190). Ironically, the Poles are described as foreigners, "others" with whom Jews are forced to interact from time to time. The analogy of Jews and Poles to parents and children not only establishes the narrator's tone but also characterizes Polish behavior in the Jewish mind and, perhaps most important, justifies Jewish behavior in their commerce with Poles. Fineman explains, for example, that shopkeepers resorted to deceitful means when dealing with the peasants, "substituting the smaller Russian pound or yard for the Polish measure" (193). At the same time, he suggests that these actions were prompted by the "childish greed" of the Poles who tried to demand lower prices. Although Joseph, the narrator, refuses to deal dishonestly with his Polish customers, his own view remains that of a parent toward children.

When Joseph introduces individual Poles, he does so with sensitivity and respect, illustrating, without seeming to notice, that the childlike quality of the Pole might be a mask used to their own advantage and, on occasion, to the advantage of their Jewish friends. Fineman devotes an entire chapter, "The Wojt," to illustrate Polish integrity and the cordial relations that often existed between Jewish and Christian Poles. The village mayor (the Wojt), Jan Ossiponski, although faced with possible punishment, refuses to indict his neighbor Joseph when Russian officials levy a large, punishing tax on Joseph solely because he is Jewish. Fineman emphasizes Ossiponski's dignity, courage, and wisdom throughout the ordeal which ends happily when the Wojt employs his supposed ignorance, his childlike naiveté, as a tactic to fend off the Russian official. The narrator adds other examples to show how Poles befriended their Jewish neighbors at the risk of their own safety. When, for example, Joseph decides to leave for America, Jan's son acts as his guide and protector on the way to the border.

When all is said and done, Fineman is still ambivalent about Poland. The mass of Poles are inferior, but some stand tall. Times of oppression alternate with times of peace and prosperity. Poland is home despite it all. As Joseph crosses the border his last glimpse of his homeland is wistful, melancholy, yet he knows that Poland can never stir in equal measure the hearts of Jewish and Christian Poles. He thinks of Slavic Jan who found peace and security on his own acres. "But what was this land to a Jew though he had lived for centuries in it," he asks (300).

Fineman's answer to this apparently rhetorical question is as ambivalent as his portrait of Poles. Although Joseph, the younger Fineman, clearly implies a negative answer to his question, the other Fineman, the sixty-eight-year-old narrator, tells us something quite different. Despite his New World success, his talented, prosperous, and assimilated family, despite his lavish wealth and Fifth Avenue address, the narrator's autobiography is almost exclusively about his European self—about his memories of life in Poland. This, his story makes clear, means more to him than all his New World achievements.

Fineman's forgotten novel draws upon the immigrant introduced by Antin, Cahan, and others, but in its portrayal of Slavic Poles, it more resembles prewar Yiddish fiction. In both cases, it serves as a valuable text to evaluate the changing image of Poland in later American fiction and as a counterpoint to a very different kind of transformation novel, Anzia Yezierska's *All I Could Never Be*.

Yezierska's New World self also has Polish roots. She grows up in a small village outside Warsaw. Although Poles live on the edge of Jewish life, her contacts with the Slavic world are enough to make her fluent in Polish, as we later learn, and to fix in her memory the landscape, rural life, and activities of her peasant neighbors. She remembers the broad fields, straw thatched huts, patchy gardens that make up "her country." Whatever antagonism exists emanates from poverty and from family disappointments. She leaves no doubt that her heritage is Polish and Jewish.

At the same time, the narrator concentrates on her attempts to transcend both ethnicity and nationality, a reflection of Yezierska's own youthful desire "to lose her heritage as swiftly as possible" (Kessler-Harris 258). While the novel thus emphasizes the narrator's New World growth, she is constantly pulled back to her Polish-Jewish heritage. In fact, Polishness in the novel is a pivotal point between her drive toward individual realization, a process which demands deethnicization as she sees it, and her equally strong wish to recover and preserve her ethnic self, rooted in Poland. As a result, the ethnic self is never far away. One of the longer episodes deals with the heroine's part in a sociological study of Chicago's Polish neighborhood. She is employed as a translator because she knows the language and culture, but she quickly assumes the role of gallant protector of ethnicity from the bloodless onslaught of the sociologist. For one who fled her native land, her sympathetic and romantic defense of Polish culture is puzzling but apparently sincere. She describes her former neighbors as "a people burning up with a million volatile ideas" (37) and accuses the research team of knowing "nothing about the heart of the Poles" (109). She visits Polish American organizations to explain the study but more so to revisit her self. As she explains to her fellow sociologists, "you've got to live our lives to feel us with the heart" (110).

Although we learn little about Polish national character, Yezierska's identification with Poland ("her country" "our lives") serves her own political interests and personal needs. From time to time, Yezierska's proletarian sympathies enter into the plot. She frets about the workers' struggle for wages, education, housing, and recreation in America and "all over the world." She complains that the cost of one bottle of champagne could buy milk for an entire block of tenement children, and she grows angry when she meets an unemployed Pole "reduced by the cruelty of existence to a mere hunt for a job" (94). The Poles, it's clear, are representative workers and ethnics to Yezierska. They are, moreover, an example of deethnicization that, in Yezierska's mind, assumes cultural and personal significance. They, like she, have lost their national heritage without having gained an American one.

Eventually, she returns to her Jewish-Polish self. Polish memories intrude: synagogues, the Day of Atonement, her father. She recognizes that she had grown ashamed of "my manners, my background . . . what I was" (192). All comes together at the end in the person of a wandering unemployed laborer, half-Russian and half-Polish whom Anzia befriends and learns to love. Pavlovich is all she ever wanted: the Old World in the New, a second father, her Polish past, the worker hero. He brings together all her conflicting and divergent interests and yet helps her to look beyond the narrowness of ethnicity and of self. His Polish heart is large; it embraces all. It connects the world of the twenty-eight-year-old who changes her name from Hattie Mayer to Anzia Yezierska and the middle-aged heroine of *All I Could Never Be,* who sees that her cultural identity is indisputably that of Jewish *Pole.*

At a glance, Yezierska's contemporary, Edna Ferber, seems all that Yezierska's narrator ever wanted to be, a popular author who moved beyond ethnicity. Few today even know about Ferber's Jewish background; and her pluralistic, melting-pot novels appear to be nothing less than celebrations of Americanness. However, certain of Ferber's novels are as ethnic as Yezierska's, and her publication of *American Beauty* one year before Yezierska's "Polish" novel ties her to the ethnic novel in general and to the Polish-Jewish tradition in particular. For Ferber, ethnicity is important only as a precondition to assimilation and the emergence of the American new-man, in much the same way that Henry Ford's education programs of the 1920s were designed to eliminate the Old World self. For Ferber, ethnicity is best when viewed from a distance and when it serves as the raw material from which a new and decidedly nonethnic American can emerge. Such is the case in

American Beauty, a depression novel like Fineman's, that emphasizes the old-fashioned qualities of perseverance, ingenuity, the land, and the resulting good fortune that would once again be America's. To develop this theme in *American Beauty,* Ferber chose to write about Poles even though she had no Polish background or direct contact with Polish culture—although some Poles lived in rural Wisconsin where Ferber grew up and others had settled in New England which she came to know as her adopted home.

It was not so much Poles, however, but a recognizable ethnic minority that Ferber needed to enable her to celebrate the American experience. She presented this experience through the biblical typology that had already become a literary mainstay in American letters. Consequently, in Ferber's hands the Poles become yet another version of the chosen people who, seeking a new life, cultivate and invigorate the American Eden. When Ferber writes about the Poles in this way, she describes them with dignity and stature. They bring to a deteriorating New England landscape vitality, industry, and a love of land. And largely through their efforts the blighted New England farm economy, a microcosm of depression America, blooms once again "as it had not since the splendid days" of the eighteenth century (244). The Poles, representing the immigrant in general, are an example to Americans who have turned away from the land and from traditional values.

When Ferber moves away from the mythic approach to talk about Polish character and culture, romanticism gives way to realism. She displays an ambivalence similar to Fineman's, although her evaluation lacks Fineman's historical support; that is to say the narrator gives no reasons for her critical comments and seems to have no knowledge of the European peasant. Her tone is often patronizing and superior. On one occasion, Ferber praises Temmie Oakes, the Anglo heroine of the novel, for her articulation, bone structure, carriage, look of freedom, and breeding; then she quickly adds, "no Polish peasant stock here" (247). Even after their forty years of labor in the fields and factories of America, the Polish Olszaks are curiously described as having "changed little, these peasant Poles" (270).

The closer Ferber looks, the less she seems to like ethnicity as far as Slavs are concerned. She complains that sex for Poles is "nothing special"; it lacks romance. She is quick to suggest that violence and alcoholism are Polish characteristics; Ondie Olszak, for example, dies in an auto accident after excessive drinking. And Ferber is especially critical of Polish women, whom she finds to be niggardly, gossipy, mean-spirited, and domineering (232). She, like earlier commentators, is shocked that Polish women work in the fields "like cattle." Her antipathy lands especially hard on Polcia, Ondie Olszak's first wife, a decent, hard-working woman who faced the impossible with courage—a run-down farm, a large family, and a new country. In Ferber's eyes, however, Polcia is a slovenly, dirty woman who "likes manual labor, who pitches hay like a man, and who except for cooking, even lacks household graces" (140).

Despite this mean-spirited portrayal of the Polish peasant woman, Ferber, for the most part, writes glowingly about Polish immigrant experiences. She hesitates, however, when she observes the values of the second generation which, in a hurry to embrace urban materialism, leaves the land. With little education and few cultural standards, the second generation emerges as a vulgar, short-sighted working class which neither retains the Polish customs of their parents nor adopts the best of New England culture. One son, Stas Olszak, leaves the farm to marry a Polish town girl and finds a job in the packing room of a factory. Eventually, he succeeds in acquiring three children, a radio, a car, a house on credit, and a "good job" in the chemical works, which quickly dissipates his health. Ferber also follows the fortunes of the Olszak family through Rozia Olszak. Like her brother, Rozia longs for the city and finds a Polish American to wed. When Ferber describes Rozia's wedding, she unmasks her feelings toward an emerging ethnic-American culture. Rozia's is a "vulgar wedding"; nothing about it is tasteful or Polish. Instead, she imitates the tacky grandeur of middle-class America, "gleaned from movies and Sunday roto gravures" (290). With her ring bearer, flower girl, long white gloves, tiara, and the matching outfits of the sizable wedding party, Rozia proudly shows that she is as "American as any of them" (293). Ferber continues her satirical portrait over the course of a few pages, rather surprising considering the fact that Rozia quickly disappears from the novel. She looks a second time at the wedding group, describing "the bare arms, the bare bosoms, the white kid gloves, the huge wilted bouquets, the cheap glass tiaras, the tulle" and how, after the church ceremony, all "were off to Kosciuszko Hall. The new Poles" (295). Ferber is clearly unhappy with those Poles who have deserted their "place" on the land and migrated to the city. Consequently, her portrait of the second generation clashes with the biblical typology that she uses to describe the immigrants themselves. At the same time, Ferber's unflattering profiles of Rozia's wedding and the character of the peasant, especially women, reflect not only her own ambivalence toward ethnic America, but the general views of Americans in the 1930s.

Ferber's dilemma is America's: how to absorb the raw ethnic vitality, exuberance, and physical stamina and to reject "undesirable" qualities, i.e., religion, peasant temperament, physical features, and so on. In *American Beauty,* Ferber's response is to blend Slav and Anglo-Saxon, a solution which perhaps helps to explain her criticism of Stas and Rozia who marry fellow Poles. Orrange Oakes is yet another matter. Brother to Stas and Rozia, the son of Olszak, the Pole, and Tamar Oakes, his New England second wife, Orrange is Polish neither in name nor in appearance. Temmie calls him "an Oakes from head to foot" (237). What is more, he bears no Slavic features. With his "long English head [and] aquiline nose," he resembles the seventeenth-century patriarch of the Oakes family. In contrast to Stas and Rozia, Orrange is destined to marry into an old, Anglo, New England family, the Baldwins. The implication is that in another generation, ethnicity will have disappeared completely—in the same sense that Ferber's own ethnicity dissolved into her literary image as a writer of middle America.

Although not herself an immigrant like Fineman or Yezierska, Edna Ferber also wrote about ethnicity in America and, like them, she shows an ambivalence about cultural pluralism. In *Giant*, for example, it is the Mexican child who is finally accepted by the Anglo-Texas family and not vice versa. That her ambivalence toward Poles is attributable to her Jewish origins remains a moot question. What her novel, *American Beauty*, and Fineman's show is that Jewish writers of varying degrees of ethnicity tended to portray Poles with a remarkable consistency in point of view. Their examination is, by and large, evenhanded—a balance of praise and criticism, of compassion and complaint.

Henry Roth's 1934 novel *Call It Sleep* points in yet another direction toward the more sophisticated ways in which Jewish American writers would develop the Polish connection in decades to come. Roth's novel, immersed in the intricacies of Jewish life on the Lower East Side and in Brooklyn during the first quarter of the century, seems to have no "Polish theme" at all. However, the often subtle references to Poles, Poland, and things Polish constitute a sizable and significant aspect. These references indicate the assumed interconnectedness of Polish-Jewish life and suggest an end to the short-lived innocence of this literary relationship as it appears in the early 1930s.

Although Roth presumes an understanding of the historical relationship of Poles and Jews, he avoids explanations, shifting this obligation to the reader. As a result, the Polish-Jewish theme enters offhandedly and with some degree of confusion. The whole matter surfaces in references to the Schearl family life in Europe, in their belief that Austria is their European home, and in the inevitable assumption by the reader that the Schearls are Austrian Jews. David's mother even buys a painting because it reminds her "of Austria my home" (72). However, the villages they come from, Servik and Veljish, are certainly not Austrian, and the language they speak is not German but Polish. In fact, Polish appears to be a first language to which they turn instinctively.

When matters are too delicate for David's ears, mother and aunt use a language that David can identify but cannot understand. "There was that Polish again" (166), he remarks to indicate his frustration and their clever ways. When Aunt Bertha grows vexed, she bays "some Polish phrases at the ceiling" (192), Roth tells us, although he does not reproduce Polish in the text. Roth never explains why the seemingly Austrian Schearls speak Polish or how David knows that the foreign language that he hears is Polish, but perhaps history supplies the answer. The most reasonable explanation is that the Schearls had emigrated from a Slavic town situated in part of Poland annexed by Austria in the late eighteenth century and that they had come to regard and identify themselves as Austrian. This phenomenon is illustrated in the statistics of thousands of Poles emigrating from Polish national territories controlled by other European nations. In the novel, Roth ignores this historical complexity for reasons not apparent. The effect is to diffuse a subject that is obviously important to Roth since he returns often to this historical connection. The Schearls, for example, make offhanded references to their former village neighbors who, though unidentified, appear to be Polish peasants, described as "vacant lumps with great shoulders and a nose on them like a split pea" (43). Moreover, the Old World sin of the Schearl family is that David's mother committed an indiscretion with Ludwig, the village organist. Despite his German name, Ludwig may in fact be Polish. Genya remembers that he participated in processions when a "Polish townsman died," an unlikely event for an Austrian church official in nineteenth-century occupied Poland. Equally unlikely would have been the possibility that Poles and Austrians shared the same church. Nonetheless, Ludwig's nationality is inconclusive.

The strong possibility that David's mother had a youthful indiscretion with a Polish Catholic may help to explain the characterization of Leo Dugovka, David's boyhood friend and antagonist. That David would seek out a playmate and that that playmate would introduce David to the mysteries of life seems natural enough. That Dugovka would be a Polish boy living in a Jewish neighborhood is more problematic. Roth's decision to characterize David's antagonist as "Polish" makes sense, however, when considered in the context of Genya's guilt and the Schearl European background.

Leo Dugovka's function is to introduce David into the non-Jewish world, into sexuality, and into Christianity in order to drive home the inexplicable and alien features of the "host culture." Roth does this by choosing an ethnic whose religion, earthiness, and otherness had already been marked in American culture and in the day-to-day contact of Pole and Jew in Eastern Europe. In their first encounter, Dugovka's challenging greeting, "I'm a Polish American, you're a Jew ain'cha!", recalls immediately the separation of Old World national groups and the Schearls' European origins. Subsequently David learns about Christianity, more specifically Polish Catholicism, as it is filtered through the eyes of a youthful Polish American and his immigrant working-class family. David is impressed, bewildered even, by the rosaries, scapulars, and crosses he sees in the Dugovka apartment. And Leo's explanation of the crucifixion and Christ's light drives David near to suicide. On a human level, Leo breaks the bond of friendship by betraying David's trust and confidence in his fellow man, and David's disappointment mirrors Genya's own European tragedy and the general predicament of the Schearls in Eastern Europe. On all sides, the Schearls appear to have been betrayed by their "neighbors," the Poles.

Roth spends little time exploring Polish culture or Polish-Jewish relations in the Old World or New, and the Polish theme disappears rather easily into the fabric of *Call It Sleep*. The Polish presence makes it clear, however, that troubling thoughts about Poles were just below the surface.

Lester Cohen's *Coming Home* (1945), discussed previously as a proletarian novel, is also important as a transition between novels about Poles and Jews written before the war and the postwar works that depict a relationship radically jarred by the Holocaust. Although Cohen takes a global view of politics and the individual, he does so by concentrating on ethnic Americans, more particularly by weaving together the fortunes of Poles and Jews in ways that make the novel something more than proletarian fiction. His choice of these two groups as representative ethnics suggests his intention to draw upon the long-standing interdependency of Jews and Poles in Eastern Europe as well as in America. At the same time, he signals dramatic changes in the ways Jewish American writers would make use of Poles.

This change is evident in the contrast between the Slavic Witowskis and the Jewish lawyer, Ben Jordan, who takes up their cause. Despite the Witowskis' role as class victims and downtrodden workers, Cohen has difficulty accepting them or seeing anything redeeming in their ethnic makeup. His tone is, in fact, disapproving and condescending. The Poles lack grace, bearing, and self-reliance. Stella, the daughter, has neither education nor ambition; her father speaks a comical English as he mostly grunts about the house; the mother's face, the color of "Polish earth," is "sorta brown" with a sunken nose "like plenty Polish people had." The family, whose behavior is regulated by gossip, the Catholic church, and what the neighbors think, possesses an inferiority complex implicit in Stella's complaint that people avoid her because "I am a Polack" (8). Even when Stella is raped and her father unjustly fired, the Witowskis will not assert themselves. Only Anglos and Jews have the conviction to fight for human rights in *Coming Home*.

If the Witowskis are typically Polish, Ben Jordan is typically Jewish. What this also appears to mean is that he is liberal, well educated, motivated by human concerns and social justice. In contrast to the Poles, he sees the need for collective action to produce change. He is a populist with a mission: to lift the oppressed, the Slavs in this case, to unite the workers, to achieve social and economic equality, to redress wrongs. Unlike the Witowskis, however, he is not confused about his heritage. His uncle Borel has taught him about the golden age when "we used to be shepherds, we tended flocks, we played lutes" (178).

The Edenic past is quickly swept away, however, by Borel's reference to the war where "we lost five million Jews, maybe more" (178) and by Cohen's equally abrupt and perplexing denunciation of Witowski, whom he accuses of anti-Semitism, although Witowski never says or does anything to justify the accusation. Instead Cohen looks into Witowski's mind and sees that "when Hitler was killing Jews, Witow-ski looked upon it with some amusement. . . . But now that Hitler had butchered Poles, he had a fierce hatred for him, the hatred . . . of one betrayed" (39). Occurring early in the novel without further elabora-tion at this point or later, Cohen's indictment appears to be almost a reflex action, one that would be repeated elsewhere in Jewish American fiction. The intrusion of history into fiction, particularly the Holocaust, foreshadows a major development in American literary history of Poles.

For Lester Cohen, ethnicity is a double-edged sword—praiseworthy, in the Jewish Jordan, problematic in the Slavic Witowskis. Cohen's proletarian impulses lead him beyond ethnicity toward Edna Ferber's ethnically integrated populist America. But ultimately Cohen is unable to see inside either his character's ethnicity or his own. It probably never even occurred to him to reverse the roles of his characters and to present a liberal, Polish lawyer, helping an anti-Catholic, backward Jew from Odessa.

2. SETTLING THE SCORE

By the 1950s, American fiction had become obsessed with the problem of identity. Tony Tanner describes the central question of the period as: Can the hero "find a freedom which is not a jelly and can he establish an identity which is not a prison?" (19). Nowhere is this more pronounced than in the works of Saul Bellow, Bernard Malamud, and Philip Roth, whose heroes are additionally burdened by ethnicity and exile, themes introduced earlier in the Yiddish literature of Poland. Citing *Herzog*

and Portnoy as particular examples, Tanner points out that the protagonists of Jewish novels are "freighted with memories and specula-
tions based on retrospection" and that they seek a psychological escape
from the past, "to disburden themselves of memories which paralyze,
in some cases, present consciousness" (296–99). Roth perhaps spoke
for all when he said in 1969 that he wanted to "kick a lot of the past"
(Junker 47). And his comic protagonist Portnoy speaks for many of the
heroes of Jewish American fiction when he says, "If I could be somehow sprung from the settling of scores! the pursuit of dreams! from this
hopeless, senseless loyalty to the long ago" (247).

By the time of Portnoy/Roth's announced desire for revenge against
the ghosts of the past, writers from Norman Mailer to Isaac Singer to
Leon Uris had already demonstrated that for many Jewish writers, the
ghosts of the past resided in Europe, particularly in Poland where a
unique culture vanished in the smoke of Oswiecim and the rubble of
Warsaw. As the world came to realize the details of the Holocaust,
accusing fingers were leveled at the Poles for their passive acceptance of
the fate of their citizens of Jewish descent and their sometimes regretta-
ble behavior. Correspondingly, the image of Poland in the mind of the
Jewish American writers was radically altered from a generally sympathetic picture of Poles as fellow victims of history (Fineman), as re-
builders of the New World (Ferber), or as working-class examples of
the need for socioeconomic reform (Cohen) to a portrait of a coarse,
spiteful, anti-Semitic people who were to some degree responsible for
Jewish suffering. In effect, the Pole became a symbol of the duplicity
and hostility of the Christian world and of the complexities of Old
World memories.

Despite Irving Howe's warning that Jewish American writers must
avoid the tendency toward "mean-spirited repudiation" (5), Rafael
Scharf makes it clear as late as 1986 that Jewish attitudes toward Poles
were too strong to escape recrimination. Writing in *Polin*, Scharf asks,
"Did it ever occur to a Pole that in a neighboring town, or for that
matter on the very same street, something was happening that could
engage his attention and deserved his interest? Not the least! The
Jewish population was commonly regarded as a 'dark continent,' backward and primitive, evoking feelings of aversion and repugnance"
(272). "Wrongs are engraved in stone," Scharf adds, "and kindness in
sand" (275). But beginning with the American publication of Isaac
Singer's *The Family Moskat* (1948) and Norman Mailer's *The Naked
and the Dead* (1948), Polish wrongs were to be engraved in American
fiction. Singer, who will be discussed at length later, has written more
comprehensively and with more authority about Poles and Jews in
Europe and America than any other writer. What is more, his works

best characterize the effort of Jewish American writers to come to terms with the memory of Poland. Although Singer, as he explains it, tried to write a literary history of the Jewish people in Poland, he also contributed significantly to the literary discussion of Poles. This is also true of writers who do not write about Poland or even consciously about Poles and Jews but whose works collectively suggest that Poland is never far from memory even in novels ostensibly about Jewishness in America. Norman Mailer, Saul Bellow, Bernard Malamud, and Philip Roth—all provide portraits of Americans of Polish descent in their postwar fiction, a commentary which when taken together comprises a puzzling page of literary history that can only be explained in the context of Jewish-Polish relations and as a literary effort to come to terms with the ambiguities of the Jewish experience in Poland.

Five years after *The Naked and the Dead,* Saul Bellow in his picaresque novel *The Adventures of Augie March* (1953) continues the dialogue between Jews and Poles begun by Mailer, despite obvious changes in setting and subject. Set largely in 1930s Chicago, the novel records the life of a young, lower-class Jew living in a racially and ethnically mixed neighborhood. Given the setting, it is not surprising that Augie might interact with Poles. Strictly speaking, however, Bellow's Poles are not so much people as they are nightmares in the Jewish imagination. We see them through the disturbed vision of Augie and his family who exhibit the kind of wariness toward their historical neighbors that is implicit in Cohen's *Coming Home.*

Bellow introduces the Poles very early in the novel, apparently to establish boundaries, set the tone, and identify the enemy. "I'll mention the Poles," Augie says, "and the swollen, bleeding hearts on every kitchen wall, the pictures of saints, baskets of death flowers tied at the door, communion, Easters, and Christmases. And how sometimes we were chased, stoned, bitten, and beat up for Christ-killers . . ." (12). Augie's comments indicate that he knows more about Poles than Bellow tells us. Augie has obviously visited Polish homes, learned about cultural practices, noted religious holidays, and formed strong opinions. Having introduced no Polish characters, Bellow's early comments ostensibly serve to establish them as a negative symbol of the Christian world.

Throughout *Augie March,* Bellow draws a line between the Jewish ethnic self and the ethnic other who—through the threat of intermarriage, violence, and economic pressures—represents forces the Jewish self must continually combat. Augie feels especially betrayed when his neighborhood friend, Stashu Kopecs, joined the "fun" as Polish thugs led by Moonya Staplanski, just out of reform school, beat him up. Augie is bewildered that ethnicity prevails over friendship, although the reader knows that what Bellow really means is that Old World anti-Semitism is stronger than newly acquired melting-pot tolerance. However, Augie's antagonism also has historical roots, passed on through Grandma Lausch who often refers to Poles in order to measure disaster. She abuses Augie's brother, Simon, for dating a "Polish" girl and warns Augie that if his school record doesn't improve, he "can go like a Polack and work in the stockyards" (29). At another point her feelings intensify when she lashes out at Simon and Augie: "Maybe you'd enjoy being an uncle to a bastard by your brother for a Polish girl with white hair and explain to her stockyards father. . . . He'd murder you with a sledgehammer, like an ox, and burn down the house" (52). Why Grandma makes such comparisons and where her hatred of Poles originates, Bellow does not explain. We can only assume, as in Augie's case, that her statements reflect Old World grievances and New World suspicions that frame the actions and attitudes of Simon and Augie and Bellow himself.

Bellow, in fact, frequently expresses antagonism that can only be attributed to the historical reservoir of history. Almost always his Poles are contraries, formidable opponents, reminders of Old World distinctions transformed into New World rivalries. When Einhorn tries to make Nails into a boxer, it is Jaworski, a Pole, who abruptly ends Nails's career. When the commissioner rents one of his stores to a Polish barber, he must tolerate the scorn from Betzhevski's "raw winter eyes." And when Augie and Simon go to "Bohunk" street to sell coal to dealers named Hrapek, Drodz, Matucynski, we are reminded of Fineman's dealings with the peasants in *Hear Ye Sons*. Once again it is the Jewish merchant who must entertain, flatter, and drink "piwa" before the peasant will agree to buy. At yet another point, Bellow provides an interesting comparison of two of the March's housekeepers, one Polish, one Irish. Molly is remembered as a "strong, lean woman, about thirty-five, who slept in the kitchen . . . and whispered or sang out to us when we came home late" (129). Sablonka, on the other hand, is remembered as the one who disliked them. Augie describes her as a "slow-climbing, muttering, mob-faced, fat, mean, pious, widow who was a bad cook besides" (129).

As Augie's adventures lead him away from his Chicago neighborhood and immediate ethnic conflicts, the Poles disappear as well. Late in the novel, however, Bellow refers once more to Poles when Augie meets Clem Tambow and they reminisce about the past and their grammar-school class with Mrs. Minsick. Tambow's memories are bitter and spiteful. He hated that "lousy classroom . . . poor punks full of sauerkraut and bread with pig's feet, with immigrant blood and washday smells and kielbasa and home-brew beer" (435). Tambow's tirade, directed as much at his own ethnic self as at Poles, contrasts sharply with Augie, who by this time has grown "aware of man's fallibility," as Eisinger sees it, and "has declared for love" (342). Having reached a degree of accommodation with himself, with his own ethnic roots, Augie remembers Mrs. Minsick as a teacher who offered the children the dream of a world of flowers. Thus, Augie's harsh view of Poles gives way to the fond memory of a Polish elementary school teacher who, apparently, had also declared for love.

In subsequent works, Saul Bellow would continue to intellectualize the Jewish experience and to universalize the ethnicity introduced in *Augie* without employing Poles as characters. In *Augie March*, however, he introduced the struggle toward accommodation that would characterize postwar Jewish American fiction in regard to Poland. Even more than Saul Bellow, Bernard Malamud is occupied with ethnicity. As Philip Roth points out, however, Malamud's Jews are not those of New York or Chicago. "They are a kind of invention, a metaphor to stand for certain human possibilities" ("Writing American Fiction" 602). Malamud's characters exist free of time and place; they are the stuff of cultural history. His 1967 novel about Jews in Russia, *The Fixer,* suggests that the nightmare of the Jewish experience in Eastern Europe is never far from his consciousness. Of Yakon Bok in *The Fixer,* Malamud says, "The past was a wound in his head" (14). This "wound" is present even in Malamud's novels with American settings such as *The Assistant* (1957), which contains ethnic and historical curiosities seemingly unrelated to the plot concerns of Maurice Bober and Frank Alpine. In this novel, Malamud transcends narrow definitions of Judaism, suggesting that all who suffer, whose vision is tragic, are Jewish. Is Frank Alpine a Jew? Don't ask, Malamud replies. Nonetheless, *The Assistant* is decidedly a novel about ethnicity in America, complicated in the particular case of Jewish Americans by Polish-Jewish history.

The novel takes place in urban America where the Bobers, like the March family, live among other ethnics. Nick Fuso, an Italian garage mechanic, lives upstairs; two Norwegians open a rival grocery around the corner; and a Greek boy passes anonymously through the plot. In the first paragraph, even before we properly meet the Bobers, Malamud introduces another ethnic, an old Polish woman who comes to the Bober store each day at 6:00 A.M. to buy one hard roll for three cents. She is always Bober's first customer; what is more, Bober seems to open the store at 6:00 A.M. just for her since he appears never to have other customers at that early hour. The woman is impatient; it is 6:10 and she has had to wait; Bober is apologetic as he kindly slices the hard roll, wraps it, and collects the meager sum from the "sour-faced, gray-haired

Poilisheh huddled there" (7). The Poilisheh, we come to learn, reappears in the novel just as she has appeared at Bober's door throughout the fifteen years he has owned the grocery. At first it appears that the woman is nothing more than another detail in an ethnic landscape in much the same way as Fuso, the Norwegians, and the Greek boy. Despite her brief appearances, however, she is more important, because as a Pole she assumes in Malamud's eyes, and in the Bober's, a historical dimension. She is part of Bober's history and identity which rankles and irritates but which Bober must bear and accept. Thus the Pole and the Jew stand as an allegory of Old World dependencies and antagonisms which Bober inherits from history. As Tony Tanner says of Bober, "History has very much happened to him, even his newspaper is yesterday's" (327). Likewise, the Poilisheh has also "happened" to Bober and, ironically, continues to happen in the present—and the future.

Bober's task—the acceptance of past and present—is made more difficult because the Polish woman is not easy to like. Malamud's negative portrayal of her leaves no doubt. Sour-faced and unkempt, she shows no appreciation that Bober rises early to open just for her. Rather she expects this from him just as he too assumes it is his duty. They reenact Old World roles of merchant and peasant, dependent yet suspicious, civil yet wary. Malamud calls attention to her "quick beady eyes" and her lack of grace. Even Alpine grows to dislike her. He resents the Polish "dame" and her "beady eyes," calling her the "Polish nut" at one point. Despite the fact that she has apparently been a regular customer for fifteen years, no conversation occurs between her and Bober, not even the usual pleasantries. The Bobers don't even know her name.

Malamud, however, supplies enough textual clues to suggest that the Poilisheh is more than an anonymous passerby in the lives of the Bobers and that they know more about her than is apparent. They know, for example, that she works in a laundry and that she has a dog named Polaschaya. When Ida Bober abruptly refers to her as "die antisemitke" (29), we sense both the role she plays in their lives and her function in Malamud's novel. Quickly Morris adds that "she had come with it from the old country, a different kind of anti-Semitism from in America" (29). Malamud at this point has no need to create sympathy for the Bobers since he has already done so through their family history, the hold-up, and the example of neighbor Fuso sneaking off to buy his groceries elsewhere. He uses the conversation to supply a context for the fictional relationship of Pole and Jew. We come to understand that the Poilisheh is Bober's fate, his obligation as a Jew. He must be deferential, polite, subservient because this, his role in Europe, must be reenacted throughout history, just as she seems destined to be what she is—at least to Morris, who suspects that "she needled him a little by asking for a 'Jewish roll' or a 'Jewish pickle'" (29).

The burden of history is transferred to Alpine when he replaces Bober in the story and assumes his new identity as a Jew. Curiously, he too adopts a suspicious stance toward his adopted Old World rival. At the same time, he becomes subservient to her daily demand for a hard roll. In one of the last scenes, we see him slicing and wrapping the role as Bober had done before him, and we see her insisting that Alpine serve her on her terms at 6 A.M. She, indifferent, insistent, "anti-semitke," has become Frank's historical burden as he becomes absorbed into the complex history of Jews and Poles.

Some ten years later in *Portnoy's Complaint* (1969), Philip Roth added another scene to the developing drama of Poles and Jews in fiction. In *Letting Go* (1962) and *Goodbye Columbus* (1964), Roth had written about the demands of ethnicity in a country rapidly moving away from Old World identities and the subsequent inability of succeeding generations to understand their historical roots. In *Portnoy's Complaint*, Roth's narrator is driven to the edge of madness by these dual, often conflicting demands. At times Roth directs his anger at the Jews themselves who, through their obsession with ethnicity, have added to their own predicament. At other times, Roth attacks the goyim world which confuses and tempts Jewish Americans away from their traditions. Although Portnoy's Newark is largely Jewish (there are only twelve non-Jews in cousin Marcia's graduating class of 250), his neighborhood, like Augie March's and Morris Bober's, brings him into contact with other racial and ethnic minorities. Among those are Poles, whose presence in the novel, appearing at first gratuitous, serves to mark the non-Jewish world in general and, in particular, to allow the Jewish American writer another opportunity to pursue the past and confront the spectre of history.

Roth's approach differs from that of his literary predecessors, however. Tony Tanner calls Roth's fiction a "fantasy of revenge" presented through "fictionalized recall" (311). Tanner's description also helps us understand Roth's use of occasional Polish characters who otherwise appear to be the object of cruel mockery. One of the Portnoy family crises involves a student at Weequahic High who becomes engaged to Portnoy's cousin Harold. For Portnoy, Alice Dembosky embodies sensuality, stupidity, and avarice. He remembers Alice, a drum majorette, "in her tiny white skirt . . . white satin bloomers . . . white boots . . . lean, strong calves" (59). She is, like the Monkey, the temptation of goyim America. Legs Dembosky, as Portnoy calls her, "in all her dumb, blond, goyische beauty" (60) stands for those bourgeois American values that threaten Jewish cultural identity. Her baton routine, Portnoy adds, is "precisely the kind of talent that only a goy would think to develop in the first place" (60). Alice, moreover, threatens the integrity of the Jewish family—no melting-pot marriages for the Portnoys, who suspect that the "Polack's plan" is to "take Heshie . . . and then ruin his life" (65). When Uncle Hymie tells her that Heshie has an incurable disease and offers her $100 to go away, her acceptance of the money confirms family suspicions.

Later, after the Dembosky threat has been thwarted, Roth introduces another Pole whose characterization helps to explain the Jewish Port-noys' attitudes toward Alice. When Portnoy boards a bus, he somehow recognizes the driver as a Pole, despite the fact that the driver never speaks and Portnoy does not know him or his name. Fearing that the driver will discover him masturbating, Portnoy immediately associates the threatening world of non-Jews with Poles. Portnoy recalls some-thing his father often said to him: "A Polack's day . . . isn't complete until he has dragged his big, dumb feet across the bones of a Jew" (142). Instinctively, Portnoy concludes without reflection, although reflection is his raison d être, that the Pole is "my worst enemy" (142). He goes on to vilify and to extract humor at the driver's supposed ethnic back-ground. His name, Portnoy imagines, is probably "all X's and Y's—if my father is right, these people are direct descendants of the ox" (143).

Since no others in the novel are identified through nationality, Roth's selection of Poles as objects of humor, carriers of bourgeois values, and the longstanding enemies of the Jews appears to be deliberate, part of Portnoy's desire to "settle the score." The Jewish urge to settle the score seems itself to be one of the tendencies that Roth criticizes. Uncle Hymie's visit to Alice Dembosky is, for example, deceitful and schem-ing, full of lies and hypocrisy despite the humor. And Portnoy carries as much ethnic prejudice as his father. Although he agrees with his father about little else, he makes no challenge to his father's comments about Poles, which suggests that this view may be a cultural attitude accepted without question.

As far as the reader is concerned, the Portnoys see monsters where none exist—in themselves and in their Polish neighbors. This, Roth suggests, is part of Portnoy's paranoia. In *Portnoy's Complaint*, how-ever, Roth allows his characters to laugh at themselves in order to disarm the enemy through self-deprecating jokes that betray Jewish aggressions. Inadvertently his novel also shows that memories of Po-land are alive and well even in Newark (as they are in Singer's Coney Island) and that ancient ethnic stereotypes persist in the New World. At the same time, Roth softens those antagonisms by exposing Jewish prejudices and overreactions to "the enemy." Unfortunately, Roth's own views are somewhat masked by his paranoid and therefore unreliable narrator. Yet enough of Roth shows through to indicate that he, like Portnoy, is also interested in settling the score—through laughter.

Leon Uris also had an argument with history, although his originated in World War II where, along with Norman Mailer, James Jones, and others he found the material for his first novel *Battle Cry,* which illustrates the panoramic sweep of history characteristic of Uris's fiction. Soon Uris turned to modern Jewish history, to the formation of postwar Israel in *Exodus* (1959), and to the Holocaust in *Mila 18* (1961) and *QB VII* (1970). Both *Mila 18,* which deals with the Warsaw Ghetto uprising, and *QB VII,* which focuses on concentration camp horrors, are set in Poland where many of Europe's Jews had felt comfortable enough to live for a thousand years. In these novels, Uris writes and revises history on a grand scale, confronting for the first time in fiction sensitive issues about the Holocaust in Poland. As best-selling successes, his novels influenced the popular imagination in regard to Poles and Poland perhaps more than any other work, with the possible exception of Michener's *Poland.* Uris chooses to look directly at an emotion-filled subject—the behavior of Poland's two largest groups, Catholics and Jews, as they experience the Holocaust. He too needed to confront, to purge, memories of Poland, but unlike Roth and Malamud he was unable to reduce the problem into metaphor or ironic comedy. Uris's novels are angry and retaliatory and his fictional Poland is a psychotic nation infected with a cultural illness emanating from a dangerously inflated romantic conception of itself and from the long-standing animosity of Slav toward Jew.

Uris's Poles and Jews are quite different from those who dot the urban landscape of memory and imagination in Bellow, Malamud, and Roth. In fact, his choice of major characters in both *Mila 18* and *QB VII* sheds some light on his intentions. In novels about the Jewish experience in Poland from 1939 to 1943, it is surprising that none of the major characters is typically Jewish, that is to say, a representative of the millions of Orthodox, Yiddish-speaking Jews who populated most of Poland's villages and cities. Gabriella Rak, half-Polish and half-American, and Christopher Demonti, an Americanized Italian, are not Jewish at all. And Deborah Bronski, Demonti's mistress, and Andrei Androfski are assimilated, Polish-speaking sophisticates whose Jewishness exists in name rather than in practice and whose contact with average Jews exists not at all. Only Alexander Brandel, whose journal is the basis of the narration, appears to speak for the nonassimilated Jewish community, and he functions primarily as a narrator rather than an active character. In short, Uris chooses his characters so that he might examine the interaction of Pole and Jew through those who would "know" both cultures, but who, in truth, may know neither.

Similarly in *QB VII,* neither of the two principals is a Jewish Pole. Adam Kelno is a Slavic Pole and Abraham Cady, a Uris surrogate, is a Jewish-American writer whose narrative, like Brandel's, acts as a document upon which the story is based.

To be sure, Uris chooses to write about urbane, cultured, glamorous people to suit his popular audience and the demands of his genre. At the same time, this strategy allows him to look at Poles and Poland from a variety of points of view—a cross-section, so to speak, of non-Jews or assimilated Jews whose perspective would be more informed. Gabriella Rak in *Mila 18,* for example, is half-Polish precisely so that Uris can have a "Pole" corroborate the indictments that issue from other characters. To this end, Uris makes her likeable, sympathetic, intelligent, and credible, perhaps the only Slavic Pole in the novel whom we can respect. Likewise, the Jewish protagonist, Andrei Androfski, is characterized as an assimilated Jew and Polish nationalist so that Uris can have a character who will later see the folly of his ways. Uris's antagonist, Adam Kelno, is the most curious choice of all. Even though Germans constructed and administered all concentration camps and were directly and solely responsible for executions, torture, and the kind of heinous medical "experiments" described in *QB VII,* the villain of the novel, the surgeon responsible for these experiments, is neither a Nazi nor a German, but a Pole, a choice which strongly suggests that Uris has more than one iron in the fire.

The force of Uris's anger is fully visible in the first part of *Mila 18* where he sarcastically sketches Polish life. The novel opens in a large room, described as "violently Polish," formerly owned by a member of the gentry who kept the house as a "nest for his mistress" (2). From the first, then, the reader regards the Polish gentry as decadent, and Polish culture as somehow distasteful despite the fact that "violently Polish" defies definition. Shortly after, Uris provides a second image of Poland, described as "a nation of thirty million with only two million newspaper readers. A nation of feudal lords and serfs in this, the twentieth century. A nation which worships a black madonna as African Zulus prayed to sun gods. . . . Five per cent Paris . . . marble mansions and ruling decadence. Ninety five per cent Ukrania . . . abominable ignorance" (13). Although this is the view of a German sympathizer, the portrait is consistent with others in the text. For example, when Uris describes Warsaw's old town, noted for its historical and architectural significance, it is with a scorn originating outside the context of the novel. Uris calls it a place where Poland's glory is preserved in "shops selling cut-glass," a "tourist trap and hearth stone of Polish sentiment" (48).

Uris is especially acidic toward the aristocracy, whose ballrooms are decorated with "Polish heroes on statuesque white horses with billowing manes leading determined troops into battle" (32). Later when he introduces the commander of the Polish Home Army, Uris says he has the perpetual arrogance of a Polish nobleman and a "medieval mentality." His class, Uris adds, has misused the wealth of Poland, legalized serfdom for private gain, and has carried the "inbred hate of centuries toward Jews" (264). And in a panoramic introduction to Warsaw, Uris with ironic humor undercuts Polish romanticism and history as well as the aristocracy. He catalogs the public monuments: "Pilsudski riding his horse, Stefan riding his horse, Casimir riding his horse, Poniatowski riding his horse, and Chopin merely standing" (62). These images prepare the way for Uris's later suggestion that Polish stubbornness, arrogance, pride, and romantic egotism were as responsible for their 1939 defeat as technological insufficiency.

Uris, however, is more interested in presenting perceptions of Jewish life in Poland. Andrei Androfsky reminds us that the Jewish experience begins well enough but turns into nothing less than a thousand years of oppression in varying intensities. Uris uses him and Alexander Brandel to review the boycotts, economic strangulation, excessive taxation, and bestial pogroms that punctuate the shared history of Poles and Jews. Uris, in fact, drives hard at Polish anti-Semitism by referring to stories of goyim beating little Jewish boys in order to steal their wares and to accounts of peasants coercing Jews bound for concentration camps to surrender their valuables before passing them a handful of snow to quench their thirst.

Moreover, the plot of *QB VII* is nothing less than the unraveling of Adam Kelno's hatred of Jews as motivation for his camp "experiments." As he is questioned at trial, prosecutors succeed in drawing out his maniacal hatred of Jews. He tells how his father always owed the village Jew money and how "everybody in the village owes money to the Jew" (246). The Jews, Kelno claims, were "always strangers in our midst, always attempting to overthrow us again," as they would later when they gave Poland to Russia at the end of the war (79). Between the wars, he charges, Jews bought all the university seats so that Poland had to establish a quota for Christian Poles to become students. Jews were "always pushing their way in," Kelno complains (100). Kelno's charges are a summary of the typical complaints that were hurled against Jews in 1930s Poland by the radical right, but, unfortunately, he appears to be a spokesperson for all of Poland. In fact the question of Kelno's guilt or innocence, a metaphor for Poland's culpability, hinges on the admission of anti-Semitism in Poland, an issue Uris hammers at in *QB VII*. Kelno's trial is actually Uris's way of documenting historical anti-Semitism and his explanation for the presence of the death camps in

Eastern Europe. Uris's prosecutor drives home this point when he asks Kelno, "Poland was anti-Semitic in nature, substance, and action, was it not?" To which Kelno grudgingly agrees that "there was some anti-Semitism in Poland" (319). The pity and irony of it all, Uris concludes, is that it was not a Nazi doctor who performed the torturous operations but Adam Kelno, "a Pole, a fellow ally" (491). Late in the novel when we see Kelno in a rage, slapping his son as a "Jew! Jew! Jew! Jew!", we see Poland's madness turned against itself.

Uris records instances of anti-Semitism to support his theory about the chosen locations of death camps. Midway through *Mila 18*, in fact, Brandel charges that the Holocaust could have occurred "only in Poland, the Baltics, and Ukrania" (298). Uris implies that the climate was abetted by an invisible conspiracy of the Polish Catholic church, the Polish government in London, the underground, and the general population. Uris indicts the apathy of Slavic Poles to events in the ghetto when he describes how Warsaw's strollers stopped outside the ghetto walls to enjoy the Nazi artillery barrage which to them resembled a monumental fireworks display. The government-in-exile ignores the plight of its Jewish citizens and instead "gathers to hear Chopin and recite poetry and live memories of Warsaw in the good old days" (270). The underground army refuses Jewish requests for assistance of any kind; and Roman, the commander, is more sinister and contemptible than the Nazis. As for the bastion of Slavic spiritual and moral guidance, Uris has only contempt. The one great voice of power and conscience, he writes, "the church, remained silent" (140). The problem, according to the archbishop of Warsaw, who refuses to help the Jews, is that Jews are "not really" Poles and that, in any event, his duty is to minister spiritual, not social, assistance. All of Poland's important institutions contribute in silent conspiracy to the Holocaust.

What makes this response even more troubling is that according to Uris, Jewish Poles tried to accommodate themselves to Slavic culture. Andrei Androfski, a brilliant officer in the crack Ulani regiment, and Paul Bronski, dean of the medical school at Warsaw University, are evidence of Jewish success in this regard. The major difference between them is that Bronski wants to forgo Judaism entirely while Androfski asks to be an equal participant in Polish life as a Jew. When Androfski makes his sympathies known, Uris implies that Andrei speaks for all Jewish Poles: "I don't want to go to Palestine, now or ever. Warsaw is my city. . . . I am a Polish officer and this is my country" (69). History shows, however, that most of Poland's Jews were neither Androfskis nor Bronskis, as far as assimilation and Polish nationalism are concerned. To shape his argument, Uris has dealt as freely with facts as he has with the issues themselves. His characters tend to represent extreme positions: the Slavs are villains, the Jews usually virtuous. And the intricacies of Polish-Jewish relations before and during the war are oversimplified for dramatic purposes and mass-market success.

Uris's task as destroyer and preserver is a necessary one, however, just as it is for Singer and Kosinski in their first novels about Poland. Isaac Singer in *The Slave* (1962) and Jerzy Kosinski in *Painted Bird* (1957) present a picture of life in Poland as harsh as that of Uris. Kosinski's renunciation is so bitter that this protagonist cannot bear to state the name of the country where the events occur. And Singer's *The Slave* offers a horrifying portrait of life among the Poles. In the last analysis, Uris must purge himself and the postwar collective memory of hatred before he can come to terms with memories of Poland in more introspective and rewarding ways. This explains why he offers as the hero of *Mila 18* a patriotic, assimilated Jew who must renounce his earlier convictions about the Polish nation, and why Gabriella Rak, the half-American, half-Slavic Pole, will not allow herself to bear her child in such a place. By the end of *Mila 18* and *QB VII*, all have been forced to admit, as Brandel does, that the Holocaust in Poland was the product of historical conditions peculiar to Poland.

Consequently, Uris presents his novels as texts that relate historical events. He pretends that *Mila 18* is based on the edited journals of Alexander Brandel, which were buried in the ruins of Warsaw and discovered afterwards. He includes a "factual" prologue about an archeological team that locates the only journals upon which a true history of events can be based. Moreover, another character, the American journalist Christof deMonti, writes his history on the basis of Brandel's massive journals. DeMonti's fictional mission—to preserve history— mirrors Uris's own conception of *Mila 18*. In *QB VII*, Uris also takes to the high road of history offering the text as a case study of the crimes of Adam Kelno prepared by a Jewish American writer, Abraham Cady, himself a surrogate for Leon Uris. Cady cannot rest until Kelno and Poland have been exposed, a retribution of sorts for the death of his son in the June 1967 war. This is Cady's way of settling the score, just as Uris's novels bring to a close mid-century attempts by Jewish American writers to address old wrongs. By then, Jewish novelists, as Alfred Kazin explains it, had apparently decided that "the world is a very bad place indeed" (137). And for some, Poland stood inside the gates of Hell from which Jews could not escape either in fact or in fiction.

3. ISAAC SINGER'S POLISH SIDE

The title of Philip Roth's 1962 novel *Letting Go* serves as a metaphor for much postwar Jewish American fiction. For some like Roth, the demands of tradition and the obsession with Jewishness stand in conflict with New World aspirations. For others, the metaphor points more toward Europe and to a cultural experience that continues to live in individual and collective memory.

Without question, the fiction of Isaac Bashevis Singer best expresses the Polish experience as an ever-present factor in Jewish consciousness. For the first thirty years of his life, Singer lived in Warsaw and in the Lublin area. Such works as *A Day of Pleasure: Stories of a Boy Growing Up in Warsaw* and *In My Father's Court* re-create the richness and adventure of those days and the particular experience of living as a Jew in Poland. In fact, all of his work is an attempt, as he describes it, to provide a "literary history of Jewish people in Poland" (qtd. in Rosenblatt 32). Understandably, Singer's readers have been interested primarily in his Jewishness: his tales of shtetl life, of pious Jews, talmudic scholars, yeshiva boys, and urban secularized Jews yearning to breathe the spiritual fragrance of Orthodox Judaism once again. Somewhat more indirectly, even haphazardly at times, Singer offers a second "history" as well: an outline of Polish culture, a view of Slavic, Christian Poland, and an important study of the complex relationships and shared history of the Jews and Christians in Poland.

Singer's "history," his depiction of Poland, is that of a culture that is no more. Having left Poland forever in the 1930s, he has necessarily perpetuated an image that bears little resemblance to the People's Republic or the age of Solidarity which Americans have seen on the evening news, or to the new generations that comprise the Polish American community. As anachronistic as it is, however, Singer's fiction is regarded by many as one of the most direct and primary sources of knowledge about Poland. As a result, the Singer canon holds a remarkable place in the literary history of Poles in America and in popular attitudes toward Poles.

Taken together, Singer's stories comprise a short course on Polish history as well as on those people, places, and times associated with Jewish history. We learn about political figures from Sigismund to Kosciuszko to Pilsudski, about writers such as Zeromski, Prus, and Przybyszewski, and about significant political events, including the Chmielnicki uprising, the partitions of the 1790s, the 1863 uprising, the 1920 war with Russia, the rise of Fascism, and the first days of World War II. On other occasions Singer acquaints us with the folklore, traditions, and superstitions of Slavic Poland—its foods, holidays, social system, and religion. Moreover, Christian Poles appear in virtually all of Singer's works, and Wanda (*The Slave*), Lucian (*The Manor* and *The Estate*), and Yadwiga (*Enemies: A Love Story*) approach major status as characters. In short, images of Slavic, Christian Poland permeate his work.

Singer's attitudes toward the country of his youth are, understandably and even necessarily, ambivalent. Even his public comments on the subject emphasize this ambivalence. To a direct question about his thoughts on Poland, Singer somewhat evasively replied, "The truth is ... I'm still living there. I lived there my first thirty years and so for me the Poland of my youth still exists" (Kresh 340). At other times Singer's response has been more nationalistic, even to the point of expressing delight that "a Pole became Pope" (Kresh 457), and of praising the merits of Adam Mickiewicz, who rendered a "wonderful picture of how Poland and Lithuania used to be in his time" (Rosenblatt 15). Other of Singer's remarks have, however, revealed a darker, more cynical view. "For years as a Jew in Poland," he explained, "I had known I was a second-class citizen—maybe even third class. They didn't really want us there. There was no place for us ... why keep a minority, strangers in your house?" (Kresh 154). Singer's attitude (and the corresponding Polish view of Singer) is inadvertently yet perfectly captured in the interplay of the title of a Polish review of *The Family Moskat* and Singer's response to that review. Apparently prepared for the worst, the reviewer calls Singer's work, "A Novel about Poland Written by a Jew without Hatred." Singer's pleased reply emphasizes forgiveness but not forgetfulness: "They felt there was no hatred in my writing toward Poles," he stated. "Even though there were pogroms and all kinds of trouble, still I see the Polish side" (Rosenblatt 36).

In truth, Singer's portrait of Slavic Poland is two-sided—shaped by intense love-hate feelings suggested even in certain of his titles: *Enemies: A Love Story, The Slave, Lost in America*. The range of these feelings is perhaps best seen in his Slavic characters, who also help us understand his fictional techniques. In many ways, Singer's depiction of Poles is conventional, resembling pre- more than postwar literary traditions. With the possible exception of Yadwiga in *Enemies*, he does not include contemporary Poles or Polish Americans in his stories. Moreover, those we do meet represent a social stratification more typical of nineteenth- than twentieth-century Poland; that is to say, Singer's Poles tend to be either princes or peasants. In contrast to the tradition established in American literature, however, his aristocrats are barbarians, not beau ideals, and his peasants are rogues, not redemptive agents. In a sense, all of them are cultural stereotypes whose fictional roles are designed primarily to illuminate the Jewish experience. Considering that many of his Jewish characters also tend to be stereotypes—a point made by such readers as Irving Malin (*Singer* 106)—

this method is not as surprising as the uniformity and predictability of certain of Singer's views. In general, Singer dislikes Slavs when they represent a social group or institution. He scorns peasants, views the gentry as decadent, and portrays males as violent, bigoted, ethically and spiritually bankrupt threats to the Jewish community and to themselves. When Singer brings together female Jews and male Slavs, as he does in *The Manor* (Lucian and Miriam), *The Estate* (Stefan and Mirale), and *The Family Moskat* (Yanek and Masha), he intends to show how the Slavic male turns love into sorrow and even death.

Both the prince and the peasant receive rough treatment by Singer. Slowwitted, superstitious, animalistic—his peasants possess all the vices charged to them by anti-immigrant writers in the periodical press and in fiction, without the virtues of work, solidity, family, patriotism, and ambition which literary history had attributed to them. In *The Slave*, Singer describes a typical peasant village: "The women were unclean and had vermin in their clothes . . . their skins were covered with rashes and boils. They ate field rodents and the rotting carcasses of fowls. Some of them could scarcely speak Polish, grunted like animals, made signs with their hands . . . the village abounded in cripples, boys and girls with goiters, distended heads and disfiguring birthmarks; there were also mutes, epileptics, freaks . . . men and women copulated in public" (9). Singer carries this image forward into the twentieth century, suggesting that the coming of modernity and the industrial age has affected the peasant very little. In the short story "Something Is There," peasants are introduced as a "bedraggled lot of men . . . smoking cheap tobacco, eating coarse bread with lard, and washing it down with vodka. Their wives reclined on the baggage and dozed." "Bumpkins such as these," a rabbi tells us as he covers "his nose from the stench, killed men, raped women, plundered, and tortured children" (*Collected Stories* 336).

The gentry receives equally harsh treatment. "Crazy rapists" who "did nothing but drink, fornicate, whip peasants, and quarrel among themselves over the distribution of honors, privileges, and titles" (*The Slave* 110), they are uniformly rascals, thieves, and butchers. Wisniewski (*Satan in Goray*) impales Ukrainians; Zagayek (*The Slave*) "steals everything." Zazhitsky (*The Family Moskat*) forbids his son to marry a Jew, one of "those who ruined Poland." In "A Friend of Kafka," an exiled aristocrat beats his lover, places a revolver to her head, and ultimately dies in prison. In "Moon and Madness," crazy Karlowski and his unfaithful wife wrangle, fornicate, and drink until he drops dead and she solaces herself "with her coachman or some other servant." Singer's most damning portrait of the upper class occurs in *The*

Manor and *The Estate* where he traces the decline of the Jampolskis and, by extension, "old Poland," and in the process creates a portrait of the aristocrat antithetical to the Polish beau ideal.

Singer's negative treatment of gentry, peasants, and men in general is tempered by the presence of Christian Poles who, like the ferryman in *Satan in Goray,* share hearth and good fellowship with all passersby. Such Christian charity is especially evident in Singer's Slavic women. Quite the opposite of their male counterparts, Singer's female Slavs are another cultural stereotype, a latter-day version of the Polish women introduced into American fiction by Edith Miniter in *Our Natupski Neighbors.* Poorly educated, lower-class domestics, or more typically peasants, they are earth mothers all—symbols of fertility, nourishment, love, and hope. Janina, the daughter of a Warsaw janitor, possesses a "rustic amiability" that reminds Lucian of the "country girls who herded geese or goats" (11). To the narrator of *Shosha,* Tekla, another house servant, has cheeks "the color of ripe apples." Even Yadwiga, prowling about her Coney Island apartment, reminds Herman of the soil, the summer, the smell of cooking beets. In *The Slave,* Wanda is the most fully developed example of the earth mother. In all cases their primary function is to serve as mistress, lover, and wife—often to the Jewish protagonist. To a woman, they are naive, wholesome, selfless, and hopelessly love-stricken: Magda commits suicide rather than live without Yasha; Wanda, disguising herself as a mute Jew, ultimately dies, a victim of her unabridged dedication to Jacob; and Kasia chooses the misery that accompanies Lucian wherever he goes. Lady Pilitzky excepted, all are pure in spirit and simple hearts—moral centers of sorts. In the security of their personal relationships and their social and moral identity, they contrast markedly with Singer's Slavic men. Aware of the plight of the Jews in Poland, attracted by the integrity of Judaism, faithful to others, incapable of wrong doing, Slavic women comprise the best of humanity in general and the best of Slavic culture in particular. Nonetheless, they suffer from two-dimensional development and stereotyping, and ultimately from Singer's insensitivity to them as women, as individuals, and as Slavs.

Although Yadwiga is far removed from her native Poland, she is the best extended example of the strength of Singer's Slavic women and his weakness for surface characterization. In certain ways, she is a cultural stereotype, in others, the culmination of all who precede her in Singer's fiction. From peasant stock, uncultured and unlettered, she spends her time listening to Catholic sermons and mazurkas on a Polish-language radio station and thinking of ways to please her Jewish husband, Herman. Like many of her fictional predecessors, she has risked her life for a Jew, having hidden Herman from the Nazis for three years on the family farm. Intellectually and socially inferior to Herman, Yadwiga converts to Judaism and assiduously learns the complexities of Orthodox Jewish life. Like Wanda in *The Slave,* she is a symbol of goodness in a corrupt world, a moral constant who contrasts with the indecisive, spiritually troubled Herman who, trying to love everyone, can love no one. Deserted ultimately by her husband, Yadwiga assumes the servant status "natural" to her culture and thus plays the only two roles that Singer creates for his women: house servants and subservient sexual partners.

Through Yadwiga we can see how well Singer presents the "Polish side." Unfortunately, as with his other females, Singer's method of characterization concentrates on surface features. Yadwiga's past is brief and generalized—a few lines to indicate her early years on a farm in southern Poland; but Singer never looks into her thoughts, never adequately explains her desire to convert to Judaism or her desire to have "a Jewish child." Although virtually all the characters in Singer's post–world war settings are haunted by memories of the Holocaust, Singer does not tell us how Yadwiga is affected or what the Holocaust means to Christian Poles like her. Instead, Yadwiga shuffles about the kitchen, reverting to her peasant-servant mentality when she is in the presence of others. When the novel ends, she is conveniently stored away, a burden to Tamara, one of Herman's other wives.

With that, Singer tosses away the chance to compare the assimilation problems of the Jewish Pole, Herman, and the Catholic Pole, Yadwiga. Instead he seems to suggest that cultural transition is no problem for the Slav content to live outside the Polish community, divorced from her ethnic traditions. Considering that Yadwiga is Singer's only significant Polish American character, his approach is a loss to the Jewish experience in literature and to the Polish tradition in literary history.

Whether Singer's depiction of Slavs is influenced more by his style than by his attitudes toward Slavic culture is difficult to say. Jewish ethnocentrism complicates the issue even more. In story after story, Singer makes it clear that Jews historically regarded themselves as superior to their Slavic neighbors. The result is often an insensitive comparison of Jews and Slavs. Whereas the Slavic peasants in *The Slave* are portrayed as little more than animals, Jacob, in contrast, is "a good student," writes in "a fine bold hand," has "a good singing voice," and is "a gifted draftsman and wood carver" (52). Tekla, the uneducated servant girl in *Shosha,* instantly recognizes the superior education and manners of Jews: "The Jewish boys read newspapers and books. They know what's going on in the world. They treat a girl better than our fellows do" (173). Even the rural Jews outshine their Slavic counterparts in cunning and cleverness. They have, Singer writes, an ability "to get the peasant women to purchase all sorts of trinkets," partly because they are "better informed . . . than the peasants" (*The Destruction of Kreshev* 95). One of Singer's most powerful comparisons of Slav and Jew occurs when Yanek, a Christian Pole, compares himself to his Jewish friends and discovers that "he had all the qualities attributed to the Jews. He shunned fighting, could not stand liquor . . . read serious books, avoided athletic sports, visited museums and art shows" (*Family Moskat* 296).

In the realistic "trilogy" consisting of *The Manor, The Estate,* and *The Family Moskat,* Singer's primary concern, however, is not in exploring cultural differences, but rather in recording the shared fate of Christians and Jews as an essentially medieval society gives way to industrialization. Viewing the 1863 revolt against tsarist Russia as the pivotal, final attempt by the gentry to preserve the feudal ways of old Poland, Singer, in his trilogy, succeeds in capturing the political life of the nation between 1863 and 1939. He documents the decline of the gentry, the resulting political vacuum, and the turmoil that eventually produces the new left and the new right. In his analysis, Singer is at his best, writing neither with animosity nor with sentimentality but rather with the eye of the historian who sees his native land caught between more powerful neighbors, swept up by the dramatic changes occurring in the late nineteenth century, and debating a national direction that would lead ironically to the Holocaust.

The Polish antagonists in these novels, the Jampolskis, are representative of old Poland. Like many of their fictional ancestors, they are aristocrats, patriots, landed gentry. Hardly models to imitate, however, the Jampolskis have contributed to the worst of times and have themselves degenerated far beneath their former station. Having lost his estate and fortune because of his role in the 1863 insurrection, Count Jampolski "seldom changed his clothes"; his "mustache became ragged" and his "language grew as coarse as a dogcatcher's" (*The Manor* 1, 2). Singer is more interested in the count's son Lucian, imprisoned for his role in the insurrection. An exile, an outcast, a man without a country or home, Lucian is also without any redeeming qualities except perhaps the courage ultimately to shoot himself in the head. Seducer of the naive Miriam Leba, debaucher of the adolescent Kasia and the equally young Janina, murderer, drunk, and deserter, Lucian wanders through two novels as the Polish heavy. Late in *The Estate,* he sums up his life: "Nobody loves me and that's the truth. I hate everybody and they hate me. I'm a hounded beast" (273). If Lucian's life and death are not enough to document the dissolution of the gentry, Singer introduces a third generation of Jampolskis, Lucian's son, Bolek, who is "forever involved in unsavory affairs." Bolek bears witness to the fact that "there is such a thing as heredity" (283). In his interview with Rosenblatt and Koppel, Singer suggested that the decline of his fictional Jampolski family "was in the genes . . . in heredity . . . in the circumstances" (2), and thus emphasized his belief that the fortunes of Poland were tied to a cultural perspective: a romantic view of itself as a courageous and noble society, incapable of constructive action, doomed instead to defeat and despair.

In Singer's fiction, Lucian Jampolski embodies this state of mind. "Everyone knew we were doomed," Lucian says of the 1863 insurrection. "Some races enjoy bleeding, and with the Poles it is a sort of passion. We were beaten and we begged for more" (*The Manor* 118). As a typical Pole, Lucian had a "foreboding sense of some approaching catastrophe" (*The Estate* 98), but Singer makes it clear that the catastrophe is the fulfillment of "a cultural deficiency." In *The Slave*, Adam Pilitzky waits for a miracle to save Poland from seventeenth-century enemies. He expects that the Virgin's tears, flaming stone crosses, and marching dead armies will invigorate the nation's spirit and "renew its belief in heaven" (175). Two centuries later, Lucian's sister Felicia still waits for miracles, in this case a Polish savior who, riding a white horse, quoting poetry, and loving the manorial life of old Poland, will rescue her from her unpleasant life. The exiles whom Lucian meets in Paris sing patriotic songs, make conspiratorial plans, form organizations, seek aid from Garibaldi, Bakunin, and President Hayes, but devote most of their time to trivial arguments about the distribution of goods to immigrants. Miriam Leba comes to understand that the exiles are "a collection of the names of dead people" (*The Manor* 208). Lucian mistakenly identifies the liberation of the peasant, the suffrage, and positivist movements as the reasons for "national corruption." More accurately, he knows that an era has ended, that the gentry are obsolete. He tells his sister, "We've become isolated from everything. We live amidst gloom and despair" (*The Manor* 104).

At the same time, Singer documents the national debate over new directions. Lucian's father, in fact, is one of the first to call for changes in outlook and in priorities. The count ironically reminds Felicia that "the middle ages have past. Too much idealism, too much poetry, too much easy patriotism. Smokestacks are what we need in Poland, towering smokestacks spewing smoke; and fertilizer for the fields—mountains of artificial manure" (*The Manor* 48). Even the Polish press, Singer tells us, constantly preached the same sermon—"industrialization and culture." But the country's aspirations are as confused as one of Singer's characters who had periods when he believed that "Poland's salvation lay in forgetting her national aspirations and getting down to the business of industrializing herself and educating her citizens. At other times, he regarded the ousting of her oppressors as her most important task" (*The Manor* 287).

These conflicting positions led eventually to a polarization in politics, a situation Singer depicts through the contrasting figures of Stefan Lamanski (*The Estate*) and Yanek Zazhitsky (*The Family Moskat*). Introduced as a disconcerted young radical, Lamanski praises the socialist movement, glorifies the worker, describes the various socialist factions and splinter groups, and identifies the breach between the peasant and the reactionary nobility. Singer uses Lamanski in only one scene. But when he later explains that Lamanski is not at all a political idealist but rather a government informer who betrays even Mirale, the mother of his illegitimate son, Singer conveys the complexity of the political intrigues of the time.

In *The Family Moskat* Singer gives us the other side of the political coin. Yanek Zazhitsky is a sensitive artist who defies his parents to marry the Jewish Masha. His conversion from a liberal to a reactionary to a fascist suggests the drift of Polish nationalism. At the outbreak of World War I, Yanek volunteers to help the Germans who promised an independent Poland. Next he joins Pilsudski's military organization and, regarding Pilsudski as a messiah, eventually rises to the rank of colonel. More to the point, he who had once been attracted to Jews and Jewish culture becomes a mouthpiece for the fascist element in Poland. "Those damn Jews of yours," he tells Masha, driving her to attempt suicide, "are eating up the country like a bunch of termites. And they'll never rest, the bastards, until the red flag flies over the Belvedere" (507).

The turncoat Lamanski and the fascist Zazhitsky, both failed idealists, represent the mainstream of a cultural deterioration whose springs originate in the seventeenth century where Adam Pilitzky complains that "everyone in Poland could be bought" (*The Slave* 149). Ironically, Singer's Slavic characters are the ones who provide the most intense and the most damning cultural self-examination. Lamanski reminds us that the gentry itself participated in the partitions and that the last Polish king cooperated in Poland's enslavement. He even indicts the 1863 patriots as concerned only with the return of the nobility to power and the removal from the people of "those shreds of rights that Alexander granted them" (*The Estate,* 47).

The gentry's decline, the break-up of the manorial system, the ensuing political vacuum, and the new wave of political extremism—all associated with the excesses of romantic nationalism—prompted renewed discussions about the legitimate place of Jews in the new Poland. At the center of Singer's realistic trilogy, this discussion is carried on primarily by Jewish assimilationists; but the Slavic Katchinski echoes the sentiments of all when he points out that it is "quite impossible to be a Polish citizen and at the same time make every effort to discard that citizenship" (*The Family Moskat* 518). This argument, however, is no more, and yet no less, than a new version of anti-Semitism—documented by Singer as the other great flaw in the Slavic temperament.

Everywhere, Singer's Slavs identify the Jews as the scapegoat for Poland's historic ills. Jews are usurers, communists, blasphemers, spies, enemies of the nation. Colored somewhat by the times, the views of an unidentified barber in *Shosha* are nonetheless typical. "They've taken over all Poland," he complains. "The cities are lousy with them . . . they swarm like vermin everywhere . . . they babble away in their jargon . . . they swindle . . . make treaties with our worst enemies . . . root out us Christians and hand over the power to the Bolsheviks . . . have a secret pact with Hitler" (162–63). Although these are clearly comments of the 1930s, anti-Semitism is not exclusively a product of neonationalism, Singer argues in other works whose settings encompass one thousand years of Polish history. Even in seventeenth-century Poland the Jew was left in peace only "as long as the village did not suffer from famine, epidemic, or fire" (*The Slave* 7). In the mid-nineteenth century, as Singer shows in *The Manor* and *The Estate,* the Jews are held responsible for every conceivable problem.

According to Singer, anti-Semitism had become institutionalized in Poland. The press, the legal system, the Catholic church—all participate. The press attacks converts to Judaism ("Something Is There"), blasts the Jewish minority "as if it were the nation's greatest danger" (*Shosha* 229), and accuses Jews of trying to "foist Western European decadence on Poland" (*The Estate* 255). The legal system is no less reactionary. In fact, for Singer the system seems to exist only to intimidate Jews. In "Zeidlus the Pope," he describes a law that condemns to public burning those who converted to Judaism; officials are introduced as "predatory beasts" ("Something Is There"); legal sanctions on Jews, especially during the 1920s, are often noted; anti-Semitism and corruption corrode the system. Hertz Yanovar is interrogated by an officer who concludes, "There's only one thing to do. Get rid of them. Like rats into the Vistula with the whole lot of 'em" (*The Family Moskat* 514).

What is more, the most venerated of Slavic Poland's institutions, the Catholic church, is in Singer's eyes an enemy of Judaism and a friend to racial and religious bigotry. The church's passion, Singer suggests in "Yentl the Yeshiva Boy," is to convert Jews. When Anshel disappears, the villagers conclude that he "had fallen into the hands of Catholic priests and had been converted" (167). This idea is repeated elsewhere. "What better merchandise is there for a priest than a Jewish soul?" the wicked narrator of "Zeidlus the Pope" wonders. In *The Estate,* a Catholic publication attacks liberals, suffragettes, socialists, atheists, and, in the same breath, rich Jews. The few priests that appear in the fiction are universally unattractive. The village priest in *The Slave* fathered "a half-dozen bastards" and advises the peasants to dispose of the Jewish Jacob "in God's name." The church, Singer concludes, is no more than a part of the national hypocrisy that characterizes Polish-Jewish relations. "The priests," he writes, "particularly the Jesuits, harangued against infidel medicine from the pulpits . . . petitioned the Sejm and the governors to disqualify Jews from medical practice, but no sooner did one of the clergy fall ill, than he called in a Jew to attend him" (*The Slave* 127).

The tragic irony of it all, Singer seems to say, is that despite the oppression of the Jews, despite anti-Semitism and Jewish ethnocentrism, the two cultures, sharing a thousand years of history, are inextricably linked. Zipkin, for example, is quite aware that after the events of centuries he is "a crazy mixture" of Polish and Jewish. The Polish countryside reminds Asa Heshel of both King Casimir and the Jews who came to Poland by his leave. Even Ezriel believes that Poland deserves his allegiance. Arele announces the last act of the Polish-Jewish drama when, days before the outbreak of war, he concludes that the same powers that drove the Christian Poles and the Jewish Poles also drove a galaxy billions of light years distant. "We were fated," he notes, "to play our little games and to be crushed" (*Shosha* 257).

In *The King of the Fields* (1988), Singer probes the origins of Polish-Jewish history to see, as it were, how it all began. Set in pre-Christian southern Poland, the novel follows the misfortunes of a Slavic tribe, the Lesniks, a primitive hunting people ridden by superstition and savagery during a period when four singular events are taking shape: the formation of the Polish state, the advance of civilization, the coming of Christianity, and the first appearance of Jews in Polish lands. This configuration, Singer shows, is the catalyst for all that follows in the Polish-Jewish saga—the fate that Arele mentions in *Shosha* and the first act in an extended tragedy for both cultures.

Midway, Singer introduces Ben Dosa, who is brought as a slave to Poland from Babylon where he was a merchant. In contrast to the Lesniks whom he serves as shoemaker, Ben Dosa is spiritually and culturally enlightened. The traveled Ben Dosa speaks several languages, knows how to read and write, and introduces crafts, trade, and a moral code to the Lesniks. It is the Jew, Singer suggests, who brings light into a darkened land. In turn, the Lesniks grow wary of Ben Dosa's strange religious practices and beliefs, prompted in part by his assumption of superiority as one of God's chosen. When Bishop Mieczyslaw appears from faraway Miasto, the Lesniks are quickly Christianized, Jews are excoriated as Christ-killers, and Ben Dosa flees the village where he had introduced the seeds of Western civilization. Singer's history lesson in *The King of the Fields* is clear: anti-Semitism and the formation of the Christian Polish state are synonymous.

Singer thus completes his history of Jewish people in Poland by providing an introductory frame for his fiction. Setting out to preserve the history of Jews in Poland, Singer does more. He traces the main currents of historical change, particularly the period 1863–1939, provides insights into Polish character and culture, and investigates the complexities of Polish Jewishness. His persistent exploration of his dual identity as Pole and Jew occupies a central place not only in his own work but in a tradition preoccupied with memories of Poland.

4. THE SOUNDS OF SILENCE: MEMORIES OF POLAND

Singer's Polishness, a lived and felt experience for those of his generation, is not, of course, shared by contemporary writers of Jewish descent. Nonetheless, Cynthia Ozick, Johanna Kaplan, Grace Paley, Meyer Liben, Herbert Wilner, and Jerome Rothenberg have all written about Polish-Jewish connections—although they write about an experience that has retreated into history and distant memory. Yet the very act of writing such stories proves that the subject is very much alive in present consciousness. Their works deal with New World Jews haunted by the past, by memories that call them back to another time and place, to another cultural experience. What characterizes this latest phase of Polish-Jewish literary history is the struggle for memory and what Eva Hoffman calls "the retrospective maneuvers to compensate for fate" (115). In addition, these writers collectively address the central question raised by Irwin Zarecka and Hoffman: What does it mean to remember Polish Jewishness?

Although this kind of story appears to belong almost exclusively to the postwar generation, Jerome Weidman in the 1930s wrote two masterful short pieces that perhaps say it best. "My Father Sits in the Dark" is a quiet, understated tale of fathers and sons and the closeness and distance that exist between generations of American families in which parents or perhaps grandparents have grown up as "foreigners." A son cannot understand why his father sits in the darkened kitchen all night, although Pop appears normal and healthy otherwise. "My father has a peculiar habit" is Weidman's way of opening the story and expressing the conflict. Repeatedly the son asks his father why he sits alone in the dark, but the father's only response is, "Thinking." When the young man asks what his father thinks about, Pop replies "nothing." Eventually, we learn, rather offhandedly, that father has "led two lives"; that is to say, he grew up in Europe and has experiences about which he prefers to remain silent and about which the son knows only through the filter of parental anecdotes. What Weidman suggests is that for the son's generation, the lived experiences of the European-born have assumed a fictive dimension. Unlike his father, the boy cannot form clear images of his ethnic roots and, therefore, cannot fully understand the cultural attitudes and frame of reference that shape his own thinking and behavior, although he suspects they originate in Europe. At one point Pop explains that he sits in the dark because he "can't get used to the lights. We didn't have lights when I was a boy in Europe" (121). "Maybe he is thinking of his brothers in the old country or of his mother and two step-brothers. Or of his father. But they are all dead," the boy reflects (119). For postwar readers, the boy's words, prophetic, tragic, bone-chilling, could have been uttered by Elie Wiesel or any Holocaust survivor, for that matter. Weidman closes the sketch with the image of a small boy crouched on a pile of twigs next to a huge fireplace, "his starry gaze fixed on the dull remains of the dead flames. The boy is my father," the narrator tells us (121).

Weidman returns to this theme in "I Thought about This Girl," a companion story of sorts to "My Father Sits in the Dark." Once again, the young narrator is curious, puzzled by the behavior of others. He cannot understand the abrupt and devastating melancholy of the young girl who works in the family bakery. She had always been bright, fresh, cheerful, invigorating to Mom and Dad as well as to the narrator. Like the father in "My Father Sits in the Dark," the young girl is taciturn when asked, then pleaded with, about her personality change. "Nothing," she replies, "nothing is wrong."

In this story, Weidman has two surprises for the reader, both of which in their simplicity and in their incredibility capture the "Polish" obsession of the Jewish American writer. Midway we learn that the girl is a Polish immigrant, recently arrived, penniless, an employee only because the narrator's family wishes to extend compassion and charity, for which she is reciprocally thankful. After insistent prodding by the family about her decision to leave the bakery, the girl herself unveils the second surprise and the point of "I Thought about This Girl." She explains that she must quit because she received a letter from her mother in Poland chastising her because "it isn't right to work for Jews" (311). If Weidman's story about Polish anti-Semitism is clear enough, so too is his decision to use a Polish character as exemplar. As in "My Father Sits in the Dark," the Polish experience reaches out over distance and time to touch the lives of Weidman's characters, to release itself from memory into experience. Weidman suggests that there is an inevitability at work, one that needs neither clarification nor postscript. The characters add nothing to the girl's statement; the narrator accepts, without necessarily understanding, his Polish connection.

And yet Weidman tells more; he introduces the theme of distant memories that would preoccupy later writers. His image aptly fits Isaac Singer, whose entire work may be described as a starry gaze at the dull flames of Jewish life in eastern Poland; Jerzy Kosinski, whose vision emanates from his ashened memories of war-torn and socialist Poland; and other lesser known but no less remarkable writers such as Meyer Liben, Johanna Kaplan, Cynthia Ozick, Herbert Wilner, and Grace Paley, all of whom write stories that not only share Weidman's sensitivity but also employ similar images, motifs, and perspectives. Their works are also marked by darkness, distance, and silence, by the search through memory for understanding, for connections with the past and with another place, which ultimately elude the protagonists. The mood is one of loss and aloneness and of the impossibility of ever knowing or regaining that which is, alas, too far away. In the stories this grief is connected in a vague, generalized way to Eastern Europe and to Poland, although the protagonists, often young, cannot transform their bits of knowledge and intuitions into clear conceptualizations. Some cannot translate their feelings or received impressions into thought; others are reluctant to admit the past into the present. In either case, memories of Poland emerge as momentary intimations, as a state of mind, and as metaphor.

In Meyer Liben's 1959 story, "Homage to Benny Leonard," young Davey Flaxman tries to come to terms with the past and with his own Jewishness which, on various levels, must be vindicated. On a plot level, Davey asserts his approaching manhood and the integrity of his neighborhood by fighting an "outsider," an older boy named Gates. But Davey's fight has symbolic overtones. For one thing, he idolizes the lightweight champion Benny Leonard, a Jewish boxer whom he sees as a defender against the known and unknown enemies of Jews, just as many in the Jewish community at that time saw Leonard. Davey's victory over Gates vindicates Leonard's loss the day before, an event that greatly troubles the young boy. Davey's actions have an Old World dimension as well, a connection with history: in his mind, he associates Leonard and his newly assumed role as "Leonard's successor" with Jewish history. He makes this association after repeatedly hearing his grandmother tell about the coming of the Cossacks to her unidentified Eastern European village and the humiliation and suffering that occurred. Davey thus senses that these Old World wrongs and failures must be vindicated in the New World, a characteristic of Jewish American literature from *The Rise of David Levinsky* to *Seize the Day*.

Liben develops this theme by contrasting Davey to his father and to his best friend, Chick, two New World Jews who have no sense of the past and therefore no sense of the need for historical vindication. Davey's father cannot (or will not) even remember his own childhood. He claims instead that childhood is "twice as far off for the immigrant as for the native born" (178). Chick differs from Davey because, Liben writes, he had "more easily thrown off his ghetto past . . . he was well-adjusted historically" (179). Through these brief comparisons, a reference to Benny Leonard, and Davey's encounter with the "outsider," Liben manages brilliantly to convey the Jewish struggle to vindicate the past, as well as the haunting presence of Slavic Europe in the Jewish imagination.

In her 1968 story, "Sour or Suntanned, It Makes No Difference," Johanna Kaplan writes about middle-class Jewish girls at a summer camp, participating in an Israeli play about the Warsaw Ghetto. The girls play Nazis, Jews, and Polish partisans and have, as one says, "phlegmy Polish names, Dudek, Vladek, Dunya, Renya" (452). The children, however, do not enjoy or understand the play because as Americans and as New World Jews they have lost contact with their history and tradition.

Kaplan dramatizes this New World predicament by contrasting the children in the camp with their parents, whose frame of reference—other places and other times—confuses them. Mr. Imberman speaks Polish Yiddish; Mother talks about a strange city named Warsaw; and Uncle's comments appear ambiguous and distracted. When he tells Miriam, the protagonist, how much he likes her summer camp, Miriam senses that "he was describing someplace else entirely—maybe a place in Poland he remembered when he was a boy" (458). Miriam's mother appears, to Miriam, equally distracted and dislocated. She refers often to memory: "Who could have believed," she explains, "that any place could be as big as Warsaw. . . . I was the first girl from my town ever to be sent there to school" (448). Mother's comments (and her sobs) have no meaning for Miriam, except that she is puzzled that her mother, like her uncle, seems at these times to speak to "someone who wasn't there at all" (448).

In "Sour or Suntanned," Kaplan uses the play about the Warsaw uprising in ways similar to Liben's allusions to Benny Leonard; that is, as Miriam rehearses, she awakens to her cultural past and to a sense of historical place in the way that Davey Flaxman does through Grandma's stories and Leonard's boxing defeat. At one point she begins to identify with the gas streetlights, trolley-car stops, and the streets of a shrunken Warsaw. And during the performance itself, she "becomes" the girl who survived and thus triumphed in the woods "outside the finished-off Warsaw ghetto" (460). Her song stirs in her a closeness and a feeling for the past which her friends, concerned with trivialities, cannot share. Miriam, like Davey Flaxman, is stronger precisely because she learns about Jewish life in Eastern Europe.

In *Bloodshed and Three Novellas*, Cynthia Ozick also uses a Polish context to depict the Jewish postwar search for wholeness and happiness. Her protagonist in *The Mercenary* is a Jewish Pole who has remained in Poland, a devotee of the new socialist state. Ozick's point is that even those who remained must come to terms with their past and with conflicting memories of Poland—a notion confirmed in the postwar novels of Jewish Poles such as Brandys and Stryjkowski. Ozick's hero, Stanislav Lushinski, a Polish diplomat, has served his country well for many years. He has forsaken Judaism because, he believes, Judaism had abandoned him. In particular we learn that during the war, his parents turned him over for safekeeping to a Slavic peasant family, although he suspects that, in reality, they may have sacrificed him to save themselves.

In either case, he has disturbing memories and conflicting attitudes toward the past. He remembers his brutal treatment by the peasants who fear him because "he's too black. . . . He'll expose us, there's danger in it for us . . . too black. . . . Get rid of him" (27). And he remembers that neither his family nor his religion were of any value during his crisis. Consequently, he has rejected his cultural past. "I am not part of the Jews," he exclaims. "I am part of mankind" (41). Lushinski's denial notwithstanding, Ozick makes it clear that even those who willingly try to assimilate into socialist Poland cannot leave their Jewishness behind. Lushinski's new identity is an ironic one. He has come to believe that he and history are "one and the same" and that "the future can invent nothing worse" (37–38), without necessarily understanding that history is something that has happened to him, transfigured him into the universal Jew, like Morris Bober, carrying the weight of the past on his shoulders. Lushinski does so, however, without the consolation and assistance of Judaism. Nonetheless, Ozick seems to say of him, as the rabbi does of Bober, "Is he a Jew? Don't ask!" *The Mercenary* closes with Mon, Lushinski's black assistant, praying for the blacks of the world, those "emptied out creatures" who have lost touch with their spiritual, cultural selves. The analogy to Lushinski (he's too black) is immediate. We see him finally, like the man in "My Father Sits in the Dark," transfixed, staring into a memory, an emptied-out creature unable to hate or love.

Herbert Wilner writes yet another piece about repression, release, and the Polish past. In "A Gift Every Morning," two elderly immigrants share a bench in a Brooklyn park: a garrulous lady from Budapest who enjoys her European memories, although she admits to having suffered there; and an old man who "never speaks of Europe any more," although he grudgingly remembers that Warsaw, where he grew up, was clean and that he lost a son during the war. Late in the story, Wilner shows that his protagonist has repressed his Polish memories which, we soon learn, lie at the heart of his bitterness and despair. Suddenly, memories of cafés, writers, his meeting with Sholem Asch, the theater, villages, acting, his bearded father in a skull cap, his first Shakespeare play—all rush through his consciousness, triggered by the woman's references to Budapest. He can no longer "put up the wall to hold back the flood of Warsaw," Wilner tells us (135).

The old man's predicament is twofold. For years he has buried his Polish self deep within, refusing to acknowledge his Polish experiences, his Polish identity. These memories have nonetheless affected his personality, outlook, and his relationship with his surviving son who cannot understand (the recurring motif in these stories) his father's bitterness precisely because he cannot know, as the father admits, of a cultural connection preserved only in memory. Like his fellow writers, Wilner teases these memories back into consciousness to fill in the missing pages.

The old man's plight and that of Lushinski, Miriam, Davey Flaxman, the young narrator in Liben's short story and, by extension, all those victims of displacement and culture shock is perfectly expressed in the title of Grace Paley's collection, *Enormous Changes at the Last Minute,* stories about Faith, a Jewish New Yorker whose despair and confusion are rooted in her lost ethnicity. Paley's stories are a final stage of sorts in Polish-Jewish literary history. Whereas other writers ultimately traced the predicament of many New World Jews to their Polish pasts, the protagonist of Paley's stories is too far removed from her past to make that connection. Ironically, Poland lurks tauntingly in the shadows of her life. Faith's friend, for example, tells about her parents who came from Poland and who now are two forlorn and lonely people, holding hands in the darkness. Faith is prompted to wonder "who are her antecedents" and to observe that, like herself, her family also suffers from dislocation. Her mother plans to go to Israel because "I have spoken altogether too much English in my life," and her grandmother has had to change national identity as well, pretending at one time to be German "in just the same way that Faith pretends that she is an American" (33).

Faith seems to know little of her European past except that her immigrant father arrived at Ellis Island and "shot into the middle class like a surface to air missile" (122). Like the school girls in "Sour or Suntanned," she shows no real interest. At this point and for many in her generation, Paley seems to say, it makes no difference whether their roots are in Germany, Hungary, or Poland. The specifics of history, of time and place, have become blurred into the disinterested guess that "maybe it was Austria." Even so, Faith admits that she has grown up in the "shadow of another person's sorrow" as we learn in "The Immigrant's Story." And Paley implies that the sorrow originates somewhere in Europe, perhaps in Poland. Now, Paley writes, it is all gone in America just as it is in the snow of "finished off Warsaw." For Faith, a "finished off Warsaw" is replaced by a New York neighborhood where African Americans now tell her she doesn't belong. They have no memory of the Jews, Poles, or Irish, who lived there earlier. Like Neil Klugman in Roth's *Goodbye Columbus,* who surveys Newark's changing landscape, Faith wonders "what in the world is coming next" (198). Fright, loneliness, stasis are all that she has left. Even the memories have disappeared.

Whereas Poland in these stories exists solely in memory, in Jerome Rothenberg's *Poland/1931,* memory becomes metaphor—a state of mind, universal, timeless, but ultimately inexpressible. His "ancestral poems," published in 1970, are the dying ember of Weidman's "dead flames" and the soundless echoes of distant memories. Through fragments, images, and scraps of detail, he remembers, recounts, presents the ways of Polish-Jewish life. The ancestors are shadows of the past, mothers, brothers, uncles brought back almost to life. But it is really Poland that Rothenberg recalls, the mystical and ordinary life of a vanished culture and the historical union of Slavic Christians and Semitic Jews. In his opening poem, "The Wedding," he scrutinizes this union through a dream haze. "My mind is dreaming of Poland," "mad Poland," he tells us, where "we have lain awake in thy soft arms forever." The macabre embrace of timeless lovers dissolves into rhetorical awe and wonder. "Have we not tired of thee Poland," he asks, and abruptly responds, "no." The elegiac tone of "The Wedding" punctuated with the refrain, "Poland, Poland, Poland, Poland, Poland" culminates in the grim image of executioners, "standing inside thy doorways" where they "begin to crow." As there will always be Jews, there will always be Jewish life in Poland, he implies in "The Connoisseur of Jews," and this life will live in the words of those who write the Jewish poem. In "The Idols," he remembers Poland as "my country," a place, however, where the light is "without light" and where grey "makes grey the day," a land of milk and honey which turns out to be only "a thin line around the mouth."

In the final two poems, elegy gives way to cynicism. In "A Poem for Christians," Rothenberg refers to a "land that was not sown for us," a place where the holy name is "destitute of good works," one where the

Sabbath is disfigured by the rubber, gasoline, and chrome of "two Buicks of the previous year" and bodies "gone for a burnt offering." In "Fish and Paradise," the landscape turns to ice and corpses and a couple who "cast no shadow." The poem recalls the union in "The Wedding," but hope has grown chill and love has turned into a past-tense affair. The speaker feels foolish, empty, and reluctant. He concludes that memory words are futile and offensive, good only with which to "paper rooms," impossible to preserve, pointless to translate into nonmeaning. *Poland/1931* ends in self-imposed and historically wrought silence.

By the 1970s Jewish American writers had passed through several stages in their attitudes and fictional treatment of Poland: ambivalence, hostility, reconciliation, introspection, silence. In each stage the task of confronting the past has been doubly difficult, marked by centuries of ancient prejudices that have at times reduced a thousand years of shared history to caricatures. Yet their work shows that Poland has become a fixed frame of reference in Jewish American literature. As ethnic writers, their fictional mission is simultaneously to destroy and preserve the past—that they have done so in the case of the Polish past remains to be seen. On the one hand, perhaps Rafael Scharf is correct in saying that "the paths of two of the saddest nations on this earth have parted forever" (277). On the other, the persistent appearance of Polishness suggests, as Alfred Kazin said of Saul Bellow's work, that Jewish American writers are still "putting it right by thought" (130).

PART
II
★

AMERICAN SELVES—ETHNIC PERSPECTIVES

8

RECONSTRUCTING ETHNICITY

The View from the Inside

*Natura Ciagnie Wilka do lasu—what's bred in the bone,
can never be out of the flesh.* —POLISH PROVERB

I. SELF-DEFINITIONS

Compared to the surprisingly large number of Americans who in one
way or another have written about the Polish experience, descent
writers constitute a minority. Even so, perhaps as many as fifty writers
of Polish descent, most of them third generation, have, especially in the
last two decades, explored ethnicity with varying degrees of commitment and purpose. Some resist being identified as Polish American or
labeled as ethnic writers. In a few cases they reject even the notion that
they are writing about the Polish self. Darryl Poniscan, for example,
despite authoring a number of novels about ethnic exiles, says, "It
would be a stretch to call me an 'ethnic' writer" (ALS, 2 March 1989).
Richard Bankowsky, whose Rose tetralogy stands as one of the most
artistically successful and extended literary treatments of ethnicity,
comments, "I've never considered myself an ethnic writer. I'm just a
writer who writes about Polish Americans" (qtd. in Wrobel 396).
Similarly, the half-Polish Gary Gildner, prominent poet and writer of
fiction, insists that he had no good reason to make the protagonist of
his novel, *The Second Bridge,* Polish. "It just felt right" (Interview,
10 March 1988). To be sure, these writers and their works are more
than ethnic. More accurately, they regard ethnicity, particularly the
Polish self, as a universal rather than a parochial experience. They are
also undoubtedly aware that works dealing with the older immigrant
groups are not, at present, a valuable literary commodity.

Others have been more quick to admit the ethnic quality in their
work and to define the role of Polishness in their art. In Victor Contoski's anthology, *Blood of Their Blood,* writers speak to this issue in
appraisals that range from contradictory impulses to wholehearted
acknowledgment. Douglas Blazek claims, on the one hand, that he is
too far removed from his heritage for it to have "any immediate influ-

ence," but on the other, admits that because of that heritage, "my poetry tries to keep its feet on the ground, its images tangible" (12). Likewise, John Minczeski believes that the ethnic influence on his work "has been fairly negligible," although "I think I'm turning more of my attention to Poland now" (72). Laura Ulewicz acknowledges the "Polish tenor" in her poetry but claims that she "cannot isolate it from the rest of me" (116). Terry Kennedy and Leonard Kress go one step farther, crediting their Polish background, Kress explains, as the "basis for my work" (54).

These sometimes reluctant admissions of ethnicity are balanced by more expansive comments that attempt to define the soul of the Polish self. For Douglas Blazek, Polish character is "stoicism and grace in facing adversity, a determination to see things to their end, an acceptance of pain and discomfort, a humble disposition to life . . . commitment to honest muscle and the pure graces of simple pleasures" (12). To this, Karl Kulikowski adds "the work ethic, respect for the elderly, a religious feeling . . . and a Polish thick headedness that does not know how to quit" (60). More penetrating, if not less romantic, than the observations of most host-culture writers, these comments do not (and perhaps cannot) differentiate between national character and an Americanized version of Polishness acquired through decades of transplant and acculturation. What emerges rather is a conception of ethnicity filtered through and influenced by New World experiences. It is, by and large, Polish American culture that these writers define, and it is an ethnicity created, altered, and transformed that they write about. As Mark Pawlak explains, "Within my extended family there was little awareness of the 'high culture' of the 'Old Country'—I discovered Chopin on my own through a mail-order record company" (80); and John Rezmerski adds, "We never listened to Chopin or read Mickiewicz when I was a kid . . . we listened to Polkas and jokes and hunting stories at the St. Joseph Society's 'Polish Hall,' and we called each other 'Polack'" (92). Anthony Bukoski, probably more than anyone else, puzzles over the culture about which he writes. For him, it is birthright, religion, history, a tradition that "in this country includes being subject to others' insensitivity," and yet something else beyond his grasp (TLS, 16 December 1989). All this makes up the thrust of Bukoski's fiction as it does, to a great extent, that of other descent writers who, somewhat uncomfortably, are still trying to locate their territory in the literary landscape.

To a degree, that territory adjoins and even overlaps that of host-culture writers; that is to say, many of the surface characteristics and literary contexts that mainstream writers attributed to Poles for over a century and a half reappear in descent literature. The peasant attachment to the land, prominent in 1930s fiction, resurfaces in the stories of Monica Krawczyk, Wanda Kubiak, and Anne Pellowski, with the distinction that the immigrant farmer moves from immediacy to reflection about a time and experience on the wane. Making a home in Pellowski's adolescent novels gives way to continuity and stability as family and place become new markers for ethnicity. The same might be said of the urban experience, where neighborhood and childhood in Stuart Dybek's South Chicago dominate the folk symbols and ceremonies that had captivated Karl Harriman almost a century before. Descent writers, such as Matt Babinski, Jan Kubicki, and Lois Lenski, continue to portray ethnicity as a working-class phenomenon, not exclusively within the political framework of the proletarian novel but almost always with overtones of class consciousness and socioeconomic struggle. For the Polish American writer, a working-class point of view, charged alternately with uneasiness, protest, and regret, seems both natural and inescapable.

At the same time the legacy of Poland's rich and illustrious history punctuates the atmosphere, whatever the subject, through allusions to names, events, and attitudes that, in the hands of nineteenth-century writers, were the exclusive markers of Polishness. In this case, however, certain characteristics used to identify a cultural beau ideal become markers of the ethnic "other" in twentieth-century America. So too, Old World customs and ceremonies, usually associated with folk culture and Catholicism, continue to play an important but diminishing role in defining the ethnic self. Whereas host-culture writers depended almost exclusively on these particularities for purposes of local color and their perception of ethnicity as exotic, descent writers use proverbs, music, and customs with the easy grace of familiarity. For them, the stuff of Poland is at times an object of wonder, especially in regard to the generation of grandparents whose ethnicity is decidedly different from their own.

This is especially true in regard to Catholicism which represents, for Richard Bankowsky and Anthony Bukoski, the mysterious center of the ethnic world. Host-culture writers tend to look at Polish Catholicism from a distance, noting only the externals of ceremony and ritual associated with festival days. But descent writers chronicle the influence of the church in day-to-day life and focus on the parish as the heart of the community. In addition, for Paul Milewski, Stuart Dybek, and Gary Gildner, Catholicism Polish-style is an experience central to childhood and adolescence. Their poems and stories about serving Mass, assisting in church functions, attending parochial school, and fathoming the depths of practice and belief are fused with the mystical wonder of childhood and the throwing off of old demons, dogmas, and superstitions that haunt them as adults. For Anthony Bukoski, parish, priest, church, and faith are a sanctuary for ethnicity, a haven from cultural interference and social disorder. To be Polish, as most in Poland and many in the United States would say, is to be Catholic, and Bukoski's fiction makes it clear that if ever two were one, then surely they.

For others, notably Gary Gildner, ethnicity has become a magnet, pulling them toward a clearer resolution of their literary voice. Gildner's poems about Poland open new territory for the exploration of the Polish and American self; Bukoski has determined that he will define Polish American culture. What these and other descent writers have done is to internalize and deepen experiences that host-culture writers have ignored or presented in two-dimensional, semiotic terms. Descent writers have looked inside the ethnic self and the inner life of ethnic America, heretofore an object *in,* but not the subject *of* literature about Poles. As one might expect, the insider view of ethnicity differs from generation to generation. Those writers most closely associated with the immigrant generation operate with an eye turned toward Poland which, for many third- and fourth-generation ethnics, has no more relevance than Timbuktu. Anne Pellowski shows the almost geometric decline of physical and intellectual connections to Poland with each succeeding generation. Whatever the age differentiation though, Poland, through anecdote, memory, and legend, finds its way into the fabric of ethnicity. For one and for all, to be Polish is to accept ethnicity as a synonym for an identity that differentiates the self of childhood and beyond from that of others, and that provides a touchstone for experience and memory.

At best this satisfaction is private and internal, a melancholy, Americanized version of *zal,* so often attributed to Poles from Rupert Hughes to William Styron. Publicly, descent writers are, as we have already seen, sensitive about the ethnic self. Like John Minczeski, they are angry that from the beginning they have been robbed of name, status, and culture. Anthony Bukoski believes that America has determined that Poles shall be as invisible as Ralph Ellison's African Americans. Darryl Poniscan's Buddusky brothers are cultural exiles. Richard Bankowsky implies that the Polish experience is yet another expression of man's eternal status as an immigrant. Their characters seek the security of name and home and a way to balance an ethnic past with which they are relatively secure with a postmodernist, deethnicized present. Polishness, whatever that might mean to them, exists in childhood and in memory poems and stories about the death of grandparents. There is the sense that the world is upside-down, that the landmarks of the ethnic experience (St. Adalbert's for Bukoski, the neighborhood for

Dybek) have disappeared with the immigrants themselves, that the end of things approaches, and that ethnic culture may already be gone.

Even as they mourn, descent writers preserve their heritage through the act of writing. What is more, their efforts affirm the paradoxical destiny of the ethnic writer to separate beginnings from ends and to distinguish what was from what is. Many of the narrators and fictional protagonists, consequently, are travelers, unsure of yesterday, in search of tomorrow, reexamining and reinventing their ethnic past to provide food for present thought. In some instances, this has produced genuine art; in others only sentiment. In all cases, however, descent writers have tried to fashion a voice for a largely unvoiced experience and to offer a literary profile of "the other" with a human face.

2. THE IMMIGRANT ON THE LAND REVISITED

Writers who portrayed the Polish farmer in novels of the 1930s did so by characterizing him as an embryonic Puritan, replete with New England values, on a mission to reclaim a distressed America, often with mixed results for the immigrants and their descendants. This typology served well to translate ethnicity into terms Americans would understand and to make foreigners into acceptable Americans. Although postwar writers continued, with variations, to employ this format, they also looked at the other side of the Polish experience: the perils of transplant, the loss of cultural identity, and the conflicting messages of dual heritage in a country where ethnic reality does not always mirror immigrant ideality.

Descent writers have been equally infatuated with the fictional possibilities for the ethnic farmer and the pleasing prospect of presenting ethnicity in terms compatible with the agrarian dream vision. From Monica Krawczyk's stories of Poles in rural Minnesota, to Wanda Kubiak's 1962 novel, *Polonaise Nevermore,* to Anne Pellowski's recent tetralogy of Wisconsin farm life, they offer an extended survey of Polish American farm life and a convenient vehicle by which to compare ethnicity from the inside to that on the outside. On the surface, these works are not dramatically different from host-culture models. Both groups of writers look back at the formative years of the late nineteenth and early twentieth centuries; both feature a decidedly regional perspective; both look at the transition of newly arrived immigrants over a period of time; and both deal with cultural conflicts of various kinds.

At this point, however the road divides. The immigrant journey in host-culture works tends to lead toward Americanness; in those of descent writers it leads toward multiculturalism. So it is with the central conflicts that descent writers describe more as intra- than inter-cultural. Additionally, the Poles in host-culture works about the peasant farmer are usually isolated, cut off from Old World contacts and New World ethnic communities. Living in a cultural vacuum, they exemplify a European mentality soon to be sloughed off for a newer and better American skin—a view of ethnicity as a prelude to authenticity. Locating their characters within ethnic communities, descent writers are, of course, equally interested in assimilation, but define ethnicity as a set of evolving cultural markers influenced by social patterns inside and outside the community. They combine the particulars of the Polish self with the characteristics of the majority culture and suggest that ethnicity resides, perilously perhaps, with a foot in both worlds and in values shared across cultures.

Consequently the notion of ethnicity as home, place, family, and religion cuts across these works, evidence of the attempt by descent writers to transform ethnicity from otherness into yet another ideological concept: the Pole as repository of traditional (American) values, perhaps already lost in postwar America. Thus grandpa's song in Pellowski's *Willow Wind Farm* is a comment on a fading Old World idyll and on ethnic romance.

> Where are the golden times gone,
> Those olden times?
> Those times when we dressed for merrymaking,
> In petticoats and dress of our homeland. (160)

Once again the immigrant farmers have created agricultural Edens, from Krawczyk's filled barns, good land, and bountiful fields to Pellowski's blooming, healthy Latsch Valley where almost everyone is Polish. But even here their emphasis differs from that of their host-culture counterparts whose aim is the Americanization of the ethnic garden. The motivation for these farmers is to transplant a little bit of Poland to Wisconsin and Minnesota and to keep it Polish as long as possible. All three writers tell this story differently, depending on their distance from the immigration process itself. As a result, ethnicity assumes different dimensions in each work.

Monica (Kowaleski) Krawczk was born to immigrant parents in 1887 and later married an immigrant. She never lost contact with the Polish community and, as Edith Blicksilver points out, had a lifelong interest in disseminating information about Polish culture (43). Associated with the Minneapolis Polonia Club which she helped to organize, she wrote dozens of stories in the 1920s and 30s, published in regional and national magazines directed toward a female audience (*Woman's Day, Good Housekeeping, The Country Home*). The stories—some of which were collected and published under the title, *If the Branch Blossoms* (1950)—provide glimpses of domestic life framed within rural settings in Poland and America.

Like Harriman's *The Homebuilders*, *If the Branch Blossoms* reveals a peasant culture transforming itself into working-class America. Although the stories deal with ordinary problems and situations, Krawczyk establishes ethnicity by casting familiar incidents in the context of an Old World framework that helps to organize experiences from a Polish viewpoint. She juxtaposes universal tales of a wife's disappointment with marriage and status with Polish traditions: the celebration of Postnik, the singing of Kolenda, the breaking of Oplatki, the peasant wedding. In these information-giving stories, female protagonists waver between allegiance to tradition and change. In "Quilts," a coarse husband warns his wife to "tend to your housework" (60) and to stay away from female socials. In "For Dimes and Quarters," the husband will not allow his wife to attend night school, insisting that "a woman's place is in the home" (91). In her opening story Krawczyk portrays a dictatorial father who stubbornly refuses his daughter permission to court a village boy she has loved for years. This "Polish" story introduces the image of the patriarchal family, which in her "American" stories undergoes modification. In many of her stories, Krawczyk contrasts authoritarian peasant behavior with enlightened New World practices, almost always in conjunction with gender issues. Time and again, Krawczyk's women turn to Anglo school teachers (Misses Taylor, Bates, Leonard, Rice, Worst, Cook) for approval, encouragement, and advice which they then use to reorganize family life.

The theme of family and social reorganization carries over into those farm stories that deal with gender and generational attitudes toward ethnicity. Mr. Kowalek isolates himself from American influences. Peasantlike, he exercises complete control over his wife and son, Antek, by refusing to give his blessing to Antek's proposed marriage to a non-Polish girl. He will not divide his land in order for Antek to become independent and he stubbornly refuses to attend local Grange meetings. In the United States for twenty-five years, Kowalek clings to his peasant upbringing. He is suspicious of strangers, resistant to change, and frightened by differences. At all turns he protects his Polishness. Nonetheless, Antek's marriage precipitates change, as Krawczyk in these stories emphasizes transformation. "Everything now that comes along, Antek takes to it right away" (137), Mrs. Kowalek proudly observes. In "No Man Alone," Kowalek reluctantly agrees to attend Grange programs and, in the process, discovers that Americans are genuinely interested in cultural diversity. His daughter wins a prize for her traditionally decorated braided rug, the men ask where he learned his skillful farming techniques, and the entire group enjoys learning a Polish song. Immigrant defensiveness changes to ethnic pride as Kowalek begins to weigh the relative value of Old and New World behavior.

Like the Poles in Miniter's, Ferber's, and Carroll's agrarian novels, Krawczyk's characters are insular, ahistorical, simple, enduring, and adaptable. But by assigning the point of view to her Poles and elevating them to major character status, Krawczyk shifts the idea of "other" from minorities to "majority" Americans who must themselves consider changing to accommodate their new kin. In "After His Own," Krawczyk emphasizes this ironic turn of events when Edith, Antek's Anglo wife, tells her mother-in-law that she would be happy to learn "half what you know I mean of the really important things" (120).

In tone and substance, Wanda Kubiak's *Polonaise Nevermore*, written a generation later, more closely resembles the agrarian novels of Castle, Hindus, and Chase than it does *If the Branch Blossoms*. For one thing, despite its Wisconsin setting, the novel has a decidedly New England flavor. Kubiak calls attention to the New England–style architecture of the farmhouses, refers to the residents as Yankees, notes that Sundays resembled "the inactivity of a typical New England Sabbath" (31), and observes that the area "was a bit of New England transplanted to Wisconsin" (30). Given that the greater number of settlers are Polish, Kubiak's New England model seems explainable only in terms of the typological format she employs. Like the New England novelists, she celebrates the reclamation of cut-over lands as Edna Ferber did in her Wisconsin novel, *Come and Get It* (1934). She also emphasizes affinities between "Yankees" and Poles by comparing their religious convictions, democratic heritage, rugged individualism, and intense patriotism. At one point, one of her American characters drives home the idea of kindred cultures in the style of 1830s writers: "I suspect that Poland had historical milestones which are similar to ours. I mean, the stream of western culture as it flowed through your country, must have produced similar reactions" (93).

Within a framework that emphasizes cultural likenesses and a familiar typology, ethnic peculiarities seem less important than Polish and American kinship. Kubiak is, nonetheless, as eager as Krawczyk to capture and to praise the uniqueness of Polish traditions, offering numerous examples of folk culture: the bowing letter, customary salutations, druzba (a wedding custom), Swieconka (the blessing of Easter food), Dingus (Easter Monday rituals), and All Souls Vigil. She also talks about regional Polish music from the Krakowiak and Trojak to the Mazur. In fact, Kubiak is quick to show that Poland is a nation of distinct regions and that Polishness is ill-defined even by Poles as she moves from colorful surface features to the more complex struggle for dominance within the ethnic community itself.

Kubiak's Poles are divided into nationalists and assimilationists, into those attracted by the powerful pull of Europe and those with an equally strong desire to slough off the old ways and emerge as Americans. In the novel, this conflict takes the form of a debate about a newly constructed Polish Catholic church. For the nationalist, Antoni Grosz, the church is an extension of the Polish homeland; for Victor Topolski, the church is a bridge to assimilation. He knows that in fifty years the name St. Stanislaus will have little meaning to succeeding generations of parishioners. Kubiak voices her own views through her narrator who tells us that the Poles had for a time "allowed their Old World repressions and resentments to cloud their New World aspirations" (9).

Actually Kubiak takes a middle road, suggesting the kind of social pattern described by Milton Gordon in *Assimilation in American Life*. Like Gordon, Kubiak senses that assimilation is a complex layer of structures within which ethnicity may continue to exist relatively unhindered. In her novel, Pan Paradowski speaks for such a "solution": a Polish community assimilated in the larger context of the American family, but separated in regard to religion, family, recreation, and the like. Kubiak/Paradowski sees a society where Poles will be "equally at ease with each . . . attracting their own people to them but securing for them a place in the highest circles of American society" (115). In *Polonaise Nevermore*, however, interethnic in-fighting results in few opportunities for Poles to mingle with Americans, and the third generation's ignorance of their cultural heritage suggests that Paradowski's plan for ethnic preservation has not succeeded. Instead we see Polish groups cut off from the larger community and individuals suffering the effects of cultural isolation.

In this respect, *Polonaise Nevermore* resembles Lampell's *The Hero*, Tabrah's *Pulaski Place*, and Algren's *The Man with the Golden Arm* more than it does earlier accounts of the immigrant on the land. Many of the Poles are simply overcome by the demands and conflicting values of the New World. Frania is driven toward isolation: "Why can't we just stay Polish and live by ourselves?" (118), she wonders. Jozefa sees herself as an alien: "I feel I don't belong anywhere, not among our own people, and, of course, not among the English" (164). Jozefa's tragic death produces sympathy for the Poles but not a distinct or permanent change in community attitudes. Kubiak's ending, like Krawczyk's, seems forced, designed more to produce empathy than to record meaningful change. The fact that the narrator, a dean at a local women's college, has moved away from her ethnicity and seems to regard it as part of a quaint but vanished past indicates that Kubiak's vision of a pluralistic America may have been only a wishful thought or one that she never really wanted.

In her biographically based tetralogy, chronicling the life of the Pellowski family in Wisconsin from 1862 to the mid-1960s, Anne Pellowski adds another chapter to the ongoing story of the immigrant on the land. The novels for children center around what Bernard Koloski in "Ethnicity for Children" calls "wish motifs." Each of the child protagonists wishes for excitement: visitors (Betsy), schooldays (Rose), continued residence on the farm (Annie), and a visit to Poland (Anna). Significantly, only Anna does not get her wish, although the author seems to get hers—a chance to re-create a somewhat idealized past and a history of American ethnicity as traced through an extended family.

Pellowski's Poles in *First Farm in the Valley* mirror the great American westering experience. Sod-busters and sod-housed, they create a happy valley through self-reliance, industry, and perseverance—Old World qualities adaptable to New World requirements. In succeeding novels, Frank Pellowski's descendants continue to insure the health and vigor of the Latsch Valley. Although Pellowski's typological format is subtle, it is clear that America is better off because of the Poles. They never swear, scheme, steal, or harbor mean thoughts. They love animals, the farm, each other, and the daily routine. Nothing in the world, of which they seem unaware, bothers them including their heritage or status as outsiders. They are secure, they are busy, they are Polish. Read chronologically (against the order of publication), the tetralogy quickly develops into a celebration not so much of ethnicity but of social stability and the peaceful and purposeful integration of immigrants into the American mainstream.

Perhaps because of her young audience, Pellowski—even in *First Farm*, her most ethnic novel—treads lightly in presenting otherness. Cultural maintenance is important but never a pressing problem and ethnic observances lack the thrust of Krawczyk's "let's be Polish" tenor. Anna, we are told "thought of herself as Polish even though she knew Poland was far, far away" (9). Anna wishes, moreover, to see the country of her parents, but Pellowski quickly neutralizes any would-be conflict by portraying this as the naive wish of a little girl, taken seriously neither by the reader nor the writer. The Pellowskis have no second thoughts about their exodus and no intention to return. From the beginning the cultural magnet for the family has been American-ness, a value embedded in the novel's structure, which opens with a chapter called "Anna's Family" and closes with "Fourth of July." In the pivotal middle chapter, "100th Birthday," Pellowski symbolically brings her family from their Polish farm to the American town to participate in the nation's centennial.

In this work and the succeeding two, a sense of community holds the immigrants together. The Cierzans, Wickas, Kukowskis, and Zywitskis like, respect, and depend on one another. They draw sustenance from, and order the calendar year around, Old World ceremonies: Dyngus, name days, Easter, the Christmas Eve visit of the gvsozdki (animal-masked gift-givers and moral inquisitors). But even in the early days of the settlement, social and moral order comes not from folklore but from family, stability, continuity, and religion—although Pellowski spends little time on Polish Catholicism except to note feast observances. Her community represents the kind of ethnicity that not even the harshest critics of immigration could fault. After all, who could object to a closing scene in which Anna dances with "English girls," and Poles and Anglos clasp hands "high and arching, like a bridge" (181).

The second novel, *Winding Valley Farm,* follows Annie Durawa who at the turn of the century lives on an "old-fashioned family farm" in a valley settled long ago by "old Frank" who emigrated from Poland. These children know little about their ancestry, although at least one is aware that local farmers still cart hay as they did in Poland. Although each chapter shows evidence of Polish customs, they are not themselves the subject of the chapter. Instead, Polishness appears only occasionally: mother makes paczkis and sara (a Polish American corruption of sere [cheese]), father reads from a Polish book, the children celebrate name day, and seeds are blessed on Rogation Day. Most of the chapters concentrate on daily rituals, on childhood delights in farm life, and on Annie's introduction to the public school system. In one generation, the child's wish shifts from Poland to an enthusiasm for institutional America. Whereas other children's novels typically use this event as a way to illustrate the anguish of otherness in a majority culture (Gray, Estes, Hayes), Pellowski plays this theme in a minor key—in a scene where Annie learns that school is an inappropriate place to speak Polish.

Pellowski vaults her story forward to the 1930s in *Stair Step Farm,* in which many readers may not recognize her third-generation farmers as Polish. Rarely does she refer to ethnic customs: a polka is mentioned without comment, Grandpa is said to speak Polish, Dyngus must be explained to the children. Ethnicity enters through the back door as Pellowski shifts from otherness to us-ness. Anna Rose's adventures are those of any American farm child, and Pellowski treats ethnicity as family, religion (undifferentiated), place, and stability. Anna Rose's problem is that father is considering leaving the family farm for a new job, but the bonds of home and continuity prevail. For all intents and purposes, Pellowski views these values as the core of ethnicity.

Nowhere is this better illustrated than in *Willow Wind Farm,* set in the 1960s in the same neighborhood. In this story of fourth- and fifth-generation Polish Americans, ethnicity has undergone further dramatic changes: Betsy's surname is Korb; her mother has married into a German family; and except for Mrs. Kulinski, few Poles seem to reside in the valley—even the parish priest is not Polish. The events are exclusively farm-based and the family is only remotely Polish. Grandpa greets the children in the Polish style, Mother remembers a word or two of the language, and Polish sausage (not called kielbasi) is served at the reunion dinner while Grandpa, through song, wonders "where are the golden times gone / those olden times?" (160).

Ethnicity in rural Wisconsin of the 1960s has passed away without regret or much remembrance. When a visiting aunt speaks to the children in various languages, they recognize German, French, and Spanish, but when she counts in Polish, they are dumbfounded until one guesses wildly, "I think it's Polish." Ethnic Polishness takes on new features in *Willow Wind Farm:* eating roast beef, kohraba, cucumber salad, and sliced tomatoes instead of blood soup, pierogi, and halupki. Polish Catholicism changes from the mystical union of Virgin and nation to frying doughnuts in the church basement on Sunday mornings. Many of the family live in distant parts; even Betsy's family lives thirty minutes away from the old homestead. At times, Pellowski, a long-time employee of the United Nations, emphasizes internationality and one worldness—as seen in the visit of Mrs. Kalula, an African, who talks to the schoolchildren about the third world. At other times, Pellowski continues to insist that ethnicity is alive and well and resides in home, place, family, and continuity. Betsy, the descendant of the little girl whose wish was to see Poland, has become the quintessential American. Echoing Dorothy of Kansas, she exclaims near the end of the novel, "there's no place like home" (173).

The tetralogy moves toward the incorporation of ethnicity into the larger national and international family held together by a transnational appreciation of family, land, religion, and traditional Western values. Ironically, when read as written (Pellowski wrote them in reverse order of chronology), the novels deny this theme. Like the world of the Leather-stocking in Cooper's romances, Pellowski's valley grows more intense, alive, and youthful, and the tetralogy gains in cultural diversity as Pellowski looks back to the springs of the immigrant experience. Her own experience in writing the novels bears this out. What began as a suggestion by a sympathetic editor developed into a passionate research project on the ninety-one pre–Civil War Polish families that settled the valley. And what begins with the notion of ethnicity as a "certain fervor that I believe is Polish in origin" (TLS,

12 October 1989) becomes the stuff of history. In her fourth volume, "all the names and events," Pellowski explains, "and the characteristics each family assumes, are based on historical records combined with some personal reminiscences" (TLS, 12 October 1989). In her first novels, Polishness expands into multiculturalism. In novels to come, Pellowski plans to uncover the "many layers of ethnicity buried in the past" (TLS, 12 October 1989).

3. THE NEW OLD PROLETARIAT

As recently as the early 1970s, the percentage of Polish Americans identified as blue-collar workers was higher than any other minority group except Hispanic; in fact, one study shows that nearly two-thirds could be described as blue-collar (Greeley 41). These figures not only help to explain the persistent appearance of Poles in prewar proletarian literature but also serve to comment on much of the literature written by Americans of Polish descent. Bill Costley's "For Dad and the Factory, Lynn River Works GE," is a case in point. The poem is about fathers who have accepted their destiny as factory workers and sons who have not, although they too stand forever in the shadows of working-class America. Costley explains how the factory had dominated family life, working its way through all their senses. "We heard it . . . we smelled it . . . it was etched into my retinas . . . [it] eats us," he writes (Contoski 29). Costley's 1970s poem is cynical about modern business mentality with its slick approach to "employee relations." He suggests that "advocate planning" and "corporate profit-sharing" are nothing more than new phrases to mask old problems. From all appearances, "For Dad" is not an ethnic poem; there are no references to cultural markers nor does the name Costley suggest an ethnic background. It is, nonetheless, one of many works by descent writers which have a hidden agenda that radiates, in this case, from Costley's perspective as the son of a factory worker of Polish heritage. That Costley would write such a poem, equating ethnicity with the working class in ways reminiscent of proletarian literature, not only links "For Dad" with that tradition but also offers evidence that for many descent writers, the Pole as proletarian had by the second half of the century become a literary assumption too obvious to state.

As Dad's years at the factory continue to plague Costley's speaker, so too the historical reality and socioeconomic status of Polonia haunt the works of descent writers, cutting across genre, time periods, and issues. Even those concerned primarily with the universals of the human condition and the inner life of contemporary America (Gildner, Poniscan, Dybek, Bankowsky) perceive the Polish experience in working-class terms without necessarily embracing the ideology that had typically portrayed the Pole as representative worker struggling to break the chains of economic slavery. In descent works this condition persists as a troubling legacy to be confronted and transcended and as the starting point for an assessment from the "inside" of the meaning of ethnicity in contemporary America.

Literature for younger readers written by descent writers is no exception. In *The Little World of Nellie Musial* (1954), Nellie (Kowalczyk) Musial tells about the trials of a young cleaning woman and her factory-worker husband, both of whom must accept their menial jobs and their status because, as recent immigrants, they have no alternatives. Lois Lenski, a prolific and well-known writer of adolescent literature seldom writes about her Polish ancestry, but when she does, as in "Auto-Worker's Son" (1965), her story turns out to be a children's version of the struggle for economic parity at the expense of cultural legacy. Ethnicity in this story is rooted in community (the setting is Hamtramck, Michigan), church, family, and occupation. The Baroszewicz's are auto workers threatened continually by "accidents, unemployment, and lay-off" (21); and, as young Josef awakens to the reality of ethnicity in America, he sees that to remain Polish is to be sentenced to the life lived by his father. Eddie, an older brother, is convinced that his name is his worst enemy, an obstacle to upward mobility, and that his family has been doomed to the assembly line by being "dirty Polacks." Against his family wishes, he changes his name to Barton and promptly finds a white-collar job. Josef, on the other hand, decides that, for now at least, he is "glad to be Polish . . . old country customs made life in America so much richer" (68). Lenski's obviously mixed messages illustrate the conflicting desires of Polonia. To be Polish means working class, which in turn brings isolation and economic exclusion. For this she offers no ready solution. We see that even in works directed at young audiences, ethnicity is a working-class phenomenon.

In addition to descent writers like Costley, who employs ethnicity behind the scenes, and Lenski, for whom class and ethnicity operate hand in glove, others have turned to the more traditional form of proletarian literature with varying degrees of political enthusiasm and commitment. In *Burning Valley* (1953), Phillip Bonosky examines ethnicity in Marxist terms, even as his *New Masses* colleague V. J. Jerome did in *A Lantern for Jeremy* (1952). In *By Raz 1937* (1978), Matt Babinski recollects his Polish boyhood as part of the left/right conflict of the 1930s. And in *Breaker Boys* (1986), Jan Kubicki returns to the formative period of labor unrest in the early years of the century. Although politics is the agenda, stated or implied in all three, the novels also show the steady transformation of the Poles from representative but decultured ethnics into individualized characters whose working-class status becomes a permanent consequence of ethnic identity.

Bonosky's *Burning Valley* is a transition novel—a bridge between standard proletarian fiction with its collectivized ethnic image, and postmodern works in which ethnicity dominates political ideology. Published by *Masses and Mainstream* where Bonosky was a long-time, influential contributing editor, *Burning Valley* follows a sociopolitical literary format already dated but somewhat rejuvenated in the McCarthy era of the early 1950s. Set in Hunky Hollow in what appears to be western Pennsylvania or West Virginia, the novel recounts the classic struggle of rich and poor, workers and owners, capitalistic oppression, labor agitation, strikes and repression in area mills, foundries, and railyards during the 1920s. Throughout, Bonosky replays the party line in the political awakening of his naive, young protagonist, Benedict Bulman, who comes to realize that industry, church, and government form an unholy class alliance designed to exclude the masses from their just share of the American dream. The rhetoric is predictable but also emotionally effective as Bonosky captures Benedict's emerging social conscience. For example, in the midst of the turmoil, Benedict questions his parish priest, a role model whose path he had always hoped to follow. "I met a man whom they beat in jail, Father, and they call him a Communist. But he wants to save our homes and to build a union—is he evil Father?" (161).

In the style of James Oppenheim, Upton Sinclair, and postwar writers such as Lester Cohen, Russell Janney, and Willard Motley, Bonosky offers ethnic composites; that is, virtually no differentiation is made among the Poles, Slovaks, and Lithuanians who populate the community. He is satisfied to characterize ethnics as victimized others and to stress ideology rather than diversity. Consequently we learn little about Polish culture and character except for perfunctory references to names, phrases, and foods which promote local color at the expense of culture. At the same time, Bonosky moves away from the bifurcated view of his host-culture contemporaries, who featured Poles as secondary characters, who relegated ethnicity to the edges of their works, and who established "otherness" through the point of view of nonethnic protagonists. His novel is decidedly ethnic centered: the major characters are Slavs, the viewpoint is Vincent's, and the sense and sensibility are that of the "other."

Significantly, even in this overtly political text, Bonosky seizes control of his ethnicity, heretofore represented by sometimes sympathetic, sometimes hostile host-culture writers. Although he is studiously careful not to favor one social group over another, his decision to tell his "own story" marks a turning point in proletarian fiction dealing with Poles and, in a way, with ethnic literature in general. In a "Salute to Mike Gold" (1954), Bonosky credits Gold's influence on his life, and he comments on his own awakening as an ethnic writer. His insights are additionally directed at a literary canon which had traditionally excluded "otherness." "In short, *I* was missing in American literature— that is, my town, the people I knew . . . the men who died workers just as they were born . . . Lithuanian Kilbasai and Serbian Tamburitzas and Joe Margarac . . . who wrote about all that? Nobody. It didn't exist" (45). Bonosky's recognition of the exclusionary nature of mainstream literature goes beyond subject matter, for he sensed that this world had to be written about from the inside by writers who stood squarely in the center of it. "I felt I stood on the outside of the permissible literary realm" he explains. "I had pride in myself . . . but the books I read did not" (46). The importance of *Burning Valley,* then, lies not in cultural insights or in new thinking about ethnicity at mid-century but rather in Bonosky's decision to appropriate his own story, to write it as an ethnic piece, to wedge ethnicity into the canon and into proletarian fiction. His is an act of self-determinism, the equivalent of Krawczyk's and Kubiak's ethnic versions of the immigrant on the land.

In *By Raz 1937* and *Breaker Boys,* Matt Babinski and Jan Kubicki continue to define the Polish experience in working-class terms but without the ideological passion of *Burning Valley.* Both writers, nonetheless, have a political agenda. Babinski frames his novel with opening references to Franco's Spain and the bombing of Guernica and with closing images of the symbolic death of the American elm trees in central Massachusetts where the story takes place. Throughout, Babinski's politics are clear. The National Recovery Act represents the last hope for the declining industry of Worcester, where most of his Poles are employed and where the depression has brought the working class to its knees. Worcester is yet another burning valley, replete with mills, foundries, waste, and the sweat of the Poles whose situation has changed little over generations. Raz's nightly visits to his uncle Eevon at the mill introduce the boy to his past and to his future unless, through Raz's own tenacity and with a little bit of luck, he can do better.

As Babinski shifts the emphasis from political to ethnic transformation, Raz's growth is predicated on his discovering his ethnic self. For this, Uncle Eevon is model and tutor to the twelve-year-old Apolinary Raz, not as a teacher of history, legend, and custom but as an example of Polish character, a subject generally avoided by proletarian writers. When Babinski introduces Eevon, he talks about Eevon's inner strength, pride, capacity for sacrifice, faith, work ethic, and his experience with oppression (Eevon knew many who had been sent to Siberia). Like Pellowski, Babinski also emphasizes Polishness as a commitment to land, family, church, community, and the past and a sympathy for otherness. These give Eevon his identity; and his neighborhood, where he has taken new roots, gives him security. He tells Raz: "I know all the families . . . on my street and adjacent streets" (49). St. Mary's is his church and the parochial school is his as well. Within this ethnically defined geography, Eevon and his neighbors feel comfortable; they know who they are.

Community life, moreover, is organized in traditional ways. Religious feast days anchor the calendar year as the neighborhood devoutly observes the religious and secular customs associated with traditional holidays. The older generation maintains ties to the old country. Raz's mother regularly goes to the park to hear news from Poland and to chat with women from Lwow, Gdansk, and Warsaw. Eevon has a small farm on the outskirts of town where he, in peasant fashion, can touch the land and where he can feel the "fullness of earth at harvest" (208). In short, Raz comes to believe that his neighborhood is "not much different from any one of a hundred villages in Poland" (72).

What appears to be the successful transplant and healthy maintenance of Old World ways is, however, deceiving. After all, as Eevon indicates, he knows *only* his neighborhood which, while self-sustaining ("an immigrant could shop in this area for most of his life, and not learn a word of English" 23), is also culturally isolated. In addition, troubling signs are evident in the excessive drinking, the hopeless resignation to a lifetime in the mills, the harsh landscape, and Raz's doubts about his future as an ethnic American. In truth, for the Polish peasant, it "was no longer the same" (156).

For the second generation, the Polish self must necessarily be defined anew, and Raz and Eevon undertake an ethnic journey that Babinski compares to Huck Finn's. He introduces the parallel early as he talks about the Blackstone River that flows through Worcester. But all illusions of romance are dispelled quickly when Raz comments that some "may think of it as the Mississippi, but to me it's the sewer overflowing and nothing else" (19). Raz's initial cynicism differs from Huck's early romantic tendencies, just as Raz's journey is distinctly an ethnic one. Nonetheless, like Huck, Raz finds himself engulfed in a struggle to stave off the pressures of mainstream values in much the same way as the protagonists of Lampell's *The Hero* and Tabrah's *Pulaski Place*.

Raz's mother, aware that "what's there is there and what is here is here" (89), has at least the benefit of a lived European experience which she can turn to in memory and as a yardstick for comparison. Raz, the second generation, does not know what's there or how here and there are different. To learn, he questions his father and Uncle Eevon about village life, history, the wars, the experience of being Polish—none of which are explained at length by Babinski, who is interested more in the immediate experience of the second generation and the conflicting demands of a dual heritage. Like the neighborhood itself, Polishness is surrounded by Americanness, New England style, much of which has worked its way into the ethnic mentality. Eevon, for example, is equally passionate about Chopin and the land and his 1928 Model T and American elm trees; Paul Revere has become as familiar as black bread and cabbage soup; and Cape Cod houses and rock walls have replaced peasant cottages. If mother has managed to differentiate between Pilgrim and Pole, Raz has not, particularly since opportunity, the essence of the American dream, appears to lead away from ethnicity.

The ethnic journey, Babinski shows, involves constant evaluation and a capacity to adapt. Befriended by the influential O'Leary sisters, Raz, at their encouragement, enrolls at the art institute because the O'Learys convince him that "it's a possibility for a new life for you . . . for a different life" (307). Raz also sees that change is the nature of things. When Abigail tells Eevon that her family "settled the land . . . built the stone walls . . . this house too" (255), Eevon is not impressed. Abruptly, he replies that all that has changed and that she would no longer be accepted by the present neighbors. Ironically, there is no place for the Puritan inside the Polish community, as there is no place for Faith in Paley's "The Immigrant Story," even as Raz senses that someday there will be no place for the world of his parents. Even ethnicity must change, must throw off provincial notions and social restraints. Abigail explains that Raz's notions of art as religious iconography, learned in parochial school, limit his artistic horizons. She shows him Rembrandt's "Polish Rider," poised to master the unknown while secure in himself. The painting strikes home and Raz decides to carry the Old World into the New, assuming his father's name Apolinary and dedicating himself to artistic enlightenment. Ready for change but comfortable within his ethnic world, "where I belonged . . . felt at home" (312), he is ready to seek out new territory without rejecting, like Huck, the old.

For Babinski the ethnic dilemma, rooted in proletarian issues, turns into a more complex, cultural dilemma for the second generation. His look back at Polishness in the 1930s is, at times, nostalgic but not fearful or angry. If anything, Babinski believes that Polish character, passed on from Eevon to Raz, is perfectly suited to a good life in America and that Poles bring a readiness for change and an ability to transcend their working-class status while retaining their cultural uniqueness. In an epilogue, Babinski moves forward to 1978 and Polon's (Raz) fight to keep the American elm as the official tree of Massachusetts. In doing so Raz continues in the footsteps of Uncle Eevon, for whom the American elm had become symbolic of the immigrant experience.

In *Breaker Boys*, Jan Kubicki also looks at the immigrant experience in industrial America, specifically in the anthracite coal regions of northeastern Pennsylvania. *Breaker Boys* is actually a historical novel about the major strikes and civil disturbances in and around Jeddoh, Pennsylvania, in 1900 and the formation of the United Mine Workers Union, led by Johnny Mitchell. Since this subject lends itself so willingly to political treatment, it is sometimes difficult to decide if Kubicki is a neutral observer of radical history or a writer inspired by the call for socioeconomic justice. In either case, Kubicki's Poles are involved in an economic struggle that has overtones of class warfare. The novel tells a familiar story: the mistreatment of workers, pay-lines, company stores, evictions, the hazards of coal mining. Even the historical catalyst for the worker revolt (inaccurate measurements of coal mined) appears in Musmanno's *Black Fury* written in the 1930s. Predictably, the oppressors are Anglo mine owners represented by J. Markham, a Jay Gould figure, who threatens to "hire one half of the working class to kill the other half" (193). He responds to complaints by exclaiming, "I will hear no talk of union today or any day" and retreats to his fortresslike home, around which stretched the yard, "like a moat" (115). In turn, the Poles and Welsh respond enthusiastically to Mother Jones who compares their life to that of plantation slaves. Like the Poles in Russell Janney's *The Miracle of the Bells*, they come to understand that a union is their only alternative. In spite of Markham, the miners unite and in the close of the novel march down the hill together to proclaim that "the union had finally come to Jeddoh" (388).

Kubicki's historical plot, labor unrest and class oppression in the mining communities, is not much different from those of host-culture writers except that, like Bonosky, Kubicki stakes an ethnic claim to social history. Assuming a stance as historical revisionist, he writes his history from an ethnic point of view, employing Anglos in secondary roles. More to the point, Kubicki strips away sentimentality from traditional portrayals of Poles—an unusual turn of events in proletarian fiction and in the literature of descent writers. His Poles are tough, coarse, untutored immigrants without high culture, love of fatherland, and the usual attachment to the rituals of folk culture. They are, moreover, unmoved by ideological abstractions, usually characterized as patriotism, an enthusiasm for education, and a desire to be free, to be American. Their horizons are limited to day-to-day survival which they confront with unadorned emotions and peasant ferocity. Kubicki wastes no time establishing the ethnic writer as tough-minded commentator. "By day," he writes, "the women worked barefoot in the house and yard, shouting their gibberish and singing while their babies cried unattended. At night, when the men came home, there was arguing, endless arguing, an endless racket" (14). In addition, the nonhistorical villain of *Breaker Boys* is Zakrzewska, a Pole, a good-for-nothing, violent brute who turns out to be a traitor to his own kind when he spies for the company. In general, Kubicki shows the Poles to be timid, frightened, and suspicious toward the new union. "Ve don't vant union! Union can go to hell!" they cry (269), as he challenges romantic notions of Poles as eager unionists.

Kubicki emphasizes kinship between ethnic groups rather than Polish and American historical cultural links. His Poles and Welsh recognize the fact that they are all subject to socioeconomic exploitation and that they must turn to one another for support. Consequently, Kubicki joins together Welsh and Polish characters—people who historically have had little in common—into a new ethnic-American coalition. "We're all the same," Rhys, the young Welsh protagonist, tells the other boys. "We're just outsiders stumbling through the fog" (184), a sentiment echoed by Myfanwy who appeals to his Polish "brothers," explaining, "I am like you . . . I know how you feel. I know your heartache. I know . . . I know" (269). On the one hand, these passages closely resemble the proletarian rhetoric of Joseph Vogel and V. J. Jerome. On the other, they represent Kubicki's successful attempt to ethnicize proletarian fiction by shifting the call to arms and the recognition of mutual working-class interest to an ethnic spokesperson.

Not necessarily convincing in this case, this technique illustrates the uncertainty of descent writers in dealing with subject matter which in literary history has not been their own. How much to disassociate Poles from host-culture portrayals and literary models plagues Kubicki throughout. He is at times eager to introduce caricatures of peasants in regional costume, piously celebrating religious feasts, or carousing on weekend, backyard picnics. On other occasions, he seems uncertain that he has captured the Polish self at all. What he leaves us with are conflicting images of Poles: pro- and antiunion, intemperate but religious, suspicious yet inclined toward other "others," familiar yet mysterious to non-Poles. Historically, the UMWA succeeds, but he leads his readers to believe that Poles may not have. Writing about events almost a hundred years past, Kubicki seems unable, ultimately, to fathom Polishness. Through his spokesman Rhys, he can only say that "they were strangers to him, and he to them" (61).

Rhys's overstated verdict is not especially applicable to descent working-class literature in general, nor is Kubicki's novel necessarily reflective of contemporary interest in Polish Americans. That he would turn, however, to sociopolitical struggle occurring almost a century ago bears witness to the lasting association of Poles and the proletarian movement and to the descent writer's desire to redress old wrongs. What is more important is that Kubicki and his colleagues have ethnicized proletarian literature much more than previous writers had done. They have seized the opportunity to appropriate their own story, to add dimension to ethnic characters, and to redefine a broad social movement in ethnic terms.

9

HOME AS FOUND

He lives indeed in a no man's land. . . . He is nobody's son. —BURT
*We came here, we are a little lost. Always in this country
we will be a little lost.* —DRISCOLL

I. 3:00 O'CLOCK IN OUR EXPERIENCE

Two recent anthologies, *Blood of Their Blood* (1980), edited by Victor
Contoski, and *Concert at Chopin's House* (1987), edited by John
Minczeski, represent the diverse and extensive efforts of contemporary
descent writers to capture the Polish experience. The selections and the
authors are far-reaching: poems, short stories, chapters from a novel,
essaylike narratives by writers representing a broad spectrum of attitudes toward their own heritage. Some, such as Jerome Rothenberg, Diane Wakoski, Ed Ochester, and Victor Contoski, have already
achieved deserved recognition; others wait for public approval. Some
like Charles Bukoski arrogantly disclaim ethnicity: "All I know about
Poles is that they've lost a great many wars" (qtd. in Contoski 16).
Others rush into ethnicity headlong. The writers themselves defy categorization: exiles writing in Polish, recent immigrants experiencing
English as a second language, those who have spent time in Poland,
those for whom Poland is a sight yet unseen. Some are Jewish Americans, some Polish Americans, some write only as Americans. A few
know Polish culture intimately; others have only memories handed
down through generations. Their writings range as far as their backgrounds and talents allow: from the Jewish experience and the Holocaust, to stories of childhood; from travels to Poland, to political
comments on a changing nation; from distinctly ethnic subjects, to
poems and stories not about Polish selves at all.

Within all this variety a singular theme occurs with regularity: the
notion that, for many, ethnicity has become only a distant memory and
that the culture they experienced in childhood has rapidly receded into
history. In this respect, these anthologists echo the sentiments of virtually all descent writers, from Helen Bristol to Wanda Kubiak to
Anthony Bukoski, who worry about the loss of ethnicity and, consequently, the loss of self. This is especially true of Stuart Dybek and

Darryl Poniscan whose writings amount to an extended and sustained elegy for ethnicity. Poniscan's antiheroes are forever separated from region and home; Dybek's young protagonists can no longer find security in place. For them as well as for the voices represented in the anthologies, ethnicity is memory recollected, even as Poland is in the works of Jewish American writers. They turn to images of ancestors, events, and scenes snatched from childhood. Theirs is an organizing literature which tries to make sense of ethnicity transformed in time and which tries to restore identity to a contemporary self, disconnected—sometimes willfully—from its roots. A sense of urgency characterizes this writing: a rush to record a culture vanishing even before it had become permanent, a recognition that attention must be paid before it is too late. The tone is elegiac. Where has it all gone?, these writers ask in stories and poems about the loss of childhood, home, and the past.

A number of poets express their loss in poems about name changes (a fate few Americans of Polish descent have escaped), from those who were abruptly given a new identity by immigration officials to those who sought to avoid the pressures exerted on non-Anglos. What to some was acculturation and assimilation was to others, including these poets, a symbol of dislocation. In "My Name," John Minczeski, for example, captures the universal immigrant experience—the journey to America and the subsequent quest for a sense of place. Minczeski focuses on anonymity, however, on language and cultural dissociation, and on cultural nakedness. Minczeski's ancestor is, in fact, nameless, languageless, cultureless. "My name did not know English," he writes. "Without a passport . . . toothbrush or brown shopping bag," it swam to Staten Island where "it was taken in by potatoe farmers" (Minczeski 199). Apart from indicating that his name arrived "from Poland in 1910," Minczeski makes no other references to cultural identity, which, he implies, has dropped away into New York Harbor along with his name. Minczeski's roots are anonymous, undiscoverable, identifiable only in terms of archetypal experience. All this has brought him years of suffering, the consequence, in part, of a name "cut in half by a harrow." The speaker's emotions are controlled, steeled by time. "My name has forgotten how to cry," he concludes in a poem that expresses the resignation of the culturally disenfranchised.

Linda Mizajewski's ethnicity also originates in anonymity, in a grandmother who has "no language, no name: / her X on her papers / marks the spot / where we disappear" (Minczeski 12). In "Keeping My Name," Mizajewski writes about the particular dilemma of the ethnically Polish woman whose lifelong struggle is doubly difficult. Mizajewski's nameless grandmother twice loses her identity—through immigration and again through marriage. Like her, the speaker must also confront name change, although her father remains the "banker of syllables." "Love shouldn't make it vanish," she protests while acknowledging that identity loss is a fate common to "aunts and grocers, even my father." After having been singled out on classroom lists as an "exotic weed." Mizajewski holds onto her name "like stolen goods" and wonders how "could I grow another one." She complains that she has never been anything other than someone else's name. Whoever she is floated away "like the Holy Ghost at the moment of incarnation." She will always be "Mrs. Other," an outsider as woman and as ethnic, in maidenhood and in marriage.

For Margaret Szumowski, names are the legacy of the past, the connection between a culture almost forgotten and an ethnicity waiting to be born. In "Bronislaw," the speaker, seemingly secure within a tradition of borscht, pierogie, sausage, and poppyseed cake, remembers a fateful day when his uncle Victor revealed a family secret that affected him deeply and that clarified for him the meaning of descent. Ashamed of his Old World name, the young boy tells his mother, "I didn't want to be Bronislaw any more," bringing tears to her eyes. But Victor helps the boy to understand his "name" as he recounts his own imprisonment in a concentration camp and the day he saw his father, also a prisoner, for the last time: "I tried to rush up to him . . . a door shut between us and that was all" (Minczeski 46). The "secret" introduces the boy to his Polish past, to a family decimated by war, and to a history of suffering hitherto unknown to him. When Uncle Victor tells him that the "man" in the camp was named Bronislaw, the boy is speechless and Szumowski ends the poem with the clear implication that names embody the past.

In contrast to "Bronislaw," Ed Ochester's "Changing the Name to Ochester" is more New World than Old, more American than Polish, more concerned with familial relationships on a psychological level than on an ethnic one. Ochester writes about fathers and sons, guilt and forgiveness, desertion and reconciliation, "about forgiving Grandpa for my not knowing him" (*Changing* 17). Furthermore, he distances himself from the archetypal immigrant experience. Other grandfathers with names like Sergius Bronislaus Jygzywglywcz found themselves renamed Sarge Jerko, he explains, "but my grandfather was born in this country." But Ochester's opening anecdote, despite his insistence on differences, ties together ethnicity and identity in the fashion of Minczeski's "My Name." In this case, name change (Olshevski to Ochester) is one of the few facts about Grandfather that Ochester can determine, but not nearly as important as Grandfather's desertion of his family and the years of subsequent estrangement between family members who "refused to go to his funeral." But even as the speaker expiates for his and his father's disavowal of Grandfather, he releases the resentment of generations, originating in the immigrant experience. The poem begins as Sarge trundles from the pier to the Lower East Side "with a lead cross and a sausage wrapped in a hair shirt." Grandfather's desertion, his son's unforgiving response, and Ochester's guilt for living a life appreciably easier than his father's are rooted in this experience. Changing the name to Ochester is indeed a pivotal and far-reaching event in the lives of three generations—a marker separating consent and descent.

For Bill "Kulik" Costley, names serve to bridge his Polish and non-Polish heritage (he has adopted Boles Kulik as a type of allonym for poems on Polish subjects). "Kulik/Krrulik" is such a bridge. The poem opens as Costley explains that his half-Polish sister has given his son a Christmas present, a bird whistle "joined from a handful of unfinished pieces of Central European birch" (Contoski 30). At Easter, he learns that his mother's name, Kulik, is "one of the brood of peasant names 'taken from the birds.' " This Easter "gift" adds meaning to the painted bird given to his son for Christmas and helps to order the fragments of ethnicity which permeate the poem: half-Polish sisters, unfinished pieces of Central European birch, pieces of a lithographed bag, the dislocated American branch of the forests of Poland, the puzzling purling of his mother's "Krrulik, Kuulik, Krrulik." Disconnectedness and fragmented images are pulled together into Costley's enriching discovery that his name reverberates with his heritage.

In *Let the Blackbird Sing*, a verse novel, Helen Bristol laments her loss of identity on two fronts: she is forever cut off from Poland, "the music that I used to hear," and equally out of joint in American society. She worries about the survival of Polish culture transplanted and writes:

> Must we perish then?
> Are we such feeble sprouts as cannot root themselves?
> And this new soil, is it not for us?
> Must we surrender, despite our will to live? (167)

As in *Blackbird*, written almost a half century after Helen (Ogrodow-ski) Bristol's journey from Zyrardow to Philadelphia, the threat of extinction hovers about the imagination of succeeding descent writers whose work often expresses fears about the fate of their cultural heritage. Many of their poems and stories provide a vision of ethnic apocalypse, expressed primarily in the deaths of the tradition-bearing generation and in the frustration of descendants who, losing contact with the past and the old ways, can only mourn and preserve isolated pieces of tradition.

Where are they now, the writers ask in "obituary" literature about the passing away of relatives and, by extension, the ethnic self. In "Grandfather," John Rezmerski, recollecting his grandfather on the anniversary of his death, observes the changes around him: Few friends noticed, Grandma wilted a bit more, the garden yielded little. The narrator's emotions are gripped by the hard reality of time marching toward the end of things. He sees that it was his grandfather that held life together. Now "the family never gets together . . . the chicken house is empty, even the dogs are gone" (Contoski 93). That Grandfather has dozens of descendants seems no more consequential than the new stoplight and paved street. Rezmerski never tells us what makes Grandfather Polish: his "still half Polish" voice, perhaps, or the quart of peach brandy in the cellar and a tobacco can "hidden with some emergency money." The speaker reads in the newspaper that "Poland is still there," but the assurance is hollow and irrelevant in the face of Grandfather's passing. John Pijewski's "Burying My Father" also looks at a death in the family on a personal and cultural level. Father is the repository of Polishness: old nursery rhymes, fables, anecdotes about the way it was. As in Bristol's *Blackbird,* Poland is alluded to as a "certain music," which in Pijewski's case he wished he had paused to hear. Karl Kulikowski uses the same frame of reference in "Music in Greenpoint," a poem about family in the Polish neighborhood of Brooklyn in the 1920s. In the poem, ethnicity represents coherence, stability, and clarity. Kulikowski recalls family evenings, "the Grudzinskis visiting us on a Saturday night" and the music they brought with them, piano, accordion, and the squeaky violin of Pan Mayewski, another neighbor. In contrast, his present life is empty. "They are all gone now"; only his mother remains of what once was a thriving community. "All Greenpoint," he reflects, "had moved into the cemeteries, buried far in the suburbs." In his *Buffalo Sequence,* Mark Pawlak moves beyond elegy although he, too, mourns for the loss of his Polish past with the passing of the immigrant generation. He recalls grandfathers and "the tunes they sang when we were little," grandmothers who "passed on their recipes of duck's blood and love," and Joe "what's-his-name-ski" who suffered silently, "dreaming he was a time-card" in the factory where he worked. But whereas some poets accept passively what appears to be inevitable, Pawlak's poems ring with anger as he indicts the deliberate erosion of ethnicity by a culture unappreciative of diversity. He criticizes an educational system that eliminates "accent," that teaches everyone to march "single file, after lunch," and that suppresses the immigrant story (written by one of the children) and promises rewards for those who do "what's expected of us." Pawlak knows what this has done to Polonia and concludes by admitting, as the other writers do, that it is "3 o'clock in our experience," enough time only to "make confession" for what we have lost.

Quite obviously, these poets represent a polarity of attitudes: disturbing fears that what has been lost is gone forever, and a quieter insistence that ethnicity persists in unmeasurable ways, as if Polishness has become a place in the heart if not in the culture. Most avoid the cozy familiarity of folklore and peasant customs, believing instead, as Pellowski, Bankowsky, and Poniscan do, that ethnicity resides in family, place, community, and, perhaps, in the mind of the poet as the inheritor of tradition. In Anna Wasecha's "Babushka," for example, the poet returns home for the last time to visit her grandmother and her "crazy bright colors." She is struck by the resemblance of the flatlands of the Minnesota forest and those of Poland. She is conscious that Polish-speaking people "once found good soil, a church, a familiar tongue" in this region, but that now the end has come. The scattered family returns only for Grandma's burial, but all they are left with are "pieces of that peasant woman," enough nonetheless to make a child's bed. Wasecha, like Kulikowski, Pijewski, and the others, carries away a bit of the past preserved in memory and in her art. In this way, these writers are the legitimate descendants of Victoria Janda and Helen Bristol who, while bridging two cultures, introduce the ethnic poet as the preserver of what Janda calls that "ever burning flame."

2. THE LONELINESS OF THE LONG-DISTANCE ETHNIC

In the 1970s, Darryl Poniscan—whose heritage is partly Polish—wrote four "ethnic" novels, three of which deal with the Buddusky clan. *The Last Detail* (1970) follows Bill (Badass) Buddusky, a career navy man as he escorts a fellow "swabby" to the Portsmouth brig. *Goldengrove* (1971) features Bill's brother, Ernie, a teacher in southern California; and *The Accomplice* (1975) deals with Cousin Harold, a drifter and dropout, during his stopover in Colorado Springs. Although the Budduskys do not physically appear in *Andoshen, Pa.* (1973), a novel about a predominately Polish coal-mining town in northeastern Pennsylvania, Andoshen and its surroundings are the geographic center for all the novels and the spiritual home for the Buddusky exiles.

Poniscan's novels are autobiographical in nature. A native of Shenandoah (Andoshen), a former teacher and navy veteran, he draws upon these experiences for his fiction. As a graduate of the Pennsylvania State University system (teacher-training colleges during Poniscan's years there), Poniscan associates his characters with these institutions. Bill and Ernie's father receives an A.B. in English from East Stroudsburg State and teaches in Andoshen. Ernie, also an English teacher, graduates from Bloomsburg State before moving to the Los Angeles area. Moreover, Bill Buddusky's sojourn in the peacetime navy roughly parallels Poniscan's own experience which, in a way, is a microcosm for thousands of young ethnics from the anthracite region of Pennsylvania who turned to teaching and the armed service as an entry into the middle class. More than that, Poniscan, like his protagonists, is one of the many third- and fourth-generation ethnics who, having come of age in the relative stability of the 1950s, suddenly finds himself separated geographically and culturally from the familiarities of place and tradition.

Reviewers have praised Poniscan for his satiric skills, tragic-comic patterns, and eccentric characters. C. R. Andrews called for more of the "depressing but fascinating Buddusky clan" (2793). And J. S. Phillipson claimed "never to have met people like the inhabitants of Andoshen" (537). Ironically, but typical of those reviewing descent writers, these same critics fail to discuss the works as ethnic literature or to connect the Budduskys with Poniscan's oblique but sustained interest in the regional, largely Slavic culture of his protagonists. To be sure, Poniscan's novels, like Updike's Rabbit series, speak more directly to the spirit of the 1960s and 1970s. All three of the Budduskys are rebels without a cause, ground down by the unyielding might of military and institutional bureaucracy and by a society searching for new, more convenient creeds. *The Last Detail* satirizes a system that betrays and crushes individuality. *Goldengrove* gives us Ernie, newly arrived in the middle class and soon overwhelmed by the jargon and ineptitude of the educational system, the scramble for materialism, and hollow California values. In *The Accomplice*, Poniscan's rebel finds himself in an advanced stage of disintegration and hopelessness. Without education, family, or stability, Beef drifts from prison to odd job, from one failed relationship to another. He is one of the "rag-tag army of young men who muster along the highway's edge" (5). And in *Andoshen*, Poniscan portrays a world out of joint—a collapsing, provincial subculture of hapless misfits reminiscent of Steinbeck's oddballs in *Cannery Row* and *Sweet Thursday*.

It is easy to neglect the ethnic quality of these works, especially since Poniscan makes only scant references to heritage or to Polish culture, preferring instead to emphasize "an odd little place, made to order for a writer" (TLS, 23 September 1989). The spirit of place in Poniscan's fiction owes much, however, to the ethnicity of its people—a fact Poniscan insists on in offhanded ways that characterize the precarious position of the Polish self in mid-century America. In *The Last Detail*, Bill rarely mentions his background other than to identify himself as "a Polack," but Poniscan intrudes by providing a minihistory of the immigrant experience in abbreviated but significant references to nine-teenth-century immigration patterns, officials at Ellis Island changing the family name to Buddusky, his grandfather's inevitable drift to the mines of eastern Pennsylvania, and to "assimilation." He also captures the second-generation drive toward socioeconomic mobility in the form of Billy's father's education at East Stroudsburg State Teacher's College and his subsequent teaching career in the public schools. In *Goldengrove,* Poniscan establishes Ernie's ethnicity through similar references to his background and in occasional flashes of Polishness such as Ernie's appetite for "pierogies fried in butter." Likewise Harold (Beef) identifies himself through the Polish phrases he uses, his appre-ciation of the polka, and in his childhood memories of traditional Christmas dinner: goose stuffed with sauerkraut, boiled potatoes, and caraway seeds.

In terms of surface details and cultural markers, Poniscan spreads his Polishness thinner than most other descent writers. But the Buddusky mentality and posture and their predicament as members of a lost generation are directly traceable to their ethnic background and to the geography of the Andoshen region with which they are no longer directly connected. They are, in short, "individual threads that aren't forming anything," as Anthony Bukoski describes certain of his third- and fourth-generation Poles in *Twelve Below Zero.* Nonetheless, it is Andoshen—a polyglot "European" town of Ukrainians, Lithuanians, Jews, Irish, Italians, Slovaks, and mostly Poles—to which they turn wherever they are, and from which they take what little cultural iden-tity they still have.

Virtually all the characters in Poniscan's *Andoshen* are Slavs (Pon-iscan does not always differentiate Poles from other Slavic groups) named Bistricky, Wowak, Robel, Grotzki, Przewalski, and the like. Even the character known only as Reader seems to be Polish. They are, however, far removed in practice from the tradition-bearing generation and give no thought to the homeland; nor are they actively involved in rejuvenating those traditions. On the contrary, they seem unaware of themselves as a distinct ethnic community. Ethnicity is simply an inher-itance. Similarly, Poniscan is not interested in revealing or reaffirming ethnic values or even in defining "otherness" in strictly ethnic terms. Instead he concentrates on the socioeconomic legacy of immigration on an ethnic group isolated by geography and, to some degree, by its own parochialism.

With the closing of the mines, the economic livelihood and the magnet for Poles beginning in the 1880s, Andoshen has become a world unto itself. The people, mostly elderly, live on meager pensions, hand-to-mouth businesses, and from the few strip mines still operating.

The economy is depressed, the spirit broken, the future without hope. Daily life consists of backyard gossip, small-town antics, and failed dreams revisited. The sweet smell of success teases the minds of Fingers, Jack Robel, Shakey, and Reader; but, in truth, only the cigar factory offers a steady income for the few, mostly women, lucky enough to find work. Estelle Wowak in "Not Goin Anywhere" speaks for all when she says, "I never realized how stinking poor we are" (152). Andoshen is a museum of the failed: R. K. Bistricky who "didn't make it" in California; Ella, who in midlife, regards herself as "a fat old Polack woman" with "stockings rolled below her knees" (194); the "rum-dums" who regularly philosophize in the corner tavern; and the intellectual who "wanted to shake the world" but finds himself employed as a reader to help time pass for the women at the cigar factory.

These are angry and frustrated ethnics. The brutish, antisocial Przewalski hates everything from "goats to garbage cans to Mostly Holy Reverend Fathers" (6). Reader knows that his ambitions will never be realized: "I wanted to do a couple thousand lines on America: the working people, the politicians, the leisure class, the fields, the rivers, the deserts, the mountains, the past, present, and future. I wanted to say it all" (98). But like Przewalski, his undereducated counterpart, he sees no way to escape; nor do the rest of Andoshen's citizens, who live in a Fitzgeraldian landscape of ashes. It is clear from the outset that a pall has settled over ethnicity in this region when Poniscan writes that in Andoshen "you know for certain that you have left a reasonable world behind" (2).

Poniscan attributes Andoshen's decline to a socioeconomic vision that offered immediate satisfaction to the immigrant generation but few long-term prospects to its descendants. He indicts a cultural temperament not able to see beyond the horizon. Mr. Wowak verbalizes this limitation when he admits to Reader that "we never knew anything else," but then ironically advises him to seek his fortune in the same blue-collar world that trapped his own generation—a tragic dilemma not unnoticed by Bill Costley, Lois Lenski, and others. "Get a job somewhere," Wowak tells Reader, "maybe in the car plants" (194). Similarly, the misfit Przewalski, who believes that most Poles "sit on their dupas," thinks that a job in the coal-breaker will bring him status, self-worth, and security; but Poniscan undercuts Przewalski's dream when Thunder is killed in a mining accident soon after getting a job. Except for Reader, who seems powerless to act, the community does not connect its pathetic situation with its own history and cultural attitudes. For them, ethnicity does not explain the past or the present.

And yet this sense of place, this unspoken kinship with the past, and a felt sense of ethnic community holds these lives together and sustains them. If Andoshen is their punishment, it is also their salvation. It is the home to which Bistricky can return as if he had never left, the place where Thunder Przewalski's rebellion is tolerated and understood, the neighborhood where the eccentric Mrs. Grotzky will be comforted by her equally bizarre friends, and the town where Reader can walk familiar streets and speak in knowing terms to like-minded neighbors. Compared to Algren's Chicago, Andoshen offers home and identity—geographic and cultural—just as Milltown and Pulaski Place do for Lampell and Tabrah.

This cultural landscape radiates outward to the Buddusky novels (*The Last Detail, Goldengrove, The Accomplice*) and defines what otherwise appears to be the hero in space. The Budduskys are social rebels, antiheroes in the style of Yossarian, the invisible man, and Holden Caulfield. Solitary individuals on seemingly aimless odysseys, they possess no particular social vision or ideology, although as working-class ethnics they resemble the Polish proletariat in contemporary fiction. They see themselves essentially as outsiders and unwilling accomplices to a stultifying system that erodes individuality and provokes their anger. In this respect, Poniscan's protagonists can take their place among modern American literary heroes. However, by fixing upon the ethnic as ironic hero, Poniscan establishes new parameters in the literary treatment of the Polish self.

In *The Last Detail*, Poniscan takes on the military. Its meaningless tasks and authoritarian structures reduce enlisted men to errand boys doing the system's bidding. "We Buy-Sell-Trade-Everything," Buddusky comments as he reluctantly participates in the imprisonment of a youthful recruit whose crime is largely his innocence. Mule Mulhall, Buddusky's African American sidekick, also knows that they have no choice except to obey orders. Yet their journey helps them realize that they are but pawns in a game they do not control. For Buddusky, their fate is linked to their minority status: "You and me," he tells Mulhall, "are a string of Polish sausages, forty-nine-cents-a-pound-stuff. It took this Portsmouth detail to bring it all home to me" (148).

In *Goldengrove*, despite his "status" as a teacher, Billy's brother Ernie shares Billy's frustration. He wants to drop out, become a kennel owner and work with animals. "There aren't even any odds," he concludes, to living a meaningful life in California's plastic culture. The educated Ernie verbalizes his condition in philosophical terms as well. Everything is in flux, he believes, without beginnings or endings. "In between nothing's begun or finished because there's nothing there except us, trying to figure out where we are" (139).

In *The Accomplice*, Harold is cut from the same mold as his cousins. Described by one reviewer as a "lumpen proletarian" (Prever 503),

Harold at age thirty has already failed in college (one semester on a football scholarship); in the navy, which prepared him for nothing at all; in the social world (he is an ex-con); and in the economic system where he lives from day to day without prospects. His is the voice of the drifter and the reject ("Born to Lose" is tattooed on his arm), but his modest hopes are those of the ordinary working class, which still clings to the American dream. "What I'd like out a life," he reveals, is "a good steady job that I can count on and that I can show what I can do, and a decent woman to come home to . . . a couple kids . . . I'd like to buy a pick-up and take them all campin" (119). Instead Harold becomes an unwitting accomplice to a murder, narrowly misses a second prison term, and retreats into further anonymity where he will try to repent for personal failures in an impersonal world.

From Harold to Bill, Ernie, Thunder, and Reader, Poniscan's well-meaning Polish protagonists rage internally, but theirs is a private protest of the spirit doomed to defeat—as it is in *Easy Rider,* to which Poniscan refers in *Goldengrove.* His antiheroes lead, as J. S. Phillipson says of Ernie, "lives of quiet desperation" (303) that end in untimely deaths in three of the novels. Whereas Poles in more traditional proletarian fiction represent the masses in conflict, Poniscan's novels do not argue for social revolution or even ethnic parity in a pluralistic society. Instead what his characters mourn for, as his allusion to Hopkins's "spring and fall" in *Goldengrove*'s title suggests, is a loss of self, a wholeness they believe existed in the environs of Andoshen and in the shadows of ethnicity. In *The Last Detail,* Billy explains how far he and the others stand outside the mainstream. "Why am I always for the badguys, the shits of the world who'd probably sell their mothers for a beer? Why can't I be part of the decent world?" (154). Typically, Billy looks to Andoshen in order to measure the world but receives only mixed signals. He is proud of his father's college education and teaching career, yet he knows that his father never escaped his cultural label as a "dumb Polack." Similarly Billy measures himself as a cheap Polish sausage. Despite it all, his ethnic-minority status allows him to identify with all those who suffer by descent. The kindest tribute he can pay the African-American Mulhall is that he is a "good Polack."

For Billy's brother Ernest, ethnicity is equally confusing. He sees that his colleagues regard Jose Poluski, one of their fellow teachers, as a social pariah precisely because he is Polish, and that Poluski naively thinks he is immune to old prejudices. Although still a young man, Ernie believes that his best years exist only in memory—in the Andoshen of his youth with its antiquated movie-house, dilapidated high school, and the comic poverty of the basketball team with its mismatched sneakers and over-laundered uniforms. He thinks about St. Stanislaus Church and the parish cemetery and the distance that separates him from his Polish roots. When he hears a friend in the shower singing, "Oh Shenandoah, I long to see you," Poniscan's own long-distance loneliness shines through for discerning readers able to connect fictional events in *Andoshen,* the novel, to Shenandoah, Pennsylvania, Poniscan's home town. As for Ernie, he, like his brother, cannot distinguish between the attractions of youth, place, and ethnicity and the status of a minority culture that has in part contributed to his outcast state. He identifies instead with the vagrants on Los Angeles's skid row, "all the unconnected and disconnected men . . . standing idly alone . . . because the loneliness was a permanent and terminal affliction" (182). He cannot and will not return to Andoshen even for Billy's funeral.

In *The Accomplice,* Harold (Beef) Buddusky suffers a similar fate: exile and a longing for home. He would like once again to "sit on the front porch and follow the patterns of smoke from the nearby stacks, to lie on the glider on his mother's porch, nestled between the anthracite strippings, drinking Moxie and watching the high school girls . . . the rattling coal trucks" (9). He misses the "comforting odors of home" (10) and the "protection of a parent" (18). He hears whispers of "an earlier security, though lost forever when his father disappeared and he was set out against the world, as though to find him" (53). Like his cousin Ernie, however, Beef cannot return. When he calls his mother, she can only say, "You go off on your own now" (8). Wandering through the Midwest, he is forever cut off from family, place, and heritage. His grandfather's long-ago odyssey and his own ethnicity exist only in dim memories of Christmas rituals and a few Polish phrases. Once he was part of something, he reflects, as Poniscan gathers place, the past, and ethnicity into a common but fading frame of reference for all his protagonists. The Budduskys have become a lost generation of lonely ethnics.

While Poniscan's vision is sustained and powerful, the issue of ethnicity is largely undeveloped. His characters are too far removed from their Polish past to explain what it means to be Polish, and Poniscan himself does not think to raise the question in sophisticated ways. He is content to equate ethnicity with the low rung on the socioeconomic ladder and to concentrate on seventies-style alienation, although he appears to have decided that these spirit-numbing conditions are the legacy of the children of immigrants. For the most part, ethnicity in the novels is a marker for the disenfranchised and the disaffected, the residue of history's misfortune, and the puzzling legacy of the third generation. Having lost its spiritual and cultural tradition, this generation can only view ethnicity at a distance, as an ill-defined but integral part of a past bound up in region and in childhood.

3. THE MYSTERIOUS PRESENCE OF THE LOST:
STUART DYBEK

Stuart Dybek's fiction immediately invites comparison to Nelson Algren's stories about "outsiders and underground men," as Howard Kaplan describes Dybek's characters (319). A winner of the Nelson Algren Award, Dybek—like Algren—is essentially a realist-naturalist with a touch of fantasy and a commitment to the proletariat—"an interest in class," as Dybek phrases it (TLS, 25 November 1989). More to the point, Dybek also writes about Chicago's Poles, although his characters, urban guerrillas of a sort, are worlds apart from the semiliterate, brutish, and hapless victims in *Never Come Morning* and *The Man with the Golden Arm*. Dybek's protagonists constantly assess themselves within the context of place. Even when they have left childhood and other neighborhoods behind, place remains with them as it does with Poniscan's wanderers, those ethnic outsiders who continue to look to their eastern Pennsylvania origins despite their long separation. But unlike the Budduskys, who have only foggy notions of heritage, Dybek's protagonists (often adolescents or teenagers) associate place with their ethnicity even though they are innocents not quite sure of their world. Dybek's commingling of place and ethnicity is recognized in Reginald Gibbons's suggestion to a round table of Chicago writers that they may be "memorializing a certain cultural reality in reaction to pressure to de-ethnicize, de-identify, and de-materialize the urban landscape" (325). Dybek replied that he does indeed worry about formerly distinct neighborhoods and regions that have become "placeless," such as the South Chicago area where he grew up and about which he writes.

Descended from Algren, and literary cousin to Poniscan, Anthony Bukoski, and Anne Pellowski, with their firm sense of place, Dybek is equally aware that ethnicity is "a strong component of my voice as a writer" (TLS, 25 November 1989). This voice echoes the complaint of Poniscan's long-distance ethnics and the elegiac tones of contemporary poets, all of whom preserve the past even as they bury it. His stories and poems also record the loss of ethnicity in a rapidly changing society and the coming of age in a seemingly disordered and fantastical urban environment. Ethnicity remains at the forefront, although Dybek does not envelop his work in Polish traditions as Anthony Bukoski does. Two of Dybek's most recent poems illustrate his method and provide an overview to stories and poems previously published. In "The Immigrant," the speaker talks about "returning to the Old Country." He's been "homesick" and "lonely" for the gas stations that "smell like garlic" and the butchershop where skinned rabbits hang next door to

the funeral parlor. Nowhere does Dybek mention the immigrant's ancestry, nationality, or place of origin, or whether the Old World is a
physical or metaphysical place—although the garlic, skinned rabbits,
and rosary beads suggest a Catholic, probably Slavic, point of reference.
In "Autobiography" the narrator's melancholy is more easily traced to
his implied Polish connections, but even here Dybek works only through
allusion. The poem is steeped in Catholicism: feast days and surplices,
crucifixes and confessionals, the clang of the evening Angelus and streets
transfigured by "a reverence I can't explain." Nonetheless, the narrator's
story is muted, darkened by distance from his neighbors and his own
history. There are autobiographies at every corner, he explains, "autobiographies, but no history." Were it not for references to the Black
Virgin of Czestochowa, "my girlfriend," and to his habit of calling any
old woman "babushka," the narrator would remain an everyman, a
Catholic catholic. But Dybek's allusions to Polish language and history
change all that and his poem assumes a specific shape through which the
narrator's thoughts are contextualized.

In a general sense, the narrator worries about the past into which the
dead slowly vanish, but Dybek has a particular past in mind: "a parish
of phantoms," shadows "under a crucifix," grandmother with her
"babushka." The abandoned past, we learn, is a particularly ethnic
problem in this case, a matter of generational indifference and contrasting expectations. "It's not that I didn't listen," he explains, "but it
wasn't my language." For succeeding generations, even the common-
place of tradition "has assumed / the mysterious presence / of the lost."
On the one hand, the speaker is relieved to be freed from the burdens of
tradition; on the other, freedom leads to exile. His story, he fears, will
ultimately recede into "a solo . . . noodling through broken English."

By and large, Dybek's characters in *Childhood and Other Neighborhoods* are young, third-generation Americans occupied with friends
from varying ethnic backgrounds, engaged in the rough and tumble of
the street, and the problematics of initiation. None seems especially
conscious either of ethnicity or of Old World connections. The peasant
culture in Krawczyk's stories and Bankowsky's *A Glass Rose* is not a
felt presence or a unifying element in the community. Nor does Dybek
try to make it so. His protagonists, unlike Anthony Bukoski's, undergo
no ethnic epiphanies, make no singular commitments, refuse to be
burdened by time. Their unobtrusive Polishness is largely assumed or, if
anything, reduced to a cultural residue.

To them, it is the older Poles who are the "other," part of the social
fringe within their vision but not at its center. More frequently than not,
the more "Polish" the character, the more bizarre are Dybek's stories.
The Palatski man and his rag-peddler colleagues exist in a wasteland, a

shantytown where they "stammered in foreign English" and reenact, mysteriously, the Easter passion. Old Buzka and her crazy grandson Swantek drown unwanted neighborhood cats. Pan Gowumpe lives in a crumbling tenement with "poultry in his room." The workers in the ice-cream factory are "Slavs missing parts of hands and arms that had been chewed off while trying to clean machines." Tadeusz's uncle spends his nights cruising the highways picking up the debris of a culture on the move and the dead animals (for stuffing) it leaves in its wake. Big Antek, a local drunk, leads two boys to an abandoned ice house where years before a grieving immigrant entombed his drowned daughter. In short, most of the immigrant Poles and their near relatives, as seen through the eyes of the young, are grotesques in a distorted landscape. Few, if any, are three-dimensional "normals," although most possess an odd sort of dignity and mystery.

Only in "Blood Soup" does Dybek examine the interior of the peasant culture. Stefush recalls Busha's house with its holy pictures, "flaming hearts crowned with thorns, pierced by swords, and dripping blood" (27), vials of holy water, Polish phrases, zupa, czarnina, rozumiesz, and the Easter blessing of eggs, ham, kielbasi, horseradish. In other cases, Dybek's characters implicitly reject this culture even though they ironically use it to measure their movements. In "The Wake," for example, Jill decides that she "wasn't going to hang around this neighborhood forever while she walks the streets, locating herself vis-à-vis St. Casimir's Church.

In "The Wake," as in other stories, ethnicity is less a problem than social class which, for many descent writers, has become an abrasive ethnic marker. Actually Jill fears the prospects of life in the working class, getting "knocked up, tied down with a bunch of kids, married to a truck driver" (104). Frank Marzek in "Sauerkraut Soup" shares Jill's fears. He regards his father's factory years as time surrendered: "It was what my father, who'd worked in a factory all his life, had wanted to tell me. But he's never been able to find the words" (131). The environment in virtually all of Dybek's stories is working class, although he does not use these settings to politicize his work. It is clear, nonetheless, that his Chicagoans have been run down by poverty, the harsh landscape, and limited opportunities. They are conscious of their lack of status and have, in some cases, accepted the blight which surrounds them. Dybek is not interested in particular indictments, in a call to collective arms, or in proletarian rhetoric, but his message is clear enough. The Poles, three generations after the great immigration, have sunk into the underclass; pride in work, a hallmark of ethnicity for the first generation, has given way to images of the working-class prison.

Like his colleagues, Dybek continues to define ethnicity with a religiosity that permeates his school memories, neighborhood geography, and childhood adventures: from Busha's iconic wall decorations, to Tim Vukovich kneeling at school detention; from Jill's awareness of St. Casimir's steeple, to Eddie Kapusta's reminiscences about his youthful days as an altar boy; from the children's references in "The Palatski Man" to Father Mike, communion, and the Holy Spirit; to Marzek's cynical appraisal of the church's power. Catholicism in these stories is as suspect, however, as the eccentrics who roam the streets. Like their working-class heritage, the religion of the church has become a cross almost too heavy to bear, the specter of unpleasant memories, a creature of habit although not necessarily of comfort, a sign of a culture unable to transfer its values to the present. Christ images in "The Palatski Man" become confused with the distorted landscape for children brought up with religious mystery. The story's religious imagery serves only to highlight the characters' inability to sort out the facts and fictions in their surroundings. When Eddie Kapusta tours the churches on Good Friday, he is moved by habit and training, not by piety. He turns away from the chanting old women, muttering to himself, "same as ever." In "Sauerkraut Soup" Frank Marzek verbalizes what Kapusta and many of the others must think. Reflecting on his own Catholic upbringing, he critically remarks, "Suspect what they teach you, study what they condemn" (127). Despite his rough treatment of religion, Dybek knows that his characters cannot escape their religious backgrounds which have become an indelible feature of their identity.

Ultimately, Dybek shows that too much has changed, that ethnicity, and consequently identity, is in transition and disarray. Demographic shifts, urban blight and renewal, the rejection of the past have produced anxiety and doubt. His "Poles," unable to resist these changes and yet part of them, sense that something has vanished: the old neighborhood, cultural promises, the assurance of heritage. Alienation, exile, and anonymity, new passwords for ethnicity, govern the lives of Big Swantek in "The Cat Woman," Sterndorf in "Neighborhood Drunk," Kapusta in "Hot Ice," and the protagonists of "Blight," one of Dybek's most recent stories. In "Blight," the musical group the boys form is significantly dubbed "The No Names." The Korean War vets who languish in the streets and taverns "have actually chosen anonymity." Even the neighborhood is known only by the postal code "2 one 8" in contrast to other Chicago areas identifiable by name. Dybek writes about the breakup of the old gang, constant moving, the absence of beauty, addresses unknown. When after a few years he returns, the neighborhood is almost unrecognizable, "mostly Mexican now." His return is terrifying, a reminder of his lost self. He is back "but lost, everything at once familiar and strange" (249).

Aimlessness, strangeness, and a sense of being lost are recurring themes in Dybek's accounts of the wandering ethnic. The children in "The Palatski Man" try to find their junkyard home doubting, on occasion, even its existence. The boy in "Blood Soup" enters unknown parts of his neighborhood in search of the elusive duck's blood for his grandmother's soup. Tadeusz and his uncle in "The Apprentice" conduct nightly odysseys on back roads. In "Hot Ice" the long evening of Eddie Kapusta stretches into timelessness. Their journeys lead, Prufrockian fashion, to deserted streets that yield few answers to time's eternal questions. Eddie and the others have stepped out of place and even outside themselves. In "Hot Ice," Dybek explains that "they felt as if they were no longer quite there themselves, half lost despite familiar street signs, shadows of themselves superimposed on the present, except there was no present—everything either rubbed past or promised future" (25).

Their odysseys carry them into the recesses of the past, toward disconnected glimpses of their roots as Dybek links the predicament of the contemporary urban self with ethnicity. Big Antek, for example, explains how it was when he came to a place filled with "mostly people from the Old Country" (22). Similarly Pan Gowumpe talks about life in the packing plants years before. "All those DPS working there . . . Polacks, Lugani, Bohunks. People who knew how to be hungry" (45). The listeners in these stories recognize how little they know and how much is irretrievable. Frank Marzek comes to believe the immigrants "knew something they were hiding" (129), and young Steven in "Blood Soup" penetrates and redefines the legacy of his past when he thinks about his "Busha." She embodied "the kind of love [that] must have come from the Old Country—instinctive, unrequesting—like her strength, something foreign that he couldn't find in himself, that hadn't been transmitted to his mother or any of Busha's other children" (26). This is Dybek's most concise, penetrating explanation of the Polish legacy and the closest he comes to epiphany in his fiction, although in "Sauerkraut Soup" something similar occurs to Marzek. Stopping at a Polish restaurant to savor once again the soup of his youth, he observes that "there are certain mystical connections to these things" (131).

Although ethnicity reexperienced breaks through occasionally in Dybek's fiction, cultural exile dominates the stories in *Childhood and Other Neighborhoods* and *The Coast of Chicago* (1990). In "Hot Ice," Eddie Kapusta confronts his own uprootedness and the specter of the past. Eddie's problem is that he has no past by which to order the present. He knows little of Polish culture (Old or New World versions) and nothing about Poland itself. What knowledge he has of his transplanted heritage resides only in memories of childhood and neighborhood. But with the death of his family and the bulldozing of his neighborhood, "the past collapsed about them," he realizes. Resembling Anthony Bukoski's stories about the razing of St. Adalbert's, but without his reverence for old ways, "Hot Ice" explains contemporary exile as a consequence of lost ethnicity. Eddie has lost the language he knew as a child so that now he can hardly distinguish Polish from other languages. He tells his friend Manny about his visits to "Busha, my grandmother" before the cranes and wrecking balls removed all the physical traces of his ethnicity. The only legacy of his once-thriving neighborhood is the twenty-sixth-street bus, the Polish Zephyr, and the old women "dressed in black coats and babushkas." Eddie tries to understand what it is they mourn, to discover the source, "to give the feeling a name [but] it eluded him as always" (40).

In "Chopin in Winter," Dybek, as he had done in "Blight" and "Autobiography," returns to the claims of memory in what is perhaps his most romantic and sentimental treatment of the Polish self. "Chopin in Winter" is a memory tale told by a narrator looking back nostalgically on his childhood. Two principal events occur: the return of the boy's grandfather, Dzia, after a long absence, and the return and departure of Marcy Kubiak, the girl upstairs whose dreams of becoming a concert pianist are cut short by pregnancy. The music of Chopin, which the girl plays nightly, strikes home to Grandfather and unleashes in him "the jumble of the past" eagerly absorbed by the boy Michael, who learns something about his ancestry. Dzia Dzia talks about his trek from Krakow to Gdansk to avoid impressment into the Prussian army, his American wanderings, and Chopin's death, piano, and heart (buried in Warsaw). Chopin sustains the old man even as it does Marcy in the winter of her discontent, and as it subsequently does Michael who continues to hear the music after Marcy moves away. Dybek's story works on a universal level: a boy and his grandfather, first infatuation, a sense of home, and an awareness of changes in the offing. But in his choice of Chopin, Old World anecdotes, and a neighborhood where old women wearing babushkas drone "endless, mournful litanies before the side altar of the Black Virgin of Czestochowa" (116), Dybek particularizes the experience as an ethnic one impressed on a boy's mind, as the stuff of Polishness long gone even though he can "still hear the silence left behind" (166).

In this and other stories, the Polish connection dominates, but Dybek, like other of his colleagues, also hears the music of transethnicity in the making. Anne Pellowski, for example, moved beyond the confines of Polishness through interethnic marriages and, more important, by showing the younger generation's acquisition of a global perspective. Anthony Bukoski also writes about the new alliance of Poles and oth-

ers—Native Americans, Jews, Scandinavians—not as a united proletariat but as Polish Americans redefining the meaning of otherness.
Perhaps not by choice, Dybek's Poles have expanded their territory
to include Hispanics and other minorities whose presence sometimes
transmogrifies Polish identity. In "Chopin in Winter," Michael does not
literally understand Mrs. Kubiac's Bohemian, but he recognizes that
through Chopin (and their own humanness) he and the Kubiacs are one
family. Interaction with the Czechs, the boy's closeness to Mrs. Panova,
a Russian neighbor in "The Cat Woman," Pan Gowumpe's years with
the "Lugani and Bohunks," young Tadeusz's visits to the Spanish Blades
restaurant—all have prepared Dybek's protagonists for change, new
cultural patterns of assimilation, and a revised sense of self. In "Hot
Ice," Eddie Kapusta and Manny Santora are more than best friends.
Eddie has become partly Hispanic. He sings in Spanish and appreciates
the Spanish words which, to him, perfectly express the contemporary
landscape. The word "juilota" (pigeon) captured, he thought, "both
their cooing and the whistling rush of their wings. He didn't remember
any words like that in Polish" (28). In "Blight," the young boy's sidekick
is Stanley Pepper Rosado, called Stash by his mother. Dybek tells us that
this new alliance is not always easy, but his story of Rosado, Ziggy
Zilinski, Joey DeCampo, and the jukeboxes filled with polkas and Mexican songs shows that the Polish self is undergoing deepseated change.

At one point in "The Apprentice," Tadeusz's uncle gives him good
advice. "You're starting to sort it out . . . [but] there's no in-between.
People who find an in-between live foolish lives" (196). Inadvertently,
the uncle describes most of Dybek's characters: the old whose ethnicity
has fossilized and the young who stand between a tradition already lost
and another they are about to launch: a mixture of Chopin, the music
of grandfather; the "She's Too Fat Polka," the music of their fathers;
and "CoCoRoCoCo Paloma," the song the narrator of "Blight" listens
to on his visit to the old place. Like Jerzy Kosinski's characters, Dybek's
ethnics know the in-betweens intimately. Alternately they seek to transcend their ethnic past and to search through it for clues to their present
altered state and to the future that awaits them. Dybek's appraisal of
the past is tough-minded enough to suggest ethnic uneasiness and
disavowal. When all is said and done, however, his fictional journey is
headed more toward the heart of ethnicity than away from it, just as his
younger characters are more attracted than repelled by their somewhat
strange ancestors. They return to the scenes of childhood to savor the
cultural flavor of people and places, echoing Dybek's own frequent
visits to his South Side Chicago neighborhood.

10

HOMEWARD BOUND

And oh, we should be so far away from every-day gossip
and malice, near to God, and better. —MODJEWSKA

I. THE BEARERS OF SOMETHING: ANTHONY BUKOSKI

The ethnic concerns of descent poets—the passing of generations, the buried self, the loss of tradition—appear, as one might expect, in contemporary fiction as well, in K. C. Frederick's "What Can You Do with a Fish?", in certain of Stuart Dybek's stories, and especially in the fiction of Anthony Bukoski, who is perhaps more intensely involved with these themes than any other current writer of Polish descent. To date, Bukoski has published seven stories about Poles and Americans of Polish descent. Of these, "The Eve of the First" is the only one not set in the Polish American neighborhoods of the Great Lakes region where he grew up. Instead, it is set in 1939 Germany during the weeks between St. John's Eve and September 1, the invasion of Poland. The principal characters are not Germans, however, but Poles, John Brozek and his mother, who grew up in Bóry Stobrawski to the east but currently own an impoverished general store somewhere in Germany.

Despite its European setting, "The Eve of the First" comments on the whole of Bukoski's ethnic fiction. For one thing the Brozeks are cultural exiles: Mother talks helplessly about her country to the east; her son also feels that Germany is a foreign land, that he belongs to a country that had been at war "for centuries . . . enough to shape the features of sad men" (369). For another, Poland is itself threatened; the story leads up to the invasion and subsequent destruction of Poland, an apocalypse that permeates, metaphorically, Bukoski's American stories. Finally, Brozek is a typical Bukoski protagonist. Exiled, burdened with history, sensitive to his own nationality, defensive about and yet a defender of cultural traditions, Brozek cannot stand by and watch it all disappear; but he is, for all intents and purposes, powerless. He imagines himself multiplied in the store mirrors into an army of illusions-turned-soldiers who would protect his homeland. Unfortunately the witches' mischief of midsummer's night turns into history on September 1 and Brozek— alone, invaded, fallen—disappears into the depths of a nearby pond, seeking his own reflection as Poland disappears into the map of Germany.

In many ways, "The Eve of the First" is analogous to Bukoski's Great Lake stories where another kind of struggle is taking place, an attempt to protect ethnicity from the threat of different—but equally insidious—enemies. In these pieces, Bukoski's protagonists, often young people, assess and reassess, discover and confront cultural loyalties, the ethnic self, the buried past. Often this occurs, as it does in many of the poems of descent writers, upon the death of a relative, usually associated with the immigrant generation. Such confrontation ends in the recognition that the world in which they had defined themselves, consciously and unconsciously, is breaking apart.

In effect, there are two ethnic communities in Bukoski's fiction: the older generation, basically secure in its identity, and a new one testing and sorting out the conflicting allegiances of past and present. For the immigrant generation, Poland is still a felt presence. Many have ties, real and symbolic, to the Old World. In "A Chance of Snow," Agnieszka's family owns worthless Polish government bonds that "a good Pole would never cash" (86). Roza Mizinski in "Tango of the Bearers of the Dead," like some of her neighbors, has close relatives in Poland. Mrs. Syzmonski in "The Pulaski Guards" expresses herself best through proverbs ("Glod Wilka z lasa wyprowadzie"—Hunger will lead a fox out of the forest). Frania Pomerinski, her immigration papers tucked away in her dresser, talks about her village landscape, and Roza Mizinski refers often to her life as a new bride and mistress in Bialy Brzeg and her husband's forced service in the Russian army. Parishioners sing "Jeszcze Polska nie Zginela," while red and white bunting hangs in the church hall, where Chopin and Paderewski exist within the easy reach of memory.

More important than these valuable but tangential connections is a pervading and deeply experienced spirituality that binds the community together—a belief in Catholicism which organizes the social structure and dominates perspective. The focal point, morally and geographically, in Bukoski's fiction is St. Adalbert's, the parish church, and Skola Wojciecha, the parochial school. The city assumes identity in relation to the church/school buildings. "From there you can look out," the narrator of "The Children of Strangers" proudly explains, "and see King Midas Flour, the oil dock, Hog Island and Minnesota Point" (21). Podgorak in "Old Customs" attends St. Adalbert's and learns the way of the world, if not of the flesh, from the sisters who teach there, as does Agnieska in "A Chance of Snow." In "A Concert of Minor Pieces," the church cemetery and church site (Adalbert's has been razed) are the catalyst for the plot and the point of reference for

Leo Pulaski. On one level, the church as a symbol of the old faith is what distinguishes Polishness from its ethnic kin. That this faith originates in Poland's distant past "made it special and added to its mystery," Bukoski explains (TLS, 4 November 1989). On another level, faith provides historical identity and a sense of ordered direction. "What Polish immigrants have over the newcomers is continuity," Josie Slipkowski believes, "a faith that has lasted long and travelled far" ("Children" 21).

If St. Adalbert's and Skola Wojciecha are cultural repositories, identity markers, and indicators of national character, they are also the sure signs of a petrified culture, frozen in time. No new Poles have arrived in years; school attendance has fallen so that the pictures on the school walls say more about the 1920s than the present; the nuns have died or moved (Sister Bronislaw is retiring in "Strangers"); the parish buildings, the church, and the neighborhood are growing "shabbier and shabbier." In fact, in "A Concert of Minor Pieces" we learn that church and school have been torn down by the bishop's order.

Bukoski best captures the end of St. Adalbert's, with all its consequences, in "The Children of Strangers," a story about the Slipkowskis and their painful realization that their ethnic generation is nearing the end. For this elderly couple, the parish is a touchstone for heritage, time, and belief. Mrs. Slipkowski remembers when the cornerstone was laid and that Sisters Stella, Cecelia, and Appolonia have long gone. At the church hall where the school's graduates have gathered over the years to honor the last remaining nun, Mrs. Slipkowski wonders, "Beyond St. Adalbert's, what remains? Beyond Sister Bronislaw . . . ?" (21). The old hall rings out with haunted melodies that "hurt a person with their sadness." And when two intruders, new residents of the formerly Polish neighborhood, disrupt the ceremony, it becomes clear even to her husband Ralph that the community is only marking time. You could tell them all about Poland's past and they wouldn't care, he thinks. For all intents and purpose, ethnicity, as the Slipkowskis and their generation practice it, resides "in the mirrors in the Polish homes and in the wrinkles of the old faces and in the eyes and deep within the memory" (23).

The Poles cling to St. Adalbert's, feeling after all these years, like cultural intruders, isolated, alone, unprotected, their American dream vanquished. "How we're losing," Josephine tells Ralph. "Except for their years at Skola Wojciecha what will distinguish the young who change their names and move away?" (21). For Bukoski's spokeswoman, there is no hope, no tomorrow, no ethnicity reinvented. When Josephine cries, "We are in decline, Ralph, and I'm afraid," Bukoski expresses a sociological predicament and a human tragedy reminiscent of Mrs. Loman's plea for Willie and herself. Anonymous intruders are replacing the Polish residents, and Poland, as in "The Eve of the First," has been invaded once more—"the way they've been coming for centuries" (22), Josephine observes.

In other stories, Bukoski juxtaposes the end of ethnicity through the death of the immigrant generation with the ethnic awakening of the younger generation. For example, in "Old Customs," Podgorak must come to terms with his great-aunt's death. Although he has heard her speak about her life in Poland, he has no sense of that place until he finds a map of Poland in the parochial school and decides that Poland looks like a butterfly. In "Tango of the Bearers of the Dead," seventy-five-year-old Mrs. Mizinski watches over the death of her husband, and their grandson watches over both. He realizes how little he knows about them, especially about their Polish lives and she responds telling him about Polish soldiers singing "Tango of the Bearers of the Dead." Grandma thinks, however, that it is too late for explanations, that Vincent cannot understand who and what she was. "Time," she tells him, "has shrouded things. . . . It's like a knot. . . . How do you untie it?" (91). She cautions him to forget about "all of us who've gone before you," paints her dresser mirror black, and says, "I am done remembering" (95). In "The Pulaski Guards," Walter probes Mrs. Szymonski's aging memory and listens to her accounts of famine and wars, reflecting back to stories he had heard but not quite understood as a child. At her request, in homage to her Old World self, he joins the Pulaski Guards, a local fraternal organization where he discovers the legion of the dead and dying and a culture frozen in the past. Not much is left, a few white-mustached "officers," a display case with a few books on Polish history, and a sabre with flowers engraved on the handle. Mr. Zawacki tells Walter that eighty years ago the Guards dressed in the style of Pulaski in the American Revolution. "Do you think anyone remembers him?" he asks. Walter has stepped through time into a world of ghosts, of octogenarians remembering eighty-year-old uniforms. He knows that the faded blue pamphlet of the organization, *Konstytucja i Reguly,* is as anachronistic as the group it describes. He knows also that he can do nothing to save his grandmother and her times from the ravages of *Twelve Below Zero,* as the title of Bukoski's collection of short stories implies.

Even as Bukoski despairs for the past, for lost traditions, for a cultural identity that can never be replaced, for old values and old ways, he points toward a redefined sense of ethnicity, an awareness by the young that something out there must be preserved, and toward a new dialogue, a new expression of ethnicity. At the same time that his young protagonists must witness and acknowledge endings, they are forming beginnings, gathering together fragments and images, filtering them into the self and becoming more comfortable with themselves as a result. Tireless questers, they prompt the past to unveil its secrets, the mirrored reflections so prominent in his stories. Vincent in "Tango" probes his grandmother's past to fill in the missing chapters of history, trying desperately to unravel what his grandmother refers to as "the knot." In "Old Customs" the young boy rushes frantically to find a map of Poland, and Agnieszka in "A Chance of Snow" turns to a Polish-English dictionary and the old picture on the school walls to penetrate the unknown. Similarly, Walter in "Guards" tries to clear away "the place of shadows" where his grandparents have always dwelt by joining their, and now his, "Pulaski Guards."

The past haunts and informs the present in Bukoski's fiction, a situation not unnoticed by the characters themselves. The ethnic past, as we have seen, especially troubles the Slipkowskis, Roza Mizinski, and Leo Pulaski who, with the razing of St. Adalbert's, see the past reduced to rubble. Roza attributes Walter's melancholy to "dreams and memories" [which] intoxicate my grandson and make him a lover of the past" (92). The spectre of the past operates differently on each. The older people see themselves slipping out of history; the younger characters are slipping into history, discovering the continuum of time. For Podgorak, it is his discovery of his grandmother's immigration papers; for Walter, the sabre and uniforms of the Pulaski Guards; for Vincent, the song of the Polish soldiers who "had no reason to be happy and they weren't" (91); for Agnieszka, the school photographs and the Polish sailor who jumps ship in Duluth harbor, immediately transforming past into present and memory into experience.

In all these stories, a new understanding occurs in the minds of these young, mostly third-generation characters who had come to associate ethnicity only with their parents and grandparents. Consequently, even as these stories document the end of ethnicity, ethnicity is reconstituted, rediscovered as the past takes on new meanings in a world forever changed. Perhaps Agnieszka best represents Bukoski's vision of ethnicity reborn. To her, Polishness is a curious and somewhat baffling phenomenon somewhere in the distant past—in the photographs of long-ago students, in their parochial school dress, and in the few remaining nuns who still teach there. That she knows enough Polish only to insult her little brother suggests that she regards ethnicity as a mark of inferiority. The appearance of a Polish sailor in her house, befriended by her father after the sailor has jumped ship to defect, causes her to examine herself for the first time in terms of consent and descent. Immediately she becomes "different," conscious that her school friends are "the same kids with the same experiences as an hour ago. But not me" (84). The sailor, she thinks, resembles the faces in the old photographs at school whose images assume an authenticity that they never had before. The predicament of the sailor caught indecisively between two worlds brings the immigrant experience to life for her. She becomes fascinated by him because he reminds her of delicate spider strands, "individual threads that aren't forming anything" (88); and, we are led to believe, he is a living example of the "other" in distress, personalizing what had only been an abstraction of history. Agnieszka's own otherness strikes her as never before; she now identifies with the photographs in the hall, "those faces with their sadness as if the students were torn from something" (89). Her secure world is disturbed and she pictures herself drifting, wishing not to be "drawn back to sea like the waves" (91). She witnesses how Lukasz, the sailor, is immediately targeted as a foreigner by Mr. Guenard, the grocery store owner, and how to many "he doesn't fit here" (91). Agnieszka is perplexed. She senses her connection to the past and sees the dilemma of the immigrant experience. Like Mrs. Slipkowski, the Polish sailor, Walter, Roza Mizinski, and others, she too is "placeless and floating," more securely connected to her past but more uncertain of her future. At the same time, she is drawn toward her roots. She wonders what there is about Poland that would cause Lukasz to turn his back on America because he misses "the stones in the road," as he phrases it. Bukoski leaves no doubt, however, that Agnieszka will never be the same. She thinks now about "the people who've come here, about their pictures," about "the haunted dream of Poland" and the living experience of otherness. She is primed, as Bukoski's other youthful protagonists are, to step into their ethnic shadows.

Agnieszka and Podgorak turn emotion, confusion, and loss into affirmation. Their older counterparts, Walter and Vincent, move toward a conscious commitment to their ethnic traditions. Vincent's grandmother's past becomes a catalyst for resolving his own doubts and for recognizing that "we're the bearers of something," echoing Josephine Slipkowski's belief that Polishness is tradition and a force for continuity. Walter's decision to join the Pulaski Guards, essentially an aging group waiting out their time, becomes a symbolic attempt to enter history. The oath of initiation strikes him as something more than the past outworn. The words, "the gathering of our members under their own standard, for mutual and moral support, also the fostering among us of the feeling of love and brotherhood," indicate to him that he too is the "bearer of something" (25).

Ethnicity rekindled and reconstituted is not limited, however, to symbolic gestures to the past or a reexamination of the self. In fact, it is not insular at all in Bukoski's stories. To the degree that they recognize their own cultural dilemma, his characters reach out to other marginal groups with sensitivity and liberality. Loyal to their own heritage, they nonetheless identify with otherness in ways that cut across racial and ethnic boundaries. Many of Bukoski's stories feature such examples of ethnic kinship through the formation of new alliances and a reassessment of old ones. In "The Pulaski Guards," Bukoski looks at the sensitive subject of Polish Jewish relations. The older generation at the club condescendingly tolerates the Jewish peddler who regularly stops by to sell his trinkets. "We don't understand his Yiddish," they complain. Instructed not to pay attention to him, Walter, moved by his own sense of otherness, sees in Mr. Kaner another cultural exile like his grandmother or perhaps like himself. Mr. Kaner has an "odd foreign look" that calls to mind the Polish sailor, the old photographs in "A Chance of Snow," and a number of characters in other stories. Having helped Mr. Kaner to his car, Walter later remembers his grandmother's anecdote about the sudden appearance of a Jewish merchant at their cottage door in Poland, who, on Christmas Eve with nowhere to go, was received warmly as a guest. Walter connects the story with Mr. Kaner and with his own image of himself as a wandering exile. Attending his grandmother at the hospital, Walter again sees Mr. Kaner who, similarly, is comforting either a wife or mother. Walter senses the parallel between Jew and Pole, the universality of their humanness, and their special relationship as cultural exiles who must observe the passing away of their Old World connections. The "Guard" closes with Walter quietly singing an old Polish song to his grandmother while Mr. Kaner, in the next room, hums softly to himself—perhaps in response.

In "The River of the Flowering Banks," Bukoski juxtaposes Poles and Chippewas through the friendship of two young boys. Gerald Bluebird and Warren Walczynski serve Mass and "hang around the river together" without any apparent awareness of the difference between themselves or the cultural majority. Indeed, Warren considers the marriage of Trudy Bluebird to Richard Bozinski to be the highlight of the summer. "The Polish people were hugging the Indians," each speaking different languages. "I'd never seen anything like it," he exclaims (118). This familiarity and kinship is tested, strained, and ultimately reaffirmed when the state decides to move an old Indian burial site. As in "The Pulaski Guards," Bukoski contrasts old animosities with new sensitivities. The workers callously toss the Indian remains into piles, refusing to bury them in the local cemetery because "they ain't Catholic." Warren, with the help of Father Novak, comes to understand the bond between Native Americans and Poles and, by extension, between all "strangers." "You've got to look at 'em differently," Father Novak explains, "we didn't none of us discover America . . . we're Polish"

(123). As he senses the universality of the human condition as immigrant and outsider, Warren grows unsure of his formerly comfortable identity as a Polish American: "I sure thought I knew who I was before all this happened" (124). With Father Novak and Gerald, he participates in a religious ceremony at the new burial site with a deepened and redefined sense of the meaning of ethnicity.

In this story, as in "The Pulaski Guards" and certain of Bukoski's non-Polish stories, the characters see their own situation mirrored in other minorities—Jews, Native Americans, Scandinavians—whose own world is often disintegrating as rapidly as that of the Poles, while simultaneously expanding beyond ethnicity. The two stories mark a turning point in Bukoski's ethnic consciousness, from a notion of ethnicity as exclusivity to an awareness that all minorities are the "bearers of something," and that that something is both the particulars of a given culture and the universals of the human experience. If, as Thomas Napierkowski rightfully contends, Anthony Bukoski challenges the image impressed on his community by outsiders ("Neighbors" 14), he does so by extending this image outward, suggesting that the story of America's Poles is central to America's experience.

2. THE IMMIGRANT IN TIME: RICHARD BANKOWSKY

Over a ten-year period Richard Bankowsky published four novels: *A Glass Rose*, 1958; *After Pentecost*, 1961; *On a Dark Night*, 1964; and *The Pale Criminals*, 1967. These novels follow the family of Stanislaw Machek who, with his wife Rozalja and her two brothers, Pyotr and Jozef, immigrates to the United States from a village near Lublin early in the century. The tetralogy explores these immigrants and their descendants over more than a half century. Its setting moves from Poland to Anderson, a factory town in New Jersey; to Dupont, a coal mining community in eastern Pennsylvania; to Korea, to New York City, and to the Southwest. However, the focus and feel of place remain in the house and garden in Anderson, where Machek raised his large family and, to some extent, in father Machek's Old World garden.

Bankowsky explains his Rose tetralogy this way: "After finishing *After Pentecost*, I discovered that its characters, as well as the characters of the earlier *Glass Rose*, refused to lie still. . . . I convinced myself (perhaps presumptuously) . . . that my characters were aspects not only of my own psyche but perhaps of the collective psyche as well" (qtd. in Bolling 62). In this interview, he goes on to talk about his multiple viewpoints, the interrelated structure of his novels, and his style of "seeing experience in mythical and scriptural terms" (63), without once referring to or being asked about the obviously ethnic interiors of a

four-novel sequence about Polish immigrants and the legacy of immigration. Reviewers have on this subject remained equally silent except
to note, as Alice Mayhew does in *Commonweal*, Bankowsky's "sensitive understanding to the lonely destiny of the immigrant" (515). Only
Anzia Yezierski, writing in the *New York Times*, chose to read *A Glass
Rose* as an ethnic work. For her, Bankowsky is an "articulate literary
voice of the Polish peasant in America," and his novel is about a world
"intensely Polish and yet so universal" (4). Yezierski, whose background differs from other reviewers of the novel, correctly emphasizes
the world of the Polish peasant, although in succeeding novels Bankowsky moves away from the immediate experience of the first generation—without, however, losing sight of their journey.

Bankowsky is not a sentimentalist, information-giver, or preserver of
either folk culture or high romance. While he does refer to Polish
history and culture, he does so only to explain the temperament and
motivation for his timeless travelers. In *A Glass Rose*, we learn something of the history which shapes the family's perspectives; of Polish
bravado, in the example of an aristocrat's (the family landlord) efforts
to free a comrade from an Austrian garrison; of the partitions of the
eighteenth century, both world wars, the Gestapo roundups, Auschwitz, and the postwar displacement of hundreds of thousands. Bankowsky is not Michener, however. His historical references collectively
amount to little more than a chapter in the thousand or so pages that
make up the tetralogy. Similarly, his portrait of the peasantry, most of
which occurs in *After Pentecost*, provides only the barest outlines of
village life and custom; so too do his references to ethnic pluralism in
Poland—the Germans in Nowy Targ and the Jews in Krakow, who
assume greater significance as the tetralogy develops.

Actually, Bankowsky's interest in a folk culture transplanted and
transformed is minimal, occurring in widely scattered allusions to
polkas on a summer's eve and other such conventional markers. When
he describes the inside of a typical Polish American home, for example,
he writes with an air of irony that resembles Edna Ferber's description
of a second-generation Polish American wedding or Saul Bellow's sense
of wonder and distance as he peers into a Polish house in *Augie March*.
Bankowsky notes the sanctuary parlor, the lace doilies on the backs and
arms of chairs, the satin pillows with their reminders of weekends in
Asbury Park, and the "pathetically peasant" housewives. In short,
Bankowsky feels no need to equip his fiction with familiar cultural
baggage.

At the same time, he is bound to a history that few of his readers
understand except in the most basic terms, and he needs to teach them
in order to move toward a metaphorical level. This he does through

stream-of-conscious narration and multiple points of view in ways comparable to Faulkner's *Absalom, Absalom!* In chapter two of *A Glass Rose,* Bankowsky reviews the long journey begun in an unnamed village with the patriarchal Machek, who regrets his son's decision to go to America although he and everyone else has endured a history of hardship in Poland. Jozef remembers the leave-taking: Old Machek "scraping the stone on the scythe," the dogs howling, the wagon clattering on the cord road, the weeping, the relief at escaping from the Austrians, the packing of seeds to transplant in the New World. We next see the family in Anderson, New Jersey, working in the mills, locked into ethnic neighborhoods, involved in labor disputes leading to defeat and tragedy. Stan's dismissal from the plant, in spite of his loyalty to management during a vicious strike, and his subsequent death (he is mangled by a textile machine) are in the best tradition of Oppenheim, Vogel, Kubicki, and other proletarian novelists. In *After Pentecost,* Bankowsky parallels the Machek family journey with others originating in the Carpathians in southern Poland. The arrival, between 1920 and 1946, of Eva, Groszek, Martha, Magda, and Jan Novak, and their tangled, almost baffling, relationships occupy much of Bankowsky's time in the last two volumes of the tetralogy. Yet these latter stories, unconventional in comparison to that of the Machek family, keep the cycle alive and allow Bankowsky to look beyond periodization and the reductive notion of the immigrant in history.

In effect, Bankowsky takes seemingly parochial ethnic concerns and translates them into universals. In this sense, his ethnicity may be compared to that of Saul Bellow's or to any writer who uses ethnicity as raw material for his art and who transcends, simultaneously, the restrictions implicit in that material. One might say of Bankowsky what Jules Chametzky said of Bellow: that by the late 1950s he had moved to a stage where traditional literature about ethnicity was no longer necessary. Bankowsky's vision of the Polish experience vis-à-vis the United States has little to do with an ethnic journey or movement. It is rather an extension of man's yearning to get "back to the eternal, to Eden, to a mythical golden age which exists only in the human soul" (TLS, 23 December 1988).

The Rose tetralogy is quite different, then, from typical versions of assimilation and promises fulfilled or from the notions of stability, reclamation, and redemption in works about the immigrant on the land. Instead, the New World garden rapidly becomes Eden after the fall—an analog to the Polish garden already fallen. The chain of desertions, incest, failure, and aloneness that links the four novels begins in Poland with old Machek's prophecy, a warning to those who hold naive ideas about America where, Jozef thinks, "it would never be cold, and how in the big cities . . . the streets were cleaned and snowless even before you got out of bed in the morning" (*AGR* 29). Machek tells his son that by turning his back on family, land, and place he will be forever doomed: "At least here what you have, though it is not much is at least yours. There, nothing will be yours, and you will lose even that which you take away with you—lose yourselves, and what is worse, your children" (*AGR* 35). Stan recognizes the truth in his father's statement. He admits that it is "a sin for a son to leave his home and his father like that. . . . Someday he would wake up," he thinks, "in the new land and find that he has lost everything" (*AGR* 35). For Bankowsky, the Polish journey thus assumes the properties of modern tragedy, as his characters inescapably act out the fate of immigrants and of all mankind.

Bankowsky represents the rapid deterioration of hope and promise in the image of Stanislaw's backyard in Anderson, New Jersey, a fixed point of reference for the characters in their worldwide odyssey and a symbol of man's eternal condition. Stan and Rozalja bring seeds from the old country. Stan plants the seeds as his father had done before him, and for a time the flower-filled garden becomes a haven from their gray and dreary environment. On Sundays the family gathers in the garden as it had done in the village near Lublin. In Jozef's mind, the garden is Eden regained: "It was a small beginning, just a small garden that first summer with more manure in it than flowers. But there was the next summer and the next and the next . . . and the garden progressing each year with more flowers and more trees until it was really something of beauty" (*AGR* 45). Stan's wife regularly places a rose in his lunch pail, with the result that, as Jozef observes, we even had "the garden there in the factory with us" (*AGR* 46). Crushed by the factory strike, the loss of his job, and his act of incest with his daughter, Stan, after a few brief years of apparent happiness, destroys the garden in a fit of rage, ripping out the roses and chopping down the trees. In ensuing years, the garden is nothing more than a run-down backyard, as the family—ripped by greed, anxiety, and depravity—self-destructs. Throughout the years the garden remains a symbol of promises unfulfilled to the children, to Stan's brothers-in-law who remember packing the seeds, and later to Wadzio in *The Pale Criminals.* Wadzio learns about the trunk "full of everything they owned and a pillow case full of rose seeds from the old country" (242) as he takes care of Stan, a ruined old man.

The image of a garden in ruins, a metaphor for the illusions and disappointments of immigration, occurs elsewhere in Hindus's *Magda* and in Chase's *A Journey to Boston.* But the implications in Bankowsky's fiction, ever more forbidding, transcend ethnic matters and testify to the spiritual disintegration of the extended family of mankind. The

Macheks are doomed to disappointment because their dream fails to account for "man's fallen animal nature," as Bankowsky explains it, and for "the impossibility of achieving perfection in time" (TLS, 23 December 1988).

Eden, the rose garden, is lost and with it the moral center necessary to deal with old Machek's fateful warning. Along with Stan, the family sinks rapidly. Brother-in-law Pyotr violates his niece and steals money sent to support another niece's child. Jozef becomes a hopeless drunkard. Stella is raped by her father, Stan, and flees to New York. Jan and Groszek lust and fight over Eva and Magda, new arrivals in 1927 and 1946, and tumble to their deaths as daughter Marya is made pregnant by son Johnny. Rozalja loses her mind and sits aimlessly in the deserted family house. By the mid-1950s, the era of *The Pale Criminals* and *On a Dark Night,* identities have become almost too tangled to unravel as Roman Novak, son of either Jan Novak or Roman Groszek, wanders through New York, eventually retreating to the monastery of the Carmelite Friars of Ascension in the Arizona desert. The novels themselves resemble a grotesque dance of death and disintegration. Pyotr is discovered suicidally "tied to a meat hook." Jozef is found drowned in a gutter. Kaz also commits suicide; Roz is committed to an asylum. On Wadzio's order, Johnny's heart is cut out; and Wadzio himself is murdered by the mob boss who, Bankowsky cryptically explains, is "going about his father's business" (PC 294). Machek's curse and the sins of the fathers are visited upon all.

Occupied with the idea of the father, the loss of Eden, sin and redemption (although Bankowsky offers redemption only to Roman), Bankowsky does not clarify lines of descent or guilt except to suggest that something is rotten in man's spiritual makeup. Needless to say, he does not suggest that all this is exclusively Polish or somehow a consequence of the Polish experience. Nonetheless, certain of his characters look upon their ethnicity and its immigrant beginnings as a cross they must bear, as if they—closer than most to the immigrant in time—are more aware of the futility of utopian dreams. During a Christmas conversation somewhere in Germany in 1946, "brothers" Johnny Groszek and Roman Novak sense that the source of their despair is rooted in Poland or in their status as cultural outsiders. Others are more specific. In *After Pentecost,* Martha indicts Poles (men actually) as a people "who dreamed impossible dreams and blamed everybody . . . but themselves when those dreams did not come true" (64). Helcha, one of Stan's daughters, believes that we are "all dirty inside," and Emily, her sister, concurs that "it takes a Pole to be that stupid" (AGR 72). Johnny Groszek regards himself as an "unsophisticated, simple, regular army Polack moron" (PC 46). What is more, he has no sympathy for Poland's suffering during the war. "What's a couple of million Polacks more or less," he tells Roman (*AP* 288).

Romantic notions of a brave and dignified people bound to land, family, tradition, and church have no place in these novels. Even the much-revered Polish Catholicism cannot redeem these Poles from their fate. Although religion hovers in the background of the Anderson and Prescott neighborhoods, the characters are not engaged either with Catholicism or the church. On the contrary, the church appears to have had no lasting influence on Jan Novak who, we learn, was formerly a priest in Poland before his fall from grace, or on Pyotr Popek who also studied at the seminary near his village. And Roman Novak's ultimate retreat behind the walls of a desert monastery has little to do with any former religious training or devotion to the faith and practices of his forefathers. If anything, Bankowsky dismisses the church's message as yet another expression of an unrealistic dream. In *After Pentecost*, he offers the church's response to the human dilemma in the pastor's Easter-day sermon. The priest insists that "with the aid of grace and complete faith, men could still make miracles in the world, and how with much hard work and much faith, even the poorest of our people could someday hope to build a great castle in this country" (164). The "castle," just as the rose garden, offers no real direction or solution to a predicament which is beyond the temporal; and Polish mysticism remains a confusing legacy which troubles more than uplifts the descendants of immigrants. Faced with the loss of garden and castle, one might think the Poles would consider returning "home," but only Jozef, who confesses that he has not been happy since leaving Poland forty years before, does so. After a short time he returns to Anderson, complaining that there was "nothing for him there." For Jozef and all the "immigrants" in the Rose tetralogy, it is too late to return to the homeland to which they have become strangers. And yet home is the illusion that they, like all weary travelers, must eternally seek.

The universality of this paradoxical journey is further enhanced in the tetralogy's complex relationship of Pole and Jew, the "immigrant *par excellence*," according to Bankowsky (TLS, 23 December 1988). At first glance, this subject—always sensitive—appears to be a way for Bankowsky to deal with Polish anti-Semitism, which frequently rears its head in the novels. The cynical speaker in the opening of *A Glass Rose* sets the tone when he berates Stella for "laying for those New York Jews" (3). Later, Emily thinks about finding "some rich Jew" as sister Stella had through her marriage to Harry Greenglass. And Johnny Groszek in *The Pale Criminals* hates Roz's Jewish husband "for being such a pig with a wife like her, a Polish girl" (280).

What these passages reveal is the frequency of intimacy and marriage between Poles and Jews, so much so that, as the tetralogy progresses, few of the characters can be said to be exclusively Polish or Jewish. Their issue is ambiguous, their blood freely mixed, and more important, their fate interchangeable. Moreover, all of this has European origins. In *After Pentecost,* Isaac Abraham Sadovi sends to Poland for a Slavic wife, "because a Jewess always expects too much from a husband" (59), and marries the Christian Martha. He is also the brother of Jan Novak's mother who, having adopted Catholicism, dies at Jan's birth. Thus Novak and Sadovi have common Jewish and Slavic ancestors in Krakow as well as in America, even more so when Jan marries Martha upon Sadovi's death. Given the complexity of Stella's marriage to Harry Greenglass, Roz's intimacy with the painter Geldstucker, and other entanglements, the majority of the primary Slavic characters, including the Jew-baiting Johnny Groszek, either have involved and extended familial relationships with Jews or are part-Jewish themselves. Even Roman Novak, who ends up in a Catholic sanctuary as the tetralogy closes, is probably Polish-Jewish, although Bankowsky's shifting viewpoints and his passion for intricacy and ambiguity cloud Novak's ancestry.

Like Singer, Bankowsky draws these two "Polish" groups together, with the result that Polishness in the Rose tetralogy means something more than Christian, Slavic, and geographic. For one thing, a Jewish-Slavic heritage is part of the historical condition that Machek's children carry with them to the New World, just as they carry seeds to transplant. For another, it is a territory of the heart in which the Pole, as immigrant in time, dwells wherever he goes. With this knowledge, there is some reason to believe that old Machek's descendants are finally homeward bound. For despite the fact that by the end of *The Pale Criminals* not much is left of the shattered human spirit, Bankowsky writes in his epilogue that Roman "advanced in wisdom and age and grace before God and men" (295).

3. PRIMARILY WE MISS OURSELVES AS ETHNICS: GARY GILDNER

In 1987, Gary Gildner, poet and short-story writer, published his first novel, *The Second Bridge.* Set in 1967 and 1980, primarily in upper Michigan, the novel follows the crack-up of the half-Polish Bill Rau, the death of his child, the end of his marriage, and his attempt to forge a future from a past freighted with happiness gone sour. In this "memory" novel, the main characters, Rau and his wife, act as a world unto themselves. Rau, the sometimes narrator, is distinctly unaware of the world beyond self or of a past other than his own. In midlife crisis, he holds on to sanity in the style of Hemingway's Nick Adams, counting his steps, rationing his cigarettes, substituting a rigid personal routine for an elusive cosmic order. A grown up Tom Sawyer, he is a romantic whose philosophy has shot him.

Rau's ethnic background seems irrelevant to the novel's universal concerns, made more so by Gildner's own dismissal of the ethnic refrain: "I didn't try to say anything about being Polish or what it means. It just is; it felt right to make Rau half-Polish because it had the feel of truth" (Interview with Gary Gildner, 10 March 1988). To be sure, ethnicity passes by almost unnoticed, although its presence adds something more than "naturalness" to the novel. For one thing Rau's point of view is shaped by his ethnic past; for another the novel marks a turning point in Gildner's writing.

Gildner draws on his Polish past in only a handful of poems from his five volumes of verse published before *The Second Bridge*—although ethnicity finds its way, masked by universality, into another dozen or so poems. In *First Practice*'s "Banal Story" (1969), Gildner alludes to his ethnic upbringing only through Burt's insensitive and hostile greeting to Eddie: "Hey Polack! Burt used to say to Eddie," and continues to do so years later after Burt's wish for status has been shattered by "four snotty kids" and a job on the assembly line while Eddie, the supposed ethnic inferior, sits in the front office with a "clean white shirt and gartered socks." "Banal Story" is about an ironic turn of events in the lives of two "friends," but it also reveals Gildner's sensitivity toward ethnicity, which he defends through Eddie's success.

In *First Practice* the only poem that looks directly at the Polish self is "Szostak," a reminiscence about the old Pole who "died at one a.m.— reading Conrad in the can by kerosene." Gildner celebrates Szostak's toughness and durability. Szostak, who spits tobacco juice and drinks a nightly pint, had been "kicked by mares, wore scars / forked out shit." Gildner establishes Szostak's heritage by alluding to Chicago (where his pretty nieces live), to Catholicism (beads and priests), and to Joseph Conrad, apparently a favorite of the old Pole. In this family poem, Gildner is struck by Szostak's singularity (cake crumbs stuck in his mustache), individuality, strength, and self-reliance, which Gildner offers as aspects of Polish character and his own legacy. Other poems in *First Practice* radiate outward from "Szostak," in the sense that ethnicity is detectable only in reference to Gildner's boyhood training in Polish Catholicism. In "Rainy Afternoon between Jobs," for example, the speaker's mother sleeps in a room with "three ivory virgins / and the prayer that glows green in the dark / for the repose of anyone's soul." In "For My Sister," Gildner describes a girl who might become "a nun yourself someday," leading the "penguin caboodle through a perfect learned hoop." Even in the most secular of these early poems, the wonderful "Letter to a Substitute Teacher," Miss Miller has eyes blue "like the Blessed Virgin's."

Nails, published six years later (1975), also contains ethnic poems, although once again ethnicity is buried among images of family, baseball (Gildner's second love), parochial school, and childhood. In "Around the Kitchen Table," Gildner brings all these together in a tribute to his ethnic past. The speaker, conscious of being "out of shape," remembers his "run-ins with the nuns who always had our number" and the young blonde Polish priest sitting next to Grandma as he "bites into his chicken." The family, Uncles John and Andy, Grandpa and Grandma, a beautiful cousin with red hair, the kids with their "skinned and bleeding shins" gather together to review, to remember, and to reconsecrate life. Their Polishness—"loaves of Polish rye . . . steaming kielbasa"—is as much a part of them as the kitchen table around which they sit. John's impulse to dance a polka with Uncle Andy is natural and yet particular, an identity marker absorbed into the fiber of the observer turned narrator.

As in First Practice, other poems in Nails reveal Gildner's ethnic consciousness primarily when read against a poem such as "Around the Kitchen Table." In "Banal Story" for instance, ethnicity appears as a derogatory reference to Eddie, "the Polack," but Gildner says nothing else about Eddie's Polish self. For Gildner, ethnicity is blended with action and movement, comradeship and youth. Eddie reappears in a number of poems in Nails as a catalyst for the speaker's internalized response to past and present, but we know from "Banal Story" that Eddie is, among other things, a bearer of ethnicity. In "Around the Horn," Eddie is "on the mound . . . I'm at shortstop"; but as time shifts to present, Eddie "packs a gun . . . and I won't grow up." In "Burn Out," the speaker revisits Eddie's Sundries and his widow who "sighing returns to her page." He watches two young bruisers "burn a baseball back and forth" and reflects that despite seasons that have gone by, he still belongs to her—and to Eddie. In "The House on Buder Street," Eddie (named Hill) appears to be deethnicized. In fact, nothing about the poem directly identifies the characters as Polish, although the speaker talks about attending Catholic school, Mother worries about "the Baptists on the street," and the family and neighborhood are working class. Like Szostack, the Eddie of these poems is a role model, someone who throws the high, hard one, hits the nail straight, knows that Shirley crosses her legs in algebra. A repository of a romantic, idealized past, Eddie as baseball player and childhood chum is the deethnicized ethnic who roams through Gildner's poetry and stories disguised as the all-American boy.

In "Wheat," a selection from Gildner's *Blue Like the Heavens,* the speaker remembers his American landscape: fields of wheat, Grandma's hot biscuits, school, the log bridge over the creek, the barn's full mow. Gildner's American dream is, however, freckled with unobtrusive images of ethnicity as natural as the trout's black pool on his grandfather's land. Pie crusts cooling on the window blend with the toasting of "Na zdrowie" by his Polish uncles, "establishing order and chaos around the table." His school lunch, a pickle and a braunschweiger sandwich, is eaten at St. Joseph's parochial school. Grandpa's farm chores are punctuated by "Psia krew," the curse of dog's blood. The hay and sweat rub against "the scapular Grandma gave me." Reminiscent of Frost's "Birches," "Wheat" integrates ethnicity, boyhood, and the classical American setting in ways that enrich Gildner's American self without necessarily calling attention to otherness.

Gary Gildner's poetry is, for the most part, ethnic-free to the naked eye, but taken together, his poems show his continued, if infrequent, allusions to an ethnic self so happily at home in a majority culture that even the most Polish of his poems seems to be mainstream. Nonetheless, directly and indirectly, Gildner bridges two cultures even as Bill Rau does in *The Second Bridge.* Rau is not a practicing ethnic; that is, he has no ties to the Polish community, does not think of himself as an ethnic outsider, and pays little attention to his heritage. Many of his deepest memories, however, are tied to his Polish self. His grandmother appears to have been born in Poland and his mother "acts" Polish, but Rau apparently knows nothing about their lives as Poles. In the novel, ethnicity is strictly third generational: foods (czarnina, pierogi, golamki), folk culture, and phrases. Surprisingly, considering Gildner's obsession with his parochial school training, Catholicism is not mentioned either in Rau's visits home or in reference to his inner turmoil.

Quite early, however, Gildner shows that Rau defines himself in ethnic terms without much thought to their significance. He tells his mother that Jay is attracted to him because "she knew I had Polish blood" (13), and later fibs to her that "Jay's part Polish . . . at least she sure looks it" (93). When he is at home, Rau's standard for naturalness is ethnic even as his mother's is. When Jay compliments her on the taste of her golamkis, she is happily embarrassed at the thought that her cooking is Old World. "Everybody makes golamki," she responds, not needing to explain her world further. Similarly, when Jay and Bill attend what appears to be a Polish wedding, Gildner reduces ethnicity to a casual "Na zdrowie"—the necessary ring of truth as he describes it. Gildner develops Rau's ethnicity in similarly innocent terms when Rau visits Freddy Zielinski, a close boyhood friend and fellow athlete paralyzed in a hunting accident at age eighteen. Freddy is a version of the Eddie featured in Gildner's poems—youth, friendship, the sporting life of the past. Although Gildner does not say so, it is clear from his poems and from Freddy's name, Zielinski, that all of this is connected to Rau as intimately as Rau is connected to Grandma's golamkis.

In truth, Gildner does not do much with ethnicity in *The Second Bridge*. It exists along the edges in fits and starts as in Darryl Poniscan's novels. Despite Rau's own lack of curiosity about his past and Gildner's tacit assumption that Rau's character speaks for itself, it is clear that Rau's ordered past, rooted in his Polish family, contrasts sharply with his disintegrating life and his disconnected present. Ethnicity remains a known quantity and a past recollected in tranquility. Surprisingly, Gildner, assessing his novel in an interview, speculates that he may have made Rau half-Polish because he wants us to see Rau as a member of a minority fighting for his place (Interview 10 March 1988). He does not indicate, however, that for Rau as for himself, ethnicity is yet another bridge waiting to be crossed.

Soon after the publication of *The Second Bridge* and *Blue Like the Heavens,* Gildner's ethnicity vaulted across the span of time, place, and cultures with remarkable results. During his year as Fulbright Lecturer at Warsaw University, he came face to face with his own cultural past through daily contact with the myths and legends, the complexities and contradictions of contemporary Polish society.

Immediately Gildner's writing changed. Within eighteen months after his return, he published a memoir of his experiences, *The Warsaw Sparks,* centered around his time as coach of Warsaw's new baseball club. Additionally, some of his poems were translated into Polish and virtually all of the poems he published in major magazines (*Poetry, Grand Street, The Georgia Review, River Styx*) were about Poland or ethnicity. These poems reveal a poet transformed by his experiences, one who has crossed into unknown territory which, in his case, illuminates the ethnicity within and relocates the hero of *The Second Bridge* in another time and place.

In terms of ethnicity, Gildner's speaker changes from information-giver to observer and information-gatherer, from one who treats his ethnic self offhandedly, unconsciously, and with the assurance of the uninformed to one acutely conscious of cultural differences, the complexities of ethnicity, and a heritage heretofore vague. In the process, Gildner discovers a new American self and an old Polish one, transforms his American poetry into a multicultural one, and bridges the chasm between the ethnic and nonethnic voices in his previous writing—between, as he says in "String," "the two stations they commanded."

Formerly, ethnicity was semiotic, a matter of signs assumed and understood. Jay looked Polish, everybody can make golamkis, Szostak embodied ethnic character, the rituals of Catholicism are universally recognized. The speakers in these instances rarely moved beyond the obvious, nor had to. They gave information from a position of assurance. In the "Polish" poems, however, Gildner is an observer of cultural differences, not always understood, but strikingly singular. "To Live in Warsaw" consists of a series of cultural encounters. The speaker puzzles at the bounty of nude posters in shops from "the skinniest side street to the Palace of Culture." He is irritated by the "come-back-tomorrow rigmarole," curious about a crying man on a Warsaw tram and the infants wrapped up several times so that "only their eyes shown through," and about the Warsaw Zoo which is no more nor less different than Detroit's. What is there about these incidents—the narrator wonders without apparent answer—that differentiates them, if at all, from the universal? The particles of Polishness, we are left to think, are not easy to define. Perhaps like the old man's keys and coins, "they might mean something / other than what they were."

For the speaker in Gildner's pre-Poland poems, the Polish self is rather a simple affair—Conrad and cabbage, "na zdrowie," and the polka. Now it takes on baffling three-dimensional complexities. The women in the Polish P.O. have their own sense of time. String tied around packages is essential, required by law; without it "everything would fall apart during the journey," they tell him. His American mailer does not impress them, not even when he tosses it high in the air to the floor to demonstrate its strength. "She had seen bigger noises fall from the sky," he comes to understand. In "String," the narrator awakens to "other" ways, including a sense that Poles act from a historical perspective.

In the poems, the narrator takes on history, so to speak, filling in his own past as he glimpses Poland's past and its present. He sees that Warsaw is a city still pulling "bricks and books / and other fragments of history / out of holes." He knows that the street where he lives, Ulica Staffa, is rooted in tradition—in this case to the poet Leopold Staff— and that Puck and Lodz are coated in memories. He grows conscious of the long road into the past—to Grandfather Szostak's generation. In "Primarily We Miss Ourselves as Children," Szostak reappears in a Warsaw dream. Gildner's newly discovered sense of history makes Szostak something more than an old Pole "reading Conrad in the can by kerosene." The speaker makes connections between the oatmeal he had for breakfast in 1942 in America and the oatmeal he eats in his Polish apartment. Those associations lead him again to Grandfather who, in the close of the poem, rises high into the apple tree and is ultimately transfigured into light, air, and water as his ethnic self assumes spirituality and timelessness.

Wherever he goes, Gildner's speaker confronts Polish selves in ways he had never anticipated: in the Polish P.O., on the tram to the zoo, in the classroom with students, on the baseball diamond—all of which provide Gildner occasion for a reexamination of his American self, as a person and as a writer. In "Primarily We Miss Ourselves as Children," Szostak and he ride in "a wider and wider circle," an apt metaphor for Gildner's transformation from a straight-line poet, crossing bridges, to an expanding traveler absorbing and creating new parts for the self. In the Polish P.O. he admits that he may have been "a hot-headed Yankee off his nut," and that the experience was "sobering and reflective." In "A Warsaw Classroom Containing Chairs," Gildner, influenced by his students, sees a multiplicity of selves, shaped in part by cultural perspectives. He is teaching his students about the American character who always looks toward tomorrow, listening, believing that "with some luck, a new leaf / anything could happen." The students, under the spectre of history fraught with tragedy and the gloom of gray socialism, cannot sympathize with what they see as "a foolish child, a dreamer, at the end." "The writer agreed," Gildner explains, and goes on to supply alternate endings, searching as it were for one that fits a Polish outlook and his own revised sense of self. Sarcastically, he offers examples of the successful American who "asked for the banker's daughter," had "its love handles wrapped in plastic at the weekend fat farm," or said "to hell with all this noise" and took to tying flies, not "bothering anyone." Whether any of these American selves makes better sense to the Poles (or the speaker), Gildner doesn't say. He does suggest, however, that he is open to possibilities, alternate definitions and perceptions, and that perhaps "it was all the writer's fault, really."

The poet, in effect, rethinks the recurring motifs in his art: youth, comradeship, love, exhortation, precision, baseball, and the natural flow of easy grace. He recasts them, more specifically, with a different cultural stance. The result is that Gildner's American self extends into ever-widening circles as he blends old forms into new consistencies. The certainties of the ancestral farm, the setting for a number of pre-Poland poems, become confused with the uncertainties of life in Poland in "Primarily We Miss Ourselves as Children." The speaker wishes that upon waking he will be back at the farm, but his Warsaw days help him to see his own mortality and how much life has been spent since eating "oatmeal for breakfast / in America, in 1942." He visualizes the long road between childhood and his present state, between his Warsaw apartment and the toad in the mud, between the Szostak he had experienced and the Szostaks of Warsaw. The narrator of "To Live in Warsaw" identifies with the weeping man on the tram to the zoo because, in part, he, like the man, is "lost in a thing he seemed to have lost." In "String," his Polish experience sends him "reeling in the dark" and leaves him "cold," his "fires were out." The burden of history and the Polish stoical response cause him to reflect on laws he "never had much use for" and to conclude that familiar approaches may not be enough—an insight similar to the writer's in "In a Warsaw Classroom Containing Chairs."

In "Coaching the Warsaw Baseball Team," a poetic sequence included in *The Warsaw Sparks,* Gildner revisits old turf forever altered by his European experience. Previously, sports connected with childhood had represented the soul of Americanness and Gildner's own controlled but liquid response to life's dark threats. The title poem of his first volume, *First Practice,* introduces this central metaphor. The youngster listens to the coach's violent introduction to "the game," but he is too intimidated to react to Clifford Hill's exhortation to hate, to injure, to win. Gildner presents first practice as if it were a perfectly natural initiation, typical-agreeable-American! In "A Circle," however, the "Polish" sequel to "First Practice," nothing is really the same except for the situation of a coach meeting his team for the first time. Instead of the two hostile lines that face each other in "First Practice," the ballplayers form a circle, "bow like monkey-suitless diplomats and shake my hand." The speaker senses that his instructions are "jammed by consonants" and thinks back to his eighth-grade coach who would tell them, "Gentlemen the world is dog eat dog . . . It's dig and sweat . . . that's it / that's everything—let's go!" But this is Warsaw, he thinks, a city more aware of dig and sweat than he can ever be, a country of broken dreams and falling snow. The initiation is reversed in "A Circle," where the speaker sees the irony of telling "these guys to grab their feet and stretch" but has little else to offer.

In "Speaking in Tongues" and "Ravens," the coaches have similar intentions and undergo similar initiations. In the former, the speaker wants the team to understand that "the ball is part of them . . . it should travel true and beautiful," but they are tight. "They throw like stiffs / the boogieman concocted out of nuts and bolts." In "Ravens," he complains that they are too quiet. "We could be in a church . . . [or] in line for lemons, leeks, and toilet paper." He wants them to razz and praise each other, to bait the pitcher with, "hey pitcher this one's coming back / between your jollies, buddy." The Poles only blush, remain quiet, or complain, "Coach that's complicated." Ultimately what Gildner sees is that his cultural self is as tight as his players and he must readjust his own thinking. He tries to adopt a Polish frame of mind and to contextualize an American game in a multicultural frame. He draws upon their religiosity, their intimacy with the church, explaining that "God is hunkered on the bench behind us . . . He hates it

when a piece of / soul is dropped . . . God is hungry for a Warsaw win."
And in "Ravens" he urges them to hit it "all the way to Moscow . . . on
Lenin's tomb." To this, George responds, "It's going over the fence
coach," and Gildner is content that they are catching "the lingo and the
rhythm."

Clearly it is Gary Gildner who has caught a rhythm not apparent in
his pre-Poland writing. *The Warsaw Sparks,* a memoir rushing toward
the future, shows him once again as the American hero: not on a limb
as in *The Second Bridge;* or as the boy and girl who knew "the world
was still where they held it" in "In the Beginning"; but as the "other"
shading in the outlines of the ethnic self and redefining the American
character. In *Sparks,* Gildner has found a meeting point in time between America's eternal present and Poland's watchful past. In his
sequence "Coaching the Warsaw Baseball Team," he joins the timelessness of baseball and the easy flow of youthful America with the
tradition-bound civility of Poland. In "Trying to Catch Up," he laments
the fact that his players "throw—excuse me—like girls" and that they
have missed all "those long days of stepping out / and following
through." The cultural comment implicit in these lines becomes more
apparent in "A Mouse," where the Polish pitcher, after hitting his friend
with a pitched ball, hugs and kisses him, "crooning Polish." "I tried to
picture something like this in the States," Gildner writes, but concludes
that such love and good manners might only be observed in nursery
school. The speaker in these poems gives and takes, digs into cultural
behavior, and thinks of otherness as a condition of humanness. Ironically, even as he gains a cultural past, a sense of history, and deep
insights into his own heritage, Gildner's ethnic self dissolves in time,
into a field of dreams where Bill Rau, the deracinated self, emerges as
the American coach of the Warsaw Baseball Club.

CONCLUSION

Presume not that I am the thing I was. —SHAKESPEARE

The idea of ethnicity, as it relates to Poles and their descendants, has traditionally been construed in American literature as having to do with the great wave of immigration occurring between 1880 and 1914. This is certainly true of host-culture writers whose interest in ethnicity, predicated on an identifiable group measured to comfortable size, has diminished as the immigrant generation and its family have receded into mainstream America and as newer ethnic groups have assumed socio-political and literary attention. Similarly, descent writers, whether they look into transethnicity, interethnicity, or the search for self among third- and fourth-generation Poles, have for the most part defined themselves in the context of late nineteenth- and early twentieth-century versions of ethnicity and through symbols, icons, and territorial markers associated with both a peasant culture and, to a lesser degree, an aristocratic tradition.

Since the mid-1950s and the heightening tensions of what was once fashionably known as the Cold War, the Polish community in America and our own perceptions of Poland have changed considerably, especially in recent years with the election of a Pole to the papacy, the emergence of Solidarity, and the awarding of Nobel Prizes to Czeslaw Milosz and Lech Walesa—both of whom are regarded in Poland and the United States as symbols no less significant than Kosciuszko and Paderewski. Currently, Poland's transition from a Moscow-dominated socialist state to a market-driven economy and pluralistic government led by a noncommunist for the first time in almost fifty years occupies the thoughts almost daily of political analysts, the media, and the public. Thus, America is certainly better acquainted with surface details of Polishness while remaining relatively uninformed about what it means to be Polish.

In the aftermath of World War II and political events since, thousands of Polish refugees and tens of thousands of others seeking economic opportunity have, like their ancestors, fled to urban America where "connections" over a century old have provided them some measure of cultural security. These immigrants, as Danuta Mostwin points out, are quite different from their predecessors. Of those arriving between 1945 and 1968, forty-seven percent have some postsecondary education and fewer than half have gravitated to Polish American neighborhoods, which they regard as restrictive. Moreover, the new Poles, Mostwin observes, are more aggressive and less willing to accept their social status as a permanent condition. Since arriving in the United States, thirty-nine percent, for example, have completed additional education (5–14). Post-Solidarity arrivals have, we might expect, affected demographics even more, since many are former professional and labor leaders.

All this suggests that America's Polish community has undergone considerable demographic change, outdistancing conventional scholarly and literary models of the Polish self. No one who has spent much time in Poland or with newly arrived Poles has escaped noticing the chasm that exists between American Polonia and the new immigrants, who think of "Polish Americans" as an archaic form of Polishness, and as a group that resembles contemporary Polish culture only remotely because it derives its identity from customs, attitudes, language, and institutions more properly associated with prewar Poland. The difference between ethnicity then and now is perhaps nowhere better illustrated than in the person of Czeslaw Milosz. In "Separate Nations: Poetry and the People," a *New York Times* excerpt from *Conversations with Czeslaw Milosz,* he establishes his distance from those who call themselves Poles, here or abroad, and in the process confronts head-on the idea of ethnicity. He denies that he is the poet of the Polish diaspora, as Eva Hoffman describes him, or that he is a moral ideal and model for contemporary Poland. As for his Polish American ties, he—despite his frequent associations with such groups—chastises the "cultural crudeness" of ethnically Polish Americans and asserts that his work is "completely alien to them" (30). Apart from his poorly chosen words and the absence of an extended explanation, Milosz's commentary is a rather accurate insight into the relationship of ethnicity and modernism—literary and otherwise. What he means is that he is no longer (or perhaps ever was) the Milosz who wrote as a tenant in German-occupied Warsaw or the Milosz whose environment and temperament produced *The Captive Mind.* "I never wanted to be involved in history," he explains in reference to World War II, to Socialist Poland, and to his enthusiastic reception and reputation in Poland as one of the nation's leading symbols (30). Milosz's sensitivity to change (personal and historical) and his contention that no one knows who we really are since the whole self exists, if at all, outside time and place, stand behind his reluctance to be dubbed a spokesperson for any group at any time.

He adds, in fact, that "I can't call myself a Polish-speaking Lithuanian because that beast is really extinct now" (30). The implications of Milosz's remarks are that the nature of ethnic groups and ideas about ethnicity never stand still and that an individual writer's relationship to any given group ultimately defies description.

Milosz's insights, the demographics of Poles in America, and the rapid changes in contemporary Poland have ramifications for literary ethnicity and American writers. It is likely that as writers respond to a reconstituted Polish self, they will discard literary models that featured typology and subject matter suited to particular social stratifications and ideological currents no longer relevant. In keeping with Erik Erikson's notion that childhood identifications become the foundation of ethnic heritage as "persistent as Jungian archetypes," the literary history of Poles in America may reflect childhoods spent as a captive mind in an urban, socialist, industrialized world far removed from village and folk culture and as an experience having little to do with immigration as it is fashioned in the popular imagination. In other words, while arbitration between consent and descent may continue to dominate the literature of a pluralistic America reenergized by immigration but plagued by unresolved problems of social belonging, writers will likely draw upon a different set of cultural symbols and markers and present yet other facets of the Polish self.

There is good reason to believe that this process is well under way. A new wave of emigré writers like Milosz offers the possibility that the works of Jan Lechon, Danuta Mostwin, W. S. Kuniczak, and others to follow may find their way into a rapidly expanding literary canon or that they may begin to venture, as Eva Hoffman does in *Lost in Translation,* into new explorations of the Polish self. If so, Polishness will assume a literary configuration quite distinct from host-culture models and even different from those of contemporary descent writers who have already enhanced our vision of ethnicity by transporting us from outside to inside the self. Gary Gildner, as we have seen, has enlarged a two-dimensional observer into that of a questioning cultural explorer in his Polish poems in which the ethnic self gains texture, sensitivity, and new words of wonder. Others, such as Margaret Szumowski, have also written about the wellsprings of the newer ethnic selves. In "About My Cousin," she travels through the ambiguities of socialist Poland with its fictitious truths and untruthful fictions, and in "Biala Wieza," she escapes into the primeval forest of eastern Poland, back into the beginnings of "this long journey" (Minczeski *Concert* 49). Eva Hoffman reveals her various selves—Pole, Jew, American, ethnic, woman—against a backdrop of life in Poland and America. And Anthony Bukoski balances the apparent incongruities of old and new selves in "A Chance of Snow," a brief encounter between a young Polish American girl hardly aware of any of her selves and a ship-jumping Polish sailor whose self was left behind in his village.

There is substantial evidence that the Polish literary self is once again on the road and that American ethnicity is itself in flux. That so many of late have written about this self may mislead some into believing that this is an early sign of a volcanic upheaval that will burst forth into the kind of literary tradition called for by Stanislaus Blejwas and Thomas Napierkowski, who have done more than their share to nurture descent writers. Unfortunately, this prospect is far from assured because current academic interest in ethnicity appears concentrated on the works of African, Asian, Hispanic, and Native American writers. This situation, while not unwelcomed, confines ethnicity once again within narrow borders. In addition, university curricula and professional conferences continue to define ethnicity with a parochial adherence to exclusivity and insiderism and insist on descent rather than the more expansive notion of literary ethnicity as a way to approach texts that may not necessarily be "by, for, or about" a particular group. Although the relative success of Bankowsky, Pellowski, Dybek, Poniscan, Bukoski, Gildner, and others suggests that something Polish may be afoot, the sociopolitical interests now setting priorities for the literary canon will undoubtedly shape, as Jane Tompkins has demonstrated in *Sensational Designs,* the central codes of American ethnicity.

BIBLIOGRAPHY

PRIMARY SOURCES

Alcott, Louisa May. "The Baron's Gloves." *Frank Leslie's Chimney Corner* 20 June 1868: 61–63; 27 June 1868: 78–79; 4 July 1868: 34; 11 July 1868: 111.

———. *Little Women.* New York: Modern Library, 1983.

———. "My Polish Boy." *The Youth's Companion* Nov.–Dec. 1868: 191–92.

Algren, Nelson. *Conversations with Nelson Algren.* With H.E.F. Donahue. New York: Hill and Wang, 1963.

———. *The Man with the Golden Arm.* Garden City, N.Y.: Doubleday, 1949.

———. *The Neon Wilderness.* 1947. Gloucester, Mass.: Peter Smith, 1968.

———. *Never Come Morning.* New York: Harper, 1942.

———. Preface. *Never Come Morning.* By Algren. New York: Harper, 1969. ix–xiv.

Allen, Frances. *The Invaders.* Boston: Houghton Mifflin, 1913.

Babinsky, Matt. *By Raz 1937.* N.p.: n.p., 1978.

Bahr, Jerome. *All Good Americans.* New York: Scribners, 1937.

Bankowsky, Richard. *After Pentecost.* New York: Random House, 1961.

———. "An Exchange between Richard Bankowsky and Doug Bolling." *Par Rapport* (Winter 1978): 62–65.

———. *A Glass Rose.* New York: Random House, 1958.

———. Letter to the author. 11 Nov. 1989.

———. Letter to the author. 23 Dec. 1989.

———. *On a Dark Night.* New York: Random House, 1964.

———. *The Pale Criminals.* New York: Random House, 1967.

Bell, Frederick. "The Shipmate Spirit." *Blue Book Magazine* Feb. 1948.

Bellow, Saul. *The Adventures of Augie March.* New York: Viking, 1953.

Berezowsky, Alice. "Pavel Gets a Job." *The Atlantic Monthly* Feb. 1943: 46–50.

Bonosky, Phillip. *Burning Valley.* New York: Masses and Mainstream, 1953.

Bristol, Helen O. *Let the Blackbird Sing.* New York: Exposition Press, 1952.

Bukoski, Anthony. "A Chance of Snow." *Writer's Forum* 13 (Fall 1987): 81–95.

———. "The Children of Strangers." *Twelve Below Zero.* St. Paul: New Rivers Press, 1986. 17–24.

———. "A Concert of Minor Pieces." Unpublished story, n.d.

———. "The Eve of the First." *Literary Review* 33 (Spring 1990): 367–75.

———: Letter to the author. 4 Nov. 1989.

———. Letter to the author. 16 Dec. 1989.

———. "Old Customs." *North Dakota Quarterly* 58 (Winter 1990): 129–33.

———. "The Pulaski Guards." *Southern Humanities Review* 22 (Winter 1988): 19–31.

———. "The River of the Flowering Banks." *Beloit Fiction Journal* (Fall 1988): 116–27.

———. "Tango of the Bearers of the Dead." Minczeski, *Concert* 88–100.

Burt, Katherine. *Strong Citadel.* New York: Scribners, 1949.

Cannon, Cornelia. *Heirs.* Boston: Little Brown, 1930.

Carroll, Gladys H. *As the Earth Turns.* New York: Macmillan, 1933.

Carver, Robin. *Stories of Poland.* Boston: Carter, Hender & Co., 1833.

Castle, William, and Robert Joseph. *Hero's Oak.* New York: The Readers Press, 1945.

Cather, Willa. *My Antonia.* Boston: Houghton Mifflin, 1918.

Chase, Mary Ellen. *A Journey to Boston.* New York: Norton, 1965.

Cobb, Jack Fletcher. "Polak Joe's Finish." *Harper's Weekly* June 1909: 22–24.

Cohen, Lester. *Coming Home.* New York: Viking, 1945.

Contoski, Victor, ed. *Blood of Their Blood: An Anthology of Polish American Poetry.* St. Paul: New Rivers Press, 1980.

Coons, Joan. *Without Passport.* New York: John Day, 1943.

Cooper, James Fenimore. "An Appeal to the American People." *New York American* 5 Sept. 1831. Rpt. in Jerzy Lerski. *A Polish Chapter in Jacksonian Democracy.* Madison: U Wisconsin P, 1958. 167–71.

———. *Letters and Journals.* Ed. James Franklin Beard. Cambridge: Belknap Press, 1960–68.

Costley, Bill. "For Dad and the Factory, Lynn River Works GE." Contoski 29.

———. "Kulik/Krrulik." Contoski 30.

Cromwell, Oliver. *Kosciuszko, or the Fall* of *Warsaw.* Charleston: W. Riley, 1826.

Dixon, Thomas Jr. *Comrades.* New York: Grosset and Dunlap, 1909.

Driscoll, Paul. *My Felicia.* New York: Macmillan, 1945.

Dybek, Stuart. "Autobiography." *Poetry* Dec. 1986: 161–64.

———. "Blight." *Chicago* Oct. 1985: 193–249.

———. *Childhood and Other Neighborhoods.* New York: Viking, 1986.

———. "Chopin in Winter." *Chicago* Mar. 1984: 154–66.

———. "Hot Ice." *The Coast of Chicago.* New York: Knopf, 1990.

———. "The Immigrant." *Porch* 2 (Summer/Fall 1979): 18.

———. Letter to the author. 25 Nov. 1989.

———. "The Writer in Chicago." With Reginald Gibbon. *Tri-Quarterly* 60 (1984): 325–47.

Emerson, Ralph Waldo. "Ode Inscribed to W. H. Channing." *Selections from Ralph Waldo Emerson.* Ed. Stephen E. Whicher. Boston: Houghton Mifflin, 1957.

Estes, Eleanor. *The Hundred Dresses.* New York: Harcourt, 1944.

Esty, Annette. *The Proud House.* New York: Harpers, 1932.

Farrell, James T. "A Casual Incident." *The Short Stories of James T. Farrell.* New York: Vanguard, 1934. 89–93.

——. "Comrade Stanley." *An Omnibus of Short Stories*. New York: Vanguard, 1942. 228–66.

Fast, Howard. *The Proud and the Free*. Greenwich, Conn.: Fawcett, 1950.

Ferber, Edna. *American Beauty*. New York: Country Life Press, 1931.

Fineman, Irving. *Hear Ye Sons*. New York: Longmans, Green & Co., 1933.

Fletcher, James. *The History of Poland*. New York: Harper and Brothers, 1831.

——. *The Polish Revolution of 1830–1831*. London: J. Cochrane, 1831.

Florizel. "Roll on, Roll on." Arthur P. Coleman. *A New England City and the November Uprising*. Chicago: Polish Roman Catholic Union, 1939. 50–51.

Frederick, K. C. "What Can You Do with a Fish?" Minczeski, *Concert* 27–44.

Friedman, Isaac K. *By Bread Alone*. New York: McClure, Phillips & Co., 1901.

Gallico, Paul. "Welcome Home." *Further Confessions of a Story Writer*. New York: Doubleday, 1961.

Gildner, Gary. *Blue Like the Heavens*. Pittsburgh: U Pittsburgh P, 1984.

——. *First Practice*. Pittsburgh: U Pittsburgh P, 1969.

——. "In a Warsaw Classroom Containing Chairs." *Grand Street* 8 (Winter 1989): 157–59.

——. *Nails*. Pittsburgh: U Pittsburgh P, 1975.

——. Personal interview. 10 Mar. 1988.

——. "Primarily We Miss Ourselves as Children." *River Styx* 29 (Winter 1989): 66.

——. *The Second Bridge*. Chapel Hill: Algonquin, 1987.

——. "String." *Poetry* Dec. 1988: 127.

——. "To Live in Warsaw." *Georgia Review* 42 (Fall 1988): 605–6.

——. *The Warsaw Sparks*. Iowa City: U Iowa P, 1990.

Gray, Eunice. *Steffi, a Novel*. New York: Exposition Press, 1951.

Greeley, John. *War Breaks Down Doors*. Boston: Hale, Cushman & Flint, 1929.

Greene, Josiah. *The Man with One Talent*. New York: McGraw Hill, 1951.

——. *Not in Our Stars*. New York: Macmillan, 1945.

Gronowicz, Antoni. *Bolek*. New York: Thomas Nelson & Sons, 1942.

——. *Four from the Old Town*. New York: Scribners, 1944.

Harriman, Karl E. *The Homebuilders*. 1903. Freeport, N.Y.: Books for Libraries Press, 1969.

Harring, Harro Paul. *Poland under the Dominion of Russia*. Boston: I. S. Szymanski, 1834.

Hayes, Florence. *Joe-Pole: New American*. Boston: Houghton Mifflin, 1952.

Hindus, Maurice. *Magda*. Garden City, N.Y.: Doubleday, 1951.

Hoffman, Eva. *Lost in Translation*. New York: E. P. Dutton, 1989.

Hordynski, Joseph. *History of the Late Polish Revolution*. Boston: Carter & Hendee, 1832.

H.U.C. "Poland." Arthur P. Coleman. *A New England City and the November Uprising*. Chicago: Polish Roman Catholic Union, 1939. 54–55.

Hughes, Rupert. *Zal, An International Romance*. New York: Century Co., 1905.

Hutter, Catherine. *On Some Fair Morning.* New York: Dodd, Mead & Co., 1946.

Jakubowski, August. *The Remembrances of a Polish Exile.* Philadelphia: Adam Waldie, 1835.

Janda, Victoria. *Singing Furrows.* Minneapolis: Polanie. The Lund Press, 1953.

Janney, Russell. *The Miracle of the Bells.* New York: Prentice Hall, 1946.

Jerome, V. J. *A Lantern for Jeremy.* New York: Masses and Mainstream, 1952.

Kaplan, Johanna. "Sour or Suntanned, It Makes No Difference." *Other People's Lives.* New York: Knopf, 1968. 443–61.

Karney, Jack. *Work of Darkness.* New York: G. P. Putnam, 1956.

Karsavina, Jean. *Reunion in Poland.* New York: International Pub., 1945.

———. *Tree By the Waters.* New York: International Pub., 1948.

Kerr, Annie B. "The Picture." *Strangers No Longer.* New York: Friendship Press, 1943. 123–41.

Knapp, Samuel L. *The Polish Chiefs.* New York: J. K. Porter, 1832.

Konopka, Jona. *Dust of Our Brothers' Blood.* Washington, D.C.: White Eagle Press, 1941.

Kosinski, Jerzy. *The Art of the Self: Essays a Propos Steps.* New York: Scientia Factum, 1968.

———. *Being There.* New York: Harcourt Brace Jovanovich, 1971.

———. *Blind Date.* Boston: Houghton Mifflin, 1977.

———. *Cockpit.* Boston: Houghton Mifflin, 1975.

———. *The Devil Tree.* New York: Harcourt Brace Jovanovich, 1973.

———. *The Hermit of 69th Street.* New York: Henry Holt & Co., 1988.

———. *The Painted Bird.* Boston: Houghton Mifflin, 1965.

———. *Passion Play.* New York: St. Martin's Press, 1979.

———. *Pinball.* New York: Bantam, 1982.

———. Preface. *The Painted Bird.* Boston: Houghton Mifflin, 1976.

———. *Steps.* New York: Random House, 1968.

Kraitser, Charles, V. *The Poles in the United State of America.* Philadelphia: Kiberlen and Stollmeyer, 1837.

Krawczyk, Monica. *If the Branch Blossoms.* Minneapolis: Polanie Pub., 1950.

Kubiak, Wanda. *Polonaise Nevermore.* New York: Vantage, 1962.

Kubicki, Jan. *Breaker Boys.* Boston: Atlantic Monthly Press, 1986.

Kulikowski, Karl. "Music in Greenpoint." Contoski 61–62.

Lampell, Millard. *The Hero.* New York: Julian Messner, 1949.

Langer, Rulka. *The Mermaid and the Messerschmitt.* New York: Roy Slavonic Pub., 1942.

Lenski, Lois. "Auto Worker's Son." *We Live in the North.* Philadelphia: J. B. Lippincott, 1965. 1–70.

Levin, Dan. *Mask of Glory.* New York: McGraw Hill, 1949.

Liben, Meyer. "Homage to Benny Leonard." *Jewish American Short Stories.* Ed. Irving Howe. New York: New American Library, 1977. 178–85.

MacInnes, Helen. *While Still We Live.* Greenwich, Conn.: Fawcett, 1944.

Mailer, Norman. *The Naked and the Dead.* New York: Rinehart, 1948.

Malamud, Bernard. *The Assistant.* New York: Farrar, Straus, and Giroux, 1957.

————. *The Fixer.* New York: Farrar, Straus, and Giroux, 1966.

Mankowski, Peter. "The Holy Basket." *Woman's Day* April 1943: 16–20.

Melville, Herman. "I and My Chimney." *The Piazza Tales and Other Prose Pieces, 1839–1860.* Evanston: Northwestern UP, 1987. 352–77.

Michener, James. *Poland.* New York: Random House, 1983.

Minczeski, John, ed. *Concert at Chopin's House.* St. Paul: New Rivers Press, 1987.

————. "My Name." Minczeski, *Concert* 199.

Miniter, Edith. *Our Natupski Neighbors.* New York: Henry Holt, 1916.

Mizajewski, Linda. "Keeping My Name." Minczeski, *Concert* 12.

Morgan, Susan Rigby. *The Polish Orphan.* Baltimore: Armstrong & Berry, 1838.

————. *Swiss Heiress.* Baltimore: Joseph Robinson Pub., 1836.

Motley, Willard. *Knock on Any Door.* New York: D. Appleton, 1947.

————. *We Fished All Night.* New York: Appleton, Century, Crofts, 1951.

Musial, Nellie. *The Little Worlds of Nellie Musial.* New York: Vantage, 1954.

Musmanno, Michael. *Black Fury.* 1935. New York: Fountainhead, 1966.

Nathan, Robert. *The Sea-Gull Cry.* New York: Knopf, 1942.

Niemcewicz, Julian U. *Under Their Vine and Fig Tree: Travels through America in 1797–1799.* 1805. New Jersey: Grassman Publishing Co., 1965.

Ochester, Ed. *Changing the Name to Ochester.* Pittsburgh: Carnegie Mellon U P, 1988.

Oemler, Marie C. *Slippy McGee.* New York: Grosset & Dunlap, 1917.

Oppenheim, James. *Pay Envelopes: Tales of the Mill, the Mine, and the City Street.* 1911. Freeport, N.Y.: Books for Libraries Press, 1972.

Ozick, Cynthia. *The Mercenary. Bloodshed and Three Novellas.* New York: Knopf, 1976.

Paley, Grace. *Enormous Changes at the Last Minute.* New York: Farrar, Straus, Giroux, 1974.

Pawlak, Mark. "Buffalo Sequence." Contoski 81–83.

Pellowski, Anne. *First Farm in the Valley.* New York: Philomel, 1982.

————. Letter to the author. 12 Oct. 1989.

————. *Stair Step Farm.* New York: Philomel, 1981.

————. *Willow Wind Farm.* New York: Philomel, 1981.

————. *Winding Valley Farm.* New York: Philomel, 1982.

Phillips, Charles, J. *The Doctor's Wooing.* New York: Devin Adair, 1926.

Pijewski, John. "Burying My Father." Contoski 89.

Poe, E. A. "To Colonel Sylvanus Thayer." 10 Mar. 1831. *The Letters of Edgar Allan Poe.* Ed. John Ward Ostrom. Vol. 1. Cambridge: Harvard U P, 1948. 44–45.

Poniscan, Darryl. *The Accomplice.* New York: Harper & Row, 1975.

————. *Andoshen, Pa.* New York: The Dial Press, 1973.

————. *Goldengrove.* New York: The Dial Press, 1971.

————. *The Last Detail.* New York: The Dial Press, 1970.

————. Letter to the author. 2 Mar. 1989.

————. Letter to the author. 23 Sept. 1989.

Rezmerski, John. "Grandfather." Contoski 93.

Richardson, Dorothy. *The Book of Blanche*. Boston: Little Brown, 1924.

Riley, Frank. *Jesus* II. Los Angeles: Sherbourne Press, 1972.

——. *The Kocska Formula*. Los Angeles: Sherbourne Press, 1971.

Roof, Katherine Metcalf. *The Stranger at the Hearth*. Boston: Small, Maynard & Co., 1916.

Roth, Henry. *Call It Sleep*. New York: Cooper Square Pub., 1934.

Roth, Phillip. *Portnoy's Complaint*. New York: Random House, 1969.

Rothenberg, Jerome. *Poland/1931*. N.p.: Unicorn Press, 1970.

Savage, Richard Henry. *The Anarchist: A Story of Today*. Chicago: F. Tennyson Neely, 1894.

Schrag, Otto. *Sons of the Morning*. Garden City, N.Y.: Doubleday, Doran & Co., 1945.

Scott, Evelyn. "Kalicz." *The Wave*. N.p.: Harrison Smith and Robert Haas, 1929.

Sienkiewicz, Henryk. *After Bread: A Story of Emigrant Life in America*. New York: R. F. Fenno, 1897.

Sinclair, Upton. *King Coal*. New York: Macmillan, 1917.

Singer, Isaac B. *Collected Stories of Isaac Bashevis Singer*. New York: Farrar, Straus, Giroux, 1982.

——. *Enemies, A Love Story*. New York: Farrar, Straus, Giroux, 1972.

——. *The Estate*. New York: Dell, 1969.

——. *The Family Moskat*. New York: Bantam, 1950.

——. *Isaac Bashevis Singer on Literature and Life: An Interview with Paul Rosenblatt, Gene Koppel*. Tucson: U Arizona P, 1979.

——. *The King of the Fields*. New York: Farrar, Straus, Giroux, 1988.

——. *The Manor*. New York: Farrar, Straus, Giroux, 1967.

——. *Satan in Goray*. New York: Noon Day Press, 1955.

——. *Shosha*. New York: Farrar, Straus, Giroux, 1978.

——. *The Slave; A Novel*. New York: Farrar, Straus, Giroux, 1962.

Slote, Alfred. *Denham Proper*. New York: G. P. Putnam, 1953.

Smith, Betty. *Tomorrow Will Be Better*. New York: Harper, 1948.

Southworth, E.D.E.N. *The Missing Bride*. New York: Hurst & Co., n.d.

Steele, Silas S. *The Brazen Drum; or The Yankee in Poland*. Philadelphia: Turner & Fisher, 1846.

Straszewicz, Jozef. *The Life of the Countess Emily Plater*. Trans. J. K. Salomonski. New York: J. F. Trow, 1842.

Styron, William. *Sophie's Choice*. New York: Random House, 1979.

——. "An Interview with William Styron." With Valerie M. Arms. *Contemporary Literature* 20 (Winter 1979): 1–20.

Szumowski, Margaret. "About My Cousin." Minczeski, *Concert* 44.

——. "Bronislaw." Minczeski, *Concert* 45–46.

Tabrah, Ruth. *Pulaski Place*. New York: Harper, 1949.

Todd, Mary Ives. *Violina: A Romance*. New York: Broadway Publishing Co., 1904.

"To Poland." Arthur P. Coleman. *A New England City and the November*

Uprising. Chicago: Polish Roman Catholic Union of America, 1939. 55–56.

Triton, Willie. *The Fisher Boy.* Boston: Whittemore, Niles & Hall, 1857.

Uris, Leon. *Mila 18.* New York: Doubleday, 1961.

———. *QB VII.* Garden City, N.Y.: Doubleday, 1970.

Van Zile, Edward S. *Kings in Adversity.* New York: F. Tennyson Neely, 1897.

Vogel, Joseph. *Man's Courage.* New York: Knopf, 1938.

Waldo, Harold. *Stash of the Marsh Country.* New York: George H. Doran Co., 1921.

Wasecha, Anna. "Babushka." Minczeski, *Concert* 10–11.

Wedda, Joseph. *Jasna Polana.* New York: House of Field-Doubleday, 1945.

Weidman, Jerome. *My Father Sits in the Dark and Other Stories.* 1934. New York: Random House, 1961.

Williams, Tennessee. *A Streetcar Named Desire.* New York: New Directions, 1947.

Williams, William Carlos. "Life Along the Passaic River." *The Collected Stories of William Carlos Williams.* New York: New Directions, 1961. 110–17.

Wilner, Herbert. "A Gift Every Morning." *Dovisch in the Wilderness and Other Stories.* Indianapolis: Bobbs Merrill, 1968. 125–39.

Wylie, Ida. *Strangers Are Coming.* New York: Random House, 1941.

Yezierska, Anzia. *All I Could Never Be.* New York: Brewer, Warren & Putnam, 1932.

SECONDARY SOURCES

Aaron, Daniel. "The Hyphenated Writer and American Letters." *Smith Alumnae Quarterly* July 1964: 213–17.

———. *Writers on the Left.* New York: Harcourt Brace, 1961.

Abel, Theodore F. "Sunderland: A Study of Changes in the Group Life of Poles in a New England Farming Community." *Immigrant Farmers and Their Children.* Ed. Edmund Brunner. Garden City, N.Y.: Doubleday, 1929. 213–43.

Almy, Frederick. "The Huddled Poles of Buffalo." *Survey* 4 Feb. 1911: 767–71.

Rev. of *The Anarchist,* by Richard Henry Savage. *The Saturday Review* 30 June 1984: 695.

Andrews, C. R. Rev. of *Goldengrove,* by Darryl Poniscan. *Library Journal* 15 Sept. 1971: 96.

Bailey, L. H., et al., eds. *Report of the Commission on Country Life.* New York: Sturgis and Walton, 1911.

Balch, Emily. "Our Slavic Fellow Citizens." *Charities* April 1907: 11–22; June 1907: 259–67; July 1907: 365–77; Sept. 1907: 676–90.

Baldwin, David. "The One and the Many: Comments on the Essays by Jules Chametzky and Werner Sollors." *Prospects* 9 (1984): 471–77.

Barnard, Kenneth. "The Mercantile Mr. Kowalski." *Discourse* 7 (Summer 1964): 337–40.

Barth, Frederick. Introduction. *Ethnic Groups and Boundaries: The Social*

Organization of Cultural Differences. Ed. Barth. Boston: Little Brown, 1969. 9–39.

Basa, Eniko M. "Hungarian-American Literature." Ifkovic 90–109.

Bercovici, Konrad. *On New Shores.* New York: The Century Co., 1925.

Bercovitch, Sacvan. *The Puritan Origins of the American Self.* New Haven: Yale U P, 1975.

Bicha, Karel D. "Hunkies: Stereotyping the Slavic Immigrants 1890–1920." *Journal of American Ethnic History* 2 (Fall 1982): 16–38.

Blake, Fay M. *The Strike in the American Novel.* Metuchen, N.J.: Scarecrow, 1972.

Blejwas, Stanislaus. "Milosz and the Polish Americans." *New York Times Book Review* 22 Nov. 1987: 47.

———. "Puritans and Poles: The New England Literary Image of the Polish Peasant Immigrant." *Polish American Studies* 43 (Autumn 1985): 46–88.

———. "Voiceless Immigrants." *Polish American Studies* 45 (Spring 1988): 5–11.

Blicksilver, Edith. "Monica Krawczyk's Polish Pride." *Turn of the Century Women* 1. 2 (1984): 42–44.

Blonski, Jan. "Is There a Jewish School of Polish Literature?" *Polin.* Ed. Antony Polonsky. London: Basil Blackwell, 1987. 196–211.

Blotner, Joseph. *The Modern American Political Novel 1900–1960.* Austin: U Texas P, 1966.

Boelhower, William. *Through a Glass Darkly: Ethnic Semiosis in American Literature.* Venice: Edizioni Helvetia, 1984.

Bonosky, Phillip. "Salute to Mike Gold." *Masses and Mainstream* April 1954: 43–50.

Brown, Harry Shipman. "Two Glimpses of the New England Pole." *Forum* Feb. 1914: 286.

Brozek, Andrzej. *Polish Americans 1854–1939.* Warsaw: Interpress, 1985.

Brumm, Ursula. *American Thought and Religious Typology.* New Brunswick, N.J.: Rutgers U P, 1970.

Budka, Metchie J. F. "Pulaski and Kosciuszko: Heroes Extremely Apropos." *Poles in America.* Ed. Frank Mocha. Stevens Point, Wisc.: Worzalla Pub., 1978. 11–44.

Bukowczyk, John. *And My Children Did Not Know Me.* Bloomington: Indiana U P, 1987.

Calverton, V. F. "Proletarian Art." *The Newer Spirit: A Sociological Criticism of Literature.* New York: Boni and Liveright, 1925. 139–50.

Cance, Alexander. "Immigrant Rural Communities." *The Annals* Mar. 1912: 69–80.

———. "Slav Farmers on the 'Abandoned Farm' Area of Connecticut." *Survey* 7 Oct. 1911: 951–56.

Chametzky, Jules. *Our Decentralized Literature: Cultural Meditations on Selected Jewish and Southern Writers.* Amherst: U Mass. P, 1986.

———. "Styron's *Sophie's Choice*: Jews and Other Marginals, and the Mainstream." *Prospects* 9 (1984): 433–41.

Cheney, Ednah D., ed. *Louisa May Alcott, Her Life, Letters, and Journals.* 1890. New York: Chelsea House, 1980.

Coale, Samuel. "The Quest for the Elusive Self: The Fiction of Jerzy Kosinski." *Critique* 15. 3 (1973): 25–37.

Coleman, Arthur P. *A New England City and the November Uprising.* Chicago: Polish Roman Catholic Union of America, 1939.

Corry, John. "A Case History: Seventeen Years of Ideological Attack." *New York Times* 7 Nov. 1982, sec. 2: 1, 20.

Corwin, Phillip. "Evil Without Roots." *Nation* April 1973: 566–68.

Cox, Martha, and Wayne Chatterton. *Nelson Algren.* Boston: G. K. Hall, 1975.

Daniels, R. L. "Polanders in Texas." *Lippincott's* 31 Mar. 1883: 298–301.

Darrow, Clarence. *Realism in Literature and Art.* Chicago: Charles H. Kerr & Co., 1899.

Davidson, Carter. "The Immigrant Strain in Contemporary Literature." *English Journal* Dec. 1936: 862–68.

Davies, Norman. *God's Playground: A History of Poland.* 2 vols. New York: Columbia U P, 1982.

Dickson, Vivienne. "*A Streetcar Named Desire:* Its Development Through the Manuscripts." *Tennessee Williams: A Tribute.* Ed. Jac Tharpe. Jackson: U Mississippi P, 1977. 154–71.

Dziewanowski, Kazimierz. *Tenth Anniversary of the Polish Solidarity Union.* C-Span, 27 Aug. 1990.

Eastman, E. R. *These Changing Times: A Story of Farm Progress During the First Quarter of the Twentieth Century.* New York: Macmillan, 1927.

Eisinger, Chester. *Fiction of the Forties.* Chicago: U Chicago P, 1963.

Elliott, Robin. "The Eastern European Immigrant in American Literature: The View of the Host Culture." *Polish American Studies* 43 (Autumn 1985): 25–45.

Ellison, Ralph. *Shadow and Act.* New York: Random House, 1964.

Fast, Howard. *Intellectuals in the Fight for Peace.* New York: Masses and Mainstream, 1949.

Ferraro, Thomas J. "Blood in the Marketplace: The Business of Family in the Godfather Narratives." Sollors, *The Invention of Ethnicity* 176–208.

Fiedler, Leslie. *The Jew in the American Novel.* New York: Herzl Institute, 1959.

Fine, David. *The City, The Immigrant, and American Fiction 1880–1920.* Metuchen, N.J.: Scarecrow, 1977.

Freeman, Joseph. Introduction. *Proletarian Literature in the United States.* Ed. Granville Hicks et al. New York: International Pub., 1935.

Fuller, Edmund. Rev. of *Magda,* by Maurice Hindus. *Booklist* 15 Mar. 1951: 253.

Furbank, P. N. "Fiction's Feelingless Man." *The Listener* May 1969: 655.

Gans, Herbert. "Symbolic Ethnicity: The Future of Ethnic Groups and Cultures in America." *On the Making of Americans.* Ed. Gans. Philadelphia: U Pennsylvania P, 1979. 193–221.

Garrett, Laura B. "Notes on the Poles in Baltimore." *Charities* Dec. 1904: 235–39.

Geismar, Maxwell. "Nelson Algren: The Iron Sanctuary." *College English* Mar. 1953: 311–15.

Gelb, Barbara. "Being Jerzy Kosinski." *New York Times Magazine* 21 Feb. 1982: 42–58.

Gladsky, Thomas S. "Deviancy and Diversity: Inventing the Polish Literary Self, 1890–1920." *Polish-Anglo Saxon Studies* 3–4 (March 1992): 27–37.

———. "The Immigrant on the Land: Polish Farmers and New England Novelists." *New England Quarterly* 61 (1988): 429–38.

———. "Jerzy Kosinski's East European Self." *Critique* 29 (Winter 1988): 121–32.

———. "The Polish Peasant and the Promised Land in 1930s and 1940s American Fiction." *The Future of American Modernism: Ethnic Writing between the Wars.* Ed. William Boelhower. Amsterdam: VU University Press, 1990: 273–88.

———. "The Polish Side of I. B. Singer." *Studies in American Jewish Literature* 5 (1986): 4–14.

———. "Primarily We See Ourselves as Ethnics." *The Polish Review* 36. 2 (1991): 179–84.

Golab, Caroline. "Stellaaaaaa......!!!!!!: The Slavic Stereotype in American Film." *The Kaleidoscopic Lens: How Hollywood Views Ethnic Groups.* Ed. Randall M. Miller, N.p.: Jerome J. Ozer, 1980. 135–55.

Gold, Michael. "Towards Proletarian Art." *The Liberator* Feb. 1921: 20–24.

———. "Notes of the Month." *New Masses* Sept. 1930: 3–5.

Gordon, Milton. *Assimilation in American Life.* New York: Oxford, 1964.

Greeley, Andrew. "What Is an Ethnic?" *White Ethnics: Their Life in Working Class America.* Ed. Joseph Ryan. Englewood Cliffs, N.J.: Prentice-Hall, 1973. 11–16.

Green, Rose Basile. *The Italian-American Novel.* Rutherford, N.J.: Fairleigh Dickinson U P, 1974.

Greene, Victor. *For God and Country: The Rise of Polish and Lithuanian Ethnic Consciousness in America 1860–1910.* Madison: State Historical Society, 1975.

———. *The Slavic Community on Strike.* Notre Dame: Notre Dame P, 1968.

Haiman, Miecislaus. *Poland and the American Revolutionary War.* Chicago: Archives and Museum of the Polish Roman Catholic Union, 1938.

Rev. of *The Homebuilders,* by Karl E. Harriman. *New York Times.* 30 Jan. 1904: 71.

Howe, Irving. Introduction. *The Jewish American Short Story.* New York: New American Library, 1977.

———. *Politics and the Novel.* Cleveland: World Publishing, 1957.

Hutchinson, James D. "The Invisible Man as Anti-Hero." *Denver Quarterly* 6 (Spring 1971): 86–92.

Ifkovic, Edward, and Robert J. Di Pietro, eds. *Ethnic Perspectives in American Literature.* New York: Modern Language Association, 1983.

Irwin Zarecka, Iwona. *Neutralizing Memory: The Jew in Contemporary Poland.* New Brunswick, N.J.: Transaction Pub., 1989.

Jerome, V. J. "Toward a Proletarian Novel." *New Masses* Aug. 1932–33: 14–15.

Junker, Howard. "Will This Finally Be Philip Roth's Year?" *New York* 13 Jan. 1969: 44–47.

Kaplan, Howard. Rev. of *Childhood and Other Neighborhoods,* by Stuart Dybek. *Commonweal* 23 May 1980: 319.

Kazin, Alfred. *Bright Book of Life: American Novelists and Storytellers from Hemingway to Mailer.* Boston: Little Brown, 1971.

Kessler-Harris, Alice. Afterward. *The Open Cage: An Anzia Yezierska Collection.* New York: Persea Books, 1979. 258–60.

King, Lawrence T. "Will Poland Rise Again?" *Catholic World* June 1948: 228–34.

Klinkowitz, Jerome. *Literary Disruptions: The Making of a Post-Contemporary American Fiction.* Urbana: U Illinois P, 1980.

Koloski, Bernard. "Ethnicity for Children: Anne Pellowski's Latsch Valley Tetralogy." Unpublished Essay. 1989.

Kresh, Paul. *Isaac Bashevis Singer.* New York: The Dial Press, 1979.

Krzyzanowski, Jerzy. "What's Wrong with *Sophie's Choice?*" *Polish American Studies* 40 (Spring 1983): 64–72.

Lavers, Norman. *Jerzy Kosinski.* Boston: Twayne, 1982.

Lawrence, Ellwood. "The Immigrant in American Fiction." Diss. Case Western Reserve, 1943.

Lerski, Jerzy. *A Polish Chapter in Jacksonian Democracy.* Madison: U Wisconsin P, 1958.

Lilly, Paul, Jr. *Words in Search of Victims: The Achievement of Jerzy Kosinski.* Kent, Ohio: Kent State U P, 1988.

Lyra, Franciszek. "The Letters of William James to Wincenty Lutoslawki." *Yale University Library Gazette* 51, 1 (1976): 28–40.

———. "Louisa May Alcott's Polish Hero." *Lubelskie Materialy Neofilologiczne.* Lublin (1982): 61–68.

———. "Grounds for Connections: The Pattern of Polish-American Literary Relations." *Polish American Studies.* Warsaw, 1 (1976): 89–111.

Maciuszko, Jerzy. "Polish-American Literature." Ifkovic 163–82.

Maclean, A. M. "Life in the Pennsylvania Coal Fields," *American Journal of Sociology* 14 Sept. 1908: 332–51.

Madden, David, ed. *Proletarian Writers of the Thirties.* Carbondale, Ill.: SI UP, 1968.

Malin, Irving. *Isaac Bashevis Singer.* New York: Frederick Ungar, 1972.

Mayhew, Alice E. Rev. of *A Glass Rose,* by Richard Bankowsky. *Commonweal* 14 Feb. 1958: 515.

McLaughlin, Allan. "The Slavic Immigrant." *Popular Science Monthly* May 1903: 25–32.

Milosz, Czeslaw. "Separate Nations: Poetry and the People." *New York Times Book Review* 11 Oct. 1987: 3, 30.

Rev. of *The Missing Bride*, by E.D.E.N. Southworth. *Godey's* Sept. 1886: 293.

Morse, William N. "Earning a Valley." *Outlook* Sept. 1910: 80–86.

Mostwin, Danuta. "Post–World War II Immigrants in the United States." *Polish American Studies* 26 (Autumn 1969): 5–14.

Napierkowski, Thomas J. "Anne Pellowski: A Voice for Polonia." *Polish American Studies* 42 (Autumn 1985): 89–97.

———. "The Image of Polish-Americans in American Literature." *Polish American Studies* 40 (Spring 1983): 5–44.

———. "The Image of Polish-American Priests in American Literature." *Pastor of the Poles*. Ed. Stanislaus Blejwas and Mieczyslaw Biskupski. New Britain: Central Connecticut State College, 1982. 166–81.

———. "Polish American Neighbors: The Fiction of Anthony Bukoski." Unpublished essay. 1989.

———. "*Sophie's Choice:* The Other Holocaust Revisited, Revised, and Reviewed." *Polish American Studies* 40 (Spring 1983): 73–87.

"The New Poland." *Life* 19 Nov. 1945: 109–17.

Phillipson, J. S. Rev. of *Andoshen, Pa.*, by Darryl Poniscan. *Best Sellers* 1 Mar. 1973: 430.

———. Rev. of *Goldengrove*, by Darryl Poniscan. *Best Sellers* 1 Oct. 1971: 303.

Pinkowski, Edward. "The Great Influx of Polish Immigrants and the Industries They Entered." *Poles in America*. Ed. Frank Mocha. Stevens Point, Wisc.: Worzalla Pub., 1978. 303–70.

Pleszczynski, Wladyslaw. "Dead End." *National Review* 11 Nov. 1983: 1418–20.

Plimpton, George, and Rocco Landesman. "The Art of Fiction: Jerzy Kosinski." *Paris Review* 54 (1972): 183–207.

"Poland: New Phase." *The New Republic* 16 July 1945: 59–60.

"The Poles and the Russians." *The New Republic* 10 May 1943: 623–24.

Prever, Phillip. Rev. of *The Accomplice*, by Darryl Poniscan. *Library Journal* 1 Mar. 1975: 503.

Radzialowski, Thaddeus. "The 'Final Solution' for Southern Guilt." *Polish American Studies* 40 (Spring 1983): 59–64.

Raymont, Henry. "National Book Awards: The Winners." *New York Times* 11 March 1964: 2.

Rideout, Walter B. *The Radical Novel in the United States 1900–1954*. Cambridge: Harvard U P, 1956.

Roberts, Peter. *Anthracite Coal Communities*. New York: Macmillan, 1904.

Rood, Henry. "The Mine Laborers in Pennsylvania." *Forum* 14 Sept. 1892: 110–22.

Roodkowski, Nikita. Rev. of *Poland*, by James Michener. *American* 3 Dec. 1983: 359–60.

Ross, Edward A. "The Slavs in America." *Century* July 1914: 590–98.

Roth, Philip. "Writing American Fiction." *The Commentary Reader*. Ed. Norman Podhoretz. New York: Atheneum, 1966.

Roucek, Joseph. "The Image of the Slav in United States History and in

Immigration Policy." *American Journal of Economics and Sociology* Jan. 1969: 29–48.

"Russians Pull Out, Poles Move in to Build." *Newsweek* 23 July 1945: 51.

"The Russo-Polish Wound." *The Nation* May 1943: 653.

Sanders, Irwin, and Ewa Morawska. *Polish American Community Life: A Survey of Research.* New York: Polish Institute of Arts and Sciences, 1975.

Sanders, Ivan. "The Gifts of Strangeness: Alienation and Creation in Kosinski's Fiction." *The Polish Review* 19 (1974): 171–89.

Saposnik, Irving. "Bellow, Malamud, Roth . . . and Styron?" *Judaism* 31 (Summer 1982): 322–32.

Sayles, Mary Buell. "Housing and Social Conditions in a Slavic Neighborhood." *Charities* 13 Dec. 1904: 257–61.

Scharf, Rafael. "In Anger and in Sorrow: Towards a Polish-Jewish Dialogue." *Polin.* Ed. Antony Polonsky. London: Basil Blackwell, 1987. 270–77.

Shaler, N. S. "European Peasants as Immigrants." *Atlantic* May 1883: 646–55.

Sheehy, Gail. "The Psychological Novelist as Portable Man." *Psychology Today* Dec. 1977: 52–56, 126, 128, 130.

Sheridan, Frank J. "Italian, Slavic, and Hungarian Unskilled Immigrant Laborers in the United States." *Bulletin of Bureau of Labor* Sept. 1907: 403–86.

Shmeruk, Chone. "Jews and Poles in Yiddish Literature in Poland Between the Two World Wars." *Polin.* Ed. Antony Polonski. London: Basil Blackwell, 1987. 176–95.

Sollors, Werner. *Beyond Ethnicity.* New York: Oxford, 1986.

———, ed. *The Invention of Ethnicity.* New York: Oxford, 1989.

———. "Literature and Ethnicity." *Harvard Encyclopedia of Ethnic Groups.* Ed. Stephan Thernstrom. Cambridge: Belknap Press, 1980. 647–65.

Solomon, Barbara. *Ancestors and Immigrants: A Changing New England Tradition.* Cambridge: Harvard U P, 1956.

Sprague, W. B. Introduction. *The Remembrances of a Polish Exile.* By August Jakubowski. Albany: Haswell and Fleu, 1836. 1–8.

Steiner, Edward. "The Slovak and the Pole in America." *Outlook* March 1903: 555–64.

Strzetelski, Jerzy. "Styron's Poland." Unpublished essay. 1987.

Tanner, Tony. *City of Words: American Fiction 1950–1970.* New York: Harper and Row, 1971.

Taylor, Carl C. *Rural Sociology.* New York: Harper, 1926.

Taylor, Henry. Rev. of *A Streetcar Named Desire,* by Tennessee Williams. *Masses and Mainstream* April 1948: 51–55.

Tepa, Barbara J. "Jerzy Kosinski's Polish Contexts: A Study of *Being There.*" *Polish Review* 22, 21 (1977): 52–61.

Thomas, William I., and Florian Znaniecki. *The Polish Peasant in Europe and America.* Ed. Eli Zaretsky. Urbana: U Illinois P, 1984.

Thomson, Harrison S. "The New Poland." *Foreign Policy Reports* 23 Dec. 1947: 226–34.

Titus, Edward Kirk. "The Pole in the Land of the Puritan." *New England Magazine* 29 Oct. 1903: 162–66.

Tompkins, Jane. *Sensational Designs: The Cultural Work of American Fiction 1790–1860.* New York: Oxford U P, 1985.

Tuerk, Richard. "Jewish-American Literature." Ifkovic 133–63.

Rev. of *Violina,* by Mary Ives Todd. *Overland Monthly* Oct. 1904: 482.

———. *New York Times* 6 Aug. 1904: 54.

Waldo, Arthur L. "Polish American Theatre." *Ethnic Theatre in the United States.* Ed. Maxine S. Seller. Westport, Conn.: Greenwood, 1983.

Weyl, Walter E. "Jan, the Polish Miner." *Outlook* 19 Mar. 1910: 709–16.

Wright, Richard. Introduction. *Never Come Morning.* By Nelson Algren. New York: Harper, 1942.

Wrobel, Paul. "The Polish American Experience: An Anthropological View of Ruth Tabrah's *Pulaski Place* and Millard Lampell's *The Hero.*" *Ethnic Literature Since 1776: The Many Voices of America.* Ed. Wolodymyr T. Zyla and Wendell M. Aycock. Lubbock, Texas: Texas Tech P, 1978. 395–407.

Wroblewski, Sergius. Letter. *America* 31 Dec. 1983: 440.

Wytrwal, Joseph. *Poles in American History and Tradition.* Detroit: Endurance Press, 1969.

Yezierski, Anzia. Rev. of *A Glass Rose,* by Richard Bankowsky. *New York Times* 12 Jan. 1958: 4.

Rev. of *Zal, An International Romance,* by Rupert Hughes. *Outlook* 2 Dec. 1905: 838.

Zurawski, Joseph. *Polish American History and Culture: A Classified Bibliography.* Chicago: Polish Museum of America, 1975. 169–96.

INDEX